Mastering Docker Enterprise

A companion guide for agile container adoption

Mark Panthofer

BIRMINGHAM - MUMBAI

Mastering Docker Enterprise

Commissioning Editor: Vijin Boricha
Acquisition Editor: Rohit Rajkumar
Content Development Editor: Deepti Thore
Technical Editor: Varsha Shivhare
Copy Editor: Safis Editing
Project Coordinator: Nusaiba Ansari
Proofreader: Safis Editing
Indexer: Priyanka Dhadke
Graphics: Jisha Chirayil
Production Coordinator: Nilesh Mohite

First published: March 2019

Production reference: 1010319

Published by Packt Publishing Ltd.
Livery Place
35 Livery Street
Birmingham
B3 2PB, UK.

ISBN 978-1-78961-207-3

www.packtpub.com

`mapt.io`

Mapt is an online digital library that gives you full access to over 5,000 books and videos, as well as industry leading tools to help you plan your personal development and advance your career. For more information, please visit our website.

Why subscribe?

- Spend less time learning and more time coding with practical eBooks and Videos from over 4,000 industry professionals

- Improve your learning with Skill Plans built especially for you

- Get a free eBook or video every month

- Mapt is fully searchable

- Copy and paste, print, and bookmark content

Packt.com

Did you know that Packt offers eBook versions of every book published, with PDF and ePub files available? You can upgrade to the eBook version at `www.packt.com` and as a print book customer, you are entitled to a discount on the eBook copy. Get in touch with us at `customercare@packtpub.com` for more details.

At `www.packt.com`, you can also read a collection of free technical articles, sign up for a range of free newsletters, and receive exclusive discounts and offers on Packt books and eBooks.

Contributors

About the author

Mark Panthofer earned a degree in computer engineering in 1991 and has since accumulated 20+ years of technology adoption experience in a wide variety of positions, ranging from software engineer to software executive. He is currently the vice president of NVISIA's technology centers, where he focuses on Docker-related technology adoption. As a Docker-accredited consultant and instructor, Mark's responsibilities include the following:

- Providing training to leading commercial and government agencies on the best practices with Docker Enterprise for developers, DevOps, and operations
- Providing advisory services to regional IT organizations on enterprise container adoption
- Co-organizing Docker Chicago and Docker Milwaukee meetups
- Collaborating with Docker's solution architects

About the reviewers

Nick Schultz works as a project architect for NVISIA and is a Docker-accredited consultant and instructor. He has 15 years' experience designing and developing enterprise applications using various languages and frameworks.

Eric Duquesnoy is a DevOps consultant for an engineering services company in Switzerland, where he currently applies DevOps methodologies in many IT departments. He has 16 years of experience as a production and applicative database administrator for many well-known companies. Now, his mission is to push continuous integration, containers, automation, and the cloud everywhere. Throughout his professional career, he has tried to find the best way of connecting Ops and Dev. As a nominated community leader of the Docker Geneva meetup, he likes to organize a monthly meetup around containers and share his knowledge with others. He is an active participant in French-speaking communities for DevOps, Docker, Kubernetes, and cloud.

Russ McKendrick is an experienced system administrator who has been working in IT and related industries for over 25 years. During his career, his responsibilities have varied, from looking after an entire IT infrastructure to providing first-line, second-line, and senior support in both client-facing and internal teams for large organizations.

Russ supports open source systems and tools on public and private clouds at N4Stack, a Node4 Company, where he is the practice manager (SRE and DevOps). In his spare time, he has authored several books, including *Mastering Docker*, *Learn Ansible*, and *Kubernetes for Serverless Applications*.

Packt is searching for authors like you

If you're interested in becoming an author for Packt, please visit `authors.packtpub.com` and apply today. We have worked with thousands of developers and tech professionals, just like you, to help them share their insight with the global tech community. You can make a general application, apply for a specific hot topic that we are recruiting an author for, or submit your own idea.

Table of Contents

Preface   1

Section 1: Getting Started with Docker Enterprise

Chapter 1: Making the Case for Docker Enterprise   9
  Zero to everywhere in five years   10
    The Docker story   10
    Containers change application development and deployment   11
    Containers gain popularity   13
    Docker Engine-Community – free Docker   14
      Docker Engine-Community includes key capabilities   15
      Running Docker Engine-Community on AWS or Azure   15
    Docker Enterprise – enterprise support and features   16
    Kubernetes and Docker Enterprise   17
      Kubernetes and Swarm orchestration   18
      Kubernetes and Swarm – different philosophies to solve different problems   19
      Moving Kubernetes to the mainstream   20
  New era for app Dev, DevOps, and IT operations   21
    DevOps   22
    Operations   22
  Container-first and strategic impact of containers   22
    Container-first as a cloud adoption strategy   23
    Get ready to bring workloads back from the public cloud   23
    Application modernization – the containerization path   24
    Support for microservices and DevOps   24
    Compliance   24
  How Docker Enterprise 2.0 has changed the game   25
  Summary   25
  Questions   26
  Further reading   26

Chapter 2: Docker Enterprise - an Architectural Overview   27
  Moving from science projects to production platforms   28
    The landscape of emerging container platforms   29
    Economics, features, and key components of Docker Enterprise   34
      The estimated cost of Docker Enterprise   34
      Docker Enterprise pricing illustration   35
      Docker Enterprise architecture-related benefits   35
        Docker support benefits   36
        Computational efficiency benefits   36
        Benefits of choice   36
        Rapid innovation – platform-neutral DevOps skills benefit the shift-left strategy   37

UCP and DTR benefits   37
Container-first benefits   38
Operational architecture of Docker Enterprise   38
Docker Enterprise's main components   38
Docker Enterprise operation architecture – infrastructure, platform, and
application layers   40
Breaking down the layers   42
Infrastructure layer – network, nodes, and storage   43
The platform layer – Docker Enterprise engine, UCP, and DTR   45
Application layer – interacting with the cluster   46
Docker Enterprise reference architecture   48
Simple view of the Docker Enterprise cluster architecture   50
Drill-down – high-level Docker Enterprise 2 components   53
Summary   55
Questions   55
Further reading   56
Chapter 3: Getting Started - Docker Enterprise Proof of Concept   57
Assembling a Docker Enterprise PoC cross-functional team   58
Preparing a Docker Enterprise platform for the PoC step   60
Preparing a four-node cluster   60
Set up a four-node cluster   61
Overview of a sample PoC environment   61
Installing Docker Enterprise Engine on all nodes   63
Getting a Docker Enterprise 30-day trial license and storebit URL   63
Installing the Docker Enterprise Engine on all nodes   65
Sample Ubuntu Docker Engine install   67
Windows 2016 Docker Engine install   70
Installing Docker's Universal Control Plane   72
Logging to the UCP web interface and uploading your trial license   74
Adding work nodes to the UCP cluster   74
Joining Linux worker nodes to the cluster   75
Joining the remaining worker nodes into the cluster   76
Joining a Windows server 2016 worker node to the cluster   77
Installing the DTR   79
Configuring RBAC for PoC   81
PoC application   82
Picking a PoC application   82
Installing Docker on a local workstation   84
Containerizing and testing the PoC application on a Dev workstation   85
Review application documentation   87
Containerizing and locally testing each application component   88
Containerizing the database   88
Containerizing the Webforms application   93
Creating deployment files and testing locally   99
Pushing images   100
Connecting to the PoC DTR   101
Preparing and pushing your images   101

Deploying a PoC application to a Docker Enterprise cluster   103
    The Docker Enterprise CLI bundle   104
       Using Bash with Docker API to get the CLI bundle   105
       Using PowerShell with the Docker API to get the CLI bundle   106
       Deploying the PoC application to the Docker Enterprise cluster   106
Updating the PoC application   110
Summary   111
Questions   112
Further reading   112

Section 2: Piloting Docker Enterprise

Chapter 4: Prepare the Docker Enterprise Pilot Cluster   115
Docker Enterprise cluster plumbing   116
    Introduction to Docker single-node networking   116
       No Domain Name System (DNS) for the Docker0 default network   119
    Introduction to cluster-based container networking   121
       Swarm and Kubernetes DNS and service discovery   123
       The management and control planes   125
    Docker Enterprise pilot network implementation   127
       Internal cluster users   127
       End users of Docker Enterprise-hosted applications   129
       Highly available cluster   130
       DNS, certificates, and certificate termination   131
       Hostnames for Docker cluster nodes   134
       Bare metal cluster – network setup example   134
          Step 1 – define a domain name and hostname structure   135
          Step 2 – define a certificate structure and termination plan   135
          Step 3 – design and implement a network infrastructure   136
          Load balancer setup and configuration design   138
Docker Enterprise pilot platform   141
    Preparing cluster nodes   142
       Node sizing consideration   142
       Network adapters considerations   142
       Cluster-based storage considerations   143
       Network timing and node synchronization   144
       Docker Enterprise pilot bare metal walk-through   144
          Installing the Docker Enterprise Engine on all nodes   146
          Installing the Docker Enterprise Engine onto each node in the cluster   147
          Setting up the NFS server node   150
          Installing the first manager node   151
          Joining initial DTR 1 and worker 1 nodes   154
          Installing the DTR   156
          Adding additional DTR replicas   158
          Final configuration of load balancers   159
Summary   159
Questions   160
Further reading   160

Chapter 5: Prepare and Deploy a Docker Enterprise Pilot Application   163
Planning for a pilot application   164
Sample pilot planning and execution   166
   Configure UCP pilot settings   168
   RBAC in Docker Enterprise   175
     Setting up Docker Enterprise teams and organizations   179
       Team member sync using LDAP   180
       Collection for pilot team   182
   DTR pilot settings   184
   The sample pilot wiki application   188
     Containerizing the application   189
       Collect and document application assets   189
       Containerizing and testing the Postgres database   191
       Containerizing and testing the wiki application   196
       Pushing the images   205
     Deploying the wiki to the pilot cluster   205
       Pilot application strategy   206
       Application flow for wiki pilot   206
       Deployment architecture for the pilot wiki   207
       Deploying the pilot wiki application   209
Summary   214
Questions   214
Further reading   214

Chapter 6: Design and Pilot a Docker Enterprise CI Pipeline   217
Pilot application development with Docker Enterprise   218
   Using Docker for faster developer on-boarding   218
   Using Docker to improve software development cycles   218
   Docker Containers as a Service (CaaS)   219
   What you need to know about distributed applications   221
     Key principles for container application design   221
       Docker Swarm services   221
       Swarm service networks and routing mesh   224
       Docker Enterprise layer 7 routing   226
       Defensive coding   227
       Centralized logging   229
       Secrets   229
   Docker tools for the local development and testing of the AtSea application   230
     AtSea application structure   231
     Using docker-compose as a Makefile   232
     Building and running an application with Compose and Swarm   235
       Mocking layer 7 routing and TSL termination for local Swarm testing   235
       Final steps for local Swarm testing   239
   Deploying a custom app to the Docker Enterprise cluster   243
     Layer 7 routing with Docker Enterprise   246
   Building and deploying the custom app with a CI pipeline   249
     Sample CI pipeline overview   249
     Connecting GitLab to Docker Enterprise   252
       Adding a GitLab Runner to the build machine   253
       DTR CI integration   258

Building our services   261
    Simple build and push pipeline for atsea-db image   262
    Simple build and push pipeline for the atsea-payment image   267
    Build, End to End Test, and Push pipeline for the atsea-web image 268
Pipeline deployment to Docker Enterprise   272
    Deployment pipeline file   273
    Understanding Docker Swarm resource scoping   279
    Triggering the pipeline manually   281
Summary   283
Questions   284
Further reading   284

Chapter 7: Pilot Docker Enterprise Platform Monitoring and Logging 287
Logging and monitoring distributed, containerized applications   288
Default Docker Engine logs   288
Centralized logging   291
    Publish approach with an ELK Stack   292
    Polling approach with Prometheus   294
        Simple Prometheus setup   295
        Prometheus on Docker and checking Docker   296
Logging and monitoring in Docker Enterprise   298
Docker Enterprise UCP and Prometheus   299
Docker Enterprise with Prometheus and Grafana   300
Commercial example – Sysdig   306
    Our pilot Sysdig architecture   308
        Installing the Sysdig agents   308
        The Wiki pilot dashboard   309
        Setting up alarms   311
Summary   315
Questions   315
Further reading   316

Section 3: In Production with Docker Enterprise

Chapter 8: First Application in Production with Docker Enterprise   319
Docker Enterprise production cluster   320
High-level cluster flow and concepts   320
    Image mirroring   321
    Image signing   323
    UCP production scheduling with Docker Content Trust   324
    Immutability for DTR repos   326
    Image scanning in production   327
Production cluster considerations   329
    Avoiding cluster sprawl   330
    Production-installation considerations   330
    Production manager nodes   331
    Node sizing   332
    Setup and installation considerations   334
        Center for Internet Security (CIS) docker benchmarks   334

Locking down SSH access 338
No public access to Docker nodes 338
Production UCP configuration 339
Production DTR configuration 343

Data management 343
Host volume mounts 343
Docker NFS volume plugin 345
Other volume storage solutions 348
Backing up data 348
Backing up UCP 349
Backing up DTR 350
Backing up application data 351
Applying OS and Docker updates 352
OS and Docker Enterprise Engine updates 352
UCP manager nodes 352
Worker nodes 353
Upgrading the UCP software 353
Upgrading the DTR software 354

Summary 356
Questions 356
Further reading 356

Chapter 9: Important Docker Enterprise Production Topics 359
Working with orchestrators in production 360
Health checks 360
Ephemeral containers and orchestration 361
Application startup and health checks 361
Swarm service health check for AtSea-web 364
Passing signals into containers 366
Managed and unmanaged cluster resources 367
Orchestrators and resource management 367
Container reservations, requests, and limits 368
Setting CPU and memory reservations 369
Production ingress 374
Ingress model overview 374
Layer 7 dynamic routing 374
Layer 4 simple port-based routing 375
Static host deployments 375
Key concepts of blue/green deployments 376
Blue/green deployments with Swarm 376
Kubernetes blue/green deployment 377
Layer 7 routing in production 378
Layer 4 routing in production 379
Docker service updates 383
Layer 4 blue/green deployment 384
Layer 4 canary deployment 386
Production monitoring 386
Summary 390

Questions	391
Further reading	391
Chapter 10: More on Kubernetes with Docker Enterprise	393
Overview of Docker Enterprise with Kubernetes	393
CNI networking	395
Docker Enterprise install – Kubernetes	395
Advanced Kubernetes networking philosophy	397
Coexistence – Swarm and Kube	398
Docker Enterprise Kubernetes role-based access control	398
Kubernetes persistent volume management	401
Docker Desktop to Docker Enterprise Kubernetes	401
Docker Desktop – Converting AtSea to Kubernetes	402
Setting up Docker Desktop with Kubernetes	403
Configuring an application with Kubernetes (Namespace/Secrets/ConfigMaps)	405
Converting and testing the DB	407
Creating the DB ClusterIP	409
Converting the web app	411
Creating the webapp NodePort	412
Testing locally	414
Docker Enterprise for a pilot release of AtSea Kubernetes	414
Setting up Docker RBAC for the atsea-test namespace	415
Blue/green deployment of AtSea to the Docker Enterprise Kubernetes cluster	419
Smoke-testing the AtSea Kubernetes application	420
Configuring the load balancer for blue/green deployment	421
Third-party Docker Enterprise Kubernetes integrations	422
Helm charts on Docker Enterprise Kubernetes	422
GitLab and Docker Enterprise Kubernetes	424
Kubernetes persistent volumes with an existing NFS server	425
Attaching your UCP Kube cluster to an existing on-premises NFS server	425
The setup	426
Ingress controller	428
Installing the NGINX ingress controller	429
Using the Docker demo application to test our ingress setup	432
Installing the dockerdemo application and docker-demo-svc	432
Configuring ingress rules to dockerdemo	433
Testing the ingress controller flow	434
Summary	438
Questions	438
Further reading	438
Chapter 11: Taking the Docker Enterprise Platform into the Future	441
Container-first culture	442
Life before a container-first culture	442
Life after a container-first culture	442
Container-first culture for developers	443
Container-first for DevOps	443
Container first for operations	444

Container-first adoption challenges   444
    The cloudy path to organic adoption   444
    Trying to move everyone in the same direction   445
Container-first target application areas   446
Considerations for building a container culture   446
    Keeping it simple in the beginning   447
    Recognizing enthusiastic learners and committed adopters   447
    Establishing a learning culture   447
Docker Enterprise managed clusters   449
Agile adoption for containers and beyond   450
    Agile Docker Enterprise adoption and container-first   450
    Building your future on the platform   450
Serverless and containers   451
Summary   452
Further reading   452

Assessments   453

Other Books You May Enjoy   461

Index   465

Preface

With mounting evidence (https://www.docker.com/why-docker), such as a 300% faster time to market, a 1,300% increase in developer productivity, and a 40% reduction in infrastructure cost, it is no wonder enterprises are taking an interest in container technology. However, it much more than a new virtualization technology. Effective adoption of a container platforms transform the way software is designed, built, delivered, and deployed. Ultimately, containerization impacts the entire software supply chain, and therefore container platform adoption, when done right, improves enterprise applications, platforms, pipelines, and governance. This represents a significant enterprise transformation.

This book is serves as a companion guide for application, platform, DevOps/pipeline, and governance teams as they travel along their container adoption journey with Docker EE. We introduce a broad body of knowledge and experience through an agile and evolutionary adoption approach, starting with a proof of concept and then taking an application through a pilot and onto production. The knowledge shared in this book comes from two years as a Docker-accredited instructor and a consultant working with customers during their adoption journey.

In this book I use we, the first-person plural pronoun, as a reminder to myself and the readers that the knowledge shared within goes way beyond me. As a Docker consulting partner and training partner, we get the privilege to collaborate with Docker's services team, engineers, and product managers—some of the brightest minds in the container space. Without their shared knowledge and insights this book would not be interesting or useful. I am very grateful for my informative interactions with students, clients, other Docker partners, and Docker, Inc.

Who this book is for

This book addresses topics related to the container adoption journey for application, platform, DevOps/pipeline, and governance teams. Because we provide detailed working examples to convey key concepts, some technical depth is very helpful. Therefore, hands-on technical leaders and technical architects are likely to benefit the most from the details shared during this journey.

What this book covers

Chapter 1, *Making the Case for Docker Enterprise*, covers the background and platform landscape of the enterprise containers space and where Docker *Enterprise* fits.

Chapter 2, *Docker Enterprise – an Architectural Overview*, provides an architectural overview, including budget, benefits, features, and product structure.

Chapter 3, *Getting Started – Docker Enterprise Proof of Concept*, walks through the setup of a simple PoC cluster, containerizing a simple .NET application, and deploying the application to the PoC cluster.

Chapter 4, *Prepare the Docker Enterprise Pilot Cluster*, explores important concepts related to setting up a Docker *Enterprise* pilot cluster and provides important details of a bare-metal installation using CentOS 7.

Chapter 5, *Prepare and Deploy a Docker Enterprise Pilot Application*, reviews the post-installation configuration of UCP and DTR, describes the containerization an old Java Wiki application, and concludes with the deployment of the Wiki application to our new the pilot cluster.

Chapter 6, *Design and Pilot a Docker Enterprise CI Pipeline*, describes distributed application design concepts, the containerized development process, and building containers with a Docker CI/CD pipeline.

Chapter 7, *Pilot Docker Enterprise Platform Monitoring and Logging*, introduces centralized logging and monitoring for our pilot platform and applications.

Chapter 8, *First Application in Production with Docker Enterprise*, cover the first big step on the production journey, where we present the software supply chain all way to a production cluster.

Chapter 9, *Important Docker Enterprise Production Topics*, present a final round-up of important Docker *Enterprise* topics for consideration in production environments.

Chapter 10, *More on Kubernetes with Docker Enterprise*, walks through the deployment of a Kubernetes application on your Docker *Enterprise* cluster.

Chapter 11, *Taking the Docker Enterprise Platform into the Future*, looks at what is in store for your Docker *Enterprise* cluster.

To get the most out of this book

You will need the following things to get the most out of this book:

- An understanding of current software development, DevOps, and system admin concepts.
- A basic understanding of container—start here: `https://training.play-with-docker.com/ops-stage1/`.
- Docker (CE) Desktop for Mac or Windows is helpful.
- Access to four Linux hosts (bare-metal or VMs) and an optional Windows Server 2016 host (bare-metal or VM) is ideal to try your own PoC. Cloud VMs can also be used, but we don't cover cloud-specific installs in the examples.

Download the example code files

You can download the example code files for this book from your account at `www.packt.com`. If you purchased this book elsewhere, you can visit `www.packt.com/support` and register to have the files emailed directly to you.

You can download the code files by following these steps:

1. Log in or register at `www.packt.com`.
2. Select the **SUPPORT** tab.
3. Click on **Code Downloads & Errata**.
4. Enter the name of the book in the **Search** box and follow the onscreen instructions.

Once the file is downloaded, please make sure that you unzip or extract the folder using the latest version of:

- WinRAR/7-Zip for Windows
- Zipeg/iZip/UnRarX for Mac
- 7-Zip/PeaZip for Linux

The code bundle for the book is also hosted on GitHub at `https://github.com/PacktPublishing/Mastering-Docker-Enterprise`. In case there's an update to the code, it will be updated on the existing GitHub repository.

We also have other code bundles from our rich catalog of books and videos available at `https://github.com/PacktPublishing/`. Check them out!

Download the color images

We also provide a PDF file that has color images of the screenshots/diagrams used in this book. You can download it here: `https://www.packtpub.com/sites/default/files/downloads/9781789612073_ColorImages.pdf`.

Conventions used

There are a number of text conventions used throughout this book.

`CodeInText`: Indicates code words in text, database table names, folder names, filenames, file extensions, pathnames, dummy URLs, user input, and Twitter handles. Here is an example: "Generally speaking, `sudo service docker restart` should do the trick."

A block of code is set as follows:

```
{
"log-driver": "json-file",
"log-opts": {
    "max-size": "10m",
    "max-file": "3"
    },
"live-restore": true
}
```

When we wish to draw your attention to a particular part of a code block, the relevant lines or items are set in bold:

```
mta-netfx-dev
    ├── docker
    │   ├── web
    │   │   └── Dockerfile
    │   └── web-builder
    │       └── 3.5
    │           └── Dockerfile
```

Any command-line input or output is written as follows:

```
$ docker container run -d -p 5432:5432 db-image:v1
1fe040d1acf242d4cfdb47761db2a59f1bb44b5eedf17376b9455120d86281a5
```

Bold: Indicates a new term, an important word, or words that you see onscreen. For example, words in menus or dialog boxes appear in the text like this. Here is an example: "Expand the **admin** menu and click **My Profile**."

Warnings or important notes appear like this.

Tips and tricks appear like this.

Get in touch

Feedback from our readers is always welcome.

General feedback: If you have questions about any aspect of this book, mention the book title in the subject of your message and email us at `customercare@packtpub.com`.

Errata: Although we have taken every care to ensure the accuracy of our content, mistakes do happen. If you have found a mistake in this book, we would be grateful if you would report this to us. Please visit `www.packt.com/submit-errata`, selecting your book, clicking on the Errata Submission Form link, and entering the details.

Piracy: If you come across any illegal copies of our works in any form on the Internet, we would be grateful if you would provide us with the location address or website name. Please contact us at `copyright@packt.com` with a link to the material.

If you are interested in becoming an author: If there is a topic that you have expertise in and you are interested in either writing or contributing to a book, please visit `authors.packtpub.com`.

Reviews

Please leave a review. Once you have read and used this book, why not leave a review on the site that you purchased it from? Potential readers can then see and use your unbiased opinion to make purchase decisions, we at Packt can understand what you think about our products, and our authors can see your feedback on their book. Thank you!

For more information about Packt, please visit `packt.com`.

Section 1: Getting Started with Docker Enterprise

The chapters in this section cover positioning the Docker Enterprise platform and explain its structure, reference architectures, installation, configuration, and pilot application deployments.

The following chapters are included in this section:

- Chapter 1, *Making the Case for Docker Enterprise*
- Chapter 2, *Docker Enterprise – an Architectural Overview*
- Chapter 3, *Getting Started – Docker Enterprise Proof of Concept*

Making the Case for Docker Enterprise

1

If you have been around the technology scene for a while, you have probably figured out that guiding principles are key to achieving long-term success and without them you end up running in circles—always bouncing to the next cool tech fad without actually getting anything done.

Furthermore, these same guiding principles inspire enterprise practices as a means to ensure the principles are achieved. Finally, principles and practices combine to inform our choice and style for the tools used to make it all happen. Therefore, before we jump into the details of using Docker's Enterprise tooling, it is important to understand how we got here, what running Docker means, and where Docker's enterprise tooling fits into the enterprise platform space.

The following are globally some sample principles and practices to help guide your enterprise container adoption journey:

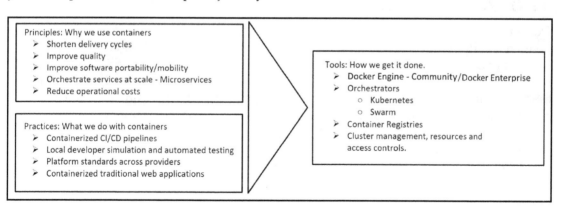

Principles, Practices and Tools for Enterprise Container Adoption

Now lets take a look at the topics which will be covered in this chapter:

- What are Docker, Inc., Docker Engine-Community, and Docker Enterprise?
- Where did containers come from and why are they so popular?
- How do Kubernetes and Docker fit together?
- How do containers impact your business?
- Why would I choose Docker Enterprise?

Zero to everywhere in five years

Technical operations teams are justifiably skeptical about new technology platforms such as containers. They are usually most concerned about hardening for security and reliability because they exist to keep enterprise applications up and running securely. At the same time, product owners within their organizations need to deliver better, often more complex, software faster. Yes, the business landscape has changed profoundly; in today's business world, software is not only used to achieve competitive advantage, it is the business and provides the frontline customer experience.

Subsequently, significant pressure is mounting to accelerate the software pipeline in nearly every organization. This section briefly explains the roots of containers and why their benefits (a secure and fast software pipeline) have driven such a rapid adoption of containers.

The Docker story

Docker was born out of a lightning talk presentation, entitled *The future of Linux Containers*, delivered at PyCon on Friday, March 15, 2013. The presenter was Solomon Hykes, the founder of Docker. On that day, the software world changed even though Linux containers had been evolving in the Linux community for nearly 13 years. It was not the technology that Solomon shepherded that got the Docker movement off the ground, it was the vision behind it and the packaging of the container ecosystem. Solomon's vision was to create tools for mass innovation and his packaging of Linux containers in the Docker experience delivered this powerful technology and put containers within the grasp of mere mortals. Today, Docker runs on tens of millions of servers around the world.

Here are some notes on Linux containers:

- They have been evolving since 2000
- **Linux Containers** (**LXC**) was released in 2008
- Google's lmctfy (let me container that for you) supports Docker's libcontainer in 2015
- Standards emerged, including OCI, and CNCF, around 2015
- Center for internet security benchmark support

Over the last 5 years, thousands of developers joined Docker's open source community to deliver what is known as **Docker Community Edition** (**Docker Engine-Community**). Docker has remained committed to an open platform and a level playing field. Docker has donated significant assets to the open source and standards community, including the Docker container format and runtime, to provide the cornerstone of the **Open Container Initiative** (**OCI**) in 2015 and the container runtime to the **Cloud Native Computing Foundation** (**CNCF**) in 2017.

At Dockercon in 2017, Solomon Hykes released Project Moby, which effectively gives anyone the tooling they need to build their own Docker. This was very cool and ultimately in the best interests of the container community. However, this well-intentioned effort led to some comprehensive repackaging of Docker community assets without community buy-in. From a big-picture point of view, Docker has demonstrated its commitment to the community and Solomon's vision of tools for mass innovation.

Containers change application development and deployment

Containers allow application developers to package up their application, along with all of their dependencies, into a portable unit called an image. These images are then stored in a remote repository where they can be pulled and run on any compliant container engine. Furthermore, the applications running on each container engine are isolated from each other and the host operating system:

- **Illustrative scenario**: Let's say I want to test out NGINX without installing anything (I already have Docker installed of course). I create a sample HTML page called `index.html` in my local directory and run the following:

  ```
  docker run -p 8000:80 -v ${PWD}:/usr/share/nginx/html:ro -d
  nginx
  ```

- **What is happening here?**
    - I'm telling Docker to run the official `nginx` image in the background on my local Docker Engine, forwarding my host adapter's port `8000` to the container's port `80` and mounting my local directory to share my HTML file with `nginx` as a `read-only` folder.
    - Then, I point my local browser at `http://localhost:8000` and I see my HTML page rendered. When I'm done, I ask Docker to remove the container. So, in the span of about a minute, I created a test web page, used NGINX to render it locally without installing anything locally, and ran it in complete isolation. The only possible collision with a host resource was around the host adapter's port `8000`, which was arbitrary.
- **This is cool, but don't VMs already do that for us?**
    - Conceptually there are some similarities, but container implementation is much more lightweight and efficient. The key implementation differences are:
        - **All containers share the host's kernel**:
            - Docker uses Linux container security futures to isolate containers from the host and other containers.
            - Since the kernel is already running, startup time for containers is usually a second or two, versus waiting a minute or two for the guest OS to boot on a VM.
        - **Containers use a layered filesystem with caching**:
            - Docker images are composed of read-only layers that can be cached and shared across multiple containers.
            - Major portions of Docker images can be shared across containers, meaning you don't have to pull the entire image every time. VMs on the other hand have a monolithic, opaque filesystem that's completely reloaded every time it's started. This leads to slow load times and inefficient image storage with VMs.

In the following figure, you can see how the applications in the VMs (right side of the diagram) have a full copy of the OS and the supporting binaries in each virtual machine, whereas the containerized applications (left side of the diagram) all share the same Alpine binaries (no kernel necessary ~ 3 MB) and runtime binaries. There have been various reports on the financial impact of containers versus VMs, but the number I have seen ranges from a 15% to a 70% reduction in operational costs. As they say, your mileage may vary based on your OS, binaries, and whether or not you move to bare metal to eliminate hypervisor licensing costs:

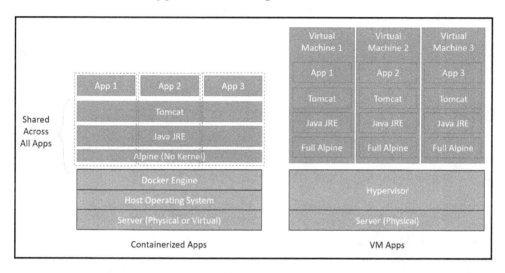

Containerized apps vs VM apps

Containers gain popularity

The following is globally a summary of what I hear from customers and students:

- **Faster developer onboarding**: Container-based development
- **Easy to run and test on dev machines**: Great for simulating production
- **Faster release cycles and shorter time to fix bugs**: No more monolithic deployments
- **Better quality software**: Consistent images across all environments
- **It is too hard to manage microservices without them**: Stacks are great for isolation and deployment
- **Easier to support legacy web applications**: Containerize old apps and manage them on a modern platform

- **Reduction of VMware tax**: Better use of compute resources through increased density and consolidation of multiple non-prod environments (using Docker Enterprise RBAC)

Even the free stuff will cost you something:
I am closing this section on a practical note by suggesting your initial operational savings will be offset by the investment required to transform your enterprise to a container platform. When done right, the impact of container adoption impacts a broad group within the enterprise, spanning the entire software development and delivery pipeline. Like any transformation worth doing, there is some investment required. More about the impact of container adoption later.

Docker Engine-Community – free Docker

The open source version of Docker is called Docker Engine-Community and it is distributed under the Apache 2.0 licence. Sometimes referred to as free Docker, this version is self-and community-supported. Docker has two packaging schemes:

- Docker Engine-Community for x86 64-bit desktop architectures for Mac and Windows 10 Pro+
- Server CE for targeting CentOS, Debian, Fedora, and Ubuntu Linux distributions

In addition to the platform packaging, Docker Engine-Community comes with two channels. It is important to note that as of Docker Engine-Community version 18.09, the stable channel will release on a six-month cadence and the edge channel will be replaced with a nightly build:

- **Stable channel**: General availability code is released through this channel after being thoroughly tested.
- **Edge channel for desktop platforms**: Monthly release of prerelease code that is in various stages of testing.
- **Nightly channel**: Fresh code is released here! Subsequently, cool new features show up here first, but this code base is not completely tested and should not be used for production. Also, if your developers use the edge channel (or run with the —experimental flag) on their workstations, you will need to be very careful to avoid the works on my machine scenario! Take care to ensure new code is not relying on unreleased GA or experimental features that will work on the developer's workstation, but will break later as images and/or configurations move through the pipeline.

You may consider having a development cluster where developers deploy their code on a Docker infrastructure that matches production versions. If a dev cluster is available, developers should always deploy to dev before their code is checked in, to ensure no builds are broken.

Docker Engine-Community includes key capabilities

Docker Engine-Community is a feature-rich container platform that includes a full API, a CLI (Docker client), and a rich plugin architecture for integration and extension. It allows you to run production applications on either a single node or in a secure cluster that includes overlay networking and layer-4 load balancing. That's all included when you install the Docker Engine-Community engine!

Running Docker Engine-Community on AWS or Azure

Please note there are AWS and Azure quickstart packages for cloud users. These convenience bundles include a Docker-supported AMI/VM image, as well as cloud utilities to wire up and support a cluster of Docker Engine-Community nodes. The real assets here are cloud provider-native IaaS templates (AWS CloudFormation or Azure resource manager), Docker VM images, and Docker4x utility containers for interacting with the cloud provider's services. For instance, the AWS bundle allows you to include the cloudstore volume plugin, where instead of using local EBS volumes, you can use EFS and S3 backed volumes across the entire cluster.

 While you might use NFS to achieve a cluster-wide storage solution on-premise, due to some unpredictable latency on cloud providers' networks, where NFS mounts may unexpectedly become read-only, I strongly recommend using Cloudstor on AWS and Azure. More information can be found at `https://docs.docker.com/docker-for-aws/persistent-data-volumes/`.

Finally, please note that Docker for AWS and Docker for Azure only apply to Docker Engine-Community installations. Docker Enterprise now uses the Docker certified infrastructure tooling, using Terraform and Ansible to target VMware, Azure, and AWS implementations of Docker Enteprise.

Docker Enterprise – enterprise support and features

Free Docker is great! But supporting yourself is not always so great. Therefore, Docker Engine-Community is usually a fine choice for learning and getting started, but as soon as you head toward production, you should consider stepping up to Docker Enterprise for the support and/or the enterprise class tooling it provides.

Docker Enterprise builds on Docker Engine-Community's already rich feature set and adds commercial support for the Docker Engine (Docker Enterprise Basic), as well as tooling that's important for managing multiple teams and production applications, including Kubernetes applications (Kubernetes is included in Docker Enterprise Standard and Advanced).

Docker offers the following support models for Docker Engine-Community and Docker Enterprise:

- **Docker Engine-Community**: Starting in CE 18.09, you will need to upgrade (deal with possible breaking changes) every 7 months if you want hotfixes and patch support. This is a recent improvement as, prior to CE 18.09, the support cycle was only four months. Docker Engine-Community relies on community-based support forums; you post an issue in a public forum and wait for someone to help you or to generate a fix. Docker has a great community, but with Docker Engine-Community there are no **Service Level Agreements** (**SLAs**).
- **Docker Enterprise**: You will need to upgrade (deal with possible breaking changes) every 24 months to maintain access to hotfixes and patch support. Docker Enteprise's cornerstone is their enterprise-grade private support channel with either a business-critical or business day support level agreement.
- **Hint**: Business critical has a faster response time SLA, but costs more.

Docker Enterprise also includes seamless support for ISV-provided Docker certified plugins and Docker certified containers. That means if you have an issue with a certified plugin or container, you just call Docker for support.

 Docker Engine-Community support issues are posted publicly for anyone to see. This can be a problem if you are, for example, a financial institution publicly announcing a security vulnerability you discovered and thus tipping off hackers. If you have concerns about the public visibility of your issues or need SLAs, you may want to consider purchasing Docker Enterprise Basic with business day support.

Docker Enterprise also comes in three tiers:

- **Docker Enterprise basic tier**: Docker Engine-Community feature set with Docker Enterprise support as described previously.
- **Docker Enterprise standard tier**: Built on top of Docker Engine-Community with Docker Enterprise support as described previously, but adds the universal control plane (UCP; integrated security with LDAP connections and RBAC through a GUI or CLI bundle for policy management, layer-7 routing, Kubernetes up-and-running out-of-the-box, and a web interface) and the Docker Trusted Registry (DTR; a private image registry tied into the UCP security model with image signing, promotions, webhooks, and full API access).
- **Docker Enterprise advanced tier**: Includes all of the features in the Docker Enterprise standard tier, but gives **Universal Control Plane** (**UCP**) additional finer-grained RBAC to allow for node isolation. The advanced tier enhances the **Docker Trusted Registry** (**DTR**) with image vulnerability scanning and images mirroring to remote DTRs.

> The advanced tier enforces a high degree of resource isolation down to the node level. This allows an enterprise to consolidate all of its non-production environments into a single non-prod docker cluster. This can considerably reduce the number of services required for non-production activities. Developers, testers, and operators are issued appropriate RBAC grants to work in isolation.

Kubernetes and Docker Enterprise

Unless you have been hiding under a rock, you have probably heard about Kubernetes. Too many times I have heard (uninformed) members of the technology community say we don't use Docker, we use Kubernetes. This is a little naive since the vast majority of clusters running Kubernetes orchestration are doing so with the Docker Engine.

Orchestrators allow developers to wire up individual container nodes into a cluster to improve scaling and availability, and reap the benefits of self-healing and distributed/microservice application management. As soon as multi-service applications needed to coordinate more than one container to run, orchestration became a thing. Orchestrators allows containerized application developers to specify how their collection of containers works together to form an application. Then, they later deploy the application using this specification to schedule the required containers across a cluster of (usually Docker) hosts.

Early on, born-in-the-cloud startups that were running at scale and usually deploying microservices became aware of a need for orchestration. Hence, the brilliant minds at Google created what has become the Kubernetes orchestration framework and later created an independent body to mange it, the **Cloud Native Computing Foundation** (**CNCF**), with Kubernetes as the CNCF's cornerstone project. Meanwhile, the Docker community started working on its own orchestration project called Swarmkit.

Kubernetes and Swarm orchestration

While there are many variations and incantations in the orchestration space, the market boils down to very different players: Kubernetes and Swarm. And no, Swarm is not dead.

Kubernetes has rapidly evolved as a modular and highly configurable third-party orchestration platform supported and used by 12-factor, cloud native developers. From an engineering point of view, it is a very interesting platform with many degrees of freedom and points of extensibility. For hardcore 12-factor folks (also known as the cool kids) who are usually delivering highly complex systems at massive scale, using Kubernetes is a no-brainer. However, if you are not Google or eBay, Kubernetes might be a little much for you, especially as you get started.

Swarm, Docker's orchestration tool, started off as an add-in, but in version 1.12 was added to the Docker Engine. As such, there is nothing to install; rather, you activate it using the `docker swarm init` and `docker swarm join` commands to create a TLS encrypted cluster with overlay networking ready to go! So, it's sort of the easy button for orchestration because there's nothing extra to install, and it is both secure and ready to use out of the box. Swarm is included in Docker Engine-Community and Docker Enterprise's UCP piggybacks directly off of Swarm.

Kubernetes and Swarm – different philosophies to solve different problems

Which is better (for you)? Well, it depends…

Getting started with Kubernetes is pretty challenging. This is somewhat because in addition to a container runtime (such as Docker Engine-Community), you need to install and configure `kubectl`, `kubeadm`, and `kubelet`, but that's just the beginning. You also have to make some decisions up front, such as picking a networking model and configuring/installing the provider's container CNI implementation. Kubernetes does not usually provide default options (some cloud services do this for you), which gives you some great flexibility, but naturally forces you to make upfront decision and complicates installation. Again, this is great if you need this flexibility and you know exactly what you are doing.

On the other hand, if you have Docker 1.12 or newer (we strongly recommend having something much newer), you only need to activated it with the `docker swarm init` command. It creates a certificate authority, an encrypted Raft store, and overlay networking automatically, as well as a tokenized `join` command for securely adding additional nodes to your cluster. However, in the spirit of simplicity and security, Docker made some default choices for you. That's great if you can live with those choices, at least while you get up to speed on enterprise container platforms.

Beyond installation, describing application deployment (using YAML files) in Kubernetes is inherently more complex. When it comes to styles of deployment, Kubernetes deploys discrete components and wires them up with a collection of YAML files that rely on labels and selectors to connect them. Again in Kubernetes style, when creating components, you have to define a wide range of behavior parameters to describe exactly what you want, rather than assuming some default behavior. This can be verbose, but it is very powerful, precise, and flexible!

Kubernetes also includes the pod as the atomic deployment unit, which can be handy for isolating a bundle of containers from the flat networking model. This leads to the use of sidecar containers that essentially interface pods to the rest of the world. This is very cool and a great way to handle networks of loosely coupled, shared, long-running services in a flat address space:

docker | kubernetes

- Best where applications are a stack of application dedicated services
- Development is application focused
- Typical 3 – Tier applications
- Lift and shift legacy web applications

-- **Bottom line** –

- Swarm is NOT dead – significant enhancements 18.09
- Easier to build, manage and secure
- Monolithic Service deployment
- Production Support for Windows with near Linux Parity

- Best where applications are composed from a network of long running services
- Development teams are service focused
- Large scale microservices applications
- Bottom-up, multi layer API services for enterprise or 3rd party consumption

-- **Bottom line** --

- Management plane as a Service (AKS/EKS/GKE) with large echo-system modules
- Modular Service deployment
- Beta, limited Windows capabilities
- Vendor lock-in with many supported versions

Swarm and Kubernetes

Swarm takes an application-centric, monolithic approach by defining a stack of related services in a .yaml file. Swarm stacks assume you are running a collection of related services, isolated by overlay networks, to support specific functionality in the context of an application. This makes it easy to deploy a typical application stack such as an Angular frontend with an application's RESTful API and a Postgres database.

Moving Kubernetes to the mainstream

Many PaaS and IaaS providers are diving into Kubernetes and providing turnkey setups. They are betting on the Kubernetes API as a specification for deploying application workloads in their service. Examples include Google's Kubernetes engine, Azure Kubernetes Service, and last but certainly not least, **Amazon Elastic Container Service for Kubernetes** (**Amazon EKS**). These are great to get you started, but what about if/when you move steady workloads back on premises due to cost or security concerns?

Finally, beware of the limitations tied to PaaS solutions. If you use a PaaS Kubernetes management plane, you may be limited to using the PaaS provider's CNI plugin and their implementation may limit your options. As an example, if you are running Kubernetes on AWS, the networking implementation may require one virtual IP/pod, but you only get a limited number of virtual IPs per instance type. Subsequently, you might need to move up to a bigger, more expensive instance type to support more pods, even though you don't really need any more/better CPUs, network, or storage.

New era for app Dev, DevOps, and IT operations

Using containers and orchestrators changes the way we look at building software and defining a software delivery pipeline. Container-based development fundamentally supports what the DevOps folks call a shift left, where developers of distributed systems become more accountable for the quality of the overall solution, meaning the binaries and how they are connected. Hence, wiring up my services in no longer the networking, integration, or operations teams' problem; it belongs to the developers. In fact, the YAML specification for connecting and deploying their application is now an artifact that gets checked into source code control!

Faster deployment of fixes and enhancements is a prime motivation for containerizing monolithic web applications built with job and .NET. Containerization allows each team to operate independently and deploy its application as soon as it is ready to go, no longer having to wait for all of the other application teams or the next quarterly release cycle.

Containerizing applications can be really helpful for breaking up the organization log jams associated with pre-container monolithic deployments, as each application gets its own runtime container. This container includes all of their specific runtime dependencies, such as Java and Tomcat, for the application to run. Because we are using containers, we become less concerned about the overhead associated with starting and operating similar containers in production by remembering how Docker isolates application execution, while sharing common layers from the filesystem for fast start times and efficient resource utilization. So, rather then having to coordinate across all of the teams involved in a deployment, each team has its own isolated stack of dependencies, which allows them to deploy and test on their own schedule. Not surprisingly, after applications are containerized, it is much easier to independently refactor them.

First containerize applications without changing any code if possible. After you have the application containerized, then take on any refactoring. Trying to accomplish both containerizing and refactoring simultaneously can be daunting and may stall the project.

DevOps

Leveraging containers in your continuous integration and continuous deployment pipeline has become a best practice for most DevOps teams. Even the pipeline itself is often run as a containerized platform. The motivation here is a higher-quality product, based on the immutable server pattern where containers are built once and promoted through the pipeline. In other words, the application is not re-installed on a new virtual server between each step in the pipeline. Instead, the same container image is pulled from a central repository and run in the next step. Environment variables and configuration files are used to account for variations between the environments.

Operations

Since the application team has taken on the tasks of wiring up and configuring the application for deployment, the operations team can shift its focus toward the container platform. This includes setting up and maintaining the container platform's operational environments, monitoring and centralized logging for applications running in the cluster, and security/policy management within the cluster to ensure that applications and users are behaving as expected.

Container-first and strategic impact of containers

Containers add some great new possibilities when approaching your enterprise application strategy, primarily with respect to cloud migration and application modernization. Containers allow organizations to elevate this conversation from the tactics around cloud migration and application stacks to a common application platform where virtually any application stack runs more efficiently while at the same time making the applications cloud-portable.

Container-first as a cloud adoption strategy

What if, before you started migrating all of your applications to a specific cloud-specific provider, you instead containerize your applications first and then migrate them to the cloud. This is sometimes referred to as a container-first strategy. There are several significant benefits to this approach:

- Abstracting platform-specific knowledge from application teams
- Gaining operational efficiency (usually in the range of 15% to 70%) from containerized applications
- It gives you the ability you move your applications between on-premise and any cloud providers with minimal effort

Container-first thinking should reduce cloud-specific staffing needs; instead of a cloud admin/application, you have a cloud admin/container cluster. Once containerized, application migrations between cloud providers and on-premise should be measured in hours and not weeks or months.

Get ready to bring workloads back from the public cloud

Moving to the cloud is fun and cool! However, it can get very expensive and hard for an enterprise to control. Most of what I see from clients is that the cloud makes sense for highly variable workloads where elastic capacity is very important. However, when steady, predictable workloads are involved, many organizations find the public cloud to be too expensive and ultimately migrate them back to their data center or private cloud. This is referred to as workload repatriation and it's becoming a very common event.

Application modernization – the containerization path

Docker customers have documented significant reductions in operational costs achieved by simply containerizing traditional web-based (.NET 2.0+ and Java) applications and establishing a Docker Enterprise infrastructure to run them. This infrastructure can run in the cloud, VMware, or even bare metal. There is a methodology used by Docker solution architects to help enterprises migrate traditional applications. It starts with accelerated PoC, moves to a pilot application, and finally to production, where each step builds on the last.

Support for microservices and DevOps

At this point in the game, most development teams won't even attempt to build and deploy microservices without containers and orchestrators. 12-factor style development teams have lots of moving part and deploy often—a perfect fit for Docker and Kubernetes! These teams use containerized, decentralized CI/CD systems that come with built-in container support to achieve low error rates using high-speed automated deployments.

Compliance

While compliance for container platforms is achievable with third-party products such as Sysdig Secure, Twistlock, and AquaSec, Docker Enterprise 2.1 adds FIPS compliance support for Windows and RHEL platforms. This means the Docker platform is validated against widely accepted standards and best practices during Docker Enterprise product development. With this, the companies and agencies get additional confidence to adopt Docker containers. **Federal Information Processing Standard (FIPS)** Publication 140-2 being the most remarkable standards, verifies and permits the use of various security encryption modules within an organization software stack which now includes the Docker Enterprise Engine.

 For more information on FIPs, please visit docker's website: `https://docs.docker.com/compliance/nist/fips140_2/`.
For more information on general Docker compliance, please visit: `https://docs.docker.com/compliance/`.

How Docker Enterprise 2.0 has changed the game

In April of 2018, Docker Enterprise 2.0 was a release. In this release, Docker added support for Kubernetes. Not some wrapped or repackaged version, but the real open source version. The advantage of running Kubernetes on Docker Enterprise 2.0 is simplicity. With Docker Enterprise 2.0, the universal control plane includes pre-installed Kubernetes, which runs alongside Swarm. This means that enterprises do not need to choose between Kubernetes and Swarm; they can have them both. This is a big deal for organizations that need to deal with both pockets of advanced microservice applications and simpler n-tier traditional applications. With Docker Enterprise 2.0, microservice teams are free get their Kube on, while the rest of the teams get up to speed with Swarm. Also, it allows an enterprise to handle a more manageable learning curve by getting started with Swarm and later introducing more complex Kubernetes configurations as required.

Additionally, at Dockercon 2018, Docker announced some very exciting features on their near-term roadmap regarding integration between Docker Enterprise and cloud-based Kubernetes Services. Essentially, Docker Enterprise 2 will be able to take an on-premise Kubernetes app running on Docker Enterprise 2.0 and deploy it to a web-based Kubernetes provider such as Amazon or Google.

While Docker Enterprise 2.0 may not be the perfect choice for a small cloud-native startup, its flexibility, integrated security model, and single platform should make it a top consideration for on premise and hybrid container platforms.

Summary

In the last 5 years, containers have come out of obscurity and into the spotlight across the software industry and DevOps. The profound organizational impact of containers spans software developers, IT admins, DevOps engineers, architects, and executives alike. From the beginning, Docker, Inc. has been at the center of the container movement and remains committed to the long term success by supporting industry standards, the open source community, and most recently enterprise customers with a Kubernetes-capable Docker Enterprise 2.

In the next 5 years, the enterprise adoption of containers will blossom. Subsequently, most organizations will begin looking for an enterprise-grade solution that balances cost and security with speed and leading-edge platform features. Docker Enterprise's single pane of glass for hybrid cloud and on-premises clusters, along with support for the latest container technologies, including Kubernetes support, is very likely to draw the attention of astute IT leaders around the world.

Coming up in `Chapter 2`, *Docker Enterprise – an Architectural Overview*, our journey continues as we explore the features and architecture of Docker Enterprise.

Questions

1. How long have containers been around?
2. What is Docker, Inc. and what does it do?
3. What is the difference between Docker Engine-Community and Docker Enterprise?
4. What is the difference between Docker and Kubernetes?
5. What is the best orchestrator for deploying simple n-tier web applications?
6. How does Docker support Kubernetes?
7. How does container-based development impact application developers?
8. Why would I need fewer cloud admins with a cloud-first strategy?

Further reading

- Docker Enterprise production information:
    - https://www.docker.com/products/docker-enterprise
    - https://docs.docker.com/ee/
- Docker Enterprise FIPS compliance:
    - https://blog.docker.com/2017/06/docker-ee-is-now-in-process-for-fips-140-2/
    - https://docs.docker.com/compliance/nist/fips140_2/

2
Docker Enterprise - an Architectural Overview

As we dive further into the details of Docker Enterprise, it is important to know where it fits within the competitive landscape of enterprise container platform providers. Informing buyers of broad provider categories can help them decide whether Docker Enterprise is the best for their organization. Additionally, we provide an overview of the economics of Docker Enterprise along with key features, architecture, and components to support open, supported products for enterprise customers.

The following topics will be covered in this chapter:

- Docker Enterprise's position in the emerging enterprise container platform market
- The cost/benefit economics of Docker Enterprise's architecture
- The architectural context of Docker Enterprise
- The key components of Docker Enterprise
- Docker Enterprise reference architecture

Moving from science projects to production platforms

In the early days, and for containers up until about the middle of 2017, Docker-based applications look more like science projects than well engineered production platforms. It seems as though no amount of technical debt was too high as long as your application was running, stable, and cool. Additionally, the hand-rolled tooling it took to support early Docker/Kubernetes applications was fully understood by only one or two members of an enterprise team, and they were usually more aligned with the developers and less aligned with the operations team, creating a huge gap in the enterprise skill set required to support containers in production. As the technical debt grew and the skill set gap widened, a large market opportunity emerged.

With Docker's explosive growth since 2013, a significant market opportunity emerged to support containers in the enterprise. To be successful, these platforms should consider the following goals:

- Give developers the ability to build, test (locally on development workstations as well as on a remote development cluster), and deploy secure multi-container applications at will
- Provide an efficient, and secure, developer-managed CI pipeline
- Allow operators (DevOps, TechOps, and SecOps) the ability to efficiently secure, manage, monitor, and scale multiple environments for development, test, QA, and production applications
- Support compliance requirements at the platform level—not at just at the application level

The landscape of emerging container platforms

Many leading technology companies are involved in the container platform game and I'll group them into three broad categories to summarize where Docker Enterprise fits in. Specific vendor names are intentionally being withheld to avoid any emotional arguments or legal warfare, so just some high-level sifting and sorting for now:

- **Container platform categories emerge**:
    - **Virtualization vendor container platforms**:
        - **Summary**: Large enterprise virtualization vendors are justifiably concerned about containers eroding their virtualization revenues. Indeed, running Docker can reduce, or in the case of Docker on bare metal can eliminate, the need for commercial virtualization products. Currently, Docker on bare metal is pretty rare in the wild, but it poses a huge threat to the multi-billion-dollar virtualization industry over the next 10 years.

            Realistically, containers and virtualization technologies will be considered complementary technologies in the short term, but in the longer term there is a real risk to the virtualization industry.

            In response to the container threat, virtualization vendors are responding with their own container platform, but they require licensing of their latest product platform to use it.

            - **Pros**:
                - Build on existing virtualization technology platforms and skill sets
                - Leverage existing legal contracts (might require some upgrades however)
                - Easy to use/same support channels
            - **Cons**:
                - Usually require upgrades to latest/advanced options

- Locked into their stack and not easy to move to different, possibly cheaper, platforms in the future
- Virtualization tax—requires full vendor stack and licensing wherever you deploy, on-premise or cloud

- **OS platform vendor stacks**:
  - **Summary**: Vendors providing enterprise support for Linux operating systems have thrown their hat in the ring as well. In the hope of maintaining market share through convenience, these vendors provide some interesting options, but lock you into their licensing models to use their version of containers. These platforms usually provide older versions of Docker (nearly 2 years old in some cases) or alternate container engines they own.
  - **Pros**:
    - Build on existing OS technology platforms and skill sets
    - Leverage existing legal contracts
    - Easy to use/same support channels
  - **Cons**:
    - Usually several releases behind their open source counterparts
    - Locked into their version of the OS and must use their licensed OS stack to be supported
    - Wrap underlying APIs—requires additional APIs and long lag times from open feature release to the vendor's wrapped version release

- **Cloud vendor-based container platforms**:
    - **Summary**: Most of the initial microservice application deployments using Docker and Kubernetes were born-in-cloud applications. Initially, these were hand-rolled with virtual networks and cloud virtual machines, but cloud vendors saw a great opportunity in the container market and began to offer container-related platform services (*CS) in 2015. Initially, these services focused on single-host container deployments, but the rapid maturity of container orchestration led to a new generation of orchestration-related cloud platform services (*KS) being released in 2017 and 2018.
    - **Pros**:
        - Easy to get started with
        - Easy to connect to the cloud vendor's other services
        - Initially low cost
    - **Cons**:
        - Need to provide, wire-up, manage, and pay for your own clusters
        - Older versions of Docker and Kubernetes
        - Isolation by resource group or VPC leads to cluster sprawl—gets expensive and complicated for centralized integrated access management
        - Sticky integration—easy to use cloud vendor's services, difficult to migrate to another cloud provider or on-premise

- **Supported open platform, extensible technologies**:
  - **Summary**: Docker Enterprise fits the category of a supported open, extensible technology. The complexity of bringing many open source products together under a single umbrella is a challenge, but is ultimately a great deal for customers. Docker customers get choice and transparency from this platform, but more integration is required. This what most enterprises would do themselves if they could, but they usually can't afford a dedicated team of rock star engineers.

    Docker Enterprise is backed by dedicated engineers and they strive to deliver a cloud-portable container platform, giving the customer the choice of running on any popular cloud/OS platform with Docker support and a stable release cycle for underlying open technologies—and doing so without wrapping or forking key technologies such as Kubernetes. Docker Enterprise includes the Docker API/container D and the real Kubernetes API out of the box.

  - **Pros**:
    - A portable or hybrid-friendly enterprise container platform that Docker supports from the engine up to the control plane, including Docker-certified plugins for networking and storage
    - Everything you need (Docker Enterprise Standard +) to run an enterprise container platform including a secure cluster, universal control plane, and a feature-rich, secure container registry
    - Very cost effective for enterprise-scale platforms
    - Because of RBAC, usually only need two clusters for all environments

- **Cons**:

  - Can be expensive for a small HA cluster—HA clusters typically require three managers/masters, three DTR nodes and therefore requires a 7th nodes to start running workloads. Please note this overhead is quickly offset by consolidating all non-production environments into a single non-prod cluster with RBAC.

  - An initial Docker Enterprise build can take some thought and time. Because Docker's open-platform approach allows for countless permutations of suitable infrastructure, preparing an enterprise-specific platform for the install takes some planning and expertise (hardware/VMs, OS, networks, storage, monitoring/alerting). Docker's professional services and authorized consulting partners can help (a lot) here, but I'll cover a lot of these setup items in subsequent chapters to help get you started on your own.

 Most recently, tech industry analysts have created a container platform software suite category. In Q4 of 2018, Forrester research claimed Docker Enerprise leads the pack: https://goto.docker.com/the-forrester-wave-enterprise-container-platform-software-suites-2018.html.

Economics, features, and key components of Docker Enterprise

When it comes to deciding on an enterprise container platform in today's digital business world, it is all about balancing innovation (usually with the goal of increased topline revenue) with the associated costs to support and operationalize these new applications. So, like most important business decisions, it comes down to the economics and in this case the economics associated with containerized applications in support of innovation, or perhaps containerizing old web apps for lower ongoing support costs to free up resources for the innovation budget. Either way, you will need to understand the costs and benefits of Docker Enterprise.

The estimated cost of Docker Enterprise

We begin our brief cost/benefit discussion with the cost side of the equation and starting with the Docker Enterprise platform and licensing.

To run Docker Enterprise, you will need virtual servers for each node, a network to connect them, and some cluster-based storage (NFS usually works great for on-premise cluster storage). Remember, Docker Enterprise can run in the cloud, on-premise, in a VM, or on bare-metal servers—the choice is yours. For cost estimation purposes, plan on six manager nodes with four cores and 16 GB of RAM for managers and **Docker Trusted Registry (DTR)** nodes. The resources required for worker nodes will depend on the types of workloads you are running on your cluster. For instance, with a Java-based application you typically need a large memory footprint of maybe four cores and 32 GB of RAM per worker node. Whereas with a node-based application, you may have more balance between CPU and memory and can run several applications comfortably with two cores and 16 GB of RAM.

Whichever infrastructure platform you choose, it is generally a good idea to target a platform where your operations team has an existing skill set, so they can focus their energy learning Docker Enterprise without having to climb a new platform learning curve at the same time.

Also, keep in mind a typical starter cluster will have about 10 nodes, because six of the nodes are used for cluster and image management, leaving four nodes to handle workloads. This might seem like a high ratio of overhead-to-workload nodes, but do keep in mind you can probably add hundreds of additional worker nodes without adding any additional overhead.

Docker Enterprise is a commercial product and may be purchased from Docker, Inc. or a Docker-authorized reseller. The following estimated costs are subject to change and are based on publicly available information from Docker's online store. When you are getting serious about Docker Enterprise, you need to contact Docker or an authorized reseller directly for up to date and possibly discounted pricing.

So, for the sake of an example, the following is representative pricing (from `https://hub.docker.com/`) for common **high availability** (**HA**) cluster configurations. Please note that business-day support is from 9 a.m. to 6 p.m. local time, Monday-Friday, and business-critical support is *24 hours/day x 7 days/week x 365 days/year*.

Docker Enterprise pricing illustration

The following table shows a sample pricing matrix for Docker Enterprise:

	Docker Enterprise standard edition (business-day support)	Docker Enterprise advanced (business-day support)	Docker Enterprise advanced (business-critical support)
Manager nodes	*3 x $150/month*	*3 x $200/month*	*3 x $350/month*
DTR nodes	*3 x $150/month*	*3 x $200/month*	*3 x $350/month*
Worker nodes	*4 x $150/month*	*4 x $200/month*	*4 x $350/month*
Total	*10 nodes = $1500/month*	*10 nodes = $2000/month*	*10 nodes = $3500/month*

This pricing chart is provided for illustration purposes only. For an actual budget planning number, please contact Docker, Inc. or a Docker authorized reseller.

Three managers and three DTR nodes are required for **HA** clusters. While this might seem like a lot of overhead, you can add hundreds of additional worker nodes without adding any more manager or DTR nodes.

Docker Enterprise architecture-related benefits

Docker Enterprise provides a wide range of benefits that are specifically geared toward Enterprise users who are looking to operate at scale with commercial levels of support. However, they also want to keep their development staff empowered to rapidly innovate and deliver secure and scalable applications.

Docker support benefits

One key reason organizations start looking at Docker Enterprise is for support. While the Community edition of Docker does provide community-based support; this requires organizations to post their issues in public forums. Not only is there no guarantee of the issue being addressed in a timely manner, it may be inappropriate to post a bug report related to a vulnerability in an enterprise's infrastructure. This is especially sensitive for users in a regulated industry.

Docker's full-stack support starts at the Docker Engine. While we are primarily focusing on Docker Enterprise Standard and Advanced, there is a basic offering that provides support for just the Docker Engine and does NOT provide UCP and DTR. This also happens to be the level of support that is included with Windows Server 2016. All Docker-supported platforms allow customers to receive patches on the same version level for up to 2 years. Without support, you are forced to upgrade every 6 months.

With Docker Enterprise Standard and Advanced editions, support extends beyond the engine to the universal control plane, Docker trusted registry, and any Docker-certified plugins or Docker-certified containers being used by the customer.

Again, as mentioned previously, there are two levels of support: business-critical, which provides 24/7 support, and business day, which is available during normal business hours.

Computational efficiency benefits

Running applications with a container architecture has demonstrated a significant reduction in operational costs for many traditional web applications. These cost reductions have been documented as high as 70%, and are generally achieved by reducing the overhead associated with virtual machines, as well as creating a higher application density per server.

Benefits of choice

Docker Enterprise provides a wide range of infrastructure choices for running your EE platform. This means you can install Docker Enterprise in the cloud, on-premise, in a virtual machine, or on bare metal. You also have a wide variety of open and commercially supported Linux operating systems to run UCP and DTR. Worker nodes can be installed on Linux, Windows Server 2016, and even on OS 390. It is common to use mixed clusters with both Linux and Windows nodes to deliver a polyglot, distributed application stack of Linux and Windows containers.

This sort of choice is really important! It allows Docker customers to migrate an entire container platform from one infrastructure provider to another with relative ease. Therefore, if an infrastructure provider becomes too expensive, a Docker Enterprise customer can pick up their cluster and move it to a lower cost provider with relative ease.

In addition to infrastructure choices, Docker also provides a choice of orchestrators. Docker Enterprise includes both Swarm and Kubernetes out of the box. While some cloud-native pundits claim to not much for Swarm, it is where most enterprises, when given a real choice, like to start because of its security and simplicity. Later they can graduate to more sophisticated Kubernetes applications.

Rapid innovation – platform-neutral DevOps skills benefit the shift-left strategy

In the DevOps world, we hear a lot about shifting to the left. This means taking responsibilities that were once part of the technical operations organization and moving them into the DevOps and application development realms. In this world, Docker becomes a really important tool for this sort of migration because the language used to describe how applications are built, wired, and deployed is based on Docker and Kubernetes platform-neutral APIs. Without this approach, your application development and DevOps staff would need to learn platform-specific details for each target environment, such as AWS, Azure, or GCE. This not only creates a steeper learning curve, it also creates another layer of locking into a vendor's platform.

UCP and DTR benefits

Docker Enterprise standard and advanced come with the **Universal Control Plane** (**UCP**) and the **Docker Trusted Registry** (**DTR**).

Docker's UCP includes critical enterprise features such as LDAP integrated, role-based access control, a certificate managed command-line interface, a web-based GUI, and the Kubernetes orchestrator installed and ready to use. UCP also provides a secure API interface for scripting and extensibility.

Rather than using a public image repository such as Docker Hub for enterprise images, Docker Enterprise uses a private image repository called DTR for security and availability reasons. If for some reason an image repository becomes unavailable to a cluster, applications cannot be deployed. So, DTR is a replicated, integral part of the Docker Enterprise platform.

Docker's DTR runs in the same cluster where the workload container images are deployed. DTR is where enterprise images are securely stored after they are built and where they are pulled from at deployment time. DTR is a critical part of an enterprise-class container cluster and is also the heart and soul of a secure image pipeline. Therefor, DTR includes image scanning (Advanced Edition feature only), image signing with Notary's TUF implementation, and webhooks for CI/CD integration and image promotion policies, and is fully integrated with the UCP RBAC system.

Container-first benefits

Setting up a container platform helps you to start realizing the benefits of serverless development. In a Docker Enterprise, container-first world, developers build and test stacks of containers using Docker's platform-independent tools, including both Docker Desktop and Docker Enterprise. Subsequently, their application can be deployed to a Docker Desktop or Docker Enterprise platform without knowing whether it is running locally on a desktop, on-premise, or in the cloud. Furthermore, containers within an application stack can freely communicate with each other, but are isolated from other containers in different application stacks using Swarm overlay networks or Kubernetes namespaces.

Operational architecture of Docker Enterprise

This section provides an introduction to Docker Enterprise's main components, puts them into an operationally oriented architectural context, and then describes each layer within the context. The goal is to present Docker Enterprise's main parts in an operational environment and describe how they work in a real-world setting. In other words, describe the components and the Docker Enterprise platform from the day-in-the-life perspective of a developer/DevOps and operations team member.

Docker Enterprise's main components

Since Docker Enterprise piggybacks off Docker Engine-Community's Swarm mode, our discussion starts with a sample overview of Swarm clusters. *Figure 1* represents a 10-node Docker Swarm cluster. It is composed of three manager nodes and seven worker nodes. Each of the nodes is a VM or bare-metal server running the Docker Engine in Swarm mode.

Our three manager nodes are members of a Raft consensus group backed by an encrypted Etcd cluster for storing things like the cluster's state, certificates, and secrets. To function properly, there needs to be an odd number of manager nodes in the health state because you need to maintain a quorum (a majority of managers need to agree on any changes to the cluster state). One manager node clusters are efficient, but if the manager goes down the cluster is dead. For higher availability, clusters generally have three and sometimes five managers for redundancy.

As the name implies, worker nodes are where containerized workloads run. There can be any number of workers and these nodes can be scaled up and down as needed:

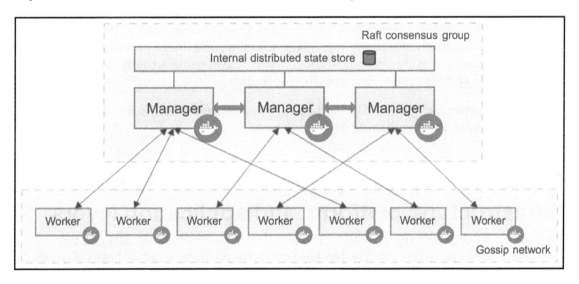

Figure 1: Highly available Swarm cluster © 2013-2018 Docker, Inc. All rights reserved

By now, most folks have heard the pets versus cattle phrase. It appears to trace back to Bill Baker's presentation (`http://www.pass.org/eventdownload.aspx?suid=1902`), but applies to container clusters too. We talk about cattle as anonymous beasts that come and go, largely without a personal connection. If there is something wrong with a cow, you don't nurse it back to health, instead you get another to replace it. Pets on the other hand are named, lovingly cared for, and we keep them around as long as possible. In a Docker Enterprise cluster, managers are your pets and worker nodes are your cattle.

Docker Enterprise adds 3 new parts to the picture:

- **The Docker Enterprise Engine**: A supported version of the Docker Engine-Community platform that includes 2-year patch support for each major version. You need a key from the Docker store to install the Docker Enterprise Engine.
- **Universal Control Plane (UCP)**: Provides GUI, RBAC, a secure certificate-based command-line interface bundle, LDAP integration, and orchestration (Swarm and Kubernetes). UCP provides secure API access through a bearer token for scripting things such as UCP RBAC structures and grants.
- **Docker Trusted Registry (DTR)**: A private image registry integrated into the Docker Enterprise cluster as a critical component of a secure software pipeline. DTR provides support for RBAC-managed repos (ties into UCP RBAC infrastructure), image signing, image scanning, and image promotion. All DTR features are made available through a secure API using an authorization token to manage both images and repository metadata.

Now, to get a better feel for how Docker Enterprise components fit into a real environment, we will take a look at using them to deploy software.

Docker Enterprise operation architecture – infrastructure, platform, and application layers

Framing up an operationally-oriented architectural perspective helps to describe the constituent user's point of view. The Docker Enterprise platform achieves both efficiency and security through a separation of concerns by isolating application developers from the infrastructure using platform-level abstractions such as services, networks, volumes, configurations, and secrets. Meanwhile, the actual implementation of these platform abstractions and their underlying infrastructure is managed by a small group of highly skilled operations folks. This approach allows application development work, including DevOps activities, to build and deploy applications using platform-agnostic APIs (Docker and Kubernetes CLIs).

Docker Enterprise's platform separation drives efficiency, security, and innovation!
Using a small operations team to back Docker Enterprise platform abstractions with
infrastructure-appropriate implementations (secure and efficient best practices for on-
premise or cloud provider platforms using Docker plugins) enables all containerized
application teams to access these abstractions through a deployment .yaml file. The
development team does not care about where the application is deployed as long as the
abstractions are implemented correctly. This gives the application powerful tools for mass
innovation (Solomon Hykes' dream realized), while a small operations team keeps things
secure and running on the underlying infrastructure.

Infrastructure skills for AWS, Azure, GCE, and VMware are hard to find!
Docker Enterprise's platform separation allows an enterprise to leverage a
relatively small team of infrastructure experts across a large number of
application teams. Additionally, platform separation enables a DevOps
shift left, empowering developers to describe their application service
stack deployment using platform-neutral constructs.

Figure 2 describes platform separation layers in action. First, the operations team installs
and configures the infrastructure using Docker-certified infrastructure guidelines. This
includes preparing the host OS, configuring (NFS) storage, installing the Docker Enterprise
Engine (image storage drivers and plugins), installing Docker UCP, and installing DTR. In
our example, the Ops team configures the Docker Enterprise Engine for central logging and
installs the plugin for NFS storage.

Then, the platform team (can be an operations function or a specialized group of Docker
Enterprise operators trained on platform configuration, operations, support, and
maintenance) configures cluster access with RBAC so users can deploy their stack using the
appropriate cluster resources. Finally, a developer/DevOps team member uses a Docker
Enterprise CLI bundle to deploy a stack of containers into the cluster using a `docker
stack deploy` command with the `ApplicationStack.yml` file. The containers are
scheduled across the cluster using the platform abstractions for services, networking, and
volumes.

Normally, this deployment process to the cluster is handled by a CI/CD
system such as Jenkins, GitLab, or Azure DevOps. The CI system user has
its own UCP RBAC user account + certificate for accessing the cluster,
managing DTR images, and signing images it built before pushing to
DTR.

In this case, the application is deployed across two worker nodes as shown below, connected by the **My-2-tier** network and has access to external data stored on an NFS mount point. Additionally, the `ApplicationStack.yml` file can describe how the application is externally exposed using layer-7 routing and can make the application immediately live. Ultimately, the application can be completely deployed without any intervention from the infrastructure/operations team:

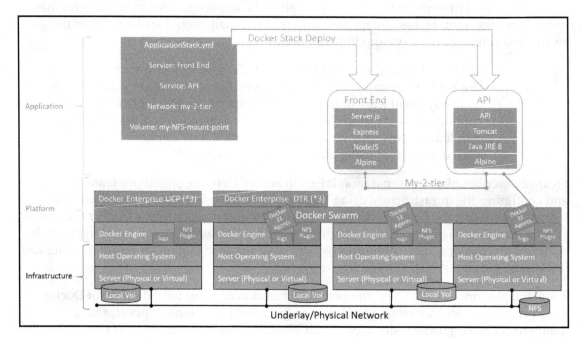

Figure 2 :Service Stacks on Swarm

Breaking down the layers

Reviewing the layers at a high level, from the bottom up, reveals their content as well as each layer's key architectural concerns. We will start at the foundational infrastructure layer by reviewing the underpinnings of Docker Enterprise. Moving up the stack to the platform layer, we will review Docker Enterprise's underlying components. Finally, we will see what the platform looks like from an application developer's point of view.

Infrastructure layer – network, nodes, and storage

At the infrastructure layer, the focus is on the operational network, computational nodes, and backend storage.

> When defining your infrastructure layer, it is a really good idea to consult the Docker-certified infrastructure documentation on Docker's website, https://success.docker.com/ (certified architecture). There are specific reference architecture guides available for VMware, AWS, and Azure. These guides provide key insights for the operations team planning and designing their Docker Enterprise infrastructure layer.

The **operational network** is primarily concerned with ingress, egress, and inter-node data flow with the appropriate isolation and encryption of Docker cluster nodes. Carving out address space and defining a network security group policy are usually the center of attention. While this is generally pretty straightforward, the Docker reference architecture covers important details. The following are globally a couple of key considerations to highlight:

- **Consideration 1**: While there is some conflicting documentation on the topic, it is a good idea to pin your manager nodes to fixed IP addresses.
- **Consideration 2**: Make sure Docker's overlay network spaces does not overlap with other address space on your network. There are some new parameters starting in Docker 18.09 for initiating Docker Enterprise's underlying Swarm cluster to carve out safe network CIDR blocks for Docker's overlay networking to use:

```
docker swarm init --default-addr-pool 10.85.0.0/16 --default-
addr-pool 10.91.0.0/16 --default-addr-pool-mask-length 25
```

For a complete introduction to Docker networking, please read the https://success. docker.com/ article on networking.

Computational nodes are the VMs or bare-metal nodes running a Docker Enterprise engine on top of a supported OS. The Docker Enterprise engine is currently supported on CentOS, Oracle Linux, Red Hat Enterprise Linux, SUSE Linux Enterprise Server, Ubuntu, Microsoft Windows Server 2016, Microsoft Windows Server 1709, and Microsoft Windows Server 1803. The key concerns for setting up a computational node are CPU, RAM, local storage, and cluster storage endpoints.

While there are no magic formulas to predict perfect-sized nodes, there are some pretty safe bets, as used for planning purposes in the previous cost section. Generally, it is a safe bet to go with four cores and 16 GB of RAM for managers and **Docker Trusted Registry (DTR)** nodes. Again, worker nodes will depend on the types of workload you are running on them. Containerized Java applications often need a large memory footprint and maybe a four-core and 32 GB of RAM worker makes sense. Most organizations have stats on applications they are currently running and can be used for estimation purposes. Do not get too hung up on sizing workers— they are your cattle and as such can be easily replaced.

Another computational node consideration is storage. There are three considerations related to storage:

- **Backing filesystems for Docker image storage drivers**: When the Docker Engine is installed (in the platform layer), you need an image storage driver to efficiently implement a layered, copy-on-write filesystem. These drivers require a compatible backing filesystem. Most modern Linux systems will automatically use the Overlay2 storage driver backed by ext4 filesystems. Older versions of CentOS and RHEL (7.3 and earlier) generally use the devicemapper storage driver backed by a direct-lvm filesystem (do not run production workloads direct-lvm in loop-back mode). On SUSE, use the btrfs driver and filesystem.
- **Local storage for node-specific volumes**: Docker volumes tied to specific nodes can be handy when you have specialized nodes in your cluster. These nodes are then labeled so that containers can be deployed specifically to these nodes. This ensures that any volumes are consistently available on these nodes and comes in handy for container-based centralized build servers to store plugins and workspaces. Please remember these volumes should be added to your backup list!
- **Cluster-based storage**: When nodes mount remote storage endpoints using something like NFS, you can then allow containers to mount these mount points as volumes to access remote storage from within a container. This is common for older on-premise deployments, but newer on-premise installations might consider installing NFS on the host and using the local volume opt: nfs, or they may consider using a third-party volume plugin that ties into your storage vendor's infrastructure for more flexibility and stability.

Please note, NFS storage generally works well for on-premise installations where you have full control over the network, but in the cloud, NFS mounts may be less reliable due to latency from noisy neighbors.

Only use NFS for on-premise implementations with predictably low latency. When running Docker Enterprise in the cloud, consider using something such as CloudStor or RexRay to avoid NFS issues related to sudden spikes in network latency. Such spikes can cause NFS to silently switch to read-only mode, resulting in cascading application failures.

Finally, here are two considerations for computational nodes being prepared to run as **manager** nodes:

- These nodes should have **fixed IPs**. There is some conflicting advice as to whether or not Docker Enterprise reconcile processing compensates for manager IP changes or not. While dynamic IPs are fine for worker nodes, when it comes to manager nodes, play it safe and use fixed IP addresses.
- They must be backed up regularly, including `/var/lib/docker/swarm`.

More about backups later in getting ready for production, but remember your manager nodes are pets and you might need to restore one from backups some day!

The platform layer – Docker Enterprise engine, UCP, and DTR

At the platform layer, the Docker software is installed and configured on top of the infrastructure layer, which we discussed in the previous section. We prepare each of the Docker nodes in the cluster by installing the Docker Enterprise Engine. Before you start this process, you need to purchase your Docker license or get a free 30-day trial license. In either case, the license key storebits link will appear in your Docker store account under **My Contents**.

We will walk through an actual install later in the book using a sample AWS installation with Ubuntu. But generally speaking, we install the Docker Enterprise engine using an encrypted link to configure a Linux package manager repository on each node, then use the package manager to install the appropriate version of the engine.

After the Docker Engine is installed and started, there are a few things you want to do:

1. Update the storage driver and the logging driver in the `/etc/docker/daemon.json` file. A service restart is required for these changes to become active.
2. Add your Linux user to the Docker group so you don't have to run Docker commands with the root privilege.
3. Install and configure any Docker plugins.

Once the engines are all installed, it's time for us to move into setting up the cluster. We install UCP on the first manager node, and then join the other nodes into the cluster. After UCP is up and all of the manager and worker nodes are joined, the Docker trusted registry is installed. Again, there will be a lot more detail as we walk through a real setup in the installation chapter.

Now, you have a new cluster with a DTR up and running. The administrator adds users to the cluster RBAC system, usually by connecting to an LDAP system and using a special query to define a sync point for UCP users with the corporation-wide LDAP directory. Docker Enterprise 2.1 also has a SAML-based single sign-on option, which we will discuss later. You can also set up new UCP users with the GUI or by running a script against the UCP API.

Once you have users created, you can give them the appropriate access to UCP and DTR resources. This is done by a grant system where you can assign fine-grained rights to clusters (Swarm collections and Kubernetes namespace resources) based on organizational membership, team membership, or by individual account. Once accounts are set up, developers can access cluster resources based on the privileges granted by the administrator. Now that UCP and DTR are installed and initially configured, we can focus our attention on the application layer.

Application layer – interacting with the cluster

Finally, we have the application layer where containerized applications run using platform APIs (Swarm or Kubernetes) to describe and deploy them, as described earlier in *Figure 2*.

Now, we'll build on what we have learned and done during our tour of the platform layer and discuss deploying the application in a little more detail. Back at the platform layer, when creating users, let's say we created a user name John Doe and granted him "full control" to his private collection of developer resources. Now, he is able to deploy Swarm and Kubernetes resources to his personal (sandbox) space, but how does it actually work?

1. The system admin provides John with his UCP credentials.
2. John is able to log in to the cluster, but only sees what he's deployed to the cluster, which is nothing so far.
3. In *Figure 3*, John opens his profile in UCP Web UI and downloads a client bundle. The bundle contains some certificates and scripts (for both Linux and Windows) to securely connect the desktop shell to the cluster Swarm and Kubernetes APIs:

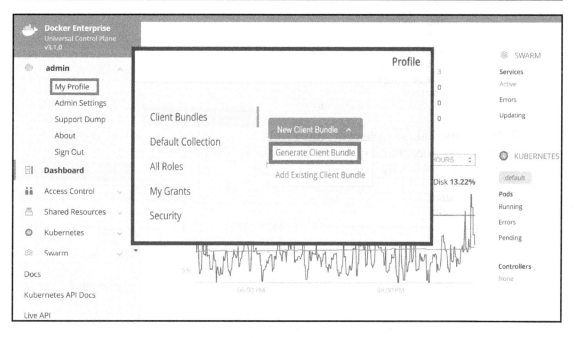

Figure 3 UCP client bundle download

4. John unzips the files and runs the connect script using either `Import-module` or source commands with PowerShell bash shell script files. John's local `$docker` and `$kubectl` commands now execute against the remote cluster, but are of course subject to his RBAC access rights.

5. John now runs the `$docker stack deploy` or `$kubectl create` commands, using the YAML file he built for his application, and deploys his application to the cluster.

6. See the following sample YAML file for a Kubernetes application use a `$kubectl create -f nginx-deployment.yml` from a command-line bundle:

```
apiVersion: apps/v1beta2
kind: Deployment
metadata:
 name: nginx-deployment
spec:
 selector:
 matchLabels:
 app: nginx
 replicas: 3
 template:
 metadata:
 labels:
```

```
app: nginx
spec:
containers:
- name: nginx
image: nginx:1.7.9
ports:
- containerPort: 80
```

7. In the previous sample code, three Kubernetes pods are deployed into the cluster, each containing an `nginx` container. Running `$kubectl get pods` command shows the running pods as follows:

```
NAME                                     READY   STATUS    RESTARTS
AGE
nginx-deployment-75675f5897-45dvt        1/1     Running   0
26s
nginx-deployment-75675f5897-hrgmg        1/1     Running   0
26s
nginx-deployment-75675f5897-vskh8        1/1     Running   0
26s
```

8. The `$kubectl get pods` command lists all three `nginx` replica pods running in the default namespace, each with 1 of 1 containers ready, and each pod status is `Running`.

Docker Enterprise reference architecture

Now, we will start to dig into the Docker Enterprise architecture. As we jump in, we need to understand that full adoption can take several months, during which enterprises gain valuable experience as they prepare their production platform. While the Docker Enterprise adoption journey will be discussed in greater detail in a later chapter, it makes sense to introduce the general concept of a phased, agile adoption approach (shown in *Figure 4*) so that new-comers are not overwhelmed. Let's understand how to best approach adopting any enterprise container technology:

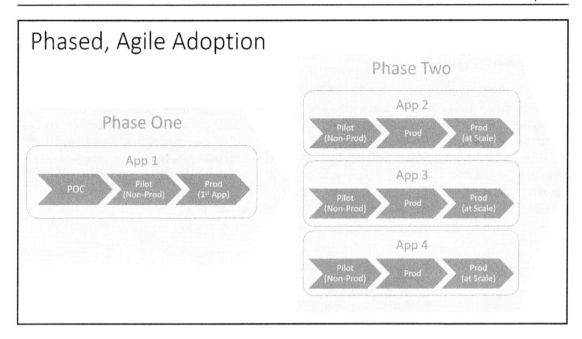

Figure 4 : Agile Adoption Cycles

It is usually best to start with a small, multi-discipline team with the goal of moving a single application from PoC, to pilot, and finally the first application into production. Additionally, the enterprise adoption of containers requires big changes with great potential upsides, but it requires a new container-first mindset. The fastest way to attain this container-first mindset and all of the associated benefits is by leveraging the experience of experts through training and advisory services that are available directly from Docker or through Docker-authorized partners. In full disclosure, as a Docker authorized partner, this may appear biased and self-serving, but to have a direct connection to the Docker source provides laser-sharp insights into the latest best practices. I say latest best practices because this rapidly evolving platform changes fast and so do the associated best practices. Be very careful not to bet your next generation platform on opinions from possibly outdated blog posts.

Simple view of the Docker Enterprise cluster architecture

Docker Enterprise provides a secure cluster management foundation that is backed by two orchestrators: Docker Swarm, built into Docker Engine-Community, and CNCF's Kubernetes, the leading born-in-the-cloud orchestration platform. When you install Docker Enterprise's **Universal Control Plane (UCP)**, both orchestrators are installed and ready to go. This includes default overlay networking to allow container network communication between containers located on different nodes in the cluster and service discovery. *Figure 5* illustrates your scheduler choice across a collection of cluster-managed worker nodes. Notice that Docker Enterprise relies on Swarm's secure cluster-based management as a foundation for both orchestrators. *Figure 6* shows a simple Docker Swarm TLS encrypted cluster:

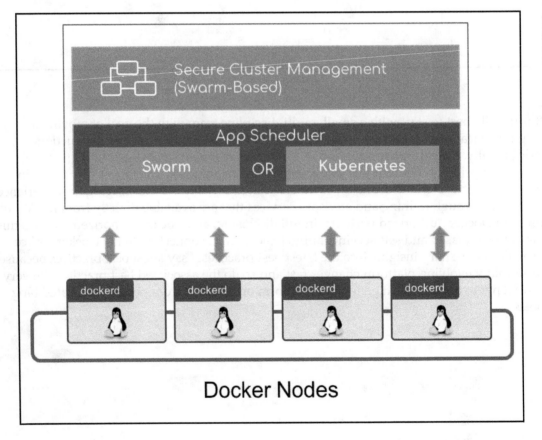

Figure 5: Swarm Cluster Overview © 2013-2018 Docker, Inc. All rights reserved

Peeling the onion one layer deeper reveals how a HA cluster includes multiple manager nodes in addition to the worker nodes, and how all intra-node communications are TLS encrypted. When a Swarm cluster is created, the first manager establishes a **Certificate Authority (CA)** and uses the CA's certificate authority to sign and secure the certificates exchanged when adding nodes to the cluster, using a secure join token. Additionally, the managers rotate the certificates at a configurable interval in case one of the certificates should be compromised over time:

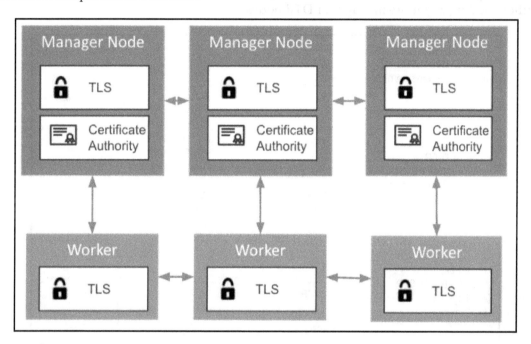

Figure 6: Swarm Mutual TLS Encryption © 2013-2018 Docker, Inc. All rights reserved

Often, in the early stages of Docker adoption and usually prior to Docker Enterprise adoption, it is common to have a simple Docker Swarm cluster with a single manager node and a few worker nodes. However, as enterprises migrate to Docker Enterprise, availability, security, and scale become the focus. The reference architecture shown in *Figure 7* reflects a highly available Docker Enterprise cluster with three UCP managers, three DTR replicas, three worker nodes, and three load balancers spread across three availability zones. Please note, you could add a hundred or more additional workers without adding any more manager or DTR nodes:

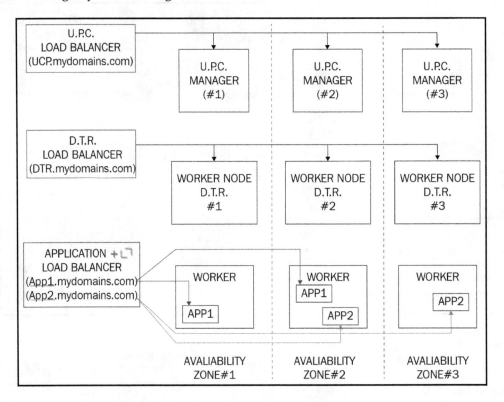

Figure 7 : Docker Enterprise with Kubernetes

Docker Enterprise UCP is installed on top of Docker Swarm managers. In this configuration, if a manager node is lost, the cluster keeps running. The same is true for the DTR. In fact, slicing UCP and DTR across availability zones allows the cluster to stay running even if one of the availability zones fails. It is important to note that, while the cluster, and more importantly the applications in the cluster, keep running, the cluster may report an unhealthy state. This means operators need to restore any unhealthy managers or DTR replicas as soon as possible to restore a quorum to the cluster ASAP and ensure that the cluster remains available.

Please note all of the primary interfaces to the cluster (UCP—admin interface, DTR—image management interface and application access) are all frontended with a load balancer. UCP and DTR both have health check endpoints for the load balancers to verify service availability. The application load balancers are usually a little different in that each application needs to implement its own health checks. Also, the application load balancing configuration is likely broken into two parts. The first part is a classic load balancer responding to the application DNS target (often something like `*.app.mydomain.com`) and it forwards traffic to instances of reverse proxy servers running in the cluster. There will be a more detailed discussion on layer-7 routing later in the book.

Drill-down – high-level Docker Enterprise 2 components

While Docker Enterprise 2 builds on Docker Engine-Community Swarm, it introduces additional components necessary to support features such as Kubernetes, **Role-Based Access Control** (**RBAC**), and a web UI. *Figure 8* depicts Docker Enterprise 2 components at a high level. Understanding these components is handy for operations teams to monitor and support Docker Enterprise for enterprise use, but most users are blissfully unaware of these implementation details:

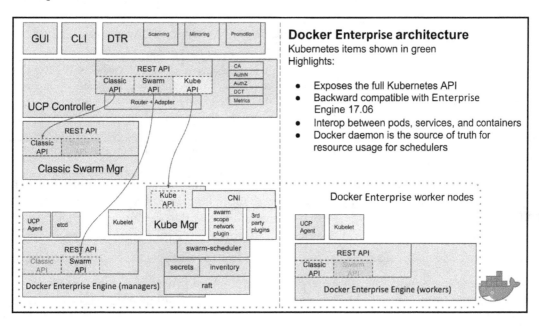

Figure 8: Docker Enterprise with Kubernetes © 2013-2018 Docker, Inc. All rights reserved

The top layer represents the components of a manager that users directly interact with. From there, the UCP controller serves as a secure controller/router to the underlying Swarm and Kubernetes services. Here are some highlights of the components depicted in *Figure 8*. Please note, this is a higher-level overview for clarity and brevity, whereas there are actually 30+ containerized components included with a UCP manager/Kubernetes master node UCP installation:

GUI	The Docker UCP web interface, running inside the `ucp-controller` container on each Docker UCP manager node, is where a user's credentials may be used to log in to Docker Enterprise's web-based portal and, based on their access rights, interact with objects in the cluster.
CLI	The Docker command-line interface is accessed using a Docker command-line bundle. The bundle contains the Docker Enterprise user's certificates and a private key for cluster authentication, as well as scripts for connecting to the cluster from a local bash or PowerShell Terminal.
DTR	The Docker trusted registry securely stores and manages images based on policies.
UCP controller	This block represents a variety of UCP components, starting with the UCP RESTful API. Using a bearer authorization token, authorized users can call the UCP API to manage UCP resources such as services, containers, networks, users, grants, and collections from scripts. Additionally, the UCP controller manages security, trust, and monitoring related to accessing the underlying orchestration APIs.
UCP agent	The UCP agent makes sure all of the correct UCP services are running on each UCP cluster node member.
Etcd	Etcd is the implementation behind `ucp-kv` where both Swarm and Kubernetes keep their encrypted cluster store in Docker Enterprise.
Kubelet	Kubelet runs inside the `ucp-kubelet` container on every Kubernetes node. The Kubelet is responsible for running the actual pods on a node, and for reporting the health of the node and resource utilization. In addition to Kubelet, you should expect to see a `ucp-kube-proxy` on each node as a means of wiring up the cluster address space across nodes, services, and pods.
Kube MGR	The Kube manager block represents the implementation for the Kubernetes controller, scheduler, and API.
CNI	This block represents the container network interface that Kubernetes needs to implement networking features. By default, Docker Enterprise uses the Calico CNI plugin. Using the `--cni-installer-url` flag during Docker UCP installation, the administrator can use a different CNI plugin such as weave or flannel.

It is interesting to see how Docker Enterprise's architecture provides a great combined experience with both Swarm and Kubernetes co-existing on a single enterprise platform.

Summary

The container movement, led by the Docker community, is changing how software is built, packaged, and delivered. The emerging enterprise container platform space is changing the way enterprises think about software platforms and virtualization. Docker, Inc. is leading the way, as recognized by Forrester Research with the Docker Enterprise platform.

Docker Enterprise 2's added support for Kubernetes, in addition to Swarm, makes it a great enterprise choice. Modernization teams can get started on the enterprise container learning curve with Swarm and use Kubernetes to bring microservices on board when they are ready. Additionally, enterprises have the choice of running Docker Enterprise on the cloud or on-premise in a VM or on bare metal.

This chapter introduced a phased and agile approach for Docker's enterprise adoption. Throughout the book, we'll build on these adoption phases as we build a pilot application and then get it ready for production.

In Chapter 3, *Getting Started – Docker Enterprise Proof of Concept*, we embark on our agile adoption journey with our PoC. We will set up a PoC cluster with Docker Enterprise, containerize a .NET application, and deploy the containerized application to our PoC cluster.

Questions

1. What's new in the platform space?
2. What should the goals be for enterprise container platform providers?
3. What are the risks of going all-in with a cloud provider's container platform?
4. How is Docker sold?
5. How many Docker nodes will I need?
6. What is shifting left and how does Docker help?

Further reading

- **Download the Forrester Reasearch report:**
    - https://goto.docker.com/the-forrester-wave-enterprise-container-platform-software-suites-2018.html
- **Docker reference architecture:**
    - https://success.docker.com/architectures
- **Shift left principle article:**
    - https://dzone.com/articles/the-shift-left-principle-and-devops-1

3
Getting Started - Docker Enterprise Proof of Concept

This chapter represents a critical first step in your journey toward the adoption of Docker Enterprise. We talked about the importance of a crawl, walk, run approach through agile adoption. So many times, in an effort to be the most efficient, we want to jump right to the answer. Subsequently, many organizations race right past the crawl and walk stages to start running (somewhere). The problem is, by skipping our crawl stage, where a **Proof of Concept (PoC)** project is used to introduce and demonstrate the Docker Enterprise platform, they miss out on discovering their own informed opinion during the PoC. Essentially, the PoC phase is a critical part of the enterprises learning experience. So start with a PoC allow the team to try things, make some mistakes and learn freely.

Here, we present the PoC phase of our agile approach, where we learn how to use and configure Docker Enterprise by working through first app phase steps where we take a single application from a PoC, to pilot, and on to production.

In this chapter, we focus on the PoC step and later we take our application to the pilot (non-production) but highly available cluster, and finally we take the application to a production environment to explore the key considerations in getting an application production-ready.

The following topics will be covered in this chapter:

- Preparing nodes, network, and storage for your PoC
- Installing Docker Enterprise for your PoC:
    - Installing Docker Enterprise Engine
    - Installing Docker UCP
    - Installing DTR
- Testing the PoC platform
- Preparing the PoC application and platform
- Building and deploying the PoC application

Assembling a Docker Enterprise PoC cross-functional team

As prescribed earlier, it is best to bring Docker Enterprise into an organization with a phased but agile crawl, walk, run approach. The agile part of the description comes from leveraging a backlog, where a prioritized list of phase-appropriate tasks is used to provide the building blocks to plan each phase. Furthermore, we sift and sort the priorities of the backlog items depending on each organization's unique needs and requirements. Docker, Inc's **Professional Services** (**PS**) team has developed a comprehensive and proprietary backlog to support their enterprise adoption methodology to support customer PoCs, pilot, and production journeys.

 Throughout this book, we draw a parallel to Docker, Inc's phased, agile approach as validation of and an introduction to the approach. We therefore intend to introduce and support Docker's approach by presenting some sample paths and important concepts, but this book is not meant to be a substitute for the Docker PS team's experience or intellectual property. Please contact Docker, Inc. for more details and professional service assistance.

The main objective of a Docker Enterprise PoC is to share an initial experience with a small, cross-functional team in an enterprise. The PoC core team normally includes one or two representatives from the application development, DevOps, platform, and governance functional areas. Ideally, the functional representatives are influential, hands-on team members with enough experience to understand which issues matter, and hands-on enough to perform the PoC work or at least closely oversee the PoC work at a detailed level.

Keeping a PoC team small and hands-on usually leads to shorter timelines for the PoC. The timeline for a PoC should be several weeks and NOT several months. Ideally, a PoC has a core team of four to six doers and, with some expert guidance, should be able to deliver the PoC in 3-6 weeks. The learning from the PoC should roll right into a pilot step, keeping the momentum going.

In *Figure 1*, you can see the various organizational areas who need to be involved in the agile adoption process. It is not just some developers or a handful of system admins. The enterprise adoption of containers will have a direct impact on governance, operations, application development, and DevOps areas, starting with the PoC:

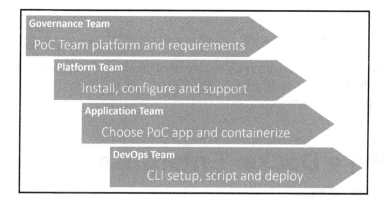

Figure 1: PoC Cross Functional Concerns

Representatives from the governance team will lead the efforts to do the following:

- Facilitate shared learning and collaboration (that is, Wiki or MS teams)
- Solicit and document objectives and success criteria for the PoC
- Begin to solicit and document compliance, security, and access requirements for the pilot phase

Representatives from the platform team will lead the efforts to do the following:

- Prepare Docker Enterprise PoC nodes, network, and storage
- Install the Docker Enterprise PoC engine with optional logging configured
- Install Docker Enterprise PoC **Universal Control Plane** (UCP)
- Install PoC **Docker Trusted Registry** (DTR)
- Configure clusters for PoC users and resources

Representatives from the application team will lead the efforts to do the following:

- Pick a sample application to containerize and deploy during the PoC
- Containerize the PoC application using official Docker Hub images
- Create a YAML file for Swarm and/or Kubernetes to deploy the PoC application

Representatives from the DevOps team will lead the efforts to do the following:

- Prepare a DevOps user Docker Enterprise CLI for remote access to the Docker Enterprise/Kubernetes APIs
- Script the PoC application deployment using the Docker Enterprise/Kubernetes APIs

- Script PoC application updates using the Docker Enterprise/Kubernetes APIs
- Run a PoC demo during the PoC wrap-up presentation

Many books have and will be written on enterprise transformation governance and DevOps. So, for the purposes of this book, we will mostly focus on the concerns of the platform and application teams.

Preparing a Docker Enterprise platform for the PoC step

The goal of this section is to get familiar with a simple, end-to-end setup of Docker Enterprise as quickly as possible. Think of it as building out an MVP Docker Enterprise platform that includes the Docker UCP and DTR as a place to deploy our PoC application. To that end, we will walk through the details of standing up a PoC cluster and we will use Amazon Web Services (AWS) to demonstrate the process to do the following:

- We'll prepare a four-node Linux cluster:
    1. Install a trial version of Docker Enterprise Engine on all nodes (configure storage and logging)
    2. Install UCP and DTR on two of the nodes
    3. Create a PoC user and Docker CLI bundles for the PoC user
- We'll build and push sample Swarm and Kubernetes application images.
- We'll deploy a sample application and test access as a PoC user with CLI to test the cluster.
- We'll update the application image and redeploy.

Preparing a four-node cluster

To get started, we need three or four Linux nodes connected on a common network where we can install Docker Enterprise and host our PoC. Keep in mind that for our PoC, one node is for UCP, another for DTR, and the remaining nodes are workers. A minimum of a four-node setup is highly recommended for PoCs to demonstrate multiple workers, and hence an actual orchestrated cluster. In Kubernetes speak, we would have one master and three nodes, where one node runs DTR and the remaining nodes run containerized workloads.

Using a single worker (three-node cluster) might seem easier or just simpler. However, a single worker starts to feel more like an old-school Docker setup using `docker-compose`. These were great in the day, but we now rely on orchestrators such as Swarm and Kubernetes to handle important cluster features such as application scheduling, scaling, availability, and overlay networking.

Please keep in mind, this is a PoC and does not reflect your final platform for Docker Enterprise; preliminary decisions on your actual target platform are not required until you move to the pilot step. These decisions are intentionally deferred because, when you are getting started with Docker Enterprise and in the PoC step, you lack the real firsthand knowledge and experience required to make informed longer-term decisions. Furthermore, trying to force these decisions during the PoC adds to the learning curve and introduces more rookie mistakes, resulting in costly delays and potentially institutionalizing anti-patterns. So, start in your comfort zone by choosing a Docker Enterprise supported infrastructure that aligns with your current skill sets. Remember, the goal here is to gain some experience with Docker Enterprise as the target platform for your PoC and not to try a bunch of new things at the same time.

Set up a four-node cluster

First, pick the platform where you are going to host your Docker Enterprise cluster. Again, this is not the time to try something new and unfamiliar. Rather and if at all possible, use your go-to platform whether it is cloud-based, on-premises, virtualized, or bare metal. To make this happen, we need four nodes with local storage and connected to a common network that we can access.

Overview of a sample PoC environment

Prepare a network with four fresh Linux nodes attached:

- Four nodes are connected to the same network, allowing all traffic/ports between nodes (please note traffic will be locked down in the pilot and production steps).

- There's a fresh install of Linux on at least two nodes (Linux required for **UCP and DTR** nodes):
  - Two vCPUs/cores for each node
  - 8 GB of RAM
  - 32 GB of disk space
  - A Docker Enterprise supported Linux distribution: CentOS, Oracle Linux, Red Hat Enterprise Linux, SUSE Linux Enterprise Server, Ubuntu, Microsoft Windows Server 2016, Microsoft Windows Server 1709, or Microsoft Windows Server 1803
- There's a fresh install of Linux or Windows on one or more worker nodes:
  - Two vCPUs/cores for each node
  - 8 GB of RAM
  - 32 GB of disk space for Linux and 80 GB for Windows Server
  - A Docker Enterprise supported Linux distribution: CentOS, Oracle Linux, Red Hat Enterprise Linux, SUSE Linux Enterprise Server, Ubuntu, Microsoft Windows Server 2016, Microsoft Windows Server 1709, or Microsoft Windows Server 1803

Figure 2 shows a working example in which we created four t2.large instances running AWS with two vCPUs and 8 GB of RAM. All have public and private IP addresses assigned to their NIC. All Linux boxes have 32 GB of disk space and the Windows worker has 80 GB of disk space:

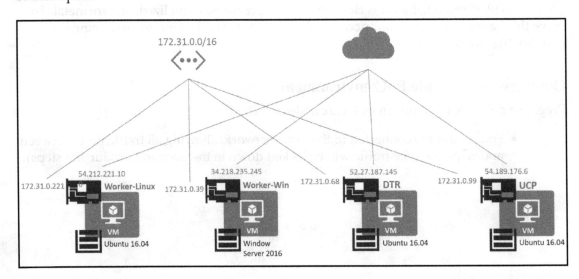

Figure 2: Mixed-Node PoC Cluster

Here, the Docker nodes communicate with each other on the local private network using the 172.31.0.x address space. However, to access our nodes externally and install Docker, we want to be able to SSH directly for the PoC. Please note for our post-PoC setup, all external traffic will come through a firewall or load balancer, where the load balancer serves as a bastion/jump host to avoid exposing the nodes externally.

Installing Docker Enterprise Engine on all nodes

Now that we have some running nodes to work with, we will install the Docker Enterprise Engine on each of your fresh nodes. To install and use Docker Enterprise, you will need a valid software license key as well as your storebits subscription URL. The storebits URL is a unique URL issued by Docker to subscription customers and allows them access their subscription-related files during installation. You can get these from the Docker store by logging in with or creating a Docker ID and registering for a free trial subscription.

 If you already have a Docker ID from Docker Hub, your same Docker ID will work in the Docker store. If you don't already have a Docker ID, just click **Sign In** in the upper-right corner of the store.docker.com home page or just visit https://store.docker.com/signup. A list of links used in this section may be found in a GitHub repository: https://github.com/PacktPublishing/Mastering-Docker-Enterprise.

Getting a Docker Enterprise 30-day trial license and storebit URL

Log in to your Docker store and use the Docker Enterprise tab to select your preferred certified platform.

Please pick a Linux distribution for the PoC, noting that any cloud products such as AWS and Azure have been deprecated. These older cloud offerings run a tiny kernel called MobyLinuxVM, which is a very lean and efficient way to run Docker, but is not something you can easily maintain yourself and is difficult to work with (it has no SSH capabilities). For these reasons and perhaps others as well, the Moby platform will only be used in special Docker managed installations such as Docker Desktop, Docker for Windows, and Docker for Mac.

Once you select your preferred Linux distribution, then click **Start 1 Month Trial**. Now, complete the trial form and submit your information. You should immediately find your license information under the My Content section of the Docker store. There is a menu selection under your profile drop-down on the top-right of the screen.

Finally, you need to click on the **Setup** button to display the information you will need to install the Docker Enterprise Engine, as shown in *Figure 3*. This is where you will find a link to download your Docker license file and your storebits URL. This is a good time to download the license to a safe directory on your local computer. Also, copy and paste the storebits URL into your favorite editor. You will need it in the next section when we configure the package manager to use the Docker repositories:

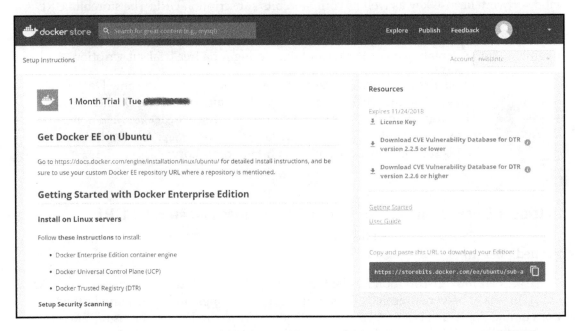

Figure 3: One Month Docker Enterprise Trial

Installing the Docker Enterprise Engine on all nodes

With your license key and Docker storebits URL saved on your local machine, it is time to install the Docker Enterprise Engine on all of your nodes. For this section, we will be using an Ubuntu distribution of Linux and a Windows 2016 server as a second worker node. So, all together we have a four-node cluster.

In an attempt to keep this information up to date and streamlined, there is a GitHub repository page for the commands in this section. It can be found here: `https://github.com/PacktPublishing/Mastering-Docker-Enterprise`.

Start by creating SSH sessions **into each of your Linux nodes** and an **RDP session into your Windows worker**. Now, you are ready to begin the engine install process. Please note the bash install commands will vary slightly on different flavors of Linux and will be completely different on Windows 2016, where we use PowerShell.

We will begin with the Linux nodes, where we will use the package manager and the official Docker repository for installing our software. Once the Docker Engines are installed, all of the other Docker Enterprise software runs in containers and will come from Docker's container registry.

Please follow these instructions carefully! Don't use the default repository from your Linux distribution to install the Docker Engine! Doing so usually results in an old or forked (sometimes called FrankenDocker) version of the community edition. Also, the following instructions assume you are using a fresh software OS install on your nodes. If that's not the case, please make sure that you remove the old versions of Docker before proceeding.

I'll demonstrate how to get started, using VS code. First, we open a couple of files using the menu bar **File** | **Open** to open two empty files. In the first file, save your connection information (public/private IPs) to your cloud servers and in the second file, just a scratch pad to store your Docker storebits URL and a place to paste commands from this chapter's accompanying repository page: `https://github.com/NVISIA/MasteringDockerEE/blob/master/PoC/install/Install-EE-Engine-notes.md`. Then, open some SSH Terminal sessions—one for each node. Now you are ready to install:

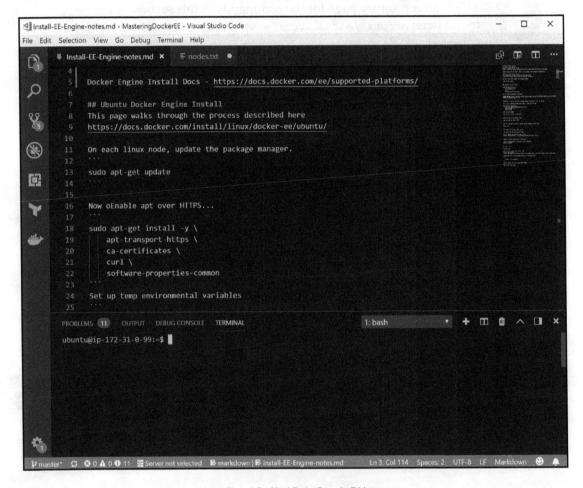

Figure 4: One Month Docker Enterprise Trial

Sample Ubuntu Docker Engine install

This section is adapted from `docs.docker.com` (Docker's official documentation for the community and enterprise editions) and walks us through the process of installing Docker Enterprise—`https://docs.docker.com/install/linux/docker-ee/ubuntu/`.

 For our PoC example, we will use the Beta3 release of Docker Enterprise of 2.1 to ensure the information is as current as possible. Since this is the third beta release of version 2.1, it should be very similar to the production release at the end of 2018. However, do note that where the Docker version information appears is subject to change.

1. **Update the Ubuntu package manager**:
    1. On each Linux node, update the package manager as follows:

        ```
        sudo apt-get update
        ```

    2. Now, enable APT to run over HTTPS using the following command:

        ```
        sudo apt-get install -y \
            apt-transport-https \
            ca-certificates \
            curl \
            software-properties-common
        ```

2. **Configure the Ubuntu package manager repositories to use the official Docker binaries**:
    1. Set up `DOCKER_EE_URL` environment variables using your Docker Store's storebits URL that you recorded earlier. Then, choose the desired Docker version. You can find them listed using your (replacing x's) storebits URL with this pattern: `https://storebits.docker.com/ee/ubuntu/sub-xxxxxxxx-xxxx-xxxx-xxxx-xxxxxxxxxxx/dists/xenial/`. Your commands should look like the following.

        ```
        DOCKER_EE_URL="https://storebits.docker.com/ee/ubuntu/
        sub-aff4b542-98da-438b-924e-8cc2c8f54b69"
        DOCKER_EE_VERSION=test
        ```

2. Here, we add Docker's repository to your Linux package manager, update APT, and then install the Docker Enterprise version:

```
curl -fsSL "${DOCKER_EE_URL}/ubuntu/gpg" | sudo apt-
key add -

sudo add-apt-repository \
    "deb [arch=amd64] $DOCKER_EE_URL/ubuntu \
    $(lsb_release -cs) \
    stable-17.06"

sudo apt-get update
```

3. **Install official Docker from properly configured repositories**:
    1. This instructs the package manage to install Docker Enterprise:

```
sudo apt-get install -y docker-ee
```

4. **Add user to Docker group (optional)**:
    1. We add your current user to the Docker group to avoid running Docker commands using root or sudo:

```
sudo usermod -aG docker $USER
```

5. **Test the install:**
    1. Log out. Then, log back in and try running Docker command (without sudo) to test Docker and Docker group permissions. Run docker info and you should see the output as in *Figure 5*.
    2. Notice the server version label is 18.09X was installed and information on the host including the kernel version, which must be > 3.10:

```
$ docker info
```

The following is the output of the `docker info` command. Please note the version:

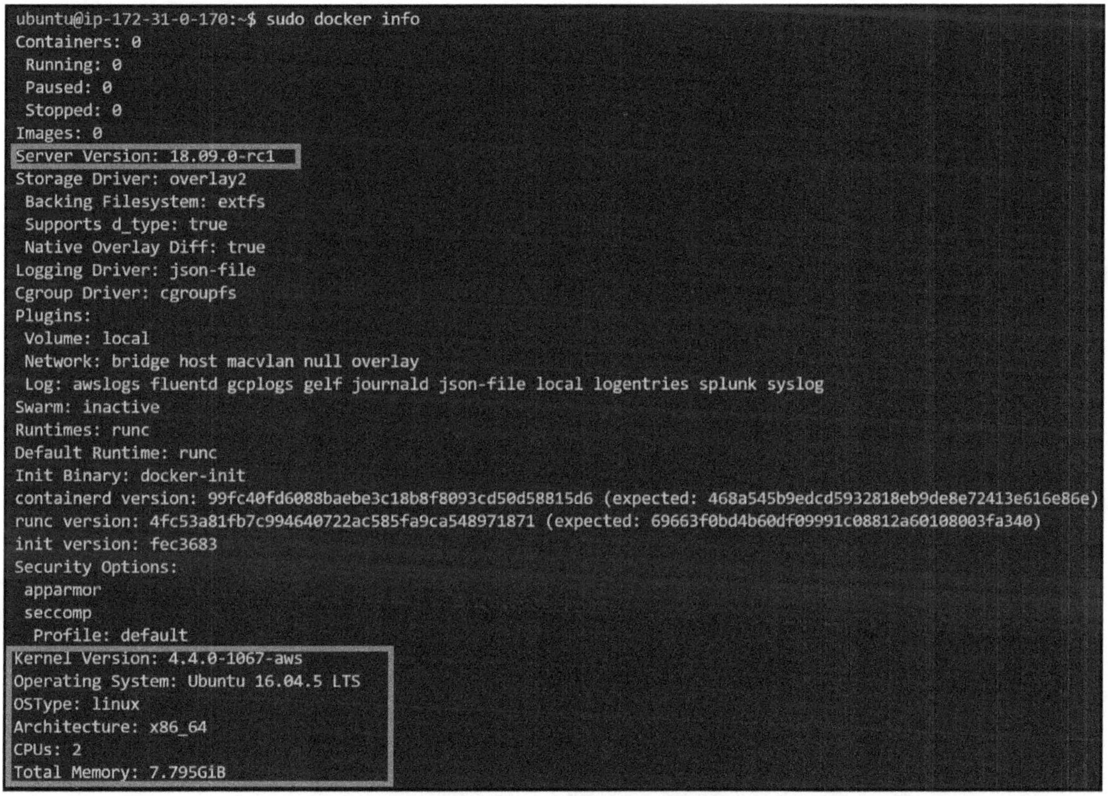
ubuntu@ip-172-31-0-170:~$ sudo docker info
Containers: 0
Running: 0
Paused: 0
Stopped: 0
Images: 0
Server Version: 18.09.0-rc1
Storage Driver: overlay2
Backing Filesystem: extfs
Supports d_type: true
Native Overlay Diff: true
Logging Driver: json-file
Cgroup Driver: cgroupfs
Plugins:
Volume: local
Network: bridge host macvlan null overlay
Log: awslogs fluentd gcplogs gelf journald json-file local logentries splunk syslog
Swarm: inactive
Runtimes: runc
Default Runtime: runc
Init Binary: docker-init
containerd version: 99fc40fd6088baebe3c18b8f8093cd50d58815d6 (expected: 468a545b9edcd5932818eb9de8e72413e616e86e)
runc version: 4fc53a81fb7c994640722ac585fa9ca548971871 (expected: 69663f0bd4b60df09991c08812a60108003fa340)
init version: fec3683
Security Options:
apparmor
seccomp
Profile: default
Kernel Version: 4.4.0-1067-aws
Operating System: Ubuntu 16.04.5 LTS
OSType: linux
Architecture: x86_64
CPUs: 2
Total Memory: 7.795GiB

Figure 5: Docker Info After Docker Linux Install

> **TIP**
>
> If you're creating virtual machine templates for your Docker Enterprise nodes from the first node setup that you already installed, you must remove the `/etc/docker/key.json` file from the virtual machine image. Then, after provisioning a virtual machine from the image, just restart the Docker daemon to create a new `/etc/docker/key.json` file.

3. Next, we move on to the Windows worker node setup.

Windows 2016 Docker Engine install

On our Docker Enterprise subnet, we install a Windows Server 2016 node and initiate a remote desktop session. Open a standard PowerShell Terminal to install the `DockerMsftProvider` module and then install the Docker package. For the latest information about installing Docker Enterprise on Windows Server, visit `https://beta.docs.docker.com/install/windows/docker-ee/#use-a-script-to-install-docker-ee`:

```
Install-Module DockerMsftProvider -Force
Install-Package Docker -ProviderName DockerMsftProvider -Force
```

In the following PowerShell block, we check to see whether a restart is necessary. If it is, we issue the `Restart-Computer` command to restart Windows 2016 Server:

```
(Install-WindowsFeature Containers).RestartNeeded
Restart-Computer
```

After a possible restart, we log back in to the server and look at the `docker info` command to see that the Docker Enterprise version is installed as shown in following *Figure 6.*

For our setup, we should see an 18.09 server running on Windows kernel 10. The `docker info` command show a lot of useful details about the Docker Engine and can be really helpful for troubleshooting:

```
PS> docker info
```

Here's the output from the `docker info` command. Please note the highlighted versions:

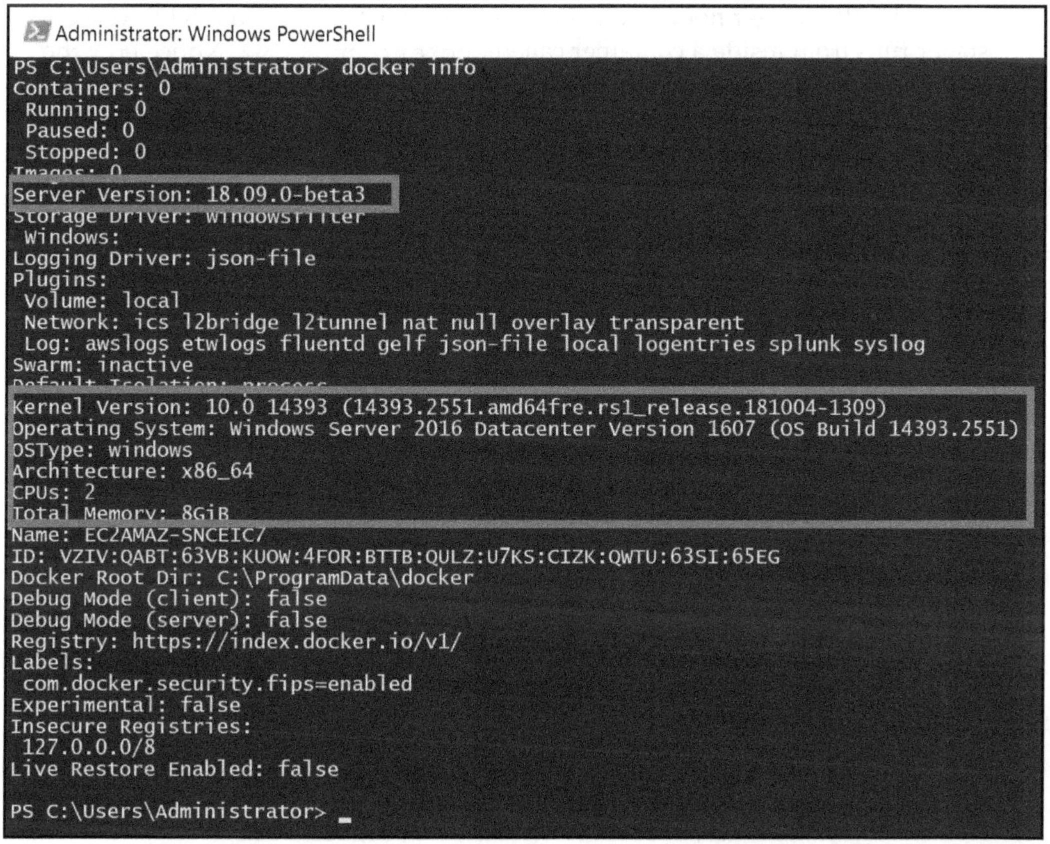

```
Administrator: Windows PowerShell

PS C:\Users\Administrator> docker info
Containers: 0
 Running: 0
 Paused: 0
 Stopped: 0
 Images: 0
Server Version: 18.09.0-beta3
Storage Driver: windowsfilter
 Windows:
Logging Driver: json-file
Plugins:
 Volume: local
 Network: ics l2bridge l2tunnel nat null overlay transparent
 Log: awslogs etwlogs fluentd gelf json-file local logentries splunk syslog
Swarm: inactive
Default Isolation: process
Kernel Version: 10.0 14393 (14393.2551.amd64fre.rs1_release.181004-1309)
Operating System: Windows Server 2016 Datacenter Version 1607 (OS Build 14393.2551)
OSType: windows
Architecture: x86_64
CPUs: 2
Total Memory: 8GiB
Name: EC2AMAZ-SNCEIC7
ID: VZIV:QABT:63VB:KUOW:4FOR:BTTB:QULZ:U7KS:CIZK:QWTU:63SI:65EG
Docker Root Dir: C:\ProgramData\docker
Debug Mode (client): false
Debug Mode (server): false
Registry: https://index.docker.io/v1/
Labels:
 com.docker.security.fips=enabled
Experimental: false
Insecure Registries:
 127.0.0.0/8
Live Restore Enabled: false

PS C:\Users\Administrator> _
```

Figure 6: Docker Info After Docker Windows Install

You may be wondering why you didn't need the storebits URL from the Docker Store to install the Docker Enterprise Engine on Windows Server. It is because Docker Enterprise Basic comes with Windows Server 2016 Datacenter, Standard, and Essentials Editions and its support is provided by Microsoft and backed by Docker. So, if you own Microsoft Windows 2016, access to Docker Enterprise Basic is already included.

Installing Docker's Universal Control Plane

SSH into your UCP/manager node and install the Docker UCP. As you might expect, the UCP installer runs from inside a container called `docker/ucp:3.1.2`. Notice how the container mounts the Docker socket as a volume so it can issues docker commands to a Docker daemon running on the host from inside the UCP installer's container. This is the preferred approach over **Docker in Docker** (**DinD**), which requires the `--privileged` flag and can lead to filesystem corruption.

At this time, Docker's UCP and DTR application are only supported on Linux platforms. Windows may be supported in a future release as Docker on Windows Server rounds out the feature set to match Linux and completes Kubernetes certification.

The following code block shows the UCP install command with an example.

```
$ docker container run -it --rm --name ucp \
-v /var/run/docker.sock:/var/run/docker.sock \
docker/ucp:3.1.2 install \
--host-address {internal IP Address of UCP Node}  \
--admin-username admin \
--admin-password {add your password here} \
--san {Internal IP of UCP node, i.e., 172.31.0.99}  \
--san {External DNS name UCP node, i.e., ucp.mydomain.com} \
--san {External IP of UCP node, i.e., 54.189.176.6} \
--interactive

## --- Actual example with my clusters values ---
$ docker run -it --rm --name ucp \
-v /var/run/docker.sock:/var/run/docker.sock \
docker/ucp:3.1.2 install \
--swarm-port 3376 \
--host-address 172.31.0.170 \
--admin-username admin \
--admin-password notReallyThePassword \
--san ip-172-31-0-170.us-west-2.compute.internal \
--san ec2-54-245-193-10.us-west-2.compute.amazonaws.com \
--san 54.245.193.10 \
--interactive
```

Looking at the Docker command in the previous code block, we see the Docker container runs the `install` binary inside the `ucp:3.1.2` container with an interactive Terminal `-it` flag (output from the container shows in the host Terminal screen and input, if prompted, is directed to the container's standard input) and `--name ucp` names the container `ucp`. The `--rm` removes the ucp container from the local node after the install finishes. We see the volume mount of the Docker socket with `-v` `/var/run/docker.sock:/var/run/docker.sock` used by the container to access the host's Docker daemon. Make sure you replace all of your node-specific values { ... } before running the install command. The next part of the command is `docker/ucp:3.1.2 install` with the following parameters:

- `--host-address` is the internal IP address of UCP node on—something like `172.o.31.2`.
- `--admin-username` is the username for the main administrator account, usually something like `admin`.
- `--admin-password` is the password for the main administrator account; this should be a strong password, where you may consider using a password generator.
- `--san` is a subject alternative name, another valid name for the certificate. UCP generates a self-signed certificate during installation and adds sans for each alternative name provided. See the following sample command, where we add any possible UCP IP or DNS name that might be used access the UCP node. This includes internal/external IP addresses as well as internal/external IP addresses. Without these, you may get x509 certificate errors when interacting with the UCP node.
- `--interactive` is for interactive mode where the installer prompts for additional information when necessary.

Once the install completes successfully, it's time to log in. Since the `--interactive` flag is used, you may be prompted for additional information.

Logging to the UCP web interface and uploading your trial license

Make sure that port 443 access is open between your browser and the UCP node. Then, point your browser to the external IP of your UCP node; make sure to start with https://. Please note, by default and for the purposes of our PoC, the HTTPS session uses a self-signed certificate. To access UCP, you will need to bypass the browser privacy warning and accept the self-signed certificate.

Get logged in and licensed:

- Use the **username/password** you provided to the previously install command to log in
- Use the Docker Enterprise trial license file you downloaded from the Docker store when logging in

Adding work nodes to the UCP cluster

After logging in to Docker Enterprise's Universal Control Plane, you will see a dashboard showing your healthy one-node cluster. Now, we need to add our additional nodes to the Docker UCP (Swarm-backed cluster). We will start with the Linux nodes and then the Windows node, noting the Windows node take a little more preparation before running the docker swarm join command.

While we use SSH to access our nodes during the installation of the Docker Engines, UCP and DTR, after the installs are complete, we should no longer use SSH access. Rather than SSH, **only allow** users access the cluster from a **UCP Client bundle.** Each UCP user has their own personalized bundle associated with their UCP role-based access account, as specified by a Docker Enterprise administrator.

Joining Linux worker nodes to the cluster

First, we add the DTR node, which is a worker node. The UCP web interface provides a GUI to format important command-line operations, including joining nodes to the cluster and installing DTR. While we still need to run these commands from the command line, the GUI tool helps us to correctly set the parameters. To join nodes, we first select the **Nodes** menu item under **Shared Resources** and click **Add Node**, as shown in *Figure 7*. Then, on the next screen, we make sure **LINUX** and **WORKER** are selected and copy the command to the clipboard, as shown in *Figure 8*:

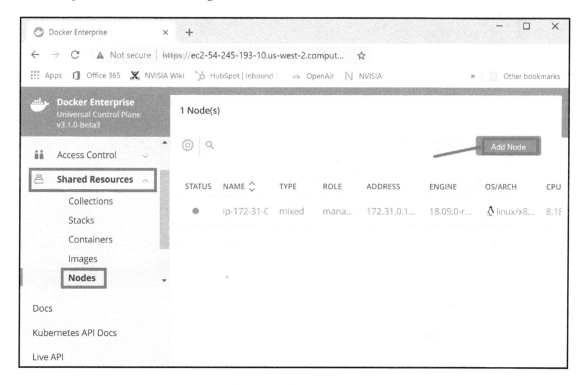

Figure 7: Universal Control Plane Nodes

The following is the **Add Node** dialog box in the Docker UCP Web UI. Select **LINUX** and **WORKER**, then click on the copy button:

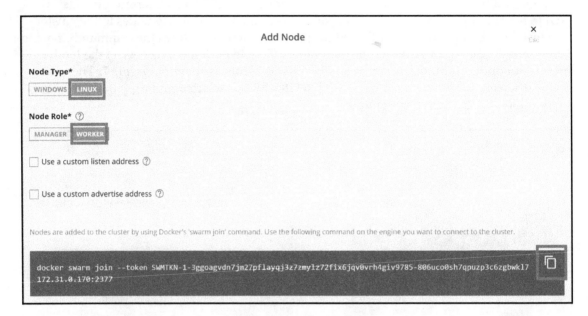

Figure 8: Universal Control Plane Add Linux Node

To join the DTR node, we SSH to the node and execute the command we copied from the UCP **Add Node** screen in *Figure 8*. Make sure you use your UCP's token, not the following example:

```
DTR-node$ docker swarm join --token
SWMTKN-1-3ggoagvdn7jm27pflayqj3z7zmylz72fix6jqv0vrh4giv9785-
xxxxxxxxxxxxxxxxxxxxx 172.31.0.170:2377
```

This node joined a swarm as a worker.

Joining the remaining worker nodes into the cluster

Now, SSH into the Linux worker node and pass the same `docker swarm join` command:

```
Worker-node$ docker swarm join --token
SWMTKN-1-3ggoagvdn7jm27pflayqj3z7zmylz72fix6jqv0vrh4giv9785-
xxxxxxxxxxxxxxxxxxxxx 172.31.0.170:2377
This node joined a swarm as a worker.
```

Joining a Windows server 2016 worker node to the cluster

We start by looking at the **UCP manager** for the Windows UCP `agent` and `dsinfo` versions. SSH to the UCP node and run the following:

```
UCP-node$ docker container run --rm docker/ucp:3.1.2 images --list --
enable-windows

docker/ucp-agent-win:3.1.2
docker/ucp-dsinfo-win:3.1.2
```

We need to make sure the same images are pulled to the Windows work nodes. Use an RDP session to access the Windows 2016 Node and open a standard PowerShell Terminal. From the Terminal, we pull the images as follows:

```
PS> docker image pull docker/ucp-agent-win:3.1.2
PS> docker image pull docker/ucp-dsinfo-win:3.1.2
```

Now, we need to run a script that:

- Verifies the Windows Server Kernel
- Verifies Docker certificates
- Secures Dockerd on port `2376` with a `tls` encrypted named pipe
- Opens inbound Windows firewall ports `2376`, `12376`, and `2377`
- Opens inbound/outbound ports `7946`, `4789`, and `7946`.
- Restarts the Docker service.

To make this easier, Docker has created a script inside the `docker.ucp-agent-win` container that can be used to generate a PowerShell script as follows:

```
PS> $script = [ScriptBlock]::Create((docker run --rm docker/ucp-agent-
win:3.1.2 windows-script | Out-String))
PS> Invoke-Command $script
```

After the script finishes restarting the Docker service, go back to your UCP and click on **Shared Resources | Nodes** and **Add Node** as shown in following *Figure 8a*. This time, select the **Windows Option** and acknowledge that you completed the previous steps by checking the step 2 box: **I have followed the instructions and I'm ready to join my windows node**. The `docker join` command appears. Copy the `docker swarm run` command to PowerShell and run it.

Following is the UCP Add Node Dialog where are adding a Windows worker node to our cluster:

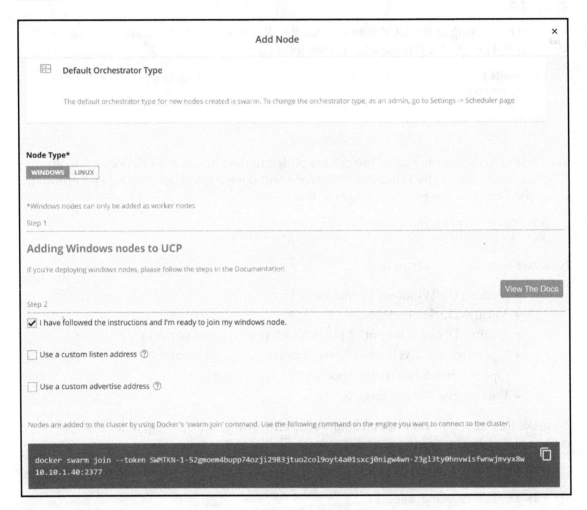

Figure 8a: Universal Control Plane Add Windows Node

Now, head back to the UCP Dashboard in our browser and wait for the new Windows node to initialize and become healthy:

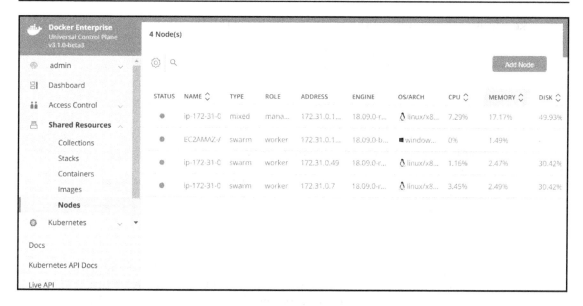

Figure 9: Universal Control Plane All Nodes Joined

Now, we have the Docker Enterprise Universal Control Plane installed onto a healthy four node cluster. Now, it's time to install the DTR.

Installing the DTR

For our PoC, we will need a private, trusted image registry to store, secure, and serve our images. For this, we will use **Docker Trusted Registry** (**DTR**). We will use an SSH Terminal for the UCP manager node.

SSH to the UCP node and run the `docker node ls` command to get a list of proper node names. For our example, the proper node name for DTR is `ip-172-31-0-168`. It can be either Linux work node. Next, from our UCP SSH Terminal, we run the DTR install as shown in the following code block. Notice how we use the UCP node name where want DTR to be installed `--ucp-node ip-172-31-0-68`.

Let's take a look at the command structure for our PoC DTR install:

```
$ docker run -it --rm docker/dtr:2.6.2 install \
--ucp-url <ucp_host_dns or IP>:443 \
--ucp-username admin \
--ucp-password <ucp password> \
--ucp-insecure-tls \
--ucp-node <name node where DTR is to be installed>

## --- Actual example with my clusters values ---
$ docker run -it --rm docker/dtr:2.6.2 install \
--ucp-url ec2-54-245-193-10.us-west-2.compute.amazonaws.com:443 \
--ucp-username admin \
--ucp-node ip-172-31-0-68 \
--ucp-password notReallyThePassword \
--ucp-insecure-tls
```

 It's important to understand that DTR and UCP work closely together and DTR can't be deployed without an associated UCP. All user, team, and organization information is stored in UCP, but is used by DTR. When you log in to DTR, you use the same credentials as UCP and you will be momentarily redirected to UCP during the authentication process.

As you probably guessed, the UCP URL is the same one you used when you installed the Docker Universal Control Plane. Subsequently, you will use the same username and password for the admin user as you did when you installed UCP. Also, note that you will be prompted to enter the node name where you want the DTR to be installed. The prompt will include a list of candidate nodes in the UCP cluster.

Once the installation completes, you can use the external IP address of your DTR to sign in. Don't forget to use the **HTTPS** prefix when accessing the DTR. And again, you will have to click through the privacy warnings to accept a self-signed certificate. Use your UCP admin username and password to sign in.

The following is the **Docker Trusted Registry** login page `https://{external-ip-DTR-Node}`:

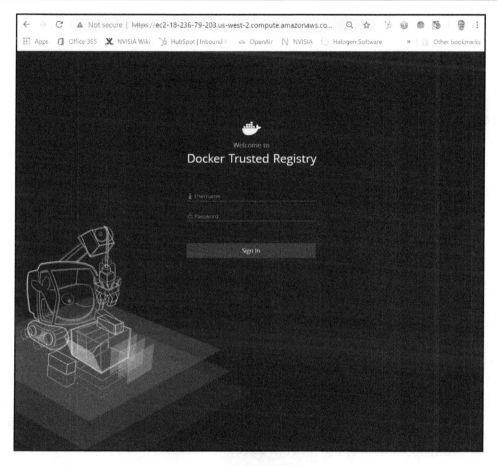

Figure 10: Docker Trusted Registry Login

Now that we have the basic platform installed for our PoC, we can take care of some of the basic configuration and testing of our shiny new Docker Enterprise installation.

Configuring RBAC for PoC

For the PoC, we will be using a minimal setup for our role-based access control. We will create a PoC developer account with full control of the Docker Enterprise shared collection. We will generate and distribute a Docker Enterprise CLI bundle to the application team using the PoC developer user's account so the containerized application can be tested and application image(s) can be pushed to the DTR. We will also create a PoC admin account used for deploying and supporting the PoC application, largely for demonstration purposes.

In `Chapter 4`, *Prepare the Docker Enterprise Pilot Cluster*, we move on to the pilot step of our Docker adoption journey, where we will spend more time delving into Docker Enterprise authentication and access features.

PoC application

Now that our PoC platform is installed and ready for PoC workloads, it is time to prepare a Docker Enterprise workload.

In this section, we will do the following:

- Pick a PoC application
- Install Docker locally
- Containerize and test the application on our local workstation
- Push the application to the PoC's DTR
- Deploy the application to the Docker Enterprise cluster

Picking a PoC application

Picking the right application for a Docker PoC can be challenging. First of all, keep in mind that the overall timeline for containerizing the application should be about three days. This timebox constraint is really important in order to keep the POC moving along. Secondly, there are a couple of fundamental competing criteria that need to be balanced while deciding which application to use for your PoC.

The first criterion is to pick an application that can be easily containerized with minimal code changes and no refactoring. Because refactoring efforts can cascade into major projects and you only have a few days to complete the containerization process, the idea of minimal code changes should make sense. The second criterion is to pick an application that will be interesting to the stakeholders because it is representative of other applications that would be beneficial to containerize. For example, if you have a bunch of old .NET applications that are difficult to support (this usually becomes an issue as Microsoft sunsets support for a long-time platform such as Windows Server 2008) and you are able to successfully containerize one of these applications as a part of your POC, it will be easy for stakeholders to imagine containerizing the balance of the old .NET applications to significantly reduce support cost. The problem is these applications might be a little more challenging to containerize without code changes.

As we dive in a little deeper, I recommend an article from
`success.docker.com` titled *Docker Reference Architecture: Modernizing Traditional .NET Framework Applications*. I also recommend another `https://success.docker.com/` article authored by Lee Namba and titled *Docker Reference Architecture: Design Considerations and Best Practices to Modernize Traditional Apps (MTA)*. I will use both Bart's and Lee's articles as supporting material as I answer the following question: which applications are the best candidates for containerization (or modernization, as the case may be)?

To give the best answer, we examine the two most common application platforms separately: Windows applications and Linux applications, starting with the Windows platform. Most commonly, custom .NET applications and Windows console applications make the best targets for containerization. WCF and Windows Services can usually be containerized with a few tweaks, while most commercial applications tend to be very challenging to containerize. Finally, Windows Desktop applications cannot be containerized, at least for now.

Picking a candidate Linux application for your PoC also favors a custom in-house developed application. These are typically three-tier Java applications with an Apache or NGINX web server frontend; a Tomcat, JBoss, WebLogic, or Websphere app server middle-tier, where the Java app is deployed in a single JAR or WAR file, and a relational DB backend. You can't have JNI bindings and you should avoid app server TLS termination. TLS can be terminated either at an upstream load balancer or at the web server frontend/reverse proxy. Also, look for any other dependent service that might make the application hard to isolate, such as messaging and remote DB connections.

Once you've identified a shortlist of three or four application candidates, take a quick look for suitable base images using `google.com` to search for something similar to `tomcat inurl:hub.docker.com` or `asp.net 2.2 inurl:hub.docker.com`. This might knock out some of your candidates. Hopefully, you'll find a reasonable base image that should work.

 Be careful here! Try to avoid the search for the perfect PoC. First, because there is a real chance you will change your mind after you start to containerize the application. Secondly, because you need to timebox the application selection process to one or two days. So, keep in mind it is very possible you will start/restart the containerization process several times. This is one of those fail/learn fast situations. So, it is handy to have a queue of candidate applications to peel through if necessary.

So to conclude the application selection process, you should have a list of three or four candidate applications shared with the PoC team as the starting point. Before we get started containerizing, we need to get our workstation set up.

Installing Docker on a local workstation

We will containerize our PoC application on a local workstation; this typically happens on a developer's desktop. These days, most application developers are using either macOS or Windows 10. So, Docker has created a free product based on the Docker Engine-Community called Docker Desktop. Docker Desktop is designed to make it very easy to install Docker Engine-Community with Kubernetes on recent versions of macOS and Windows 10 professional. The reason for using Windows Professional is due to Docker's use of Hyper-V on Windows, and Hyper-V is only available on Windows Professional and higher. The Docker Desktop install is available here: `https://www.docker.com/products/docker-desktop`.

If you are using an older version of Windows, you are going to want to use the Docker Toolbox that is available here: `https://docs.docker.com/toolbox/overview/`. The toolbox is an old-school way of installing your own virtualizer, in this case VirtualBox, onto your Windows desktop and then running Docker in Linux VMs. Behind the scenes, all of these products use a very stripped-down Linux kernel to run the latest version of Docker. This image is called MobyLinuxVM and this same image runs on Hyperkit (macOS) and Hyper-V (Windows 10 Pro+) and in VirtualBox using Docker Toolbox (Window 7 and 8).

If you are running a Linux distribution on your developer desktop, the installation process is a little bit more manual. First, you need to install the Docker Engine: `https://docs.docker.com/install/linux/docker-ce/ubuntu/`. This link is for the Ubuntu distribution, but there are others available, as you will see in the left-hand navigation menu. After you've installed the Docker Engine on your Linux box, you will also need to install `docker-compose` separately. Detailed instructions can be found by following this link: `https://docs.docker.com/compose/install/#install-compose`.

If you are planning to containerize a Windows application, you will need to run Windows containers. The Windows container option is only available on Windows hosted machines, including Docker Desktop for Windows or Windows Server 2016+. Since Docker Desktop for Windows supports both Linux and Windows containers, you will have to choose the Windows container option shown in *Figure 11*. This menu is accessed by right-clicking the Docker whale (Moby) in the Windows system tray. If the whale is not there, it means that Docker is not running. Now, open your Windows **Start** menu and type in `Docker for Windows`, hit *Enter* to select and to start Docker up. Please note that it may take 1 to 2 minutes for Docker to start. You may have also noticed the Kubernetes menu item in the context menu. This is where you would go to enable Kubernetes. You won't need it yet, but it would'nt hurt to enable it.

Figure 11 shows the Docker Desktop **Context** menu. Right-click the Docker whale icon in the Windows system tray to access it:

Figure 11: Docker Desktop Context Menu

 When changing between Linux containers and Windows containers, you are connecting to a different Docker Engine on your local machine and each engine has a its own location/file system to store the Docker image cache. So when switching from Linux to Windows, your local Linux images wont be available until you switch back. Also, some Docker updates may cause a loss of local images. So, it is a good idea to push local images to a remote repository (like Docker Hub—`https://hub.docker.com/`) before switching container types or update Docker.

Containerizing and testing the PoC application on a Dev workstation

Entire books have been written about containerizing applications and, in fact, we will discuss one such book later in this section. Containerization is probably one of the most challenging areas for organizations as they work through a PoC, and is therefore a great place to get some help if you are brand new to containers. Docker Inc and MTA enabled Docker Authorized partners have entire service offerings dedicated to the PoC process, and most of their expertise is applied to the application containerization section. However, assuming you are reading this book in an effort to work through this on your own, I will do my best to present a clear process, as well as supporting material from Docker experts.

Image2Docker is a tool designed to help teams containerize applications from VHD or WIM files. If your target application is packaged in a VM, this can help to get you started, but it is not magic. To run the tool, install Docker and the Docker2Image PowerShell 5 module on a Windows box. Then, run the application against the VHD or WIM file to generate `Dockerfile`. While the tool can be helpful as you get started, there are some limitations.

Also, the Docker professional services team and MTA-enabled Docker Partners have a more powerful version of this tool called the **Docker Application Converter** (**DAC**). They will use it to scan servers and create initial Dockerfiles for Windows and Linux applications. These initial files are refined and refactored for the PoC.

More information on Image2Docker can be found at `https://github.com/docker/communitytools-image2docker-win`.

Your goal in this section is to create a containerized PoC application that can be deployed to the Docker PoC cluster we created in the previous section. While the PoC application could be any custom application that targets Windows or Linux, for our PoC, we will demonstrate the process using a .NET web application with a SQL Server database. Java and JavaScript fans, don't despair! In `Chapter 4`, *Prepare the Docker Enterprise Pilot Cluster*, when we get into the pilot phase, we will use a Java book application with a React frontend as our example.

For our PoC application, we will follow this process for containerization:

- Review the application documentation
- Containerize each application component/process into an image
- Test each containerized image locally
- Create a deployment file app and test it locally
- Push images
- Test deploy on the Docker Enterprise PoC platform
- Review with the team

Our sample .NET application featured in the PoC is from a Docker blog by post by Elton Stoneman. We chose this application from Elton because he's a Docker expert and he provides in-depth additional material, including his blog (`https://blog.docker.com/2018/02/video-series-modernizing-net-apps-developers/`) and his related book (`https://www.packtpub.com/virtualization-and-cloud/docker-windows`).

The GitHub repository for the PoC sample is here: `https://github.com/dockersamples/ mta-netfx-dev/tree/part-1`.

Review application documentation

We begin the containerization process by collecting information about our PoC, starting with the installation process. In other words, we want to see how this application would be installed on a clean server. This information is often available from operational documentation related to the application or some sort of automated script. In other cases, where documentation or scripts are not available, a subject matter expert such as a software developer can usually help you through the process.

Our application documentation includes this diagram:

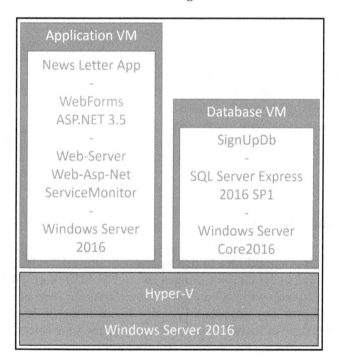

Figure 12: PoC application architecture

Our example PoC application architecture includes two key components: the application virtual machine and the database virtual machine. Within the database virtual machine, we see the application's database called `SignUpDb`, running in a SQL Server Express 2016 SP1 database on a Windows Server core 2016 operating system. Within the application virtual machine, we see our newsletter app, an ASP.NET 3.5 web forms application. The application server has the `web-server`, `web-asp-net`, and `ServiceMonitor` modules installed on top of a Windows Server 2016 guest operating system. Our application has two high-level processes, the application and the database. We will split each of these into a separate image and connect them together with a common network when we deploy them. When containerizing, it is often helpful to build from the bottom up, testing each of the images along the way. So, we will start with the database.

Containerizing and locally testing each application component

A best practice is to build Docker images using something called Dockerfiles. `Dockerfile` is a text file containing commands to build a Docker image layer by layer, starting with a base image. Our goal for the section will be to create two separate Dockerfiles. One `Dockerfile` is for the application and the other `Dockerfile` is for the database. Please note, `Dockerfile` default naming has no file extension by convention. So, be careful of text editors appending your `Dockerfile` with a `.txt` extension. If you are not familiar with Dockerfiles, please take minute to read this: `https://docs.docker.com/engine/reference/builder/`.

Containerizing the database

Our first task when containerizing a process is to find the appropriate base for our database image. During a PoC, it is a good idea to use a pre-made official image from the Docker Hub. In our case, we will be looking for images created by Microsoft. Please note that, later down the adoption path, you will probably want to create your own hardened-based images for enterprise development. We will talk more about that during the pilot chapter. There are a couple of ways to discover base images. One is to simply Google for the image and look for links to Docker Hub. Another approach is to just search within Docker Hub.

We begin our search for a base image in a most familiar way, by Googling "Docker SQL express 2016 server". The first result is a link to a Microsoft image on Docker Hub—it looks promising so we follow the link to `https://hub.docker.com/r/microsoft/mssql-server-windows-express/` and review the image information page. So far, it looks like a good fit. However, I want to make sure that I find a version that's compatible with our application. So, I click on the **Tags** tab, where we find a `2016-sp1` tag for this image. So, the address of our image is `microsoft/mssql-server-windows-express:2016-sp1`. This is an image in the Docker Hub public registry, located within the Microsoft namespace, in a repository called `mssql-server-windows-express`, with a tag of `2016-sp1`.

> Reminder! Although it might be tempting to try the latest version of an image (latest for MS SQL Server Express: 2017-latest, 2017-CU1), that is not what our application is using. Using the newer image is effectively adding an upgrade project to the PoC's critical path, as well as all of the associated headaches and momentum killing issues. Be very careful to avoid any upgrading or refactoring of your application in the PoC process, lest you get bogged down and lose your momentum. You can review any refactoring efforts when scoping the next pilot phase.

Congratulations, we have the beginnings of our database `Dockerfile`. The first line is an important practice for building Windows images. The `# escape=` tells the `docker build` command to treat the backtick (`) as the escape character instead of the default backslash (\\). On Windows, the backslash is of course used in file paths and you do not want file path characters to be confused with escape characters.

In the second line, we see the base image that we discovered on Docker Hub:

```
# escape=`
FROM microsoft/mssql-server-windows-express:2016-sp1
```

We now return to the Docker Hub repository information page for the `sql-server` express image for more instructions on how to use this image. We noticed some interesting instructions about setting environment variables. We create a section in our `Dockerfile` for setting environment variables that will be used by MS SQL when it runs in the container. One variable is for accepting the **End User Licensing Agreement (EULA)** and the other variable is the system administrator password. Please note the password used here for the DB image will have to match the connection string of our web application as stored in the `Web.config` file of our application image (we will build that next). Also, please note the use of the backtick (`` ` ``) character as a line continuation and therefore all of the following lines are part of a single `ENV` command in the `Dockerfile`:

```
ENV ACCEPT_EULA="Y" `
sa_password="DockerCon!!!" `
DATA_PATH="C:\mssql"
```

The `DATA_PATH` environment variable is used in conjunction with the Docker volume (shown in the following).

```
VOLUME ${DATA_PATH}

WORKDIR C:\init
COPY docker\db .
CMD ./init.ps1 -sa_password $env:sa_password -Verbose
```

Using a Docker volume this way stores MS SQL database files outside of the database container on the host filesystem. Later, we can use this volume to mount our database's files in this volume and share the same files between different runs of the container. Therefore, if the container running the database is stopped and restarted, the database state will be preserved across the new and old containers.

`WORKDIR` sets the active directory inside the container you are building, much like a change directory (`cd`) command, where your location on the file system is preserved as a working directory until change it again. Please note that if I issue a change directory command, it is only valid on the current line of the `Dockerfile`. This means that if you `cd` to a directory in one line, and in the next line of the `Dockerfile` you run PWD, you will see you are back to the default root directory. This relates to how Docker uses an intermediate container to generate image layers; there's more to come on this topic later, when we talk about optimizing Dockerfiles in the pilot chapter.

COPY moves files from the {my-build-context}\docker\db source into the current directory, = WORKDIR = C:\init. So, my files in the docker\db directory end up in the c:\init directory.

CMD is the default command that's executed when the container is run (without a command in the docker run command line). In our case, CMD runs the init.ps1 PowerShell script. The init.ps1 script hides the logic that determines whether there is already a database present in the C:\mssql directory. If the database files exist, it will use them. If the files don't exist, then a sequel script is run to populate the initial database. This is a pattern that can be really helpful for test applications, where you allow Docker to create an ephemeral volume and therefore generate a fresh database every time it runs:

The HEALTHCHECK section of Elton's Dockerfile (shown in the following) will be used later when we deploy our container into a Docker cluster. A health check defines code that's executed by the orchestrator in order to determine the health of a container. In our case, it's running a SQL command from inside our SQL database container. If an orchestrator finds a container unhealthy, it'll kill it and replace it with a fresh container:

```
HEALTHCHECK CMD powershell -command `
try { `
$result = Invoke-SqlCmd -Query 'SELECT TOP 1 1 FROM Countries' -Database
SignUpDb; `
if ($result[0] -eq 1) { return 0} `
else {return 1}; `
} catch { return 1 }
```

We now have a complete docker\db\Dockerfile to build our containerized database server image shown in the following code block:

```
# escape=`
FROM microsoft/mssql-server-windows-express:2016-sp1
SHELL ["powershell", "-Command", "$ErrorActionPreference = 'Stop';
$ProgressPreference = 'SilentlyContinue';"]

ENV ACCEPT_EULA="Y" `
sa_password="DockerCon!!!" `
DATA_PATH="C:\mssql"

VOLUME ${DATA_PATH}

WORKDIR C:\init
COPY .\docker\db .

CMD ./init.ps1 -sa_password $env:sa_password -Verbose
```

```
HEALTHCHECK CMD powershell -command `
try { `
$result = Invoke-SqlCmd -Query 'SELECT TOP 1 1 FROM Countries' -Database
SignUpDb; `
if ($result[0] -eq 1) { return 0} `
else {return 1}; `
} catch { return 1 }
```

We've discussed every line in the previous code block, except for the shell line in the file. The key part of this line is the $ErrorActionPreference = 'Stop' section that tells the shell to stop on the first error and not to on error, resume next, the default error preference. In other words, stop running the script if there is an error.

It's time to build an image using Dockerfile. We have copied Elton's code to our Windows build machine, which is either a Windows 10 desktop or a Windows 2016 server.

 If you create a fresh Windows Server 2016 to build and test your containerized Windows applications, make sure to update Docker on the host, otherwise you may get an ancient version such as Docker 1.12. To update Docker on Windows 2016, run this command: Install-Package -Name docker -ProviderName DockerMsftProvider -Verbose -Update -Force. You'll probably have to restart the Docker service manually after the update.

Let's assume you copied your files to the mta-netfx-dev directory. We then focus our attention on the db subtree under the docker directory to better understand the docker build command that we are going to run (shown in the following). Please note the location of the database's Dockerfile, init-db.sql, and init.ps1 files:

```
mta-netfx-dev
        ├── docker
        │   ├── db
        │   │   ├── Dockerfile
        │   │   ├── init-db.sql
        │   │   └── init.ps1
```

From the `mta-netfx-dev` directory, we run the `docker image build` command to create the `db-image:v1` image and use `Dockerfile` in the `docker\db` folder that we just created. You should see some successfully built and tagged images at the bottom of the output. Don't forget the trailing period in this command. It provides the `build` context where the `COPY` command gets its base, in this case, the `mta-netfx-dev` directory:

```
mta-netfx-dev$ docker image build -t db-image:v1 --file
.\docker\db\Dockerfile .
...
Successfully built 026c23401784
Successfully tagged db-image:v1
```

Now, we can fire up and test our database server (shown in the following). First, we are going to run a container using the database image we create. We use `-d` to run it in the background, expose port `5432` on the host, and forward it to port `5432` inside the container. These are the standard MS SQL ports. Next, we test the our database container by running an SQL command against our database from inside the container. In order to do that, we need to get a PowerShell prompt inside the container. We can use the `docker container exec` command to create a new PowerShell process and Command Prompt. Inside the container, we see the PowerShell `PS C:\init>` prompt in the `WORKDIR`. We use the SQL command module (the same one we are using for the health check in the `Dockerfile`) to query `SignUpDb`. We see that `1` is returned. You can of course run any SQL you would like to verify the data:

```
$ docker container run -d -p 5432:5432 db-image:v1
1fe040d1acf242d4cfdb47761db2a59f1bb44b5eedf17376b9455120d86281a5

$ docker container exec -it 1fe0 powershell
PS C:\init> Invoke-SqlCmd -Query 'SELECT TOP 1 1 FROM Countries' -Database
SignUpDb

Column1
-------
1
```

Containerizing the Webforms application

For the Webforms application, Elton takes a more sophisticated approach. Here, we are actually going to build two image files to create the Webform application.

Figure 13 shows the image dependency:

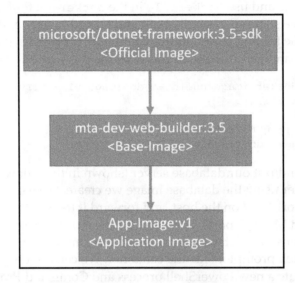

Figure 13: Image Dependency Graph (Not Image Hierarchy)

The first image file is a base builder image we can use for this application and reuse for containerizing other .NET 3.5 Webform applications. So, first let's take a look at the base image `Dockerfile` shown in the following code block:

```
# escape=`
FROM microsoft/dotnet-framework:3.5-sdk
SHELL ["powershell", "-Command", "$ErrorActionPreference = 'Stop';
$ProgressPreference = 'SilentlyContinue';"]

# Install web workload:
RUN Invoke-WebRequest -UseBasicParsing
https://download.visualstudio.microsoft.com/download/pr/100196686/e64d79b40
219aea618ce2fe10ebd5f0d/vs_BuildTools.exe -OutFile vs_BuildTools.exe; `
    Start-Process vs_BuildTools.exe -ArgumentList '--add',
'Microsoft.VisualStudio.Workload.WebBuildTools', '--quiet', '--norestart',
'--nocache' -NoNewWindow -Wait;

# Install WebDeploy
RUN Install-PackageProvider -Name chocolatey -RequiredVersion 2.8.5.130 -
Force; `
    Install-Package -Name webdeploy -RequiredVersion 3.6.0 -Force;
```

This file starts out in the usual way, by overriding the default escape character for a Windows image build, using the backtick instead of the default backslash. Then, we see the base image from the Microsoft call, `microsoft/dotnet-framework:3.5-sdk`. Please note we updated the base image reference to use Microsoft's new repository scheme from Elton's example `docker/web-builder/3.5/Dockerfile` (shown in the following). In the second section of this `Dockerfile`, we see Visual Studio build tools being downloaded and installed. In the final stage, we see the `chocolatey` provider being used to install the `webdeploy` module:

For reference, here's the docker/web filesystem tree:

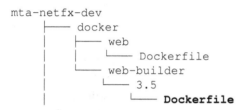

This is the complete `docker/web-builder/3.5/Dockerfile` file; we can build and tag our new base image using this `Dockerfile`, and it will act as the base image for our application's `Dockerfile`:

```
mta-netfx-dev$ docker image build -t mta-sdk-web-builder:3.5 --file
.\docker\web-builder\3.5\Dockerfile .
...
Successfully built df1102a58630
Successfully tagged mta-sdk-web-builder:3.5
```

Now, we can use this new image as the base image for the Webforms application, as follows:

```
# escape=`
FROM mta-sdk-web-builder:3.5 AS builder
SHELL ["powershell", "-Command", "$ErrorActionPreference = 'Stop';"]

WORKDIR C:\src\SignUp.Web
COPY .\src\SignUp\SignUp.Web\packages.config .
RUN nuget restore packages.config -PackagesDirectory ..\packages
COPY src\SignUp C:\src
RUN msbuild SignUp.Web.csproj /p:OutputPath=c:\out /p:DeployOnBuild=true

# app image
FROM microsoft/aspnet:3.5-windowsservercore-10.0.14393.1884
SHELL ["powershell", "-Command", "$ErrorActionPreference = 'Stop';"]
```

```
ENV APP_ROOT="C:\web-app" `
DB_CONNECTION_STRING_PATH=""

WORKDIR $APP_ROOT

RUN Import-Module WebAdministration; `
Set-ItemProperty 'IIS:\AppPools\.NET v2.0' -Name processModel.identityType
-Value LocalSystem; `
Remove-Website -Name 'Default Web Site'; `
New-Website -Name 'web-app' -Port 80 -PhysicalPath $env:APP_ROOT -
ApplicationPool '.NET v2.0'

COPY .\docker\web\start.ps1 .
ENTRYPOINT ["powershell", ".\\start.ps1"]
COPY --from=builder C:\out\_PublishedWebsites\SignUp.Web .
```

The previous Dockerfile is called a multi-stage build because the file has more than
one FROM statement. The first FROM statement designates the first stage of the build, and it is
called builder. This is where msbuild runs to actually build the application. However, it
includes a lot of utilities that we don't need at runtime. So, in the very last line of the
Dockerfile, we copy the assets from the build stage into the second and final image stage.
Therefore, all of the build components are left behind, reducing the size of the final image
and creating a smaller attack surface.

One other noteworthy item in this Dockerfile is the second to last line, where we use an
ENTRYPOINT. An ENTRYPOINT designates which binary is going to be run when this
container starts. This is different than what we did in the database Dockerfile, where we
defined a CMD. While these are similar, the CMD will get replaced by anything passed in
from the command line and ENTRYPOINT will append the command-line argument as a
parameter to the application defined by ENTRYPOINT:

```
# DB Image used CMD, easily overridden with any other command after the
image name
$ docker container run -it run db-image:v1 dir
...directory listing from working directory C:\init
...container exits

# App Image used ENTRYPOINT, command after image name is passed as argument
to start.ps1
$ docker container run -it db-image:v1 dir
... passes argument to "dir" as parameter to start.ps1 script and it's
ignored
... tries to start web application
```

For more information, see the following Docker documentation: https://docs.docker.
com/engine/reference/builder/#cmd.

Now, let's build our application image:

```
docker image build -t app-image:v1 --file .\docker\web\Dockerfile .
...
Successfully built dec1102a58630
Successfully tagged app-image:v1
```

So, we've built three images: one base image for building web apps (mta-sdk-web-builder:3.5), and two final images to run our database and application (db-image:v1 and app-image:v1). It is time to start our application up and test it:

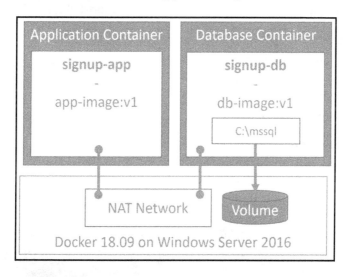

Figure 14: Local Integration Test

Figure 14 shows our local build machine's single node Docker configuration used for testing the local application containers . We have our application container, called signup-app, and our database container, called signup-db. The database container name (signup-db) is particularly important because the application container relies on that name for DNS lookup for service resolution (locally routable IP address) of the database. The following commands show how we start the database container, then start the application container, and both share a common nat network. Containers need to be on the same network to communicate and to share DNS names:

```
# Start the database container
$ docker container run --network nat --name signup-db -d db-image:v1

# Start the application container
$ docker container run --network nat -p 8000:80 --name signup-app -d app-image:v1
```

The first container run command starts the database container in the background (-d) from the db-image:v1 image, names it signup-db, and attaches it to the nat network. The second container run command starts the application container in the background (-d) from the app-image:v1 image, names it signup-app, and attaches it to the nat network.

Did you notice how the nat network is already there? On single-node Windows hosts, Docker provides a single Docker network called nat. Unlike Linux bridge networks, you can't create new networks. This is because other Windows containers may or may not be running on the same Docker deamon/host as Windows supports Hyper-V isolation (that is, docker run -d --isolation hyperv microsoft/nanoserver powershell echo hyperv). Therefore, Docker networks need to be tied together before the host level, at the Hyper-V networking level, with a Hyper-V nat network. To keep it simple, there is one network for Windows called nat; it is available at startup and it provides DNS to other named containers attached to the nat network.

On my test machine, I point my browser to my local IP address, 8000 (using localhost with IIS can be configured with some permission jostling in IIS, but we can use the dev machine's IP instead) and I see the following glorious screen in *Figure 15*:

Figure 15: Local Application Page In Browser

We can now stop our container using the `docker container rm -f` command.

Creating deployment files and testing locally

We now have the individual containers tested and it is time to create a `docker-compose` file that we can use to bring the application stack of services up and down together. Docker's compose tool (`docker-compose`) is part of free Docker. Historically, it has been a tool for defining and running multi-container applications on a single Docker node. However, in Docker 1.13, Docker introduced Swarm mode with extended functionality to run multi-container applications across multiple nodes. Docker uses the same YAML file format (although Docker Swarm extensions require version 3+) to configure your application's multiple services. When the `docker-compose` file is set up, we can start our database and application services/containers with one command.

Next, we have our `docker-compose` for local nodes. Following in our `docker-compose.yml` file, the image names are only local (no namespace in front of the image name) and need to be in the Docker host's image cache in order to be run. We will address this local image issue later. Also, notice the service names (bold in the following code), which will be used for DNS resolution when signup-app looks for `signup-db` in the connections string:

```
version: '3.3'

services:
  signup-db:
    image: db-image:v1
    networks:
      - app-net

  signup-app:
    image: app-image:v1
    ports:
      - "8000:80"
    depends_on:
      - signup-db
    networks:
      - app-net

networks:
  app-net:
    external:
      name: nat
```

To run our application on a single node, we use the `docker-compose up` command. It is usually best to run the `docker-compose` commands in the same directory as `docker-compose.yml`. Next, we see the command being run and the subsequent log entries:

```
PS mta-netfx-dev-part-2\app> docker-compose up
...
Creating app_signup-db_1_3084b8816d59 ... done
Creating app_signup-app_1_cf2adb1663f8 ... done
Attaching to app_signup-db_1_7dc594a2a1cf, app_signup-app_1_3c8d26d0a674
signup-db_1_7dc594a2a1cf  | VERBOSE: Starting SQL Server
signup-db_1_7dc594a2a1cf  | VERBOSE: Changing SA login credentials
signup-app_1_3c8d26d0a674 | Configuring DB connection
signup-app_1_3c8d26d0a674 | Starting IIS
signup-app_1_3c8d26d0a674 | Tailing log
signup-db_1_7dc594a2a1cf  | VERBOSE: No existing data files - will create
new database
signup-db_1_7dc594a2a1cf  | VERBOSE: Changed database context to 'master'.
signup-db_1_7dc594a2a1cf  | VERBOSE: Changed database context to 'SignUpDb'.
signup-db_1_7dc594a2a1cf  |
signup-app_1_3c8d26d0a674 | 2018-11-11 01:47:55,705 [1 ] INFO - Completed
pre-load data cache, took: 7020ms
signup-app_1_3c8d26d0a674 | 2018-11-11 01:48:14,908 [1 ] INFO - Starting
pre-load data cache
signup-app_1_3c8d26d0a674 | 2018-11-11 01:48:15,033 [1 ] INFO - Completed
pre-load data cache, took: 99ms

(press Ctrl+C twice to terminate)
$ docker-compose down
... clean up messages
```

Now, we have a `docker-compose` or stack file that we can use to run our application. However, if we want to be able to run that stack file from anywhere, we are going to need to rename and move the images to a central registry.

Pushing images

Currently, our application and database images are only stored on the Docker node where we ran the `docker image build` command. For our PoC, we will be using the DTR that we installed in our PoC cluster.

Connecting to the PoC DTR

Since you are using a self-signed certificate for the PoC's DTR, you will need to configure your local build machine Docker daemon to trust the DTR certificate used during the https login. If you do not configure your local build machine to trust the DTR certificate, you will get an x509 certificate error when attempting to log in to DTR. For more information on configuring the operating system on your build machine, please read this: `https://docs.docker.com/ee/dtr/user/access-dtr/`.

At this point, you will need your login credentials for the PoC's UCP/DTR from your Docker Enterprise administrator. In addition to the username and password, you will also need the DNS name or routable IP address of both the UCP and DTR. Use the following command to log a Docker Engine into the DTR; follow the prompts for credentials:

```
$ docker login url-of-docker-trusted-registry
username: dev-user
password: *******
...
WARNING! Your password will be stored unencrypted in
C:\Users\Administrator\.docker\config.json.
Configure a credential helper to remove this warning. See
https://docs.docker.com/engine/reference/commandline/login/#credentials-sto
re

Login Succeeded
```

After the warning, you should be logged in to the DTR. For the PoC, don't worry about installing a credential helper, but is not a bad idea for developer workstations that have access to the Docker Enterprise cluster.

Preparing and pushing your images

Now that you are logged in to the DTR, you will be able to push your images once you have them properly named/tagged. Images are identified by the following naming properties:

- The URL of the registry where they're stored
- The username or namespace within the registry
- The repository name
- The image tag

Docker image naming format is as follows: `Repo_URL / Namespace /Repo_name:Tag`

- `Repo_URL`: This is where your Docker DTR is located. The default value is `docker.io` (Docker Hub).
- `Namespace`: This is the organization name or user name. The default value is `empty` (Docker official images).
- `Repo_name`: This is the repository name. It's a required value with no default.
- `Tag`: This is the repository tag name. The default value is `latest`.

Examples from Docker Hub (`docker.io`) include the following:

- **Repository for official CentOS image with latest tag**: CentOS
- **Repository for official Ubuntu image with 16.04 tag**: Ubuntu 16.04
- **Microsoft organization, .Net framework image with 3.5-sdk tag**: `microsoft/dotnet-framework:3.5-sdk`

Examples from my the `app-dev` organization in my private PoC DTR on AWS include the following:

- **My app image**: `ec2-xxx-xxx-xxx-xxx.us-west-2.compute.amazonaws.com/app-dev/app-image:v1`
- **My DB image**: `ec2-xxx-xxx-xxx-xxx.us-west-2.compute.amazonaws.com/app-dev/db-image:v1`

As you can tell, my repository has an organization named `app-dev` and my user is part of that organization. Your Docker Enterprise administrator can set these up; then, you are ready to rename your images. In order to prepare your image, you will need to rename your images in the proper format for storing them in your PoC DTR. For this, we use the `docker tag` command:

```
$ docker image tag db-image:v1 {insert-your-DTR-URL-here}/{user-name or
org-name}/db-image:v1
$ docker image push {insert-your-DTR-URL-here}/{user-name or org-name}/db-
image:v1
$ docker image tag app-image:v1 {insert-your-DTR-URL-here}/{user-name or
org-name}/app-image:v1
$ docker image push {insert-your-DTR-URL-here}/{user-name or org-name}/app-
image:v1
```

After the image is pushed, enter you DTR URL into the browser and don't forget the `https://` prefix. Then, look at the repositories. You should see something like the screen shown in *Figure 16*:

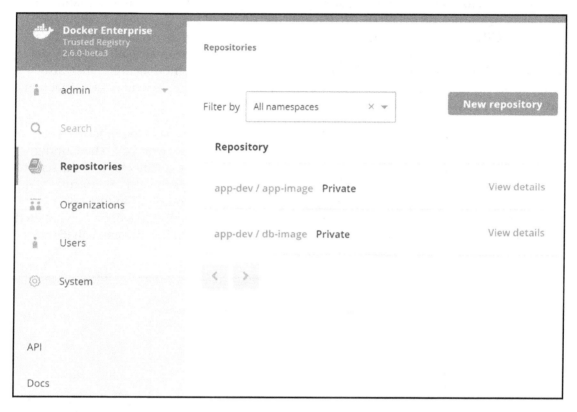

Figure 16: PoC Images in the Docker Trusted Registry

Next, we will look at deploying our PoC application to the Docker Enterprise cluster.

Deploying a PoC application to a Docker Enterprise cluster

In order to secure access to a Docker Enterprise cluster, we use Docker's role-based access control system. We will get into more details on the role-based access control system in the pilot phase, but for our PoC, we need a user with sufficient access to deploy our PoC application containers to the cluster.

The Docker Enterprise CLI bundle

Docker Enterprise makes it easy to manage access to your cluster. It gives you fine-grained access controls to resources in the cluster by generating a bundle (.zip file) consisting of your user certificates signed by the UCP certificate authority that was created when you installed UCP and scripts for connecting your Terminal to a remote cluster. The bundle's scripts support both Windows' PowerShell and Linux's Bash Terminal shell. Not only do these scripts connect you with the Docker Enterprise cluster daemon securely, they also give you access to the Kubernetes API running in the UCP cluster. Just make sure that you have port 6443 available to access the Kubernetes API.

The bundle can be downloaded in one of two ways. The first way is to log in to the web interface with the credentials that your system administrator has given you. Then, under your profile, you can generate a bundle and it will download the certificates and the scripts in a ZIP file to your local drive from the browser. *Figure 17* shows the web interface method. Expand the **admin** menu and click **My Profile**. Then, choose **Client Bundles** | **New Client Bundle** | **Generate Client Bundle**. Subsequently, a zip file will be downloaded through your browser. Unzip the contents of this file and move it to a directory that's easy to access from your shell:

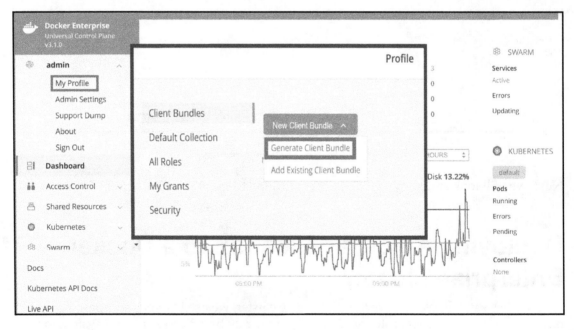

Figure 17: Download UCP Client Bundle

Another way to get the command-line bundle without using the web interface is to use the Docker Enterprise API. The API requires that you generate a bearer token by passing your username and password to the API. The results of the call will be a token that you need to pass along with the header to subsequent API calls. So, in our case, we first generate our bearer token. Then, we use it to request our UCP CLI bundle file. This is a really handy way to access the API from either PowerShell or bash scripts:

Using Bash with Docker API to get the CLI bundle

Refer to the following steps:

1. Before you start the process of downloading the command-line bundle through the API, make sure that you have the curl, jq (a lightweight formatter for JSON payloads), and unzip utilities installed:

   ```
   sudo apt-get update && sudo apt-get install curl jq unzip
   ```

2. Now, get the bearer token and call the API to retrieve the CLI files. Be sure to replace <ucp-ip> with the IP or DNS of your Docker PoC IP:

   ```
   # Stash your Bearer token in an environment variable
   AUTHTOKEN=$(curl -sk -d
   '{"username":"<username>","password":"<password>"}'
   https://<ucp-ip>/auth/login | jq -r .auth_token)

   # Download the client certificate bundle
   curl -k -H "Authorization: Bearer $AUTHTOKEN"
   https://<ucp-ip>/api/clientbundle -o bundle.zip

   # Unzip the bundle.
   unzip bundle.zip

   # Run the utility script.
   eval "$(<env.sh)"

   # You are connected to the cluster - test it.
   docker node ls
   ... listing of your Docker Enterprise nodes
   ```

Using PowerShell with the Docker API to get the CLI bundle

If you would rather connect to your EE cluster with a standard Windows PowerShell, use the following commands. Again, be sure to replace the <username>, <password>, and <ucp-ip> with the IP or DNS of your Docker PoC IP:

```
PS> $AUTHTOKEN=((Invoke-WebRequest -Body '{"username":"<username>",
"password":"<password>"}' -Uri https://<ucp-ip>/auth/login -Method
POST).Content)|ConvertFrom-Json|select auth_token -ExpandProperty
auth_token

PS> [io.file]::WriteAllBytes("ucp-bundle.zip", ((Invoke-WebRequest -Uri
https://<ucp-ip>/api/clientbundle -Headers @{"Authorization"="Bearer
$AUTHTOKEN"}).Content))

PS> Expand-Archive -Path ucp-bundle.zip -DestinationPath .

PS> Import-Module .\env.ps1
Security warning
Run only scripts that you trust. While scripts from the internet can be
useful, this script can potentially harm your
computer. If you trust this script, use the Unblock-File cmdlet to allow
the script to run without this warning
message. Do you want to run C:\Users\Administrator\PoC CLI\env.ps1?
[D] Do not run [R] Run once [S] Suspend [?] Help (default is "D"): R

PS> docker node ls
... listing of your Docker Enterprise nodes
```

Visit the Docker docs here for more information on the command-line bundle: https://docs.docker.com/ee/ucp/user-access/cli/.

Deploying the PoC application to the Docker Enterprise cluster

Now that you are connected to the Docker cluster through the command-line interface bundle, it is time to deploy your application. Up until now, we've deployed the containers on your development or build machine to make sure the application is working properly. Then, we pushed the images out to the DTR so they will be available to our orchestrator when we deploy our stack to the cluster.

Up until now, we've created our `docker-compose.yml` file and run it with the `docker-compose up` command to get our stack of containers (described as services in the YAML file) running our single/local Docker host. Now, we want to run that same stack of containers on our Docker Enterprise cluster. Docker makes it easy by allowing us to use the familiar `docker-compose.yml` file format to deploy to a Docker Enterprise (or an Swarm) cluster using the `docker stack deploy` command. However, there are some things we need to do in order to get this cluster ready. For instance, it is really important to note how the image names must use a fully qualified path to your trusted registries repository. Otherwise, the orchestrator will be unable to pull the images from the cluster nodes and the deployment will fail.

First, let's rename the `docker-compose` file to something like `stack.yml`. This will help avoid confusion when we are trying to determine which file to use for a cluster deployment. Since the Docker Swarm command for deployment is `docker stack deploy`, `stack` should be a pretty logical choice and one we often see used.

 `docker-compose` files can be used for Swarm deployments with the `docker stack deploy` command, but requires version 3.0 or newer (declared at the top of the file). Notice how we are using version 3.3, which will allow us to use to add the deploy section to our stack file.

Looking at the `stack.yml` file, we will walk through the changes to the file that are needed as we upgrade from a single-node `docker-compose` file to a Swarm cluster file. First, notice the image uses a fully qualified DTR path to your PoC registry. Second, notice the addition of the deploy section in the file. Here, we are using **DNS Round Robin (DNSRR)** endpoint mode because we are using Windows Server 2016 where VIP (Virtual IP, the preferred Docker built-in load balancing approach) is not available. Look for VIP on Windows in Windows Server 2019.

In conjunction with a DNSRR endpoint, we must use host mode for publishing IP ports for external traffic. This means the port is only published on the host adapter where the signup-app container is running. For us, that means we will have to point all incoming traffic to our Windows worker node on port `8000`. While this may seem a little bit limiting, it's a fairly common setup for some of the old-school Docker implementations.

Finally, notice the slight change to our network. Previously, we had it as an external network when we were running on a single Windows 2016 node. This was primarily due to some limitations with Docker running on a single node with Windows Server 2016, where you are limited to a preconfigured `nat` network to connect containers. So, to access the preexisting network, we used the external network. Now, however, we are running in Swarm mode and Swarm provides overlay networking, allowing our containers to communicate across multiple nodes in the cluster. The default implementation of Docker overlay networking is VXLAN behind the scenes:

```
# stack.yml file
version: '3.3'

services:
  signup-db:
    image: {insert-your-DTR-URL-here}/{user-name or org-name}/db-image:v1
    networks:
      - app-neto
    deploy:
      endpoint_mode: dnsrr
      placement:
        constraints:
          - node.platform.os==windows

  signup-app:
    image: {insert-your-DTR-URL-here}/{user-name or org-name}/app-image:v1
    ports:
      - mode: host
        target: 80
        published: 8000
    depends_on:
      - signup-db
    networks:
      - app-neto
    deploy:
      endpoint_mode: dnsrr
      placement:
        constraints:
          - node.platform.os==windows

  networks:
    app-neto:
      driver: overlay
```

For more information on creating `docker-compose` files, please check out the Docker docs manual: https://docs.docker.com/compose/compose-file/.

Now, to run the application in the cluster, you need to do the following:

```
# Deploy the test stack
docker stack deploy -c .\stack.yml.txt test

# Look at the services
docker service ls
ID              NAME             MODE         REPLICAS IMAGE
paoo6ej3ubcz test_signup-app replicated 1/1       ec2-xx-xx-x-xx.us-
west-2.compute.amazonaws.com/app-dev/app-image:v1
w321xzt14khc test_signup-db  replicated 1/1       ec2-xx-xx-x-xx.us-
west-2.compute.amazonaws.com/app-dev/db-image:v1
```

To test the application, point your browser at the Windows worker node's external IP address on port 8000. You might see this:

Figure 18: PoC Application Error Screen

This means `signup-app` came up before the database was ready. You see, the `depends_on` parameter in the `stack.yml` file is only reliable with `docker-compose` and not `docker stack deploy`. Furthermore, `depends_on` only means the dependent process's PID 1 is up and running and not that the database is completely initialized and ready. While that's certainly something we would want to attend to in the pilot phase, we can manually tweak it for the PoC. For our tweak, we will restart the application service, and the easiest way to do it is to scale down the `signup-app` service to 0 replicas and then back up to 1 replica. Here are the commands for doing it:

```
docker service scale test_signup-app=0
...
docker service scale test_signup-app=1
```

Now, we can return to our browser and refresh the page. Now, we should see the Dockercon newsletter site.

Updating the PoC application

Congratulations! You containerized your PoC application and have it running on your Docker POC platform. You should be comfortable deploying the code that you've containerized previously using the process outline. However, it is a good idea to demonstrate how easy it is to update and deploy your PoC application to the cluster.

To demonstrate the update process, try the following:

1. Make a small code tweak that will show up in the UI.
2. In the `src/SignUp.aspx` file, change the following:

```
<div class="jumbotron">
    <h1>Play with Docker is the best thing I've ever heard of!</h1>
    <p class="lead">Here are my details. Sign me up.</p>
</div>
```

3. Change it to the following:

```
<div class="jumbotron">
    <h1>Play with Docker Enterprise Rocks!</h1>
    <p class="lead">Here are my details. Sign me up.</p>
</div>
```

4. Rebuild your application container and test it locally:

```
docker image build -t app-image:v1 --file .\docker\web\Dockerfile
docker-compose up
```

5. Label your updated container with a `v2` tag and `push` it to DTR:

```
docker image tag app-image:v1 {insert-your-DTR-URL-here}/{user-name
or org-name}/app-image:v2
docker image push {insert-your-DTR-URL-here}/{user-name or org-
name}/app-image:v2
```

6. Update your stack file to use the new image with the `v2` tag for the `app-image` app section (shown in the following) and don't forget to save your changes:

```
signup-app:
    image: {insert-your-DTR-URL-here}/{user-name or org-
name}/app-image:v2
```

```
ports:
  - mode: host
    target: 80
    published: 8000
depends_on:
  - signup-db
networks:
  - app-neto
deploy:
  endpoint_mode: dnsrr
  placement:
    constraints:
      - node.platform.os==windows
```

7. With the old stack still running (the old version of app-image), rerun the `docker stack deploy` command:

docker stack deploy -c .\stack.yml.txt test

8. The updated image should be updated.
9. Verify the changes in the browser—playing with Docker Enterprise rocks!

Summary

In this final chapter of our *Getting Started* section, we kicked off our Docker Enterprise journey in earnest by building our own environment, where we can run a containerized PoC application. The goal is to be able to demonstrate how Docker Enterprise will run in your environment and what it looks like running one of your own applications.

First, we prepared the environment for the PoC. We started with some PoC nodes on a common network. Then, we prepared each node by installing the Docker Engine, as well as the Docker Enterprise components, consisting of the Universal Control Plane and the DTR. Then, with the PoC environment ready to go, we turned our focus to selecting and containerizing a PoC application.

Selecting a proof-of-concept application can be a little bit tricky. We want to find one that can be containerized without any code refactoring, and at the same time, we want to find an application that's representative of other applications that are likely to follow down the containerization path. Once we select the application and containerize it, we can demonstrate the deployment and update processes using an actual Docker Enterprise environment.

So, at this point, we have some working experience with our new container platform, as well as our first containerized application under our belt. After our PoC demonstration and discussion with stakeholders, we should be ready to move on to the pilot step in Chapter 4, *Prepare the Docker Enterprise Pilot Cluster*.

Questions

1. How many nodes do we need to PoC cluster?
2. What is a "short list" of PoC applications for?
3. What are the 4 parts of a fully qualified Docker image name?
4. How do I get a local image, my-db-image:latest into my private (dtr.mydomain.dom) trusted registry's dev/db-image repository?

Further reading

- **Running Docker commands from inside a container** (skip to the end of this discussion thread):
    - https://forums.docker.com/t/how-can-i-run-docker-command-inside-a-docker-container/337/11
- **Installing Docker Enterprise on Windows**:
    - https://docs.docker.com/install/windows/docker-ee/#use-a-script-to-install-docker-ee
- **Docker application tutorials**:
    - https://docs.docker.com/samples/#tutorial-labs
- **Docker Enterprise role-based access control**:
    - https://docs.docker.com/ee/ucp/authorization/
- **Elton Stoneman containerizing .NET applications**:
    - https://www.packtpub.com/virtualization-and-cloud/docker-windows
    - https://blog.docker.com/2018/02/video-series-modernizing-net-apps-developers/
- **Docker Trusted Registry overview**:
    - https://docs.docker.com/ee/dtr/

Section 2: Piloting Docker Enterprise

2

Moving past the proof of concept, in this section we prepare to pilot the internal release of a single containerized application to a highly-available non-production Docker Enterprise cluster. This section covers the key infrastructure, installation, application, pipeline, and operations considerations for our pilot.

The following chapters are included in this section:

- Chapter 4, *Prepare the Docker Enterprise Pilot Cluster*
- Chapter 5, *Prepare and Deploy a Docker Enterprise Pilot Application*
- Chapter 6, *Design and Pilot a Docker Enterprise CI Pipeline*
- Chapter 7, *Pilot Docker Enterprise Platform Monitoring and Logging*

Prepare the Docker Enterprise Pilot Cluster

4

As we enter the pilot phase of our Enterprise container adoption, we begin with a clean slate. Informed by our experience from the proof of concept, we will begin to make some long-term design decisions regarding our **Docker Enterprise** platform. The goal here is to have a platform ready for internal pilot deployments. Not all of the rigging is necessary for a full-blown production application, but more of an internal development platform that is ready to support multiple in-house application development teams.

In this chapter, we will get started with the pilot phase and walk through the design, configuration, and build of a Docker Enterprise pilot cluster. Before we are ready to make any design decisions regarding the pilot platform, however, we will need to review some important Docker concepts related to networking. Additionally, we need to configure our cluster by learning more about Docker's **Universal Control Plane** (**UCP**) configuration settings. Also related to configuration, is understanding how users will interact with the cluster to design a **Role-Based Access Control** (**RBAC**) scheme. Finally, in this chapter, we back up our key concepts with a walk-through of a bare metal installation of Docker Enterprise 2.1 on CentOS 7.5. While we will come back to the Docker-certified infrastructure for cloud and **Virtual Machines** (**VMs**), bare metal is a great way to learn important setup details for Docker Enterprise.

We will cover the following topics in this chapter:

- Highly available clusters for Swarm and Kubernetes
- **Role-Based Access Control (RBAC)** to isolate multiple teams on a single cluster
- Secure cluster with external client certificates
- Centralized logging
- Monitoring
- Secure software pipeline with separate organization repositories
- Image scanning and vulnerability alerting

Docker Enterprise cluster plumbing

During the PoC phase, our only networking-related requirement was to have all of the nodes on the same network, and a network configuration that would allow for a free flow of traffic between the nodes. As we move forward to the pilot phase, we need to begin understanding Docker networks in more detail. We'll start by describing the networking Docker provides on a single engine node. Then, we will get into a discussion regarding networking in a clustered environment, such as a Swarm in Kubernetes.

Introduction to Docker single-node networking

While single-node networking may seem like an oxymoron, in the early days of Docker, many containers would run on a single node. Additionally, there were no clusters. There was a need for containers to be able to communicate with one another in a safe and easy way, even on a single Docker node. So, although not typically used in the Docker Enterprise realm, we provide a quick overview here. This will provide a foundation for the relevant cluster-based container networking models used by Swarm and Kubernetes.

At the core of Docker networking is the Libnetwork's **Container Network Model** (**CNM**). The CNM is a Docker model for composing container networks in an abstract way, separate from underlying network implementation, and therefore portable. This is sort of like Docker's version of infrastructure as code, using the network API as an infrastructure abstraction. For our purposes, we are going to summarize the key points of Docker single-node networking.

Container network troubleshooting

Please refer to the Libnetwork repository, as well as Nicola Kabar's famous network troubleshooting utility container; this is the Swiss army knife of container networking utilities. For more information, please review the documentation here: `https://github.com/nicolaka/netshoot`.

When it came to container networking, Docker took a very pragmatic approach. This was tricky because they tried to balance security with usability. As a result, it is generally easy to use, but there are some understandable quirks based on fundamental design decisions. In *Figure 1*, we see a single Docker host node with a single container running. From the bottom up, we see the host adapter connected to the Docker0 Linux bridge network, attached to a single container (Docker supports multiple containers on a host, but we will focus on a single container for our first example) through a virtual Ethernet (veth) endpoint. Notice that the **host** namespace and **container** namespace are separate. This is important so that users and applications inside the **container** namespace cannot see the **host network namespace**. This is an important security feature provided by Linux bridge networks:

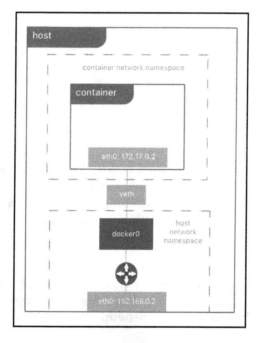

Figure 1: Docker0 Bridge Network-*Copyright © 2018 Docker Inc. All rights reserved*

The Docker0 Linux bridge network, which is the default network used when launching containers, has some special properties. By default, containers launched with the `docker run` command are attached to this default network and are reachable by other containers on the Docker0 network through their IP address (that is, `172.17.0.2` in *Figure 1*). If you wish to have your container completely isolated from other containers, run your container with the `none` network, as shown in the following code block. Otherwise, it will be connected to the Docker0 network automatically:

```
$ docker run --rm -dit \
  --network none \
  --name no-net-alpine \
  alpine:latest \
  ash
```

There are three basic types of networks used with single-node container networks, as follows:

- Linux bridge networks
- host networks
- none networks

These types of networks are created by using Docker network drivers when the network is created. We saw this when we previously created the `none` network to isolate our container. Docker uses the Linux bridge network when it creates the Docker0 default network on each Docker host. We will look at bridge networks in more depth in a moment, particularly as they apply to the custom that works. The `none` network driver, as we already described, can be used to completely isolate a container.

Using the host network driver is not recommended because it gives the container access to the host network namespace. In other words, all of the host's networking resources can be accessed as root from inside the container when using a host network driver. This obviously introduces potential security threats.

No Domain Name System (DNS) for the Docker0 default network

By default, containers can communicate with other local containers on the Docker0 network using their IP addresses only, as the Docker0 network does not provide any DNS services. Please note that, initially Docker provided a primitive mechanism for referencing containers using something called links, but links have been deprecated in favor of user-defined networks. User-defined networks, which bridge networks by default on single-node Docker hosts, can be used for both isolation and service discovery.

In *Figure 2* following, we see three containers running on a Docker host:

- The first container, **c1**, was run and automatically connected to the default Docker0 network.
- Containers **c2** and **c3** are connected to a custom bridge network called `my_bridge`. In this scenario, container **c2** can communicate with container **c3** by using the IP address, `10.10.0.254`, or by using the container name **c3**.
- Container **c3** can communicate with container **c2** by using either the IP address of `10.0.0.2`, or the container name **c2**.
- **c2** and **c3** can communicate freely on their custom bridge network, but they cannot interact with container **c1**.

Docker isolates the container that works by adding IP table-blocking rules to disallow any traffic routing between Docker networks. This means you cannot use DNS or IP addresses to communicate between containers on the Docker0 and the custom bridge network.

Figure 2 shows a single-node Docker network set up with a default (`docker0`) and custom (`my_bridge`) network:

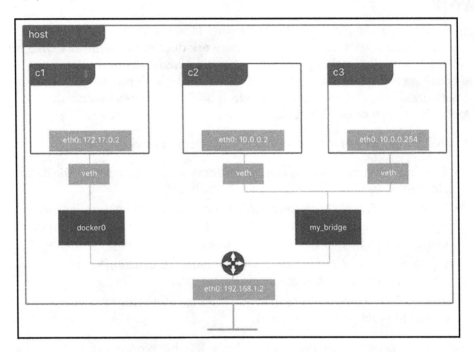

Figure 2: Custom Bridge Network-*Copyright © 2018 Docker Inc. All rights reserved*

This sort of isolation needs to be considered as you transition from the old concept of a physical DMZ and web server subnet to a container-based application on a Docker network. These same isolation principles apply to Docker networks in clusters as well as single nodes, and become a really important concept to grasp when leveraging containers in Enterprise.

Because of Docker's network isolation features, we can create our own isolated web frontend network and backend data network for each 3-tier application stack. Not only will this isolate the layers in your application, but it will also isolate each application's containers from one another. So, on the same cluster, we can have development, test, and QA versions of the same application running next to each other without interfering with one another. In `Chapter 5`, *Prepare and Deploy a Docker Enterprise Pilot Application*, we will discuss role-based access control that can be used in combination with network isolation as a powerful feature to securely support multiple teams in the same non-production cluster resources.

Introduction to cluster-based container networking

So far, our discussion has focused on a single-node Docker networking environment. While single-node Docker networking is feature-rich with network isolation and DNS, it is all still contained within a single host. This means traffic between containers doesn't have to hit an external network. Additionally, it means our platform is restricted to a single node, limiting our ability to scale and failover. So, now we extend our focus to clusters running containers with both Swarm and Kubernetes orchestrators. This means that our containers need to not only communicate with other containers on the same node, but they also need to span the network and communicate with containers running on different nodes in the cluster.

Cluster-based networking conversations are often organized around three key networking planes: the data plane, the control plane, and the management plane. The concept of inter-container communication across the entire cluster is often referred to as the data plane. While the data plane is the key feature of interest to most distributed application developers, it requires support from the control and management planes to function.

In order to facilitate the necessary housekeeping for the data plane to work – that is, which containers are running on a particular node and how to access them – there is an additional cluster-based networking component called the control plane. Finally, the category of cluster networking related to cluster management functions, with responsibilities such as adding and removing cluster member nodes and maintaining cluster health and container scheduling, is called the management plane.

Docker Swarm and Kubernetes both support data planes for cross-cluster, inter-container communication. However, they take a different approach to implementation. Docker Swarm uses VXLAN overlay networks to create isolated and optionally encrypted networks for a select subset of Swarm services.

This means we can define a custom network within a Swarm application stack, and isolate which containers can directly communicate within my application stack. This is how we can create a frontend network for your web application and API to share, and a backend network for the API in the database to connect to, as shown in *Figure 3*:

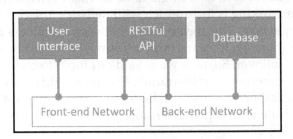

Figure 3: Example of Swarm network isolation

This sort of network isolation is easily achieved using Docker's built-in overlay networks with Swarm. Kubernetes takes a different approach.

Kubernetes achieves cross-cluster, inter-container communication with a flat overlay networking model. *Figure 4* shows how our application components are connected to the single flat network, and isolation is enforced using network policies to limit traffic flow between our application components:

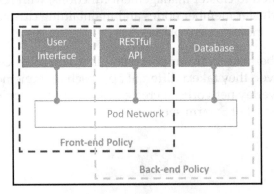

Figure 4: Calico Network Policy Isolation

The Kubernetes cluster networking model is implemented using a third party **Container Networking Interface** (**CNI**) plugin. This means Kubernetes does not provide networking out of the box, just the specification for third-parties to build suitable networking implementations. Therefore, you must install a CNI plugin when installing Kubernetes. This is where Docker Enterprise makes it easier.

Docker Enterprise automatically installs the Kubernetes orchestrator when installing the UCP. Furthermore, Docker Enterprise provides a built-in Calico CNI plugin by default when installing the UCP. Calico uses a combination of BGB and IP in IP to establish a data plane.

There are several popular Kubernetes CNI plugins for networking. Calico has become a very popular choice, but there are others such as Weave, Flannel, and Romana. Docker makes it very easy to swap out CNI plugins when installing UCP. To make this happen, you need to find the appropriate URL for the CNI provider and use the `--cni-installer-url` parameter for the UCP install command. Docker has an article on this topic, which you can read here: `https://docs.docker.com/ee/ucp/kubernetes/install-cni-plugin/`.

Docker Enterprise provides a variety of options for Kubernetes networking. This is especially important when installing Docker Enterprise on a cloud platform where there are restrictions on network protocols. For instance, on Azure, IP in IP protocol is not allowed, so the out-of-the-box Calico implementation is not an option. Both AWS and Azure offer custom Kubernetes CNI plugins to support Kubernetes networking with native networking support. Be aware that, these cloud platform CNI plugins come with (possibly significant) limitations and are platform specific – possibly leading to cloud platform lock-in, or at least stickiness.

Swarm and Kubernetes DNS and service discovery

Both Swarm and Kubernetes provide DNS services, which are primarily used to support service discovery. DNS is really important for a distributed application platform as a means of runtime, service discovery. Let's say you have two application components: an API and database service. The API needs the database service to store and retrieve data. Now, at runtime when the application is deployed (both services are deployed by an orchestrator in individual containers), the API needs to find the database service and connect over a particular port.

In our old static world, we would simply plug in an IP address or hopefully some local DNS entry that would resolve to the IP address of the database service at runtime. As application components have become increasing ephemeral, server mechanisms have emerged to accomplish this sort of service discovery for distributed application architectures, including `Consul.io` and Eureka.

While these external service discovery tools work very well, they introduce another moving part into your environment. In an effort to simplify the platform, both Docker Swarm and Kubernetes have built-in DNS. While Swarm and Kubernetes operate differently in terms of configuration and implementation, from an application perspective, they are pretty similar.

Essentially, an application running with either orchestrator can refer to a durable endpoint of a dependent and separate process, called a service. The service name resolves to a routable IP address. Additionally, these services monitor the health of underlying containers or pods and replace them if they become unhealthy. Finally, a service can act as a load balancer in front of a group of containers and a load balance request between them.

In *Figure 5*, we have a **redis** service with four pods (all using the same **redis** container image), but accessed through a single **redis:6379** service endpoint. Callers refer to the **redis** service name from their code and the request resolved to one of the four backing containers, as follows:

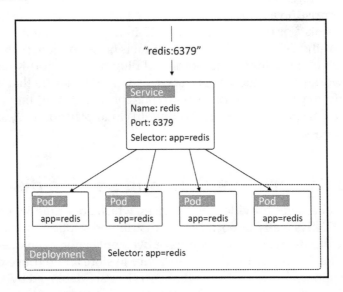

Figure 5: Kubernetes Service

As you can see, the data plane is an essential part of a container cluster. It provides not only a means of communication between containers spread across the cluster, but the integrated DNS also provides the mechanism for binding them together at runtime. Kubernetes and Swarm are designed so that containerized applications can be as portable as possible, and standard data and DNS solutions make this possible.

The management and control planes

Management and control planes are the building blocks for a large part of modern cluster technology. As mentioned in `Chapter 2`, *Docker Enterprise – an Architectural Overview*, the manager's nodes are members of a Raft consensus group backed by an encrypted Etcd cluster for storing things such as the cluster's state, certificates, and secrets. Additionally, the manager nodes are responsible for scheduling workloads to the cluster. *Figure 6* shows the management plane in the blue shading and the control plane in the green shading.

To function properly, there needs to be an odd number of manager nodes in the health state because you need to maintain a quorum (that is, the majority of managers need to agree on any changes to the cluster state). While clusters with a single manager node are efficient, should there be a problem with the single manager, our cluster will be unusable until the manager is restored. As we move to the pilot phase, it is highly recommended to use clusters with three to five manager/master nodes for redundancy:

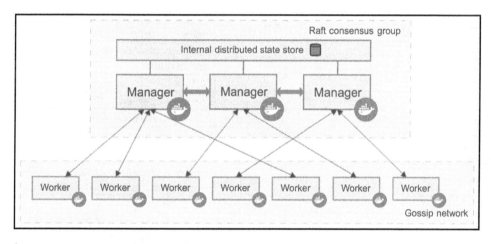

Figure 6: Swarm Management and Control Planes- *Copyright © 2018 Docker Inc. All rights reserved*

Generally, for most high-availability implementations, three manager/master nodes suffice. Some cluster operators opt for five manager nodes for more resilience during routine maintenance on the cluster. Remember, as discussed in `Chapter 2`, *Docker Enterprise – an Architectural Overview*, we need an odd number of managers. While it is nice to have five manager/master nodes, it adds network traffic, computational resources, and licensing costs to your cluster. Going beyond five manager/master nodes generally brings about diminishing returns quickly.

Remember that managers and masters are your pets, and the worker nodes are your cattle. Manager nodes are backed up and sit on fixed IP addresses, whereas worker nodes can be spun up and spun down as needed on dynamic IP addresses.

As we prepare for our pilot environment, it's important for us to understand what ports are being used by the various that work planes in the Docker EE cluster. We need to make sure that our network policies and our firewalls allow these ports to pass freely. The following table shows a listing of all of the ports used in the management control and data planes across the Docker Enterprise cluster:

The following are the network ports for various networking planes:

Nodes	Port	Plane	Purpose
managers, workers	TCP 179	Data	Port for BGP peers, used for Kubernetes networking
managers	TCP 443 (configurable)	Management	Port for the UCP web UI and API
managers	TCP 2376 (configurable)	Management	Port for the Docker Swarm Manager. Used for backward compatibility
managers	TCP 2377 (configurable)	Management	Port for control communication between Swarm nodes
managers, workers	UDP 4789	Data	Port for overlay networking
managers	TCP 6443 (configurable)	Management	Port for Kubernetes API server endpoint
managers, workers	TCP 6444	Management	Port for Kubernetes API reverse proxy
managers, workers	TCP, UDP 7946	Control	Port for gossip-based clustering
managers, workers	TCP 10250	Management	Port for Kubelet
managers, workers	TCP 12376	Management	Port for a TLS authentication proxy that provides access to the Docker Engine
managers, workers	TCP 12378	Management	Port for Etcd reverse proxy
managers	TCP 12379	Management	Port for Etcd Control API
managers	TCP 12380	Management	Port for Etcd Peer API
managers	TCP 12381	Management	Port for the UCP cluster certificate authority
managers	TCP 12382	Management	Port for the UCP client certificate authority
managers	TCP 12383	Management	Port for the authentication storage backend
managers	TCP 12384	Management	Port for the authentication storage backend for replication across managers
managers	TCP 12385	Management	Port for the authentication service API
managers	TCP 12386	Management	Port for the authentication worker
managers	TCP 12388	Management	Internal port for the Kubernetes API Server

Please note that the Kubernetes ports may change if you choose a different CNI provider. Additionally, Kubernetes with Calico requires IPv4 encapsulation protocol 4, and Swarm VXLAN overlay requires ESP protocol 50. This can be really useful information when you are setting up any type of network filtering, network security groups, or firewall rule setting.

Now that we understand a little bit about cluster networking planes and how they are used, we will start to plan the details of the pilot platform implementation.

Docker Enterprise pilot network implementation

Now, let's move on to the implementation of our management plane, control plane, and data plane. In this section, we will discuss how to plan and implement work to support the various working planes used by Docker Enterprise. While all of this may seem internal to the cluster, it's not much good without getting traffic in and out of the cluster, as well as to support two key use cases. Therefore, we will clarify the scope and requirements of our network implementation by presenting these two key use cases for the cluster, as follows:

- Internal users interacting with the cluster
- Application end users of applications hosted in our cluster environment

Internal cluster users

In a Docker Enterprise cluster, there are two primary ways that internal users will gain access to secured cluster APIs and resources. The first is through the UCP Web UI, using a username and password issued by a UCP administrator. The second is through a Docker Enterprise client bundle. This bundle is generated by UCP, and it includes certificates and scripts to remotely connect a local terminal session to the cluster, using user-specific certificates for secure access, cluster authentication, and cluster authorization. The bundle includes scripts for both Linux shells and Windows PowerShell.

Do not give SSH access to any users except for a special group of cluster maintainers and admins. Giving SSH access to a cluster manager node allows users to perform powerful administrative functions, such as recovering the UCP administrator's password. Therefore, SSH access to cluster nodes needs to be highly restricted/regulated and not available to cluster operators and application developers.

Both methods previously described our subject to the grants established by the cluster administrator, meaning that your views, from both the client bundle and the web, will be filtered based on your access control rights. Normally, cluster users will have access to their own personal sandbox, where they can create containers, networks, volumes, secrets, and configurations, all of which are isolated within their user sandbox. When using Docker Enterprise Advanced, the administrator may choose to restrict which nodes you may deploy in workloads.

In *Figure 7*, we see an illustration of how traffic flows from the command shells (Linux and Windows PowerShell) and browsers of internal users into the cluster. The UCP web UI resolves an external IP address for the UCP load balancer through some appropriately scoped DNS entry. In our following example, we called it ucp.mydomain.com. The load balancer then passes the traffic off to one of the three UCP nodes running in our cluster. Notice that this traffic is flowing on port 443 using TLS, and requires certificate exchange and verification. With UCP, this is achieved by using an SNI passthrough in the load balancer, where the certificate is terminated at the end UCP node and not in the load balancer. We will come back to a discussion about certificates after the next section. First, we need to talk about how external users access our cluster, as follows:

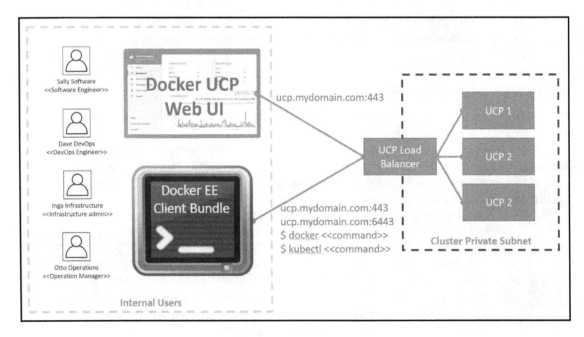

Figure 7: Remote Cluster Access with UCP

End users of Docker Enterprise-hosted applications

The next use case in terms of informing our network design and implementation is the use case of an end user of cluster-hosted applications. As the name suggests, here, we are talking about how end users access applications that we have deployed to the Docker Enterprise cluster. The method that I'm illustrating in *Figure 8,* is a pattern that provides the maximum amount of flexibility for cluster deployments. This approach allows Development, DevOps, or Ops teams (with the right access) to completely deploy an application to the cluster without making any external load balancer changes or DNS updates. This greatly simplifies deployments, and reduces the number of major moving parts in an enterprise platform. There are, of course, other approaches as well that use service clusters and headless services to create a more deterministic traffic pattern for a particular application's network path but these approaches require a more coordinated configuration of load balancers and DNS when an application is deployed.

Figure 8 illustrates the end user access to a cluster deployed application with a layer 7, reverse proxy load balancer for applications. Here, we see the end user of the application entering the application's **Fully Qualified Domain Name** (**FQDN**) into their browser. When the request is made, a wildcard DNS entry picks up the application name and forwards it to the external application load balancer. The external application load balancer then translates the request to a special port where the cluster expects application traffic. For example, we will use port 8443 for Swarm applications, and an ephemeral port (32768+) for a Kubernetes application.

Normally, this will look like a simple NAT passthrough from the load balancer external IP/port to the cluster's ingress controller internal IP/port. However, it is possible to split applications across different ingress controllers. This may be done to accommodate both Swarm and Kubernetes running in the same cluster, or using something called service clusters, to group certain services within a particular ingress controller. While you might need this at some point in time, the pilot phase is not usually where you start. Keep it simple at this point in your implementation, with a single ingress controller, if possible.

When the traffic reaches the L7 ingress controller in the cluster, the header is examined to determine whether it matches any of the reverse proxy rules using a hostname or a path. If a match is found, the L7 ingress controller forwards traffic to the appropriate cluster IP or Swarm service. Later on in this book, we will explore the mechanics of the ingress controller life cycle for Kubernetes and Swarm; but for now it is important to focus on the network traffic flow, as follows:

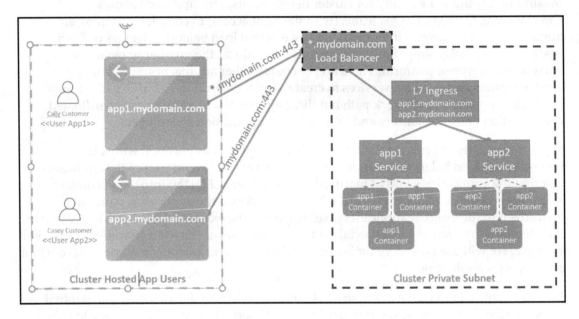

Figure 8: Remote Cluster Access with UCP

We now see how network flows for internal users and cluster-hosted app users. Now, let's talk about how we secure our connections between both internal users accessing the cluster, and end users connecting to applications running in the cluster.

Highly available cluster

A key goal of the pilot is to better understand the Docker Enterprise operational model required to support business-critical applications. Therefore, piloting a Docker HA cluster is highly recommended during the pilot phase.

The reference architecture for a Docker Enterprise cluster includes considerations for both resilience and scalability. As discussed in the Docker Enterprise architecture chapter, highly available clusters include manager nodes where the Docker UCP software is installed. Due to the nature of the Raft Consensus Algorithm, which requires an odd number of managers, the smallest redundant cluster includes three manager nodes. For most pilot platforms, three manager nodes should be sufficient to support high availability and scalability up to 100 nodes. Bear in mind that 100 nodes will be a very large cluster for a pilot platform.

 More information on Raft can be found at: `https://raft.github.io/`, and more information on Docker Swarm Raft can be found at: `https://docs.docker.com/engine/swarm/raft/`.

It is also a good idea to make sure that the **Docker Trusted Registry** (**DTR**) is highly available. After all, without a functioning image registry, applications cannot be deployed. To satisfy an HA DTR requirement, we use three replicas of the DTR running across a special subset of worker nodes, reserved for DTR workloads only.

DNS, certificates, and certificate termination

During our PoC, it was okay to use self-signed certificates generated by the UCP at install time. However, as we move into the pilot phase, it's a good time to introduce third-party certificates issued from a trusted source.

There are two kinds of certificates involved with Docker Enterprise:

- Internal cluster certificates
- External client certificates

Each type has its own CA root signing authority. The internal certificates are those used by the Swarm cluster for TLS encryption between the Swarm nodes. The external client certificates are used to access the cluster from outside sources with managed access through the UCP. The certificates we are primarily interested in for configuration are the external client certificates. These should be set up to use third-party trusted certificates to avoid both x509 certificate errors from remote servers and browser security warnings.

The industry standard for securing internet connections is **Transport Layer Security** (**TLS**). A TLS handshake has several requirements, but two key items for our discussion. First, the server must have a valid server certificate, signed by a trusted certificate authority. Second, the server certificate must be valid for the URL being requested.

The first item is pretty straightforward. When a client requests a certificate from the server, it validates the certificate that was signed by a trusted CA authority. If it is not, we get the usual browser security warnings. Therefore, we need a certificate issued by a trusted third party. These certificates are available from a variety of issuers, or your organization may already have its own CA chain established.

The second item requires a match between the certificate's common name (CN, or domain the certificate was issued to) and the URL used to route the request to the server where the certificate is installed. This means that if a certificate was issued with a CN of `app1.mydomain.com`, and a request comes to a server where the certificate is installed, with the header showing a target hostname of `app1.mydomain.com`, the secure connection will be allowed because the CN and request header's hostnames match. While this is great for security, it is very cumbersome to have a separate certificate for each URL hostname used within my cluster. To address this, there are a couple of common ways of managing the certificate challenge using either multi-domain or wildcard certificates.

The objective for both types of certificates is to allow support for multiple domains being derived from a single server with a single certificate. However, multi-domain and wildcard accomplish this differently. Multi-domain certificates have a CN, plus a list of other valid domains, using **Subject Alternative Names** (**SANs**). The main idea here is that the domain structure of the SAN can be completely different. Therefore, multi-domain certificates are great for when your internal and external domain names are different (that is, `app1.mydomain.com` and `app2.test.mydomain.local`). One other consideration for multi-domain certificates is that all domains must be known when the certificate is generated. Otherwise, the additional SAN can be added, but the new certificate with those hands has to be distributed to the servers. Finally, multi-domains are a better option if you are using your own internal trusted certificate CA chain. Otherwise, they can be expensive and clumsy to maintain from a third-party provider.

Wildcard certificates are another popular option. They give you unlimited domains, but there's a catch, as all of the domains need to share the same base. For instance, a wildcard certificate for `*.mydomain.com` works for domains such as `app1.mydomain.com` and `app2.mydomain.com`, but not `app2.test.mydomain.com`. Instead, you end up with domains looking something like `app1-test.mydomain.com` for test, and `app1.mydomain.com` for production. The good news here is that you don't need to know all of your domains when you issue the certificate, and wildcard certificates tend to be less expensive than multi-domain certificates from third-party issuers. However, it forces a consistent domain structure internally and externally, meaning that internal cluster servers will need to fit the scheme with something like `prod-ucp-1.mydomain.com`, and you will generally need to use a split/internal DNS approach for your externally accessible DNS names, such as `app1.mydomain.com`.

The results of this DNS configuration mean that when `app1.mydomain.com` is referenced internally, it gets a private internal IP address (something like 10.1.1.23). Conversely, when it is accessed publicly, the same domain name resolves to a publicly routable IP address on your firewall that is NATed to the internal IP (`10.1.1.23`). Because of DNS rebound attacks, traffic is not usually allowed to come out of the firewall and back in. Otherwise, you could just rely on NATing, but most on-premise setups will not allow it.

Once you decide which type of certificate and DNS structure is most suitable for your environment, you then need to figure out where to terminate the server-side TLS connections.

There are three common approaches for TLS termination. The first approach terminates at the external load balancer. Therefore, connections are encrypted between the client and the external load balancer and allowed to flow unencrypted on the internal network. This is a pretty typical old-school, perimeter-based security approach and has the benefit of smaller packets on your internal network and the ability to view packets on your internal network for debugging. This scheme is simple to implement and efficient for internal networking, but is typically inadequate for today's security requirements.

The second termination approach is terminating the connection at the final destination. In a container-based environment, this means terminating the TLS connection inside a container endpoint. The result is a secure connection the entire way between the client and the final server – nowhere in the network path are packets allowed to be unencrypted. This is a very secure way to connect endpoints. However it means certificates will need to be distributed to, and maintained inside, every container with a secure endpoint, using TLS. This used to be a real pain when it was time to update your certificates, but with the introduction of secrets in both Swarm and Kubernetes, it can be very manageable and secure to store certificates as secrets across Development, Test, QA, and Production environments, and injecting the appropriate secret/certificates at runtime.

The third termination approach starts off like the first, where we terminate at the external load balancer, but then we re-encrypt for the internal network using a different certificate. With this scheme, the critical external certificate is locked down, while the internal certificate is used only internally to inspect packets for troubleshooting and debugging purposes, but is only on the internal network. So, if the internal certificate key was compromised, you would still need physical access to the internal network to use it. With this approach, if your rogue application gets loose inside your network, unless it has the key to your internal certificate/key, it will be unable to see any traffic on common networks because it is encrypted with the internal certificate. The downside is that you have larger encrypted packets flowing through your internal network, but the trade-off is generally acceptable in an effort to provide high levels of security.

While you can choose any of these termination approaches for your own applications when you deploy them to your cluster, UCP and DTR expect the second termination approach, where you terminate connections in the UCP in DTR containers. UCP and DTR store their certificates using Docker volumes, `ucp-client-root-ca` and `dtr-ca-<replica_id>` (where each DTR node has a unique replica ID), respectively.

DTR and UCP certificate termination occurs inside the actual DTR and UCP endpoint containers. In other words, they should not be terminated by an upstream load balancer. Furthermore, these certificates are stored in special Docker volumes where they are accessed by the DTR and UCP containers. We can use these volumes to set up the certificates prior to installing the Docker EE software, or the DTR and UCP third-party certificates can be injected into the DTR and UCP install commands as parameters.

Another important requirement for your cluster is a DNS resolvable hostname for your cluster node.

Hostnames for Docker cluster nodes

Docker relies on an internal hostname to function properly. Before installing Docker Enterprise on your cluster nodes, you need to decide on a hostname. You can use short hostnames or FQDNs. Be consistent with your naming scheme across the cluster, as both the Docker Engine and UCP rely on hostnames. This means your hostnames should resolve with DNS on all nodes throughout the cluster.

If you are running on a cloud-based platform, make sure that you have private DNS names turned on for your Docker hosts so that your hostnames will resolve internally.

In a bare metal environment, you will need to add the hostnames for the network adapters. In a cloud setup, most platforms provide an option to enable internal DNS for your cluster nodes.

Bare metal cluster – network setup example

At this point, we have talked about enough theoretical and conceptual topics to set the stage, and highlight key decisions associated with the underlying plumbing for our cluster. Now, it's time to start walking through the steps of creating a sample bare metal pilot cluster setup to see what these decisions look like and how they are implemented.

Step 1 – define a domain name and hostname structure

For a limitation sample, we have chosen the following external domain name structure:

- `ucp.mydomain.com`: This domain address is used to access the UCP web user interface and to connect with the UCP API remotely.
- `dtr.mydomain.com`: This domain address is used for accessing the DTR web user interface and to connect with the DTR API remotely to push and pull images.
- `*.mydomain.com`: This domain is used to access applications hosted in our DTR cluster.

The bare metal internal hostnames that we have used are as follows:

- `ntc-ucp-1.mydomain.com`
- `ntc-ucp-2.mydomain.com`
- `ntc-ucp-3.mydomain.com`
- `ntc-dtr-1.mydomain.com`
- `ntc-dtr-2.mydomain.com`
- `ntc-dtr-3.mydomain.com`
- `ntc-wrk-1.mydomain.com`
- `ntc-wrk-2.mydomain.com`
- `ntc-wrk-3.mydomain.com`
- `ntc-nfs-server.mydomain.com`

A couple of important notes need to be mentioned here. First, all of these DNS names resolve properly inside the network. Second, the wildcard certificate (`*.mydomain.com`) will function properly because all hostnames share the same base domain structure of `mydomain.com`.

Step 2 – define a certificate structure and termination plan

In our example, we are using a wildcard certificate issued from a third party to secure all three domain entry points (`*.mydomain.com`). Our choice works for a relatively simple example where all of our DTR domains share the same base domain (`mydomain.com`). Not only do these domains need to share the same base domain structure externally, but they need to also share the same scheme internally. To accomplish this, we are using a split DNS setup, where we have an internal DNS forwarder to intercept requests for our domain structure from inside our network, and respond with internal private IP addresses. We will go into more detail on this later, but you may refer to *Figure 9* for more information.

The UCP and DTR certificates are covered by the wildcard certificate and are terminated inside the UCP controller containers running on the UCP and DTR nodes in our cluster. All other application certificates covered by the wildcard DNS and corresponding certificate will be terminated, either in the application container, or in the ingress controller's reverse proxy server.

Step 3 – design and implement a network infrastructure

The cluster is accessed when users address the cluster using one of the external domain names. We have three external domain entries for UCP, DTR, and a wildcard DNS entry for our cluster hosted applications. All of the these DNS entries resolve to public IP addresses on the external firewall.

Please note that, for our example, we are using representative, but fictional, IP addresses. An overview of the sample bare metal setup is shown in *Figure 9*, as follows:

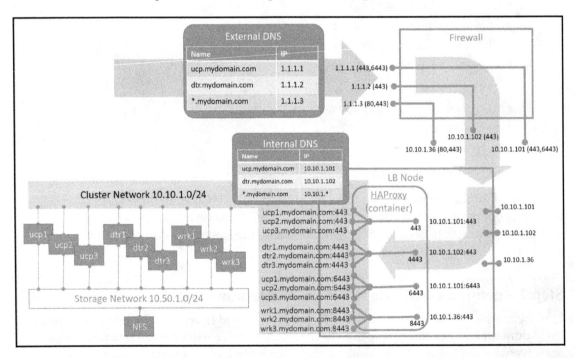

Figure 9: Cluster network diagram

Traffic coming to the UCP domain entry resolves to address 1.1.1.1 on either port 443 or 6443. Port 443 is for the UCP web UI and API. Traffic on port 6443 is for the Kubernetes API. Both of these APIs are generally accessed using a local command-line interface bundle generated from the UCP. As mentioned previously, these bundles contain certificates and scripts for securely routing traffic from a remote shell outside the cluster to the UCP ports of the cluster. The UCP traffic then hits the external IP address of the firewall at 1.1.1.1, and is translated using NAT to an internal private network address of 10.10.1.101. The internal 10.10.1.101 address is routed to the HAProxy load balancer's network adapter. From there, the HAProxy load balancer application binds to 10.10.1.101 on ports 443 and 6443, where it load balances requests across the three UCP manager nodes on the internal network – ucp1.mydomain.com:443, ucp2.mydomain.com:443, and ucp3.mydomain.com:443.

Traffic coming to the DTR domain entry resolves to address 1.1.1.2 on port 443. Port 443 is for the DTR web UI and API used for pushing and pulling Docker images. The DTR traffic then hits the external IP address of the firewall at 1.1.1.2, and is translated using NAT to an internal private network address of 10.10.1.102. The internal 10.10.1.102 address is routed to the HAProxy load balancer's network adapter. From there, the HAProxy load balancer application binds to 10.10.1.102 on port 443, where it load balances requests across the three DTR manager nodes on the internal network using port 4443 on the backend – dtr1.mydomain.com:4443, dtr2.mydomain.com:4443, and dtr3.mydomain.com:4443.

Traffic coming to the wildcard cluster-hosted application domain (that is, app1.mydomain.com) is resolved by the *.mydomain.com external DNS entry, pointing to the 1.1.1.3 public IP address. This is an external address on the firewall, which uses NATs to 10.10.1.36 on the private internal network using ports 80 and 443 attached to the HAProxy load balancer node. HAProxy binds the 10.10.1.36:443 to the frontend configuration to load balance across the worker nodes in the the cluster on port 8443 – wrk1.mydomain.com:8443, wrk2.mydomain.com:8443, and wrk3.mydomain.com:8443. Port 8443 is the cluster's assigned inbound port connected to UCP's L7 routing using Docker Enterprise's interlock 2 for Swarm.

We will talk more about Layer 7 load balancing with interlock 2 for Swarm applications when we deploy our pilot application in Chapter 5, *Prepare and Deploy a Docker Enterprise Pilot Application*. Additionally, we will look at a similar scheme using a Kubernetes ingress controller toward the end of the book.

Load balancer setup and configuration design

Using a containerized software load balancer is a great way to manage and upgrade a software firewall. There are several great load balancer options, including NGINX and HAProxy. For our example, we are using HAProxy.

In order to make sense of the HAProxy configuration, we will first need to understand how the host adapter ports are bound to the container where the HAProxy software is running. The following is a sample script used to start the HAProxy load balancer. Carefully note the port mappings (`-p host-adapter:host-port:container-port`) when the Docker container for HAProxy is launched. Ports `80`, `443`, `4443`, `6443`, and `8443` are mapped inside the container, as follows:

- Port `80` is for inbound cluster-based application traffic—it is only there as a redirect to port `443`
- Port `443` is for inbound UCP web interface and API traffic
- Port `4443` is for DTR inbound web interface and API traffic
- Port `6443` is for Kubernetes API traffic (usually from a UCP client bundle).
- Port `8443` is for inbound TLS connections to cluster-hosted applications (your apps running deployed to the cluster)

 By default, the official HAProxy image logs to `syslogd`. This means you need to either configure `syslogd` to forward logs to a (central) log agent, or redirect `syslogd` to `stdout` from inside the container. In my case, I added the following line to the end of my `docker-entrypoint.sh` file used in the official Docker `haproxy` container:

```
/sbin/syslogd -O /proc/1/fd/1
```

HAProxy start script:

The following shell script will start an HAProxy load balancer using the `haproxy.cfg` file:

```
#!/bin/sh
docker run -d --name ntc-haproxy -p 10.10.1.36:80:80 -p 10.10.1.36:443:8443
-p 10.10.1.101:443:443 -p 10.10.1.101:6443:6443 -p 10.10.1.102:443:4443 -v
~/haproxy:/usr/local/etc/haproxy:ro nvisiantc/haproxy-log-forward:1.0
```

Now, let's look at the following `haproxy.cfg` configuration file. The first two sections are pretty standard with two notable items. The first item is that I have my pilot configurations set to debug logging. This is something I may switch off shortly after my implementation, but it is really helpful to see what is going on with your load balancer. Secondly, the timeout tunnel is set to 1 hour. While it doesn't necessarily have to be an hour, the default may cause timeouts when installing UCP and DTR.

Starting at the top of the configuration file, we have the following sections:

1. In the frontend sections, we first have the port 80 binding, which we have set up as a redirect to SSL. Therefore, if a request comes to an cluster-hosted application on port 80, we will redirect the caller back to retry their request using `ssl/tls` on port 443, as follows:

```
# Sample haproxy.cfg

global
      maxconn 2048
      log /dev/log local0 debug
      log /dev/log local1 notice

defaults
          mode tcp
          option dontlognull
          timeout connect 5s
          timeout client 50s
          timeout server 50s
          timeout tunnel 1h
          timeout client-fin 50s

frontend http_80
 mode http
 bind *:80
 option httplog
 log /dev/log local0 debug
 redirect scheme https code 301 if !{ ssl_fc }
```

2. The `ucp_443` frontend binds to port 443 and forwards traffic to the `ucp_upstream_server_443` backend load balancer. The backend load balancer is set up using a round robin strategy with a health check provided by the UCP with a `/_ping` endpoint to verify the health of the UCP controller container, as follows:

```
frontend ucp_443
 mode tcp
 bind *:443
```

```
option tcplog
log /dev/log local0 debug
default_backend ucp_upstream_servers_443
```

3. The `dtr_4443` frontend binds to port `4443` and forwards traffic to the `dtr_upstream_server_4443` backend load balancer. The backend load balancer is set up using a round robin strategy with a health check provided by the UCP with a `/_ping` endpoint to verify the health of the DTR `nginx` container:

```
frontend dtr_4443
 mode tcp
 bind *:4443
 option tcplog
 log /dev/log local0 debug
 default_backend dtr_upstream_servers_4443
```

4. The `kube_6443` frontend binds to port `6443` and forwards traffic to the `kubectl_upstream_servers_6443` backend. This backend simply load balances the request across the UCP nodes on port `6443`, as follows:

```
frontend kube_6443
 mode tcp
 bind *:6443
 option tcplog
 log /dev/log local0 debug
 default_backend kubectl_upstream_servers_6443
```

5. Inbound application traffic comes into port `8443` and forwards traffic to the `interlock_app_upstream_8443` backend, as follows:

```
frontend app_8443
 mode tcp
 bind *:8443
 option tcplog
 log /dev/log local0 debug
 default_backend interlock_app_upstream_8443
```

6. The backend load balances the requests across the worker nodes on port `8443`, where it is picked up by interlock 2's ingress controller for Swarm. From there, interlock 2 will examine the request header to determine which cluster-based application will receive the traffic, as follows:

```
## Backend
backend ucp_upstream_servers_443
 mode tcp
```

```
balance roundrobin
option log-health-checks
option httpchk GET /_ping HTTP/1.1\r\nHost:\ ucp.mydomain.com
server UCPNode01 ntc-ucp-1:443 check check-ssl verify none
server UCPNode02 ntc-ucp-2:443 check check-ssl verify none
server UCPNode03 ntc-ucp-3:443 check check-ssl verify none

backend dtr_upstream_servers_4443
mode tcp
balance roundrobin
option log-health-checks
option httpchk GET /_ping HTTP/1.1\r\nHost:\ dtr.mydomain.com
server DTRNode01 ntc-dtr-1:4443 check check-ssl verify none
server DTRNode02 ntc-dtr-2:4443 check check-ssl verify none
server DTRNode03 ntc-dtr-3:4443 check check-ssl verify none

backend kubectl_upstream_servers_6443
mode tcp
balance roundrobin
option log-health-checks
server KubeNode01 ntc-ucp-1:6443 check check-ssl verify none
server KubeNode02 ntc-ucp-2:6443 check check-ssl verify none
server KubeNode03 ntc-ucp-3:6443 check check-ssl verify none

#backend interlock_app_upstream_8443
mode tcp
option log-health-checks
server AppNode01 ntc-wrk-1:8443 weight 100 check check-ssl
verify none
server AppNode02 ntc-wrk-2:8443 weight 100 check check-ssl
verify none
server AppNode03 ntc-wrk-3:8443 weight 100 check check-ssl
verify none
```

Using HAProxy with this `haproxy.cfg` configuration file will start a load balancer, which will redirect traffic to our cluster. This will enable us to start building the cluster nodes in the next section.

Docker Enterprise pilot platform

We now have a network setup with a load balancer to direct traffic to our cluster and we are ready to get started on building the nodes. We will run through a similar flow as presented in setting up the PoC Platform in the last chapter. This time, however, we will highlight important details related to an enterprise platform with a highly available and secure cluster.

In this section, we will cover the following topics:

- Setting up the cluster nodes
- Installing and configuring the Docker Enterprise Engine
- Creating/configuring a Docker Swarm
- Installing the UCP
- Installing the DTR

Preparing cluster nodes

A typical pilot cluster will include 10 nodes: 3 nodes are UCP managers, 3 nodes are DTR replicas, and 4 nodes are workers.

Node sizing consideration

At the end of the day, our pilot will help us to dial in the correct node sizing for our final non-production and production clusters. However, we want to make a special effort to get our UCP and DTR nodes sized right from the start, remembering that UCP (and, to some degree, DTR nodes) are more like pets than cattle. Therefore, plan on 4 CPU cores, 16 GB of RAM, and 32 GBs SSD for each UCP and DTR node. This recommendation is a safe bet as long as we stick with best practices, where we do not run workloads on our managers or DTR nodes.

The sizing of the worker nodes is less critical since we treat them more like cattle, and if a worker node is undersized, we can just replace it with a larger one and with minimal disruption to the cluster operations.

Please note, if the pilot platform includes Windows nodes in the cluster to run Windows containers, plan on having a minimum of 100 GBs of disk space to accommodate the larger footprint associated with Docker Windows container images.

Network adapters considerations

Generally speaking, for a bare metal implementation, we will want at least two network adapters for each node. One adapter will be attached to the cluster network for communication with other cluster members as well as ingress traffic from outside the cluster. The second adapter will be used for an isolated storage network, to provide high-performance backend storage services in support of cluster-based container volumes.

In conjunction with the network adapters, please configure a software firewall such as `firewalld`. The firewall will be configured to allow Docker Enterprise traffic as described previously in *Figure 9*.

> Install and configure the firewall completely (open ports are described in *Figure 9*) before installing Docker software. Installing the firewall after Docker Enterprise is installed may cause potential networking issues. If you experience these issues, run a `docker info` from the command line and look for warnings at the bottom of the listing. Conflicts between `firewalld` and `iptables` can sometimes lead to certain protocols being dropped by Docker. Also, always remember to follow any network adapter reconfiguration with a system reboot.

Do keep in mind that, your choice of networking technologies will impact firewall configurations. Here, we are using overlay networking implementations, VXLAN for Swarm, and Calico's BGP/IPinIP for your Kubernetes, to isolate you from the underlying network. These technologies rely on tunneling through well-known ports on our cluster nodes. We have to make sure these ports are open on the firewall.

Cluster-based storage considerations

Cluster-based storage allows container-based workloads to be moved from one worker node to another without a loss of data. In other words, if volume A appears on all of the nodes in the cluster and is mapped to the same backend mount point using cluster storage, such as NFS, an application can run on any node and find its current data in the same place.

While cluster-based storage is not a requirement for some applications in a cluster environment, it is required for Docker Enterprise HA infrastructure, as regards storage backing for the DTR. DTR requires common storage backend across the multiple replicas in order to operate properly in HA mode.

If you're planning to use a cloud-based implementation for your pilot platform, there are some excellent cluster-based storage options for both AWS and Azure using the docker4x/cloudstor volume plugin. On AWS, the cloudstor volume plugin can be backed by either EBS or EFS, depending on your requirements. On Azure, the cloudstor volume plugin is backed by a storage account.

Network timing and node synchronization

All nodes in the cluster should be placed on a common local network. The subnets may be split across multiple availability zones, but should be geographically co-located in order to reduce latency. If latency rises above 500 milliseconds, replication of important data may time out and cause instability in the cluster. In more recent releases of Docker Enterprise, the Etcd timeout values can be configured for higher tolerance, but it is not generally recommended.

Additionally, you need to make sure that all of your node clocks are synced using Network Time Protocol (NTP). Clock skew across the cluster can lead to nasty problems related to manager synchronization problems, as well as errant certificate rejections (for instance, an out-of-sync timestamp on a certificate might look like a replay attack and be rejected).

Docker Enterprise pilot bare metal walk-through

We will begin by setting up our nodes with a supported Docker Enterprise OS. Please verify your platform's compatibility using the Docker Enterprise 2.1 compatibility matrix on Docker's Success website: `https://success.docker.com/article/compatibility-matrix`.

During the pilot phase, look for an OS platform to align with your long-term support and licensing strategy. While our example is using a bare metal pilot platform, you may very well choose a cloud-based setup instead, because it aligns with your strategy. Remember, we are just using the bare metal environment to flush out any cloud magic from our examples. If you are using a cloud-based platform such as AWS or Azure, do not fret. Toward the end of the book, we cover Docker-certified infrastructure templates, including specific implementation details for Azure, AWS, and VMWare.

An overview of the bare metal pilot environment is as follows:

- 2 isolated switches connected to 10 fresh CentOS 7.5 nodes attached:
    - 10 nodes connected to 2 networks:
        - A cluster network
        - A storage network, as described previously
    - Fresh install of CentOS 7.5 Linux:
        - 4 vCPUs/cores for each node
        - 16+ GB of RAM
        - 32+ GB of disk space
        - EXT4 /var filesystem

- Dual NICs 10.10.1.x/24 + 10.10.50.x/24
- Hostname `ntc-XXX-Y` with common domain suffix of `mydomain.com`
- Internal DNS, as shown in *Figure 10*
- NTP, firewalld, IPTables, and Docker Enterprise Engine on all nodes:
    - Docker Enterprise 18.09
    - Overlay 2 storage driver
- UCP 3.1.x installed on 3 managers `ntc-ucp-1`, `ntc-ucp-2`, and `ntc-ucp-3`
- DTR 2.6.x installed on 3 DTR/worker nodes `ntc-dtr-1`, `ntc-dtr-2`, and `ntc-dtr-3`

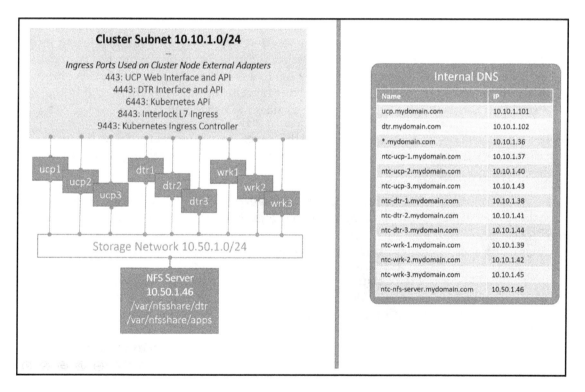

Figure 10: Cluster's Internal DNS

After your nodes are configured, it is time to install the software.

Installing the Docker Enterprise Engine on all nodes

For our pilot, we have chosen to use a CentOS 7.5 OS running on bare metal Intel-based servers. We have chosen the CentOS OS because it allows us to start off with an open source distribution and easily migrate to a commercially supported platform such as RHEL.

As discussed during the PoC, a valid software license key, as well as your storebits subscription URL, is required to install Docker Enterprise. You can get these from the Docker store by logging in with, or creating, a Docker ID.

 At this point, most customers have already run a successful PoC. Subsequently, they are ready to commit to at least a 10 node Docker Enterprise license. However, if you are not ready to make the leap, please work with your local Docker sales team to extend your trial license to cover the pilot.

After acquiring your license, you will find a link to download your Docker license file and your Storebits URL in your store.docker.com account. Right-click on your profile and go to the **My Content** menu. On the **My Content** page, click the **Setup** button next to your active subscription. Then, download the license key file to a safe directory on your local computer. Also, copy and paste the Storebits URL into your favorite editor. You will need it in the next section when we configure the package manager to use the Docker repos.

With your license key and Docker Storebits URL saved on your local machine, it is time to install the Docker Enterprise Engine on all of your nodes. Start by creating SSH sessions in each of your Linux nodes.

We start by configuring the CentOS package manager and the official Docker Enterprise repository for installing our software. Once the Docker engines are installed, we can install our Docker Enterprise platform's containerized software components on top of the Docker engines using special images from Docker's container registry.

 Do not use the default repository from the CentOS distribution to install the Docker engine! Doing so usually results in an old and unsupported version of the Community Edition. Remember, we are using the Docker Enterprise Engine.
Also, the following instructions assume you are using a fresh software OS installastion on your nodes. If that's not the case, please make sure that you remove the old versions of Docker before proceeding.

Installing the Docker Enterprise Engine onto each node in the cluster

The following instructions in this section are a summary of `https://docs.docker.com/install/linux/docker-ee/centos/`:

1. **Step 1—prepare the CentOS 7.5 node, as follows**:
    1. On each Linux node, install NTP to keep the server clocks synchronized; `yum-utils` for the Docker installation process, and `nfs-utils` for our cluster-based storage access:

    ```
    $ sudo yum install ntp
    $ sudo systemctl start ntpd
    $ sudo systemctl enable ntpd
    $ sudo yum install -y yum-utils
    $ sudo yum install -y nfs-utils
    ```

    2. Set up and enable `firewalld` with the following commands:

    ```
    $ sudo firewall-cmd --permanent --add-port=22/tcp
    $ sudo firewall-cmd --permanent --add-port=80/tcp
    $ sudo firewall-cmd --permanent --add-port=179/tcp
    $ sudo firewall-cmd --permanent --add-port=443/tcp
    $ sudo firewall-cmd --permanent --add-port=4443/tcp
    $ sudo firewall-cmd --permanent --add-port=8443/tcp
    $ sudo firewall-cmd --permanent --add-port=2376/tcp
    $ sudo firewall-cmd --permanent --add-port=2377/tcp
    $ sudo firewall-cmd --permanent --add-port=4789/udp
    $ sudo firewall-cmd --permanent --add-port=6443/tcp
    $ sudo firewall-cmd --permanent --add-port=6444/tcp
    $ sudo firewall-cmd --permanent --add-port=7946/tcp
    $ sudo firewall-cmd --permanent --add-port=7946/udp
    $ sudo firewall-cmd --permanent --add-port=10250/tcp
    $ sudo firewall-cmd --permanent --add-port=12376/tcp
    $ sudo firewall-cmd --permanent --add-port=12378/tcp
    $ sudo firewall-cmd --permanent --add-port=12379/tcp
    $ sudo firewall-cmd --permanent --add-port=12380/tcp
    $ sudo firewall-cmd --permanent --add-port=12381/tcp
    $ sudo firewall-cmd --permanent --add-port=12382/tcp
    $ sudo firewall-cmd --permanent --add-port=12383/tcp
    $ sudo firewall-cmd --permanent --add-port=12384/tcp
    $ sudo firewall-cmd --permanent --add-port=12385/tcp
    $ sudo firewall-cmd --permanent --add-port=12386/tcp
    $ sudo firewall-cmd --permanent --add-port=12387/tcp
    $ sudo firewall-cmd --permanent --add-port=12388/tcp
    $ sudo firewall-cmd --permanent --add-service=nfs
    $ sudo firewall-cmd --permanent --add-service=ntp
    $ sudo firewall-cmd --reload
    ```

3. Get rid of any existing Docker repos:

```
$ sudo rm /etc/yum.repos.d/docker*.repo
```

2. **Step 2—configure the** yum **package manager repos to use the official Docker binaries, as follows**:
    1. Set up the DOCKER_EE_URL environment variables using your Docker Store's Storebits URL that you recorded earlier. It should look similar to the following:

```
$ export
DOCKERURL="https://storebits.docker.com/ee/m/sub-xxxxx
xxx-xxxx-xxxx-xxxx-xxxxxxxxxxx"
```

With your Storebits URL set in the $DOCKERURL environment variable, it is time to install Docker:

3. **Step 3—configure the official Docker** repo, **install the Docker Enterprise engine, and start the Docker engine, as follows**:

```
$ sudo -E sh -c 'echo "$DOCKERURL/centos" >
/etc/yum/vars/dockerurl'
$ sudo -E yum-config-manager --add-repo
"$DOCKERURL/centos/docker-ee.repo"
$ sudo yum-config-manager --enable docker-ee-stable-18.09
$ sudo yum -y install docker-ee
$ sudo systemctl start docker
```

Following installation, there are a few additional steps that will make it easier to use Docker:

4. **Step 4—apply the finishing touches, as follows**:
    1. Finally, we add our user to the Docker group (so we do not have to type sudo before all of our Docker commands) and we enable Docker to run at startup. Please note that, you need to log out and back in for the Docker group membership to take hold, as follows:

```
$ sudo usermod -aG docker $USER
$ sudo systemctl enable docker
```

2. Verify the installation with the `docker info` command as follows, and notice the server version is 18.09.1 and host's kernel version 3.10 (must be 3.10 or greater) was installed and information on the host, including the kernel version, which must be greater than `3.10`, as follows:

```
$ docker info
...
Server Version: 18.09.0
Storage Driver: overlay2
 Backing Filesystem: extfs
 Supports d_type: true
 Native Overlay Diff: true
...
Kernel Version: 3.10.0-862.14.4.el7.x86_64
Operating System: CentOS Linux 7 (Core)
OSType: linux
...
```

Now, we will need to test the setup.

5. **Step 5—try running the** `hello-world` **container, as follows**:

   1. Log out, then log back in, and try running the `docker` command (without `sudo`) to test Docker and Docker group permissions. Run the Docker information and you should see something like the following:

```
$ docker run hello-world
Unable to find image 'hello-world:latest' locally
latest: Pulling from library/hello-world
d1725b59e92d: Pull complete
Digest:
sha256:0add3ace90ecb4adbf7777e9aacf18357296e799f81cabc
9fde470971e499788
Status: Downloaded newer image for hello-world:latest

Hello from Docker!
```

The previous message shows that your installation appears to be working correctly.

To generate this message, Docker took the following steps:

1. The Docker client contacted the Docker daemon.
2. The Docker daemon pulled the `hello-world` image from the Docker Hub (amd64).
3. The Docker daemon created a new container from that image, which runs the executable that produces the output that you are currently reading.
4. The Docker daemon streamed the output to the Docker client, which sent it to your Terminal.

 Repeat these steps for all Docker manager and worker nodes.

Setting up the NFS server node

Refer to the following steps:

1. Connect to the NFS server node; in my case, I use an adapter connected to the cluster network. Install NFS, create the shares, and enable the services on startup, as follows:

```
sudo yum install -y nfs-utils
sudo mkdir -p /var/nfsshare/dtr
sudo mkdir -p /var/nfsshare/apps
sudo chmod -R 755 /var/nfsshare
sudo chmod -R 755 /var/nfsshare/dtr
sudo chmod -R 755 /var/nfsshare/apps
sudo chown nfsnobody:nfsnobody /var/nfsshare
sudo chown nfsnobody:nfsnobody /var/nfsshare/dtr
sudo chown nfsnobody:nfsnobody /var/nfsshare/apps
sudo systemctl enable rpcbind
sudo systemctl enable nfs-server
sudo systemctl enable nfs-lock
sudo systemctl enable nfs-idmap
sudo systemctl start rpcbind
sudo systemctl start nfs-server
sudo systemctl start nfs-lock
sudo systemctl start nfs-idmap
```

2. To complete the setup, add a line to the `/etc/exports` file, as follows:

```
sudo vi /etc/exports
```

3. Add the following line to the file:

```
/var/nfsshare *.mydomain.com
(rw,sync,no_root_squash,no_all_squash)
```

4. Restart the `nfs` server to pick up the new `/etc/exports` configuration, as follows:

```
sudo systemctl restart nfs-server
```

5. Open the required `firewall` ports as follows:

```
sudo firewall-cmd --permanent --zone=public --add-service=nfs
sudo firewall-cmd --permanent --zone=public --add-
service=mountd
sudo firewall-cmd --permanent --zone=public --add-service=rpc-
bind
sudo firewall-cmd --reload
```

You now have the Docker Enterprise Engine installed on each node. Next, we need to create the Swarm cluster by initializing the first manager node.

Installing the first manager node

We now have all of our Docker cluster nodes initialized with the Docker Enterprise Engine and are ready to begin configuring our first manager node. Our approach here will be to create a Swarm with a specified address pool – the address pool is where Docker's VXLAN networks assign /26 networks.

There are a couple of important items to note: first, it is important that this address pool parameter's CIDR is a non-routable network block within your private address space. Otherwise, there could be conflicts with Docker's internal overlay networks. Second, this address pool parameter can only be assigned with a Docker Swarm `init` command. It is not available as a UCP install parameter. Therefore, we will initialize our Swarm with our desired address pool configuration and install the UCP software on top of it. This will work great, because UCP will use an existing Swarm if it is detected at installation time. Otherwise, it will create a new Swarm when it installs UCP. Furthermore, if the Swarm cluster with multiple nodes is already running with UCP installed, it will automatically replicate all of the UCP software across the entire Swarm cluster.

From our first UCP node, we initialize the Docker Swarm with the address pool allocation, as follows:

```
[ntc-ucp-1 ~]$ docker swarm init --advertise-addr 10.10.1.37 --default-
addr-pool 10.60.0.0/16 --default-addr-pool-mask-length 26
```

Also notice the use of the `--advertised-addr` parameter. This is because the Docker node has two network adapters with different IP addresses. We need to tell Docker Swarm which adapter we are going to use to communicate across the cluster with other nodes. Our design designated the `10.10.1.x/24` network as the cluster network and the `10.10.50.x/24` network as the storage network:

- **Copy the Docker Enterprise license file to UCP node 1, as follows**:

  Before installing UCP, copy the license key files to the `my first manager` node and store it in my home directory (~). From here, we will inject the license key into the UCP install command as a `--license "$(cat license.lic)"` parameter into the UCP install command, as shown in the following code block. If you wish to defer the installation of the license file, you may do so by uploading the license file the first time you log into the UCP web interface or, by uploading it from inside the UCP web interface using the **Admin Settings | License** menu option. Please note, if you opt to defer the licence key installation, you will need to remove the `--license` parameter from the UCP install command which we use when we install the UCP on top of our new Swarm cluster.

- **Copy the third-party certificates to UCP node 1, as follows**:

  This is also a great time to set up your third-party certificates by creating a Docker volume called `ucp-controller-server-certs`. After this, copy your certificate file into the volume. Either copy or paste the certificate values for your third-party certificates into three files—the certificate authority file (`ca.pem`), the server certificate file (`cert.pem`), and the certificate key file (`key.pem`) in your home directory, and then copy them into the container shown.

  Alternatively, you can run a bash script from inside a container that mounts both the newly created UCP certificate volume and your home directory to copy certificate files for you. In fact, if you do not have root access to the UCP manager node, you would not have access to the `/var` directory. So, the containerized script might be your only option:

```
docker volume create ucp-controller-server-certs
sudo -s
cp ./ca.pem /var/lib/docker/volumes/ucp-controller-server-
certs/_data/
cp ./cert.pem /var/lib/docker/volumes/ucp-controller-
server-certs/_data/
cp ./key.pem /var/lib/docker/volumes/ucp-controller-server-
```

```
certs/_data/
exit
```

In the first line, we create the `docker volume` where UCP keeps its certificates. When we install, we will provide the `--external-server-cert` parameter to the UCP installer so that UCP does not generate new certificates over our existing certs in the volume. The remainder of the commands involve copying the certificate files into the container using Docker's internal mount point for the `ucp-controller-server-certs` volume.

Now, we can install the UCP on top of our new Swarm cluster, as follows:

```
[ntc-ucp-1 ~]$ docker image pull docker/ucp:3.1.1

[ntc-ucp-1 ~]$ docker container run --rm -it --name ucp \
  -v /var/run/docker.sock:/var/run/docker.sock \
  docker/ucp:3.1.1 install \
  --host-address 10.10.1.37 \
  --external-server-cert \
  --external-service-lb ucp.mydomain.com \
  --license "$(cat license.lic)" \
  --interactive
```

Now it is time to test your first node's UCP installation. To do this, point your browser to the external UCP URL. Remember to use the `https://` URL prefix when accessing UCP web UI. You should see the Docker login screen from there. Use the credentials you provided during the UCP install to log in to the UCP web UI.

If you did not include the license parameter in the UCP installation process, you will be prompted to upload a license key when logging into UCP for the first time. Again, you can defer and upload it later by using the admin settings license menu option in the UCP UI.

Hopefully, your browser reaches the UCP web UI and you get to the UCP dashboard showing 1 manager and 0 worker nodes. If you cannot reach the UCP web UI, try curling the UCP web UI endpoint from inside your cluster. If the curl works and the external browser does not, it's time to trace from your external connection, through DNS, through the firewall, and through the load balancer, to see where the request gets hung up. This is where your load balancer logs can be really helpful.

At this point, we have a single-node UCP manager cluster running. While the other Docker nodes are attached to the same network, they have not been joined to the cluster. We will do this in the next section.

Joining initial DTR 1 and worker 1 nodes

Before we can add any other nodes to the cluster, we will need a secure `join` token. The join token ensures any node trying to join the cluster does so with a secure join token issued from a cluster manager. The join token itself is used as a parameter to the `docker swarm join` command. To obtain a worker join token, you must use an SSH connection to a manager node and run the following code:

```
[ntc-ucp-1 ~]$ docker swarm join-token worker
To add a worker to this swarm, run the following command:

docker swarm join --token SWMTKN-1-xxxxxxxxxxxxxxxxxxxxxxxxxxxxxxxxxxx-
xxxxxxxxxxxxxxxxxxxxxxxxx 10.10.1.37:2377
```

Copy the entire `docker swarm join --token...` command to the clipboard. Log in to each of your DTR and worker nodes to paste and run the `join` command. In a matter of seconds, the Docker engine should provide a confirmation message about the node being joined to the Swarm.

Confirm the cluster node status, and then open the UCP 1 terminal to verify that the nodes are ready, as follows:

```
[ntc-ucp-1 ~]$ docker node ls
ID                          HOSTNAME                STATUS  AVAILABILITY
1rqhb4rzj3gk4mdgk8kza53jp   ntc-dtr-1.mydomain.com  Ready   Active
1rqhb4rzj3gk4mdgk8kza53jp   ntc-dtr-1.mydomain.com  Ready   Active
x27m3yjlh6b0wczmo0mcahkjv   ntc-dtr-2.mydomain.com  Ready   Active
rw2tuw53wl34pv6sfj213845a   ntc-dtr-3.mydomain.com  Ready   Active
q5q9u0yr7p8r0mcz4ob24s2kz*  ntc-ucp-1.mydomain.com  Ready   Active
3lw64q2o818xgnberjry410o7   ntc-wrk-1.mydomain.com  Ready   Active
zxcosutrxr3rhzkz2h6ld0khj   ntc-wrk-2.mydomain.com  Ready   Active
sfuxfiwhf2tpd6q3i7fbmaziv   ntc-wrk-3.mydomain.com  Ready   Active
```

At this point, all you should see is a node list with the UCP-1 manager node, three DTR nodes, and three worker nodes. Our next step is to join the two additional UCP manager nodes. Now, we need a join-token manager token to be added to the additional UCP manager nodes, as follows:

```
[ntc-ucp-1 ~]$ docker swarm join-token manager
To add a manager to this swarm, run the following command:

docker swarm join --token SWMTKN-1-xxxxxxxxxxxxxxxxxxxxxxxxxxxxxxxxxxx-
xxxxxxxxxxxxxxxxxxxxxxxxx 10.10.1.37:2377
```

Again, copy the entire `docker swarm join --token...` command to the clipboard. This time, log in to the UCP-2 and UCP-3 nodes to paste and run the `join` command. In a matter of seconds, the Docker engine should provide a confirmation message about the node being joined to the Swarm.

Now, log in to the UCP web UI, and notice that the dashboard displays three manager nodes and six worker nodes. It may take a few minutes for the UCP manager nodes to initialize and report a healthy status. Give UCP about 10 minutes to fully reconcile the new nodes before trying to fix anything. In most cases, the UCP will straighten itself out and add the nodes successfully, as follows:

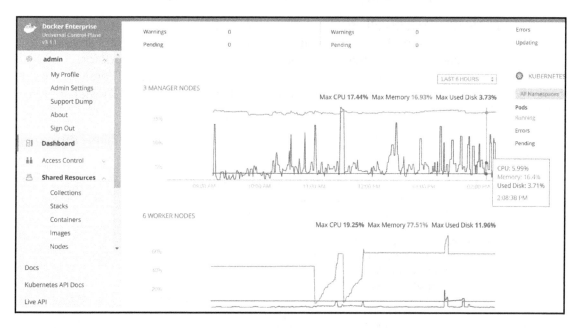

Figure 11: Universal Control Plane Dashboard

Now, our cluster is up and running, we are ready to run both Swarm and Kubernetes workloads. However, in order to support these containerized workloads, we need to install a private DTR for our cluster orchestrators to guarantee a secure software pipeline.

Installing the DTR

Now, we are ready to install the DTR. DTR software is deployed as a stack of basic containers on each target DTR node. It is important to note that, we initialize the DTR installer from either a shell on **UCP manager node,** or using a command-line bundle generated from the UCP.

 New Docker admins often make the mistake of trying to initiate a DTR install command from a DTR node. We do not initiate DTR install commands from DTR nodes. We run the DTR install commands from a UCP manager node.

In preparation for the DTR install, make sure you have your third-party certificates handy for DTR access. In our example, we are using a wildcard certificate that covers access to UCP, DTR, and cluster-hosted applications. Our sample certificates will work for dtr.mydomain.com, ucp.mydomain.com, and anyapp.mydomain.com. Therefore, we can reuse the UCP certificates we created in our home directory during the UCP installation for installing DTR as well.

Here, we kick off the DTR installation from the UCP 1 node and from your home directory, as follows:

```
[ntc-ucp-1 ~]$ docker run –it --rm docker/dtr:2.6.0 install \
--dtr-external-url dtr.mydomain.com \
--ucp-node ntc-dtr-1.mydomain.com \
--ucp-username admin \
--ucp-password yourUcpPassword \
--ucp-url https://ucp.mydomain.com \
--replica-http-port 81 \
--replica-https-port 4443 \
--nfs-storage-url nfs://ntc-nfs-server.mydomain.com/var/nfsshare/dtr \
--ucp-ca "$(cat ca.pem)" \
--dtr-ca "$(cat ca.pem)" \
--dtr-cert "$(cat cert.pem)" \
--dtr-key "$(cat key.pem)"
```

Notice that the nfs-storage-url (nfs://ntc-nfs-server.mydomain.com) is the path to the backend storage for the DTR. This is where the large binary image files are stored and will be shared by all DTR replicas. Please be aware that, the DNS name resolves to the storage network interface adapter. In other words, it uses the 10.10.50.X/24 adapter to communicate with NFS on the isolated storage network when moving image files. This is the location of the EGR back in storage that will be shared across all DTR replicas to store large image binary files. Remember, a common backend data store is a requirement for DTR high availability.

Notice the two port parameters: `replica-http-port` and `replica-https-port`. This is where we are providing alternate ports for DTR access. We specified these DTR alternate ports during our network design to correspond to our load balancer backend internal network ports for DTR. It is, of course, important for the load balancer backend and DTR alternate ports to match up.

The DTR installation process will take several minutes to complete. When it is done, you may log in using the DTR external URL, making sure that you use an HTTPS prefix. When logging in, use the same credentials as you used with UCP.

This is the point where we want to run some smoke tests on the cluster dash before we replicate to all of the nodes. Run through the following tests:

1. Log in to the UCP Web UI, as follows:
    1. Generate a client bundle (`admin > My Profile > Client Bundles > New Bundle`).

2. Alternatively, use the following approach:
    1. **Setting | General**
    2. **Set Create On Push** to **Yes**

3. Open a remote shell and source the bundle, as follows:
    1. Connect a remote Terminal to the cluster, as follows:

       ```
       $ source env.sh
       ```

    2. Or, as follows:

       ```
       PS> Import-module env.ps1
       ```

    3. Test Docker API connectivity, as follows:

       ```
       docker node ls
       ```

    4. Test `kubectl` connectivity, as follows:

       ```
       kubectl get nodes
       ```

    5. Pull a test image, as follows:

       ```
       docker image pull alpine:latest
       ```

    6. Retag a test image, as follows:

       ```
       docker image tag alpine:latest
       dtr.mydomain.com/admin/test:v1
       ```

7. Push `image`, as follows:

```
docker image push  dtr.mydomain.com/admin/test:v1
```

8. Return to the DTR web UI and look for the image.

Adding additional DTR replicas

Now that we have tested our first DTR replica, it is time to add two more replicas to create a high-availability DTR cluster. *Figure 12* shows the sample bare metal DTR replica configuration, as follows:

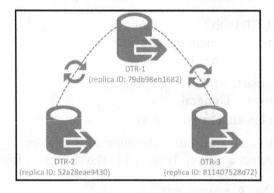

Figure 12: Docker Trusted Registry Replicas

Again, from the same place we installed DTR (UCP-1 node), we are going to join additional DTR replicas. When we run the DTR `join` command, we need to specify a target node. We use the `--ucp-node` parameter for this descriptor. In our case, we are installing the second replica on the `ntc-dtr-2.mydomain.com` node. Another parameter shown here is the UCP admin password. You need to replace the `{yourUcpPassword}` value with your admin password. You may omit the `ucp-password` parameter if you wish to be prompted for the admin password during the join process. Again, we provide the alternate ports (same ports for each of our DTR nodes) used by our second DTR node, as follows:

```
[ntc-ucp-1 ~]$ docker run –it --rm docker/dtr:2.6.0 join \
--ucp-node ntc-dtr-2.mydomain.com \
--ucp-username admin \
--ucp-password {yourUcpPassword} \
--ucp-url https://ucp.mydomain.com \
--replica-http-port 81 \
--replica-https-port 4443 \
--ucp-ca "$(cat ca.pem)"
```

When the `join` command is issued, a new replica ID is generated. Look in the logs for something like this the replica ID is set to: `52a28eae9430`. If the DTR `join` command fails, you will want to refer to this replica ID to remove the failed replica install. If this fails, resolve the issues and remove the broken replica before attempting to rejoin.

You only need to do this if the DTR join fails, as follows:

```
docker run -it --rm docker/dtr:2.6.0 remove --force --ucp-insecure-
tlsusername admin
```

When running the DTR `remove` command, you will be asked for the replica ID you wish to remove. Make sure you choose the ID in the failed `join` command output (that is, the replica ID is set to `52a28eae9430`). Additionally, you will be prompted for the ID of the main replica for notification (it should display a default replica ID to choose). Providing the main DTR replica ID stops the main replica from trying to sync with the broken/removed DTR replica.

Final configuration of load balancers

Now, we have our UCP and DTR replica set up. Remember to complete the configuration of our load balancers by adding entries for the UCP and DTR replicas. The load balancer backend for UCP should be pointing to three servers: UCP-1, UCP-2, and UCP-3 nodes on port `443`. The load balancer backend for DTR should be pointing to three servers: DTR-1, DTR-2, and DTR-3 nodes on port `4443`. Finally, the load balancer backend for Kubernetes should be pointing to 3 servers: UCP-1, UCP-2, and UCP-3 nodes on port `6443`.

Summary

Congratulations! We have walked through the initial implementation of our Docker Enterprise pilot platform. While we still have configuration work in preparation for our pilot application team's application deployment, we have worked on many important initial decisions regarding the network design, platform specifications, and security.

In future chapters, we will examine a number of network and platform topics in more operational depth in terms of performance, security, and recovery.

Questions

1. What are the main differences between the Docker0 default network and the custom bridge network?
2. Can containers running on different nodes communicate with a Docker network?
3. What are two recommended ways for cluster users (such as developers, DevOps, and system administrators) to access the cluster?
4. Where in the cluster does the UCP controller run?
5. Why do we need NTC installed on the cluster nodes?

Further reading

Here are some links for planning your pilot platform:

- https://docs.docker.com/ee/ucp/admin/install/plan-installation/
- https://docs.docker.com/ee/dtr/admin/install/system-requirements/
- https://success.docker.com/article/running-docker-ee-at-scale

Here are a number of Docker networking resources:

- https://github.com/docker/libnetwork/blob/master/docs/design.md
- https://success.docker.com/article/networking
- https://docs.docker.com/network/links/#connect-using-network-port-mapping
- https://success.docker.com/article/networking#thecontainernetworkingmodel
- https://docs.docker.com/ee/ucp/kubernetes/install-cni-plugin/
- https://kubernetes.io/docs/concepts/cluster-administration/networking/
- https://success.docker.com/article/ipv4-forwarding
- https://blog.giantswarm.io/deep-dive-into-kubernetes-networking-in-azure/

Here is some additional information on securing UCP:

- `https://success.docker.com/article/security-best-practices#ucpsecurity`

Here is some additional information pertaining to Docker Enterprise installations:

- `https://docs.docker.com/install/linux/docker-ee/centos/`
- `https://docs.docker.com/ee/ucp/admin/install/`
- `https://docs.docker.com/ee/dtr/admin/install/`

And here are some miscellaneous network links:

- `https://www.iana.org/assignments/protocol-numbers/protocol-numbers.xhtml`
- `http://droptips.com/cidr-subnet-masks-and-usable-ip-addresses-quick-reference-guide-cheat-sheet`

5
Prepare and Deploy a Docker Enterprise Pilot Application

In Chapter 4, *Preparing the Docker Enterprise Pilot Cluster*, we completed a basic pilot installation of Docker Enterprise's **Universal Control Plane** (**UCP**) and the **Docker Trusted Registry** (**DTR**). Now we will configure the access control structures for our pilot cluster to allow our pilot team to build and deploy their applications.

The main objective of the pilot is to deploy two pilot applications. For the sake of illustration, in this chapter, we will feature the first of two applications for the pilot. The first application is a containerized Java web application running with Tomcat and a Postgres database backend. The second application, featured in Chapter 6, *Design and Pilot a Docker Enterprise CI Pipeline*, is a sample custom Java application where we simulate the development process to illustrate a development team's interaction with the Docker Enterprise platform, as well as a pipeline for DevOps and operations. So, while the technology stacks for the two applications is similar, you will see the additional considerations required for the custom application deployment in the subsequent chapter.

In this chapter, we will cover the following topics:

- Pilot planning
- Configuring UCP and DTR for a pilot application
- Pilot application selection, containerization, networking, service discovery, and layer 4 routing
- Pilot application deployment script with secrets and configuration management

Planning for a pilot application

Getting ready for the actual Docker Enterprise pilot takes coordination between application developers, DevOps, and technical operations team members. To illustrate the array of typical tasks and their associated impact areas, we have provided a **Responsible, Accountable, Consulted, and Informed** (**RACI**)-style table, shown shortly, as a communication tool to describe what needs to be done and who will be involved in each task. While we are not going to cover each of these tasks in depth, we will focus our discussion on the items presented in bold.

 Generally, an RACI chart/matrix/table lists the tasks on the left column and team members across the top, with the R, A , C, or I roles placed at the intersection of a team member and a task (deliverable or milestone).

The first section of the table deals with core project management/governance activities related to organizing and kicking off the pilot. It is, of course, important to identify the pilot's goals, activities, deliverables, and timelines, and review progress being made on a daily basis.

You will notice a heavy emphasis on training toward the top of the chart. While some initial Docker training is often very helpful during the PoC phase, the following training should be considered a requirements during the pilot phase, where all members of the core pilot team should attend training as indicated in the following chart in the early stages of the pilot:

Task-role RACI chart	Pilot coordinator	App architect	App Dev	DevOps	Sys admin	Ops Mgr
Schedule training	R	I	I	I	I	I
Pilot goal capture	R	I	I	I	I	I
Pilot planning and execution	R	C	I	C	I	C
Pilot kickoff	R	C	C	C	C	C
Attend Docker fundamentals	I	R	R	R	R	R
Attend Docker Ent Ops	I			R	R	R
Attend Docker Ent Dev	I	A	R	R	I	I
Attend Docker support	I	I	I	R	R	A

R: Responsible (possibly shared) | **A**: Accountable (only one) | **C**: Consulted | **S**: Supports | **I**: Informed

Attend Docker security	I	R	R	R	R	A
Configure UCP and DTR for pilot		I	I	C	R	A
LDAP/team sync for pilot		C		C	A	R
Storage config for pilot		C	C	C	A	R
Configure DTR for pilot				R	A	R
Distribute pilot credentials					R	
Pilot app base image		S	S	S	S	A
Pilot app architecture		A	R	R	S	S
Containerize pilot app		A	R	S		
Pilot image repo config		C	I	C	C	R
Pilot image tag and push		A	R	A		
Pilot image scan		I	I	C	A	R
Pilot `docker-compose-dev`		R	A	S		
Pilot secrets		I	I	S	A	R
Pilot stack deploy		C	C	A	S	C

R: Responsible (possibly shared) | **A**: Accountable (only one) | **C**: Consulted | **S**: Supports | **I**: Informed

Prior to the pilot kickoff, a pilot coordinator (project manager, type role to expedite the pilot program) and the core pilot team will develop a plan where they define key responsibilities and timelines. It is important for the various constituents involved in the pilot program to identify their key learning objectives for the pilot initiative and to make sure the plan covers real, hands-on involvement to support their objectives. Finally, before the pilot begins, a kick-off meeting should be held to review the goals, (learning and functional) objectives, participant roles, and the timelines for the pilot.

Sample pilot planning and execution

To effectively illustrate the pilot planning tasks, we will continue to work through our sample pilot application. We'll start with a summary chart of decisions made for our pilot, where we tie them back to the key tasks described in the preceding RACI chart. From there, we will walk through the execution of the tasks along with a more detailed description of each of the decisions and how they are implemented in the Docker Enterprise environment.

For our sample pilot, we identified the following objectives:

- Set up a bare-metal Docker Enterprise install with CentOS 7.5—guided reference architecture
- Design and implement a split DNS scheme for proper internal and external resolution
- Secure the installation with NAT, firewalls, network isolation, and frontend load balancing
- Use NFS on an isolated network for backing DTR and possibly application data volumes
- Implement cluster and application logging, monitoring, and alerting (covered later in `Chapter 7`, *Pilot Docker Enterprise Platform Monitoring and Logging*)
- Deploy an internet-facing, HTTPS wiki site application for internal users, but try to maintain near-zero downtime
- Deploy a sample custom application with a representative pipeline for other custom applications (covered in `Chapter 6`, *Design and Pilot a Docker Enterprise CI Pipeline*)

Our sample pilot team includes a **core team** with five members. We list their roles and fictitious names for our following examples:

- An **operations manager** to act as Docker Enterprise administrator—Otto OpsManager
- A **system administrator** to assist with Docker Enterprise underlying infrastructure and cluster resources—Sandy SysAdmin
- A **DevOps engineer** to support the software pipeline and cluster stack deployments—Deepti DevOps
- A **software architect** to oversee containerized software design—Andrew Architect
- A **software engineer** to containerize, test, and push artifacts to source code control—Sally Software

Our timeline was 6 weeks in duration with the following **overlapping key activities**:

- Key activities covered in this chapter:
    - 2 weeks for the platform build out
    - 1 week to containerize and deploy a confluence wiki application
    - 1 week to operationalize confluence wiki application—backups, updates, and application break/fix process
- Key activities covered in Chapter 6, *Design and Pilot a Docker Enterprise CI Pipeline*:
    - 1 week to containerize custom application with local integration tests
    - 2 weeks to pilot a container-based CI pipeline to build customer application
    - 1 week to operationalized custom application platform—backups, updates, and application break/fix process
- Key activities covered in Chapter 7, *Pilot Docker Enterprise Platform Monitoring and Logging*:
    - 2 weeks of logging, monitoring, and alerting setup
    - 1 week to document platform for post pilot on-boarding

The following is a chart highlighting key decisions for our sample pilot application. Again, for consistency sake, tie the tasks back to the RACI chart shown previously:

Task	Summary key decision made for pilot
Configure UCP and DTR for pilot	• Only run workloads on non-DTR worker nodes • Use third-party certificates for cluster access (`*.mydomain.com`) and cluster deployed applications (`wiki.mydomain.com`) • Use layer 4 routing for wiki application deployment • Use layer 7 for custom application deployment • Use standard Swarm UCP ports • Use default UCP session settings • Initially configure logs for `.json` file—roll at 10 MB and keep the three latest files • Turn off usage reporting • **DTR**: Allow create on push for repos • **DTR**: Using a central NFS mount for all DTR instances • **DTR**: Enable image scanning • **DTR**: Run garbage collection at 2 a.m. local time
LDAP/team sync for pilot	• Use UCP's built-in access user management for small pilot team—add LDAP/AD integration for production phase
Storage config for pilot	• Use NFS backing for DTR image storage

Design and configure RBAC	• See *Figure 4*
Pilot app base image	• Use an official base image from Docker Hub
Pilot app architecture	• TLS termination at external HAProxy load balancer for Java application with Postgres DB backend

Containerize pilot app UCP and DTR	• Two images in pilot DTR (wiki and Postgres)
	• Use local volumes and not NFS for wiki application
	   ○ Constrain application for worker-3 node
	   ○ Prepopulate Docker volume mount points on worker 3

Pilot image repo config	• Tie images to pilot organization

Pilot image tag and push	• Pick image namespaces:
	   ○ `dtr/mydomain.com/pilot/wiki`
	   ○ `dtr/mydomain.com/pilot/postgres`
	• Use semantic versioning: `major.minor.patch`

Pilot image scan	• Manually scan images before deploying
Pilot `docker-compose-dev`	• Create a local developer build and local run file for application stack
Pilot secrets	• Secrets for Postgres image/container
Pilot stack deploy	• Use bash script from UCP bundle

Summary of pilot decisions

Configure UCP pilot settings

Installing UCP and DTR was the first step toward launching the pilot phase; now we need to configure the UCP admin settings and the **role-based access control** (**RBAC**) system. The administrative settings include configuration information and options for Swarm, UCP client certificates, layer 7 routing, cluster configuration, authentication and authorization, logs, license, DTR, content trust, usage, scheduler, and upgrades.

We begin by logging into the UCP web UI using the credentials specified during the UCP installation process. After logging in, we look at the left-hand column where we see the menu structure's six main headings (the menus are collapsed by default). From there, we expand the admin menu and click on the **Admin Settings** menu item as shown in the following screenshot:

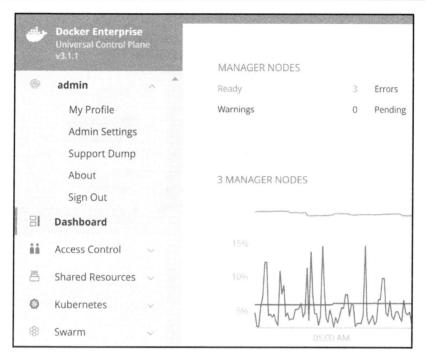

Figure 1: UCP Admin Settings Menu

The Swarm settings page (**Admin Settings | Swarm**) displays the worker and manager join tokens, allows for the rotation of cluster certificates and tokens, and provides adjustments to timing related to cluster operations. While you may find occasion to rotate the certificates/tokens (usually because of a compromise), normally the Swarm settings don't need any adjustment.

The UCP client certificates settings page (**Admin Settings | Certificates**) allows users to swap out the self-signed UCP client certificate with a trusted third-party certificate. Back in Chapter 3, *Getting Started – Docker Enterprise Proof of Concept*, we showed how to provide a third-party certificate when installing UCP. However, if you deferred during the installation process, here is the place to paste or upload your third-party certificates.

If you have already installed DTR and then updated UCP's client certificates, you will probably need to reconfigure your DTR installation with the new UCP certificates using a `docker run -it --rm docker/dtr:2.6.0 reconfigure` command with the `--ucp-ca` parameter. Otherwise, you will get an error when accessing the DTR as it redirects to UCP for single sign-up authentication.

After installing the third-party UCP client certificates, you may need to reconfigure your DTR installation. Updating the UCP certificate may interrupt the linkage between DTR and UCP and result in a DTR login problem. If you encounter this issue, it is easily fixed with the DTR reconfigure command. Also, you can take this opportunity to add your third-party DTR client certificate at the same time by using a command looking something like this:

```
$ docker run -it --rm docker/dtr \
  reconfigure \
  --ucp-url https://ucp.mydomain.com:443 \
  --ucp-username admin \
  --ucp-password {your-password-goes-here} \
  --replica-http-port 81 \
  --replica-https-port 4443 \
  --dtr-external-url dtr.mydomain.com \
  --ucp-ca "$(cat ucp.ca)" \
  --dtr-ca "$(cat dtr.ca)" \
  --dtr-cert "$(cat dtr.cert)" \
  --dtr-key "$(cat dtr.key)"
```

The UCP **layer 7 routing settings** (**Admin Settings | Layer 7 Routing**) are used to enable and configure Docker Enterprise's Interlock 2 ingress system. Layer 7 routing requires a couple of key settings. The first thing you want to do is confirm the HTTP and HTTPS ports are set correctly. In the last chapter, we talked about network design and described how our load balancer would pass inbound application traffic on port 8443 to the cluster. When we enable Interlock 2, a proxy receives traffic on port 4443 from the application load balancer, examines the HTTP headers, and routes traffic to the intended containers. We will get into more detail about layer 7 routing when we deploy our custom application later in the chapter.

The cluster configuration settings may be used to override the default settings for the Swarm cluster. The first two options are port settings for the Docker controller port and Swarm port. The controller port is used by the web UI and API and usually set to 443, but can be overridden when UCP is installed. The Swarm port, also known as the Docker daemon port, is set to 2376 by default, and is used for encrypted cluster management communication between Swarm nodes.

If the daemon port is set to 2375, it means it is using an unencrypted protocol. This is very dangerous! Anyone accessing this port can issue Docker commands on that node, including Docker commands to run in privilege mode or mount a sensitive directory on the host filesystem. Using 2375 is neither normal nor expected for a pilot cluster setup.

In addition to the port settings, the cluster configuration settings allows administrators to change the scheduling strategy for individual container deployment in the cluster. This is not for Swarm service scheduling, just containers. Swarm services are always scheduled using the spread scheduling strategy to evenly distribute containers across the cluster. For more information on deploying Swarm services, please refer to the Docker docs: https://docs.docker.com/engine/swarm/how-swarm-mode-works/services/

The last setting for the cluster setting you need to know about (we will ignore the KV store settings as they are not really used by mere mortals) is the external service load balancer URL. This should be set to how your expected URL for external access that corresponds to your CN of your certificate.

The **Authentication & Authorization Settings** page includes a number of important settings. The first setting is the default role for all private collections. This setting impacts the default access given to each user's private sandbox. By default, it is set to restricted control. In some cases, you may consider giving users full control over their sandbox, keeping in mind the additional security problems that may arise.

The next grouping of settings has to do with a login session's lifetime, renewal, and per-user limits. Generally, these can be left at the default settings of a 60-minute session lifetime, a 20-minute renewal threshold, and a 10-user limit (a given user can only have 10 sessions).

Two final sections of the authentication and authorization settings page allow for the integration with external enterprise mechanisms, including LDAP directory services and SAML 2.0 single sign on with Okta or ADFS. The SAML 2.0 feature is new in Docker EE2.1/UCP 3.1 and currently has some limitations. The LDAP integration, on the other hand, has been a part of the platform for while and is typically used by larger enterprises.

Docker UCP LDAP integration has two parts. The first part is establishing a connection to your corporate LDAP server with a reader account and then defining how to search for users in the directory. These settings are pretty straightforward and allow you to test the connection from the UCP's **Authentication & Authorization** page. We will discuss the second part when we get to adding teams to the Docker Enterprise RBAC system.

This is where we can actively sync users from (based on LDAP query parameters such as group memberships) LDAP to Docker RBAC team. By actively, I mean that if a user is removed from a LDAP, they become inactive in UCP at the next LDAP sync, but only if the **Just-In-Time User Provisioning** setting is `false`.

 Setting **Just-In-Time User Provisioning** to `true` is nice because it only sets up authorized LDAP users in UCP when they log in the first time. So, you don't have a bunch of inactive user accounts in UCP, but there is a downside. If **Just-In-Time User Provisioning** is `true` and a user is removed from a group in LDAP, UCP will deny authentication of the account at the next sync, but the user's CLI bundle will still allow cluster access! For a more secure environment, consider using the narrowest possible LDAP user search query to limit the number of user accounts synchronized with UCP and setting the **Just-In-Time User Provisioning** setting to `false`.

The **Logs settings** page is where we set the Docker UCP logging level. This restarts the UCP containers with an updated logging level and is one small aspect of logging. In `Chapter 7`, *Pilot Docker Enterprise Platform Monitoring and Logging*, we discuss the details of logging and Docker Enterprise approach to integrate with open source and commercial enterprise logging platforms.

The **License settings** page lists information about the currently installed Docker Enterprise license. It also gives you the option to upload a new license.

The **Docker Trusted Registry Settings** page lists the **fully qualified domain name** (FQDN) of the DTR associated with the cluster.

The **Content Trust settings** page allows Docker Enterprise administrators to restrict UCP's Docker Enterprise engines to only run container with signed images. When this feature is activated, by checking the **Run only signed images** checkbox, you will further specify the Docker Enterprise teams who are required to sign the images before they can be deployed. For example, the Ops team from our pilot organization may be required to digitally sign any images before they are run in the cluster. This makes it difficult for unauthorized, potentially malicious images to be substituted into production containers. This feature is typically reserved for production clusters.

The **Usage settings** page is where users configure options regarding if and how your cluster shares usage reports with the Docker product team. Like most software companies, Docker is always looking for feedback to improve their product. By reviewing your usage information as well as API and UI tracking, they are able to identify important usage patterns to guide product development efforts. If you are a little bit wary about sharing, you can always check the last box, which makes the reports anonymous by removing your license information from the reports.

The **Scheduler settings** page allows Docker Enterprise administrators to constrain workload deployments to worker nodes (non-UCP and non-DTR nodes). There are two levels of constraints for both Kubernetes and Swarm. The first level allows users to schedule work loads on all nodes including UCP managers in DTR nodes. This box is almost always unchecked—do not allow non-admins to deploy workloads to managers and DTR nodes. Allowing user workload on managers (and DTR) nodes is against Docker best practices. The second setting allows Docker Enterprise administrators to deploy containers on UCP managers or DTR nodes. Once the cluster is completely set up, this can be unchecked, but this box must be checked while you are installing DTR and other system utilities, including some logging frameworks such as an ELK stack, where log collectors need to be on all nodes.

The **Upgrade setting** page is where Docker Enterprise administrators can check the current version of the software and if there are any UCP upgrades available. If newer versions are available, you can upgrade from this page. However, always back up UCP before choosing to upgrade.

 The general procedure for maintaining a cluster includes updating/patching the OS and Docker Engine on each cluster node. This should be done before updating UCP or DTR as they may require fixes or capabilities available in the latest release of the Docker engine. Also, before updating from the **Docker Upgrade settings** page, back up UCP and DTR. While patch releases almost always work without an issue, larger update/upgrades may encounter issues and backup is rarely regretted!

Docker has also exposed the UCP configuration file API. This allows Docker Enterprise admins to use a TOML format to export/import UCP configurations rather than using the UI to configure the settings. For example, using a Docker Enterprise admin's command-line bundle, we can dump the configuration of our UCP. First, we `curl` our UCP's API endpoint by providing our admin user's CA certificate and key info, and dump the response into the local `ucp-config.toml` file. Then we can see the contents:

```
[local-CLI-DOcker-EE-Admin]$ curl --cacert ca.pem --cert cert.pem --key
key.pem https://ucp.mydomain.com/api/ucp/config-toml > ucp-config.toml
```

```
[local-CLI-DOcker-EE-Admin]$ cat ucp-config.toml
[auth]
  default_new_user_role = "restrictedcontrol"
  backend = "managed"
  samlEnabled = false
  samlLoginText = ""
  [auth.sessions]
    lifetime_minutes = 60
    renewal_threshold_minutes = 20
    per_user_limit = 10
  [auth.saml]
    idpMetadataURL = ""
    spHost = ""
    rootCerts = ""
    tlsSkipVerify = false

[[registries]]
  host_address = "dtr.mydomain.com"
  service_id = "8c599992-8996-43b5-b511-f26c94631fea"
  ca_bundle = "-----BEGIN CERTIFICATE-----\n <SNIP-redacted> \n-----END
CERTIFICATE-----\n"
  batch_scanning_data_enabled = true

[scheduling_configuration]
  enable_admin_ucp_scheduling = false
  default_node_orchestrator = "swarm"

[tracking_configuration]
  disable_usageinfo = true
  disable_tracking = true
  anonymize_tracking = false
  cluster_label = ""

[trust_configuration]
  require_content_trust = false

[log_configuration]
  level = "INFO"

[audit_log_configuration]
  level = ""
  support_dump_include_audit_logs = false

[license_configuration]
  auto_refresh = false

[cluster_config]
  controller_port = 443
```

```
kube_apiserver_port = 6443
swarm_port = 2376
swarm_strategy = "spread"
kv_timeout = 5000
kv_snapshot_count = 20000
profiling_enabled = false
external_service_lb = "ucp.nvisia.io"
metrics_retention_time = "24h"
metrics_scrape_interval = "1m"
rethinkdb_cache_size = "1GB"
cloud_provider = ""
cni_installer_url = ""
pod_cidr = "192.168.0.0/16"
calico_mtu = "1480"
ipip_mtu = "1480"
unmanaged_cni = false
nodeport_range = "32768-35535"
azure_ip_count = ""
local_volume_collection_mapping = false
manager_kube_reserved_resources = "cpu=250m,memory=2Gi,ephemeral-
storage=4Gi"
  worker_kube_reserved_resources = "cpu=50m,memory=300Mi,ephemeral-
storage=500Mi"
```

The UCP config API is a great way to initialize a cluster as well. For more information on UCP configs, see the docs at https://docs.docker.com/ee/ucp/admin/configure/ucp-configuration-file/.

Now that we have explained the UCP settings, we will configure the RBAC system for our pilot group.

RBAC in Docker Enterprise

Docker Enterprise's **Role-Based Access Control (RBAC)** system allows administrators to define user access to their cluster at a very fine-grained level. First, we will talk about the applicable RBAC concepts in Docker Enterprise. Then, we will dive into a specific example for our sample pilot application to clarify and demonstrate the concepts in practice.

To work with the Docker Enterprise RBAC system, you need to understand the four following primary constructs within Docker Enterprise:

- **Subjects**: Organization, teams, users, and service accounts
- **Resource groups**: Collections and namespaces

- **Roles**: Groupings of permissions to perform cluster operations
- **Grants**: The application of role to a subject for a specific resource group

We start our discussion with the grant because it best describes the functional aspects of all of the components. The grant is the glue that ties the subject to a set of resources through a specific role. In *Figure 2,* we can see how a grant associates a subject with a list of allowed operations (grouped into roles) on a defined set of resources.

In Docker Enterprise, the subjects may reference as an organization, a user, a team, or a service account. Resource sets are implemented with collections and namespaces (Kubernetes). Collections may hold containers, services, images, networks, volumes, secrets, (app) configs, and cluster nodes. A role lists all of the operations allowed on objects in the target collection, such as a container `create container` or `network connect` command, as shown in the following diagram:

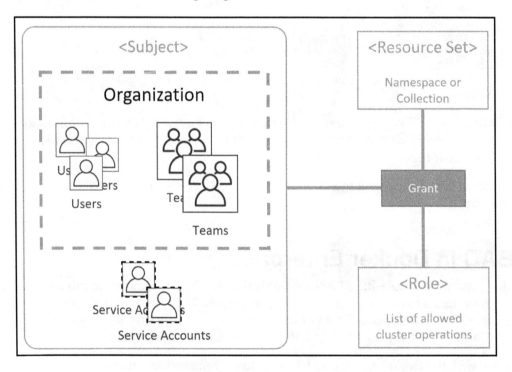

Figure 2: Docker Enterprise Role Based Access Control

For convenience, Docker Enterprise has several useful predefined roles. While you may find it necessary or convenient to define your own, these predefined roles are both typical and illustrative of real scenarios. The out-of-the-box roles included are none, view only, restricted control, full control, and schedule (for node related operations), as shown in the following diagram:

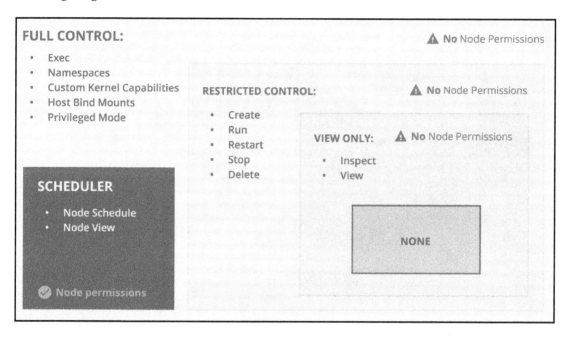

Figure 3: Docker's Built-In Roles

 Roles are immutable and therefore they cannot be modified (only deleted and recreated). This makes sense, since any modification could create confusion and lead to possible security holes. For instance, what if an admin changed a read-only user role to allow for updates and deletes? All existing grants using the modified read-only role would be compromised.

The RBAC system may be configured through the Docker Enterprise Web UI's Access Control menu or using the Docker API, but please note the RBAC settings are only available to Docker Enterprise administrative users. The **Access Control** menu has the four submenu items: **Orgs & Teams**, **Users**, **Roles**, and **Grants**.

In *Figure 4*, we show a specific configuration for our pilot example. Please note the figure shows the relationship between orgs and users to UCP (using grants) and DTR (using team-repository permissions in DTR):

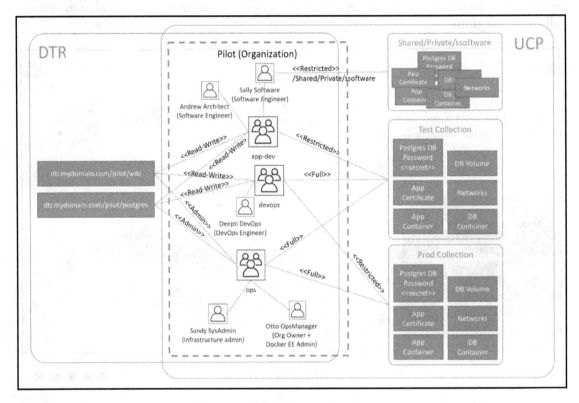

Figure 4: Sample Pilot RBAC Configuration

Setting up Docker Enterprise teams and organizations

Docker Enterprise Orgs and Teams provide grouping mechanisms for users and are the subjects for RBAC systems. When discerning options for Organizations and teams, keep in mind that organization impacts DTR repository namespaces structures. The DTR image name is comprised of the DTR_FQDN + user or organization name + repository name: tag. Enterprise images name are usually associated with the organization name rather than a user's name. These organization names could be aligned with a business unit (that is, underwriting or sales) or a pipeline phase for image promotion (development, test, QA, staging, and production), depending on your approach and access controls between business units or pipeline stages.

Docker Enterprise teams are subgroupings within organizations. Users are associated with teams and when a user is added to a team, that user automatically becomes a member of the parent organization.

The steps for setting up and manually populating a team in Docker Enterprise are as follows:

1. Log in with a Docker Enterprise administrator account.
2. Add users:
    1. Open **Access Control** | **Users** and click on the **Create** button
    2. Enter the new user's information and click **Create** to create the new users
    3. Repeat *Step 2* and *Step 3* for each new user
3. Add orgs and teams:
    1. Open **Access Control** | **Orgs & Teams** and use the **Create** button create a new organization
    2. Enter the organization information and click on the **Create** button at the bottom of the form
    3. Click on the new organization name in the list to view/create teams for the selected organization
    4. Click + in the upper right-hand menu to add a new team
    5. Enter the team name and description, then click **Create** at the bottom of the form
4. Add users to the teams:
    1. Go to **Access Control** | **Orgs & Teams** | **Name of Org** to see a list of teams
    2. Click on a **Team** and use the + in the top-right corner to add users to the team

In the Org menu, you may notice the Docker-datacenter organization. This is an internal organization to which users are added the first time they log into Docker Enterprise and by default are granted restricted control access (default access control level is configurable through **Admin Settings | Authentication & Authorization**) to their personal /Shared/Private/{user-name} collection—the users default collection (this may be overridden in a user's profile).

As you might expect, adding individual users to UCP could become very tedious in a large organization. That's why Docker Enterprise allows Docker Enterprise administrators to synchronize LDAP group members into UCP teams. Not only does this populate the team members, but as mentioned previously, in the UCP **Authentication & Authorization** settings section, it can also be used to synchronize the team members with updates made to the LDAP groups.

Team member sync using LDAP

For your pilot project, you may decide to use Docker Enterprise's built-in user access and authentication rather than synchronizing with a corporate AD/LDAP directory in an effort to limit the scope of the pilot project. While moving AD/LDAP integration out of scope may be a great way to keep the pilot moving forward, it is an important enterprise touchpoint for the Docker Enterprise platform and will need to be resolved at some point. Because Docker's built-in access control system is flexible, adding the AD/LDAP synchronization at a later time is possible. However, the pilot is a really good time to begin conversations with the sys admin and user security teams about detailed integration plans. A good compromise might be to start by manually adding the first team's users, but then start experimenting with the AD/LDAP sync feature to implement a long-term synced solution.

Before using the Docker EE LDAP sync, your UCP cluster must be connected to the LDAP server using the UCP **Authentication & Authorization** settings page. Not only will this connect to the corporate AD/LDAP server, but it will allow you to isolate a subset of candidate UCP team members through the use of an LDAP query filter.

After an LDAP connection is established between UCP and your LDAP server, you will have some new options when creating a UCP team. Then when creating a UCP team, by setting **Enable Sync Team Members** to **Yes**, you may add all members from an LDAP group or you may provide a custom LDAP query to populate your team. Remember, these will be synchronized at intervals as specified in the UCP configuration.

If members are removed from the LDAP group, their access to UCP will be reduced or eliminated depending on the just-in-time provisioning setting for LDAP synchronization:

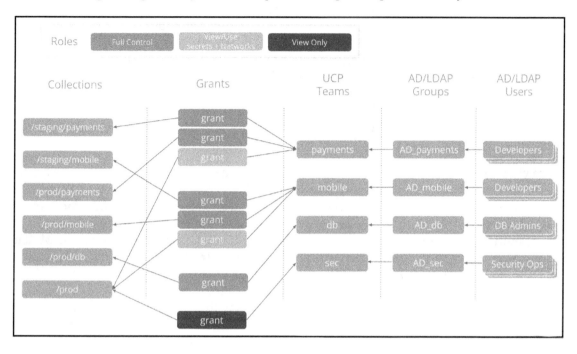

Figure 5: Base Image Hierarchy Example- https://docs.docker.com/ee/ucp/authorization/ee-standard/

In *Figure 5*, we see an example from a Docker Enterprise tutorial on `https://docs.docker.com/`. This is a great example of showing the end-to-end spectrum of how an LDAP user gains access to resources in a Docker Enterprise collection through groups, teams, and grants. On the left side, we have resource collections (or namespaces for Kubernetes) inside of our UCP access control subsystem. On the right, we have a corporate active directory or LDAP with our company's users. Again, this presumes that UCP is set up to synchronize with your corporate LDAP server.

To connect the UCP resources with AD/LDAP users, we move from right to left, from the users in the corporate directory to their associated groups that represent functional groupings. Here in our example, the developers are organized into two app groups (`AD_payments` and `AD_mobile`) and other administrative users are organized by functional concern such as DB admins (`AD_db`) and security ops (`AD_sec`).

The AD/LDAP grouping, of course, takes place inside of the AD/LDAP corporate directory (outside of the Docker Enterprise realm) and is ideally already put in place as a part of your system administrator/security team's normal practices. However, if it is not, you have a couple of options. The first option is to meet with the system administrators and security team to establish logical groupings similar the example shown previously. The second option is to create an AD/LDAP query to target users associated with a specific team. The second option may be faster, but it tends to be brittle and difficult to maintain. We strongly suggest that you work with your admin and security teams to develop a logical grouping scheme for your directory.

Once your AD/ADAP groupings are set up, it is time to head inside of the UCP's UI. Under the access control orgs and teams menu, you can click on your main org. Then, click on the plus sign in the upper right-hand corner to add a new team. Notice the enables sync team members option. This is where you can set it to yes and then you may specify how you want your UCP team to be synced with your AD/LDAP team. Usually, you'll use the **Match Group Members** option (direct bind) by providing the descriptors in the **Group DN** field that match your team in the AD/LDAP directory. The group member attribute tells UCP where to pull the group members distinguish names from the AD/LDAP directory. Once this is done, you have now connected your AD groups with your UCP teams. This connection will be synchronized at regular intervals based on your UCP/LDAP server settings.

Congratulations! You have now set up your orgs, teams, and users in UCP. The next step is establishing UCP collections for our pilot team to use.

Collection for pilot team

With our users either set up manually or imported into our teams using AD/LDAP synchronization, we may now grant them access to UCP resources. As described previously, UCP resources are organized into collections. For the pilot's collection configuration, let's refer back to *Figure 4* where we see three collections depicted.

The main collections of interest for the pilot team are the test and prod collections. For our pilot discussion, the test collection holds resources used to test the application after (automated) deployments. We will learn more about automated pipelines with Docker in Chapter 6, *Design and Pilot a Docker Enterprise CI Pipeline,* where we will trigger automated builds and deploy updated artifacts into the test collection for integration testing.

The application developers will have restricted access to the test environment for the purposes of troubleshooting any issues. The DevOps team will test their deployment scripts within the test collection and app-dev team will have full access to all resources. The test collection should not have any sensitive data or secrets shared, because app-dev team members will potentially be able to see both data and secrets in this environment.

The prod collection is a more locked-down collection and will more closely mimic what will eventually be a separate production cluster. In fact, the prod database may start with a recent copy of a production database with full data fidelity, including potentially sensitive personal or financial data. This environment may also include production secrets such as access tokens to third-party APIs. Notice that application developers do not have access to the prod collection in *Figure 4* for this reason.

An important security note: if you are using a centralized logging system for your container cluster, be careful not to log any PMI or HIPAA type data to the logs unless they are encrypted and locked down appropriately. Oftentimes, private information is shared through environment variables that may be revealed during a stack dump to the logger when an application fails.

So, for the sake of simplicity in our pilot, we have two main collections for our team with no nesting or hierarchical collection structures. The test and prod collections are flat without any overlap. However, in *Figure 4,* we see how the Docker docs team has leveraged a nested hierarchical collection structure.

The example shows three roles used:

- Full control
- View/use secrets and networks
- View only

In the example, we see a grant is given to the payments team of full control over the `/staging/payments` collection. Additionally, two more grants are applied to the payments team, allowing them full control over the `/prod/payments` collection and view/use secret and networks access to `/prod`. **Carefully note** how UCP collections are nested (unlike our pilot's flat collection design). Therefore, the `/prod` collection is a superset of `/prod`, `/prod/payments`, `/prod/mobile`, and `/prod/DB`. So, any grants to `/prod` will propagate to all the collections underneath `/prod` as well!

For our pilot project, please note that each user will receive restricted access to their own sandbox collection called `/shared/private/{username}` (for user Sally Software, `/shared/private/ssoftware`). This collection will be created and a restricted control grant added the first time the user logs in. This is where they may want to test a stack of containers using the cluster's resources rather than their own development machine. This should be carefully managed as a part of your software development process. Again, we'll talk more about that in the pipeline chapter.

DTR pilot settings

In the previous chapter, where we took care of some critical infrastructure associated with our pilot DTR configuration during the installation process, we configured NFS backing for our DTR image storage. This provides a single common backend data store for large DTR images across all replicas in the cluster. This is particularly important for the proper functioning of Docker Enterprise Advanced version's image-scanning feature. Please note that, DTR backend storage is for the binary image layers. Other repository metadata is stored and replicated across the DTR replicas using `rethinkdb`. Other DTR replica settings for the cluster are stored in the cluster's **etcd** key/value store (`ucp-kv`).

To access DTR settings, log in to DTR as a Docker Enterprise administrator. Then, navigate to the **System** menu as shown in *Figure 6*. The DTR System menu has five primary sub menus: **General**, **Storage**, **Security**, **Garbage collection**, and **Job Logs**:

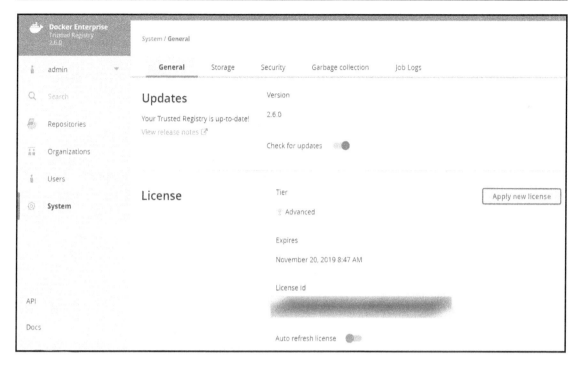

Figure 6: Docker Trusted Registry General Settings

The general settings page is broken down into multiple sections including **Updates**, **License**, **Domains & Proxies**, **Single Sign-on**, **Repositories**, **Repository Events**, **Job Logs**, **Analytics**, and **Notifications**.

The **Update** section of the general settings page allows you to see whether there are any newer versions of DTR available. By enabling check for updates, DTR will automatically look for newer versions of the software and notify users with a header banner in the DTR UI if a newer version is available. It is important to note that, while users are made aware of available updates, updates will not be automatically installed. The update process itself is a manual operation performed by a Docker Enterprise admin.

During a pilot, it may be tempting to give everyone Docker Enterprise admin access rights. This is problematic for several reasons, ranging from security concerns to the destabilization of the cluster! Users may inadvertently delete system resources and cause instability in the cluster, or users with Docker Enterprise admin rights may also perform updates on Docker Enterprise software. Usually, this happens innocently enough, where a banner with a link tells the user (with admin rights) there is a newer version of DTR or UCP available. The user clicks on the link and applies the update without reading any of the release notes, which may include required upgrades to the Docker Engine prior to the update. **Limit Docker Enterprise admins to a small group sys admins**.

The **License** section, much like the UCP settings, provides information about the current Docker license, such as the license tier expiration date and license ID. Under most circumstances, you should not need to worry about the License section as it should be automatically copied from your UCP License information when DTR is installed.

The **Domain & Proxies** settings section is where client access configuration is set for the DTR web UI. When set up for pilot mode, using an external load balancer, you will need to fill in the **Load Balancer** the **Public Address** field. This is generally the FQDN (`dtr.mydomain.com`) of your DTR externally. It also correlates to the FQDN used to generate the DTR certificate. Please note that accessing the DTR with any other IP address or domain name may result in single sign-on authentication failures.

The **Single Sign-On** setting allows you to streamline DTR logins by redirecting to UCP for authentication. This should be turned on with the slider to the right.

The **Repositories** setting allows users (with the appropriate permissions) to create repositories when they push their first image. The setting is off by default, but turning it on is typically expected behavior from experienced users. Again, if they don't have access to the repository namespace where they are trying to push the image, it will not succeed anyway.

For example, if create on push is enabled and Sally Software pushes an image to her repository namespace, `dtr.mydomain.com/ssoftware/somerepo:v1`, it should just work. However, if she attempts to push an image with an pilot organization repository namespace, `dtr.mydomain.com/ssoftware/somerepo:v1`, because she is only a member and not a org owner of the pilot organization, the operation will fail.

The **Repository Events** and **Job Logs** settings allow for the automatic housekeeping of repository events and job logs. Generally speaking, it is a good idea to put finite limits on continuous processing outputs that accumulate over time, especially logs. For our pilot sample DTR, we have set auto-deletion for repository events to seven days and job logs to six weeks.

The DTR **Analytics** settings, similar to the UCP analytics settings, send usage reports to Docker for analysis in an effort to improve the DTR product. There are two settings: one to allow sending any data to Docker and the second to send only anonymous data to Docker.

The final setting on the general page is **Notifications**. Enabling the Show "back up needed" warning does exactly that. When DTR has not been backed up for at least seven days, a banner appears at the top of the DTR web UI.

Next, the major section in the DTR settings is for external **Storage** settings. Again, we configured our pilot DTR storage when we installed DTR, using an NFS filesystem. However, if you are using a different filesystem and did not specify the parameters at install time, this is the place to do it. DTR external storage supports the local filesystem (which is the default and is not recommended for HA DTR clusters), NFS (typical standard for on-permises managed network installs), Amazon S3 or similar (AWS—hosted Docker Enterprise installs), Google Cloud Storage (Google—hosted Docker Enterprise installs), Microsoft Azure Blob storage accounts (Azure hosted Docker Enterprise installs), and OpenStack Swift (Openshift Docker Enterprise installs).

The DTR system's **Security** settings UI tab configures image scanning preferences and is only available to Docker Enterprise Advanced subscribers. The first section is for Docker Enterprise admins to specify how the image scanner obtains its vulnerability database. There are two options. The first and easiest option is the online update option, which automatically syncs everyday at 3 a.m. UTC. The second option, the offline update option, requires an admin to manually upload a vulnerability database at regular intervals, in which case you may have a link emailed to you daily. While cumbersome, the offline mode is the only option for DTRs running in an environment without internet egress, such as a secure air gap network environment that you might see in finance or a secure government facility.

There are two additional security settings. The first sets a scanning timeout threshold and is specified in hours. Because image scanning can be a resource-intensive process, it is a good idea to set a threshold. For our pilot DTR, I have set the scanning limit to 1 hour. The final security setting for DTR involves scanning webhooks.

With this setting, DTR can automatically execute an HTTP post to an external URL every time the security scanner has been updated. While certainly not necessary, this is a good nudge for the security/SecOps team to look at the CVE database and determine the potential impact on containers running in production.

The DTR system's **Garbage collection** UI tab configures how garbage collection behaves when cleaning up backend storage (deleted tags and images). There are three primary options for garbage collection. The first option runs the garbage collection task until it finishes, which, depending on your DTR traffic and backend IOP's performance, may take a long time. The second option is run for N minutes, where you set N to be a limit for how long the garbage collector should run each time it is triggered. The third option is to never run garbage collection, which you should probably only consider if you are having some performance issues with your DTR backend and you believe they are related to garbage collection. A reasonable approach here is to set it to run once per day (using the cron trigger setting) during off-processing hours and monitor DTR onlinegc actions in the job logs. If they run too long, then update the garbage collection settings.

Depending on your peak processing times, you will want to set the Repeat option using a `cron(ish)` schedule format. For our pilot DTR configuration, we used a `Custom cron schedule` set to `8 * * *` in order to trigger garbage collection at 2 a.m. central standard time.

The sample pilot wiki application

For the selection of our pilot application, we have chosen a lift-and-shift legacy wiki application from a private cloud host. This application is appealing for our pilot because of its limited dependencies. There are some web-based resources for things such as SMTP, but they require no modification to function in our containerized environment. Additionally, our stakeholders are motivated to rehost this in our Docker bare-metal data center cluster because of the $1,500 per month private cloud server charges we currently pay. In fact, the current private cloud charges are equal to licensing for a Docker Enterprise 10-node standard cluster with business-day support. So, conservatively, where we assume that 6 of our 10 nodes are consumed for UCP and DTR , we still have 4 worker nodes available in our new HA Docker Enterprise environment as opposed to 1, non-HA host in our current private cloud environment.

The goal for our sample wiki application is to simply containerize and deploy the wiki application and its database in our cluster. Over time, we will experiment with more advanced features (layer 7 routing and NFS for volume backing), but our key objective is to provide a stable alternative to the private cloud-hosted platform.

Begin by containerizing the application and testing it on a local machine. After the application is tested and verified, we will prepare it for a cluster deployment that includes— storing the images in our trusted registry, preparing persistent data volumes for the application and database, and finally creating a Docker stack file to deploy to Docker Enterprise cluster.

Containerizing the application

Earlier, in `Chapter 3`, *Getting Started -Docker Enterprise Proof of Concept*, we described the process for containerizing a sample .NET application using Elton Stoneman's example newsletter subscription application as a backdrop. Now, for our first pilot application, we are going to containerize an old Confluence Wiki application built with Java 7, Tomcat. and Postgres.

We begin the containerization process for our wiki application by identifying and collecting the application assets. The application's assets include source code, configuration, and data files. Once we have collected these assets, we document the application's components and dependency relationships.

Collect and document application assets

One proven technique used to gain a deep and accurate understanding of an application's components and dependencies is to study the installation process for the application on a clean server. If there is some solid, up-to-date documentation for installing the application on a fresh server, that works great. Otherwise, you need to schedule some time with an application subject matter expert who is responsible for installing the application. However, in either case, you will want to set up an installation walkthrough on a clean/new server. This sometimes is referred to as a sandbox install for the application. This requires the provisioning of an accessible sandbox machine, usually a VM, with the appropriate access network resources.

For our sample application, we are granted sudoer's access to the production box where the application is deployed. This is clearly a little scary because we do not want to interfere with the operation of the current production system! So, we need to proceed with great caution. Luckily for our sample pilot team, we had a Java architect to guide us through the application architecture for the confluence Wiki application and we were able to construct the diagram shown in *Figure 7*.

After looking at the Java application running with a Tomcat server, we discovered there were a few major assets we needed to capture and reproduce for our containerized application. The source code, the directory where the application stored local files, and the database files. Also, since the application uses a Postgres database backend, we can easily dump the database contents into an SQL file and use that file to initialize a new database in our containerized environment. Because of the Postgres DB's dumb feature, we are able to grab snapshots (DB dumps) of the production environment without interrupting the wiki's normal processing:

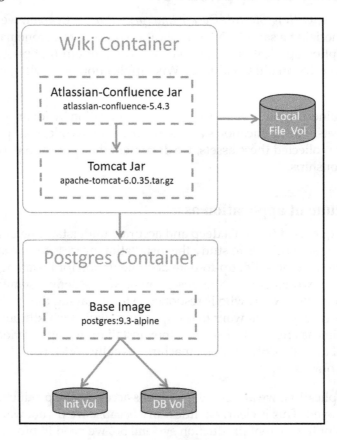

Figure 7: Sample Wiki Application Architecture

Inside of our **Wiki Container**, we have Java archive files. One archive file is for the confluence wiki application's code and the other is for the Tomcat application server. The confluence application also uses a local file volume to store documents and other blobs. For persistent (relational) data storage of metadata the configuration information, the wiki application uses the Postgres database backend server.

We begin the containerization process from the bottom up, starting with the Wiki's Postgres DB.

Containerizing and testing the Postgres database

For the `postgres` container, we are armed with the configuration (user and connection information) from the production install and the `wiki.sql` file we generated using the `pg_dump` command. This file will be used to populate our test container DB at startup. Please note that, this a copy of the the wiki's production database and is therefore subject our organization's data controls, data loss prevention, and other applicable policies and/or regulations.

We will start with an official Postgres Docker image that matches our Postgres version, in our case Postgres 9.3. We search Docker Hub to find the official Postgres repository. Then, we click on the **tags** tab to find a tag to match our the version our wiki application is expecting and we find 9.3 (`https://hub.docker.com/_/postgres?tab=tags`).

 When containerizing applications with database connections, it is really important to match the correct versions between the Postgres client in the application and the database server itself. If you try to upgrade the server, the client may fail to connect because of protocol changes that occur across versions. This situation can be really tricky to track down. So, when containerizing an application with a Postgres database, make sure the application's client version matches the your server version, to avoid possible headaches.

To learn more about the official Postgres image, from the Docker Hub description tab, we click on a Dockerfile link to any version of Postgres—this takes us to the associated GitHub repo. We notice the structure of the GitHub repo is organized by tag. We then follow that repo path the Postgres/9.3/Alpine version. Here is the repo URL for our Postgres version: `https://github.com/docker-library/postgres/tree/` `d564da5142b2e5fa235707b05d8aa0fc76250418/9.3/alpine`.
We see the Dockerfile used to build our image.

If we look toward the bottom of the Dockerfile, we can make note of a couple of items. The first is the use of the `PGDATA` environment variable and its associated volume used to specify the location for Postgres database files. It is set to `/var/lib/postgresql/data`. Therefore, this is the directory where we can volume-mount our database files on an external file system to preserve the state of our database across multiple Postgres database instances.

This means we can stop a `postgres` container and create a new one with the same volume mount point and the database will pick up where it left off, as follows:

```
# ... end of postgres 9.3 alpine Dockerfile

ENV PGDATA /var/lib/postgresql/data
RUN mkdir -p "$PGDATA" && chown -R postgres:postgres "$PGDATA" && chmod 777
"$PGDATA" # this 777 will be replaced by 700 at runtime (allows semi-
arbitrary "--user" values)
VOLUME /var/lib/postgresql/data

COPY docker-entrypoint.sh /usr/local/bin/
RUN ln -s usr/local/bin/docker-entrypoint.sh / # backwards compat
ENTRYPOINT ["docker-entrypoint.sh"]

EXPOSE 5432
CMD ["postgres"]
```

The second item to note from the preceding Postgres Dockerfile is the use of the ENTRYPOINT+CMD combination. The Postgres image uses a shell script at startup called `usr/local/bin/docker-entrypoint.sh` to initialize the database and passes Postgres as a parameter.

We can then dig into the `docker-entrypoint.sh` file to see how it is responsible for using the `wiki.sql` file to initialize the database if needed. We see the `docker-entrypoint.sh` snippet (shown following), where the script looks for the PG_VERSION file in the location where Postgres stores the data files. If it does not find the file, it assumes the database needs to be created and goes on to run/load `*.sh` or `*.sql` files found in the `docker-entrypoint-initdb.d` directory:

```
# look specifically for PG_VERSION, as it is expected in the DB dir
if [ ! -s "$PGDATA/PG_VERSION" ]; then
```

Therefore, by taking the `wiki.sql` file we created using the `pg_dump` command and copying it to the `docker-entrypoint-initdb.d` directory, we can have Postgres load a copy of our production database.

Now let's start to build our containerized Postgres DB. Here is the directory structure we are using for the sample application:

```
wiki-app
├──── docker-compose-dev.yml
└──── postgres
    ├──── db-init
    │    └──── wiki.sql
    └──── Dockerfile
```

So, the initial Dockerfile for our `postgres` container starts with version 9.3 of Postgress running on an Alpine OS. Then we set some environmental variables used by Postgres. Finally, we set up a user and group in order for the `mydomain-conf` DB to load properly from the SQL file, as follows:

```
# /wiki-app/postgres/Dockerfile
FROM postgres:9.3-alpine

ENV POSTGRES_DB mydomain-conf
ENV POSTGRES_USER mydomain-conf
#POSTGRESS_PASSWORD is supplied from the command line or docker-compose

#To load our wiki.sql file, our DB expects to find a password file
#...in specific user directory, mydomain-conf who is a member of a group
called my-domain.conf
RUN addgroup -S mydomain-conf && adduser -S -G mydomain-conf mydomain-conf
```

Remember, this first application is a lift-and-shift effort. Ideally, we would not want to have our database name, username, and user group name all being the same. This is just a byproduct of how the initial application database for our wiki was set up. If you want to do some basic refactoring during the pilot, that is up to your team. However, as you get started, we strongly recommend just getting the containerized version running as is before you start modifying it.

OK, you might be a little confused at this point, but hopefully this will become more clear as we build and test the container.

At this point, we could simply run a `docker image build` command to create an image from our Dockerfile. However, more experienced dev/DevOps Docker users like to take advantage of the features provided by `docker-compose`, where we can build and test an image by using the same YML specification file. The `docker-compose` utility allows developers or DevOps engineers to build and then run/test a set of related containers using a single command from a single YML specification file. By convention, the specification files are called `docker-compose.yml`. You can vary the filename by using the `-f` parameter to specify an alternate filename. However, when using `docker-compose` to build and test a local image, we often append a `-dev` to the base filename of the `docker-compose.yml` specification file. For us, this means that our file is called `docker-compose-dev.yml` and it is used by the pilot team to build and test our wiki application.

Let's take a look at our sample wiki build/test specification file called `/wiki-app/docker-compose-dev.yml`. The first thing we see after our comment is the version number. This tells docker-compose what features this specification file is expecting to find based on the version, and therefore ensures that the specification is compatible with the version of docker-compose installed on the build machine.

Next, we see two high-level YML constructs: **services** and **volumes**. Services specify the desired state for our Postgres container(s), but also include some build information as well. Here, the `build` attributes indicate where to find the build context for our Postgres image. For our example, when we build the Postgres image, `docker-compose` looks in the `postgres` directory for the Dockerfile and then tags the `my-postgres:v1` image , as follows:

```
# /wiki-app/docker-compose-dev.yml
version: '3.7'
services:
  postgres:
    build: postgres
    image: my-postgres:v1
    environment:
      - POSTGRES_PASSWORD=xxxxxxx
    volumes:
      - pgdata:/var/lib/postgresql/data
      - ./postgres:/docker-entrypoint-initdb.d
volumes:
  pgdata:
```

We also see that the `postgres` password is set as an environment variable where Postgres expects to find it by convention.

Finally, we declare the volumes this container expects to find at runtime. The first volume, `pgdata` is a local volume on the build/test machine where the database files are to be stored. Doing this allows you to save the data between runs of your stack and not having to re-initialize the DB for every test. The second volume uses of mount point on the local file system that is mounted inside the `/docker-entrypoint-initdb.d` directory within the container, where Postgres looks for DB initialization scripts or SQL files. This is the directory where we stashed our database dump file. So, the expected behavior is, when the container starts for the first time, it will find an empty `pgdata` volume and then use the wiki. SQL file to initialize the database.

From the `wiki-app` directory, we run `docker-compose -f docker-compose-dev.yml up --build -d` to build our `my-postgres:v1` image and start our container. From the following output, it looks like it succeeded, but we need to be sure:

```
[wiki-app]$ docker-compose -f docker-compose-dev.yml up --build -d
Building postgres
Step 1/4 : FROM postgres:9.3-alpine
 ---> e26433e300a4
Step 2/4 : ENV POSTGRES_DB nvisia-conf
 ---> Running in 0ce302897ed3
Removing intermediate container 0ce302897ed3
 ---> 579eaa40f99c
Step 3/4 : ENV POSTGRES_USER nvisia-conf
 ---> Running in eecfde4c3689
Removing intermediate container eecfde4c3689
 ---> 861d4fdf597b
Step 4/4 : RUN addgroup -S nvisia-conf && adduser -S -G nvisia-conf nvisia-conf
 ---> Running in 8728f40e1b04
Removing intermediate container 8728f40e1b04
 ---> 6779fb8a1eef

Successfully built 6779fb8a1eef
Successfully tagged my-postgres:v1

Creating network "wiki-app_default" with the default driver
Creating wiki-app_postgres_1 ... done
```

To confirm whether the database script ran to initialize the database, we need to look at the container's logs. For this, we use the `docker container logs` command. Make a note of the container name created by the `docker-compose up` command. The prefix is the directory name from where `docker-compose` was run. The `postgres` part of the container name in the middle is the name of the service and the `_1` suffix indicates the first container for that service. Yes, the suffix correctly implies we could have multiple replicas of a container running the `my-postgres:v1` image using `docker-compose` scale or replicas directives for Compose or Swarm respectively. Running the `logs` command shows all of the Postgres `docker-entrypoint.sh` and `postgress` startup messages.

Run the database container. We are looking for one specific message where the `wiki.sql` file is being executed. In the following block, I have highlighted an abbreviated log output section showing that we successfully created the database showing the `/usr/local/bin/docker-entrypoint.sh: running /docker-entrypoint-initdb.d/wiki.sql` message:

```
[wiki-app]$ docker container logs wiki-app_postgres_1
...
/usr/local/bin/docker-entrypoint.sh: running /docker-entrypoint-
initdb.d/wiki.sql
SET
SET
SET
SET
SET
SET
SET
CREATE FUNCTION
ALTER FUNCTION
SET
SET
CREATE TABLE
ALTER TABLE
CREATE SEQUENCE
ALTER TABLE
ALTER SEQUENCE
...
```

We now have the Postgres DB containerized and initializing with real data.

Containerizing and testing the wiki application

We will continue to build on our success as we create a Java 7 container to run our wiki using Tomcat. Before we install the Java application and Tomcat server, we create an empty Java container and use it to connect and test the Postgres DB backend.

First, we need to select an appropriate base image for our Java 7 container. Our journey takes us back to hub.docker.com where we search for (https://hub.docker.com/search?q=javatype=imageimage_filter=officialcategory=base) and find Docker's official Java image. We click on the Java repo, select the **Tags** tab, and look for the tag associated with the Java version 7 JDK.

There we find the **java:7-JDK** image as our starting point. Now we will add a `wiki` folder under `wiki-apps` directory and create a Dockerfile to build the `wiki` container image, as follows:

```
# /wiki-app/wiki/Dockerfile - Simple shell
FROM java:7-jdk
CMD ping localhost
```

We start off with a really simple shell for our wiki application. The goal here is to start the base image, and for our sample, we will just run a continuous `ping` command to hold PID 1 open. We will, of course, change this to actually running a Java application later, but this is all we need for now.

Now we need to update our `docker-compose-dev.yml` file to build and run the wiki shell application. In the following code sample, pay special attention to the items in bold, as these have been added to the `compose` file to support build and run the wiki shell application:

```
# /wiki-app/docker-compose-dev.yml
version: '3.7'
services:
  postgres:
    build: postgres
    image: my-postgres:v1
    environment:
      - POSTGRES_PASSWORD=xxxxxxxx
    networks:
      - db_net
  volumes:
    - pgdata:/var/lib/postgresql/data
    - ./postgres/db-init:/docker-entrypoint-initdb.d

  wiki:
    build: wiki
    image: my-wiki:v1
    networks:
      - db_net

networks:
  db_net:
volumes:
  pgdata:
```

The first bold item is the `networks` attribute added to the Postgres service specification. In order for Docker containers or services to communicate using DNS (refer to each other using the service name—service discovery), they need to share a common network. In our case, we are going to call this network `db_net`. Notice how the `networks` attribute is also declared under the wiki's service specification as well as at the end of the file in the networks section.

Notice the new wiki service section where we tell `docker-compose` where to find the build context (the Dockerfile, for now) in the wiki directory and to tag the newly built image as `my-wiki:v1`.

So, again, we build and run the services with the `docker-compose` command, this time to build and deploy the Postgres service and the wiki shell on the same network so we can test DB access from the `wiki` container, as follows:

```
[wiki-app]$ docker-compose -f docker-compose-dev.yml up -d --build
Creating network "wiki-app_db_net" with the default driver
Building postgres
Step 1/4 : FROM postgres:9.3-alpine
 ---> e26433e300a4
Step 2/4 : ENV POSTGRES_DB nvisia-conf
 ---> Using cache
 ---> 579eaa40f99c
Step 3/4 : ENV POSTGRES_USER nvisia-conf
 ---> Using cache
 ---> 861d4fdf597b
Step 4/4 : RUN addgroup -S nvisia-conf && adduser -S -G nvisia-conf nvisia-
conf
 ---> Using cache
 ---> 6779fb8a1eef
Successfully built 6779fb8a1eef
Successfully tagged my-postgres:v1
Building wiki
Step 1/2 : FROM java:7-jdk
 ---> 5dc48a6b75af
Step 2/2 : CMD ping localhost
 ---> Using cache
 ---> 9bce8d0254d9
Successfully built 9bce8d0254d9
Successfully tagged my-wiki:v1
Creating wiki-app_wiki_1 ... done
Creating wiki-app_postgres_1 ... done
```

Our first step is to verify connectivity from the `wiki-app_wiki_1` container to the `wiki-app_postgres_1` container. To accomplish this, we will execute a shell process inside of the `wiki-app_wiki_1` container using the `docker exec` command. Then we will install a `psql` client (version 9.3) and then connect to Postgres running in `wiki-app_postgres_1` and query for the Postgres table schema, as follows:

```
# Exec into the wiki container...
[wiki-app]$ docker exec -it wiki-app_wiki_1 bash

# Install the repo sources for postgres
root@424766f9fa1f:/# echo "deb http://apt.postgresql.org/pub/repos/apt/
jessie-pgdg main" > /etc/apt/sources.list.d/pgdg.list

# Get the to authenticate repos
root@424766f9fa1f:/# wget --quiet -O -
https://www.postgresql.org/media/keys/ACCC4CF8.asc | apt-key add -
OK

# Update package managers repository info
root@424766f9fa1f:/# apt-get update
...
done.

# Install the postgresql version 9.3 client
root@424766f9fa1f:/# apt-get install -y postgresql-9.3
...
Processing triggers for libc-bin (2.19-18+deb8u7)...

# Connect the client to the postgres host using service name spec'ed in
docker-compose-dev.yml
root@424766f9fa1f:/# psql -h postgres mydomain-conf mydomain-conf
Password for user nvisia-conf: xxxxxxxx
psql (9.3.25)
Type "help" for help.

mydomain-conf=# \dit
                                          List of relations
 Schema | Name | Type | Owner | Table
--------+---------------------------------------------+-------+-------------
+---------------------------
 public | AO_187CCC_SIDEBAR_LINK | table | mydomain-conf |
 public | AO_187CCC_SIDEBAR_LINK_pkey | index | mydomain-conf |
AO_187CCC_SIDEBAR_LINK
 public | AO_21D670_WHITELIST_RULES | table | mydomain-conf |
 public | AO_21D670_WHITELIST_RULES_pkey | index | mydomain-conf |
AO_21D670_WHITELIST_RULES
 public | AO_38321B_CUSTOM_CONTENT_LINK | table | mydomain-conf |
```

```
 public | AO_38321B_CUSTOM_CONTENT_LINK_pkey | index | mydomain-conf |
AO_38321B_CUSTOM_CONTENT_LINK
 public | AO_42E351_HEALTH_CHECK_ENTITY | table | mydomain-conf |
 public | AO_42E351_HEALTH_CHECK_ENTITY_pkey | index | mydomain-conf |
AO_42E351_HEALTH_CHECK_ENTITY
--MORE--
^C
mydomain-conf=# \q
root@424766f9fa1f:/#
```

We are able to connect from the `wiki` container to the Postgres server using the DNS name and list the tables. Keep in mind that once you are connected to the Postgres database, you can run any query you like, such as `select * from public.users`, to verify your database. Now we need to get the wiki application installed and running in the local container.

Once the shell container of the wiki is able to connect to the the database, we need to install the remainder of the assets for the wiki application—namely the JAR and configuration files. We add the additional assets into a `wiki` project file structure on our local build machine as shown following, where we highlight the application assets:

```
wiki-app$ tree -L 3
.
├── docker-compose-dev.yml
├── postgres
│   ├── db-init
│   │   └── wiki.sql
│   └── Dockerfile
└── wiki
    ├── Dockerfile
    ├── wiki-conf
    │   ├── confluence-init.properties
    │   ├── ROOT.xml
    │   └── server.xml
    ├── wiki-files
    │   └── current ...lots of files 19GB
    └── wiki-jar
        ├── apache-tomcat-6.0.35.tar.gz
        └── atlassian-confluence-5.4.3-deployment.tar.gz
```

Now, we head back to our Dockerfile located in the `wiki` folder. As shown previously, our assets from the production wiki have been copied into the directory structure and shown in bold. We now use the following wiki's Dockerfile to add these JAR files and configuration files to our wiki image. Then, also shown in the following wiki Dockerfile, we set the required environment variables for Tomcat (Catalina) and Java to run correctly. Finally, we add the Tomcat JAR and configuration files to find out the target locations (where Tomcat expects to find config and application files). At the end of the file, we set the container's default start to the `catalina.sh run` command, as follows:

```
# /wiki-app/wiki/Dockerfile - install confluence and Tomcat
FROM java:7-jdk

ADD ./wiki-jar/atlassian-confluence-5.4.3-deployment.tar.gz
/opt/j2ee/domains/mydomain.com/wiki/webapps/atlassian-
confluence/deployment/

COPY ./wiki-conf/confluence-init.properties
/opt/j2ee/domains/mydoamin.com/wiki/webapps/atlassian-
confluence/deployment/exploded_war/WEB-INF/classes/confluence-
init.properties

ENV CATALINA_HOME /usr/local/tomcat
ENV PATH $CATALINA_HOME/bin:$PATH
ENV JAVA_OPTS -Xms1536m -Xmx1536m -Dinstance.id=wiki.nvisia.com -
Djava.awt.headless=true -XX:MaxPermSize=384m

ADD ./wiki-jar/apache-tomcat-6.0.35.tar.gz /usr/local/
RUN mv /usr/local/apache-tomcat-6.0.35 /usr/local/tomcat
COPY ./wiki-conf/ROOT.xml /usr/local/tomcat/conf/Catalina/localhost/
COPY ./wiki-conf/server.xml /usr/local/tomcat/conf/
CMD catalina.sh run
```

Then we update `docker-compose-dev.yml` follow to mount our wiki-files (data files copied from the production wiki when we collected application assets) and we also expose our wiki's web UI port, as follows:

```
# /wiki-app/docker-compose-dev.yml
version: '3.7'
services:
  wiki:
    build: wiki
    image: dtr.mydoamin.com/pilot/wiki:v1
    volumes:
      - ./wiki/wiki-
files/current:/opt/j2ee/domains/mydomain.com/wiki/webapps/atlassian-
confluence/data/current
    ports:
      - 8080:8080
    networks:
      - db_net

  postgres:
    build: postgres
    image: dtr.mydoamin.com/pilot/postgres:v1
    environment:
      - POSTGRES_PASSWORD=xxxxxxxxx
    networks:
      - db_net
    volumes:
      - pgdata:/var/lib/postgresql/data
      - ./postgres/db-init:/docker-entrypoint-initdb.d

networks:
  db_net:
volumes:
  pgdata:
```

Notice how we also renamed the image files to get them ready to store in our DTR located at `dtr.mydomain.com`.

Again, we run `docker-compose -f docker-compose-dev.yml up -d` to build and start our containers. Then we run a `-f docker-compose-dev.yml logs` command and notice something strange. The wiki is starting before the database. To address this startup race condition, we introduce some defensive programming logic into our wiki startup using `entrypoint.sh`.

Defensive programming is a good practice in the world of orchestrators and ephemeral containers. Since containers may come and go, we can't guarantee startup order and the associated dependencies. Therefore, if our container depends on another container, such as our `wiki` container depending on the Postgres container, you should consider adding some defensive code. This code should wait for the dependency to be met before starting. This way, if both containers are deployed at the same time, the wiki will wait for the database to be ready and then it will start.

The purpose of the entrypoint script is to make sure the Postgres database is running before we start our wiki application. In the `entrypoint.sh` file there are a couple of highlights—all of them in bold. The first one is the `nc` command for Netcat, which checks to see whether Postgres responds on port `5432`. Remember, the Postgres hostname is resolved by the Docker DNS using the service name provided in the `docker-compose` file. If Postgres responds successfully, the status will be zero, we echo postgres is reachable! to standard out, and then we break from our loop, where we echo the `starting tomcat catalina in 10 seconds...` message and then sleep for 10 seconds before starting Tomcat/Catalina, as follows:

```
#!/bin/bash
while :
do
    echo "Probing postgres:5432 ..."
    nc -z -w 1 postgres 5432 </dev/null
    result=$?
    if [[ $result -eq 0 ]]; then
        echo "postgres is reachable!"
        break
    fi
    sleep 5
done

echo "starting tomcat catalina in 10 seconds..."
sleep 10
catalina.sh run
```

In order to use the `nc` command, we need to install the `netcat` package. So, we had back to our wiki's Dockerfile and add the `netcat` package install at the top of the file, as follows:

```
# /wiki-app/wiki/Dockerfile - Added netcat to test postgres port from
enterypoint.sh script
FROM java:7-jdk

RUN apt update && apt install -y netcat
...
```

Now we rebuild using `docker-compose` with up `--build` to rebuild and start our application. The following is an excerpt of logs where we see `wiki_1` probing the database port several times before reporting Postgres is reachable. Then, after 10 seconds, the wiki starts successfully. We test the wiki by pointing our browser to port `8080` on the build machine to see whether the wiki is up and running:

```
...
Successfully built 6779fb8a1eef
Successfully tagged my-postgres:v1
Creating wiki-app_postgres_1 ... done
Creating wiki-app_wiki_1 ... done
Attaching to wiki-app_postgres_1, wiki-app_wiki_1
wiki_1   | Probing postgres:5432 ...
...
postgres_1 | LOG: database system is ready to accept connections
postgres_1 | LOG: autovacuum launcher started
wiki_1   | Probing postgres:5432 ...
postgres_1 | LOG: incomplete startup packet
wiki_1   | postgres is reachable!
wiki_1   | starting tomcat catalina in 10 seconds...
...
wiki_1   | Jan 06, 2019 7:15:45 PM org.apache.coyote.http11.Http11Protocol
start
wiki_1   | INFO: Starting Coyote HTTP/1.1 on http-8080
wiki_1   | Jan 06, 2019 7:15:45 PM org.apache.jk.common.ChannelSocket init
wiki_1   | INFO: JK: ajp13 listening on /0.0.0.0:8009
wiki_1   | Jan 06, 2019 7:15:45 PM org.apache.jk.server.JkMain start
wiki_1   | INFO: Jk running ID=0 time=0/24 config=null
wiki_1   | Jan 06, 2019 7:15:45 PM org.apache.catalina.startup.Catalina start
wiki_1   | INFO: Server startup in 178492 ms
```

We have now created, containerized, and tested the wiki and Postgres containers on a local build box. Now it is time to get the application ready to run in our Docker Enterprise cluster.

Pushing the images

Now that we have the images ready to go and are prepared for the pilot cluster deployment, we need to push the images to our DTR. In the last version of the `docker-compose-dev.yml` file, we retagged the images as `dtr.mydomain.com/pilot/wiki:v1` and `dtr.mydomain.com/pilot/postgres:v1`. Now we need to log in to the DTR and push our wiki and Postgres images. Since all of the pilot team has access to our trusted registry pilot repos, we may use any of the user's accounts. For the sake of example, we will use our Sally Software developer account to log in and push our images to the DTR, as follows:

```
ssoftware::ssCLI$ docker login dtr.mydomain.com -u ssoftware
Password:xxxxxxxx
WARNING! Your password will be stored unencrypted in
/home/ssoftware/.docker/config.json.
Configure a credential helper to remove this warning. See
https://docs.docker.com/engine/reference/commandline/login/#credentials-sto
re
Login Succeeded

ssoftware::ssCLI$ docker image push dtr.mydomain.com/pilot/wiki:v1
...
ssoftware::ssCLI$ docker image push dtr.mydomain.com/pilot/postgres:v1
```

Deploying the wiki to the pilot cluster

When moving from the local build machine to pilot Docker Enterprise cluster, we need to start thinking about pilot deployment concerns, such as the following:

- How are pilot users using the application—as a sandbox or a limited production system?
- How are users going to access the application (**DNS | Wiki Service Ingress**)?
- How are we going to secure the connection between the user and the wiki?
- How are we going initialize, refresh, and backup the database?
- Who is going to deploy the application and how will they do it?

Pilot application strategy

As we start to design our pilot application's deployment architecture, we need to understand how are pilot users going to use the application. For example, will the pilot application just be a sandbox for users to play with, separate from the production system? This would be a conservative sandboxed approach where the pilot application runs in parallel with the production system, allowing users to poke around in a sandbox-type setting and where the pilot data is refreshed to match production every night. While the sandbox pilot approach is safer, it is also less engaging for users since the users, work in the pilot system is reset back to production each night. Additionally, the sandbox pilot does not force the sort of full dress rehearsal for application support as running a live pilot application with real (albeit internal) users and data does.

Depending on the goals and application chosen for your pilot, you will need to decide which approach is best for you. However, if your application can be scoped to internal users, you might want to consider an approach that covers both a sandbox and live pilot strategy, where you start with the sandbox approach to verify the application's basic function when running on the Docker Enterprise platform and then migrate the internal users to the live pilot platform, but always having a path back to the production environment as a plan B in the event of pilot failure. In either case, you will want to consult users to explain the trade-offs of duplicate work for the sandbox pilot versus the risk of losing working data/time if reverting a live pilot back to the production system becomes necessary.

For our wiki pilot example, we are going to start with a sandbox, but then migrate to a live pilot, using the old private cloud installation as a backup in case we need to revert. Our first stage is to deploy the application as a sandbox and provide limited access to test team for verification. Then, after verification, we will refresh the pilot application data from production and redirect the internal users to the live pilot application.

Application flow for wiki pilot

Regardless of your pilot strategy, you will need to figure out how targeted user's traffic will reach the pilot application in your Docker Enterprise cluster. For our sample application sandbox phase, we are going to modify the tester's local host file to point to our test load balancer (testing user in the offices) or firewall app IP (for testing outside of the office), and thus the pilot behaves just like the production wiki. However, to avoid confusion, we are going to make sure the header for the pilot wiki is clearly different from production to remind users which environment they are connected to.

When we move to the live pilot phase, we will update DNS for the pilot application to redirect all (in our case, internal) users to the pilot, where we will carefully monitor the running application—this is covered in Chapter 7, *Pilot Docker Enterprise Platform Monitoring and Logging*.

Deployment architecture for the pilot wiki

For the pilot wiki, we are going to keep our deployment relatively simple to keep the pilot moving and to demonstrate some common Docker Enterprise implementation options. In this section, we begin to transform our docker-compose-dev.yml file into a Docker stack specification used to deploy the application to our cluster, but we start with an overview of the cluster's traffic ingress flow.

In *Figure 8* , we see how traffic flows from the outside world to our wiki application running on worker node 3; from **External DNS** to **Firewall**, from the **Firewall** NAT to the **LB Node**, and finally to worker node 3:

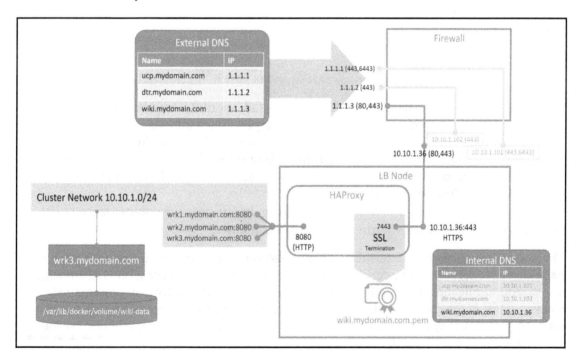

Figure 8: Wiki Network Traffic Flow

First of all, why worker node 3, and why not just let Docker Swarm place the wiki workload on any of the workers? The answer is **data**! As described back in *Figure 7*, both the wiki application and the Postgres database will require external volumes. We need these volumes to store the state of the application outside the container. Therefore, we can easily back up and restore the data as well as we restart our containers and have them resume their last known state.

In order to use volumes in a cluster, we either have to use some sort of cluster filesystem backing such as NFS across all of the worker nodes, or constrain our wiki and Postgres services to a specific worker node (in our case, we chose worker 3), so the containers consistently run on the node where the local host volume is mounted. This is the node where we will back up and refresh production data during the pilot. To constrain the node placement of our services in the cluster, we apply a label to worker node 3 using the `docker node update --label-add com.mydomain.wiki.stage=pilot wrk3.mydomain.com` command. Once the node is labeled, we can specify deployment constraint in our Swarm version of `docker-compose file.yml` in the wiki service section of the file, as follows:

```
deploy:
  placement:
    constraints:
      - node.labels.com.mydomain.wiki.stage==pilot
```

Next in *Figure 8*, working from the inside out, let's talk about the load balancer node running HAProxy in a container. Here we have mapped the load balancer network interface for `10. 10. 1. 36` port `443` report `7443` inside of our HAProxy container. Additionally, we're using HAProxy to terminate our inbound SSL (TLS) connection on `7443` using a third-party certificate for `wiki.mydomain.com`. This is a simple HAProxy configuration: we just need to have the `.pem` file in the `/usr/local/etc/haproxy/certs/` directory. In our case, we volume-mount our certificated directory when we run the HAProxy container.

There are three different TLS termination models you may consider during your pilot. We have chosen to terminate our certificate at the upstream load balancer with HAProxy for our sample application and use HTTP/layer 4 routing into the Swarm, but you may also terminate inside the container at the application server or using a layer 7 ingress controller for both reverse proxy and TLS termination. In the pipeline chapter, we will discuss the layer 7 ingress option in more detail.

Terminating inside the container is generally not preferred as it may be difficult to rotate the certificates as they expire in the future. If termination in the container is chosen, do consider using secrets to store the certificates externally in the Swarm for both security and manageability. For more information, please see `https://docs.docker.com/engine/swarm/secrets/`.

The following code block shows how we terminate our TLS certificates at the load balancer:

```
frontend wiki_80_7443
        mode http
        option tcplog
        bind *:80
        bind *:7443 ssl crt
/usr/local/etc/haproxy/certs/wiki.mydomain.com.pem
        redirect scheme https if !{ ssl_fc }
        default_backend wiki_upstream_servers_7443
```

Deploying the pilot wiki application

For the pilot wiki, our team is working with our fictitious operations manager, Otto OpsManager, to deploy the wiki application to our Docker Enterprise pilot platform. Since the load balancer box is upstream of the cluster, Otto asks a system admin to configure and run his HAProxy container.

The sample HAProxy config `frontend` section looks as follows:

```
global
    maxconn 2048
    log /dev/log local0 debug
    log /dev/log local1 notice

defaults
        mode tcp
        option dontlognull
        timeout connect 5s
        timeout client 50s
        timeout server 50s
        timeout tunnel 1h
        timeout client-fin 50s

frontend ucp_443
        mode tcp
        bind *:443
        option tcplog
        log /dev/log local0 debug
        default_backend ucp_upstream_servers_443
```

```
frontend dtr_4443
        mode tcp
        bind *:4443
        option tcplog
        log /dev/log local0 debug
        default_backend dtr_upstream_servers_4443

frontend kube_6443
        mode tcp
        bind *:6443
        option tcplog
        log /dev/log local0 debug
        default_backend kubectl_upstream_servers_6443

frontend wiki_80_7443
        mode http
        option tcplog
        log global
        bind *:80
        bind *:7443 ssl crt
/usr/local/etc/haproxy/certs/wiki.mydomain.com.pem
        redirect scheme https if !{ ssl_fc }
        default_backend wiki_upstream_servers_7443
```

The sample HAProxy config `backend` section looks as follows:

```
## Backend
backend ucp_upstream_servers_443
        mode tcp
        balance roundrobin
        option log-health-checks
        option httpchk GET /_ping HTTP/1.1\r\nHost:\ ucp.mydimain.com
        server UCPNode01 ucp-1:443 check check-ssl verify none
        server UCPNode02 ucp-2:443 check check-ssl verify none
        server UCPNode03 ucp-3:443 check check-ssl verify none

backend dtr_upstream_servers_4443
        mode tcp
        balance roundrobin
        option log-health-checks
        option httpchk GET /_ping HTTP/1.1\r\nHost:\ dtr.mydomain.com
        server DTRNode01 dtr-1:4443 check check-ssl verify none
        server DTRNode02 dtr-2:4443 check check-ssl verify none
        server DTRNode03 dtr-3:4443 check check-ssl verify none

backend kubectl_upstream_servers_6443
        mode tcp
```

```
        balance roundrobin
        option log-health-checks
        server KubeNode01 ucp-1:6443 check check-ssl verify none
        server KubeNode02 ucp-2:6443 check check-ssl verify none
        server KubeNode03 ucp-3:6443 check check-ssl verify none

backend wiki_upstream_servers_7443
        mode http
        balance roundrobin
        # server wikiServer1 wrk-1:8080
        # server wikiServer2 wrk-2:8080
        server wikiServer3 wrk-3:8080
        http-request set-header X-Forwarded-Port %[dst_port]
        http-request add-header X-Forwarded-Proto https if { ssl_fc }
```

Then, using a SSH terminal shell connected to the load balancer, Otto launches the
HAProxy container startup script as follows:

```
#!/bin/sh
docker run -d --name haproxy -p 10.10.1.36:80:80 -p 10.10.1.36:443:7443 -p
10.10.1.101:443:443 -p 10.10.1.101:6443:6443 -p 10.10.1.102:443:4443 -v
~/haproxy:/usr/local/etc/haproxy:ro haproxy:1.7
```

In addition to the load balancer setup, we also need to get the wiki files and database
initialization script into the local Docker volume mount points on worker 3. Normally, I
recommend designing your file permission scheme with the utmost care. For our sample,
the original implementation of the Postgres database used an alternative owner. I wanted to
make sure that the Postgres and Atlassian wiki container processes could access all of their
files for read, write, and execute:

```
sysadmin@worker-node-3$ sudo -s
root@worker-node-3$ mkdir -p /var/local/wiki-init-data
root@worker-node-3$ mkdir -p /var/local/wiki-db-data
root@worker-node-3$ mkdir -p /var/local/atlassian-data
root@worker-node-3$ chmod 777 /var/local/wiki-init-data
root@worker-node-3$ chmod 777 /var/local/wiki-db-data
root@worker-node-3$ chmod 777 /var/local/atlassian-data
root@worker-node-3$ tar -C ./atlassian-data -xzf
./someZipSourceDir/atlassian-data.tar.gz
root@worker-node-3$ cp ./someSQLsourceDir/wiki.sql /var/local/wiki-init-
data/wiki.sql
root@worker-node-3$ tree L2 /var/local/
├── atlassian-data
│   └── current ...
├── wiki-db-data
├── wiki-init-data
│   └── wiki.sql
```

```
root@worker-node-3$ exit
sysadmin@worker-node-3$
```

Now Otto logs into the pilot UCP web UI and generates a command-line bundle, as shown in *Figure 9*:

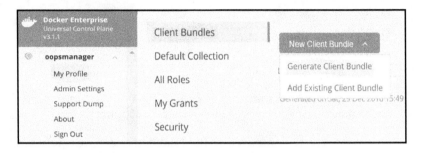

Figure 9: Create Client Bundle from UCP Web UI

Otto unzips the bundle into his `opsCLI` folder. Otto opens a Bash shell in the `opsCLI` folder and connects using `source env.sh` to the cluster with his OpsManager permissions. He verifies his connection using a `docker node ls` command as shown in the following code:

```
otto::opsCLI$ source env.sh
Cluster "ucp_ucp.mydomain.com:6443_oopsmanager" set.
User "ucp_ucp.mydomain.com:6443_oopsmanager" set.
Context "ucp_ucp.mydomain.com:6443_oopsmanager" modified.
otto::opsCLI$ docker node ls
ID                          HOSTNAME             STATUS AVAILABILITY MANAGER
STATUS   ENGINE VERSION
1rqhb4rzj3gk4mdgk8kza53jp   dtr-1.mydomain.com Ready   Active
18.09.0
x27m3yjlh6b0wczmo0mcahkjv   dtr-2.mydomain.com Ready   Active
18.09.0
rw2tuw53wl34pv6sfj213845a   dtr-3.mydomain.com Ready   Active
18.09.0
q5q9u0yr7p8r0mcz4ob24s2kz*  ucp-1.mydomain.com Ready   Active        Reachable
18.09.0
6ce10w7leu0a9my91w39j5eai   ucp-2.mydomain.com Ready   Active        Reachable
18.09.0
bd1bwcbqkpbulhwvm0f11gm55   upc-3.mydomain.com Ready   Active        Leader
18.09.0
31w64q2o818xgnberjry410o7   wrk-1.mydomain.com Ready   Active
18.09.0
zxcosutrxr3rhzkz2h61d0khj   wrk-2.mydomain.com Ready   Active
18.09.0
sfuxfiwhf2tpd6q3i7fbmaziv   wrk-3.mydomain.com Ready   Active
```

```
18.09.0
```

Otto crafts the following `docker-compose.yml`:

```
version: '3.7'

services:
  wiki:
    image: dtr.mydomain.com/pilot/wiki:v1
    volumes:
      - /var/local/atlassian-
data:/opt/j2ee/domains/mydomain.com/wiki/webapps/atlassian-confluence/data/
    ports:
      - 8080:8080
    networks:
      - wiki_net
    deploy:
      placement:
        constraints:
          - node.labels.com.mydomain.wiki.stage==pilot
  postgres:
    image: dtr.mydomain.com/pilot/postgress:v1
    environment:
      - POSTGRES_PASSWORD=xxxxxxxx
    volumes:
      - /var/local/wiki-db-data:/var/lib/postgresql/data
      - /var/local/wiki-init-data:/docker-entrypoint-initdb.d
    networks:
      - wiki_net
    deploy:
      placement:
        constraints:
          - node.labels.com.mydomain.wiki.stage==pilot
networks:
  wiki_net:
```

Otto runs and deploys the application from his command-line bundle using `docker stack deploy -c docker-compose.yml mydomain-wiki` from the directory where he stored `docker-compose.yml` file. Otto verifies the stack is deployed as follows:

```
opsCLI$ docker service ls
ID              NAME                     MODE       REPLICAS IMAGE
PORTS
2v9s2aikk80g mydomain-wiki_postgres replicated 1/1
dtr.mydomain.com/pilot/postgress:v1
3q1cxwa1mw0a mydomain-wiki_wiki       replicated 1/1
dtr.mydomain.com/pilot/wiki:v1         *:8080->8080/tcp
```

Finally, Otto sets his local host file to resolve `wiki.mydomain.com` to the `10.10.1.36` load balancer, as he is running from inside the network. Then he points his browser to `https://10.10.1.36` and begins testing the wiki.

Summary

In this chapter, we discussed the planning and implementation of your pilot application. We presented some sample roles and responsibilities for the pilot team members, as well as the configuration for UCP and DTR during a pilot. Additionally, we walked through the deployment of our sample lift-and-shift wiki application in great detail, following the journey of a sample pilot team.

In `Chapter 6`, *Design and Pilot a Docker Enterprise CI Pipeline*, we pick up on a parallel pilot journey for an organization working through a custom application development pilot.

Questions

1. What are the responsibilities of the pilot coordinator?
2. Do I have to use the UCP web UI to configure all of the UCP settings?
3. How much refactoring should I do during a pilot?
4. Can my pilot include TLS certificates?
5. Where will my application data be stored during the pilot?

Further reading

- **Managing Docker Enterprise role-based authorization:**
  - `https://docs.docker.com/ee/ucp/authorization/create-users-and-teams-manually/#authentication`
- **Setting up UCP configuration without a web interface:**
  - `https://docs.docker.com/ee/ucp/admin/configure/ucp-configuration-file/#the-ucp-configuration-file`

- **Securing a Docker Enterprise**:
  - `https://success.docker.com/article/security-best-practices`

- **Setting up and syncing Docker Enterprise teams with LDAP groups**:
  - `https://docs.docker.com/ee/ucp/authorization/create-teams-with-ldap/`

- **DTR troubleshooting**:
  - `https://docs.docker.com/ee/dtr/admin/monitor-and-troubleshoot/troubleshoot-dtr/`

6
Design and Pilot a Docker Enterprise CI Pipeline

In Chapter 8, *First Application in Production with Docker Enterprise*, we looked at piloting with a lift and shift approach with our pilot team, where we focused a good deal of attention on configuring the Docker Enterprise pilot platform for the containerized deployment to host a Java based wiki application with a PostgreSQL database. In this chapter, we will dive into building a custom, Java pilot application and supporting it with a **Continuous Integration (CI)** pipeline.

Before we configure any sort of CI solution, we need to start at the beginning with a container-optimized application design, ready to utilize an orchestrator, such as Kubernetes or Swarm's service discovery, volume management, networking, and secrets. Then, we will create a containerized local development and testing environment for our custom pilot Java application as a starting point and from there, we will make our journey through a containerized, continuous integration pipeline using our Docker Enterprise pilot cluster.

In this chapter, we will discuss the following topics:

- Key principles for distributed application development with containers
- Process for local container-based software development, build, and testing
- Sample pilot application development, build, and testing
- Designing a containerized CI pipeline with Docker Enterprise
- Implementing a CI pipeline for our sample customer Java application

Pilot application development with Docker Enterprise

For developers, containers are often introduced as a local testing tool, creating third party application components locally, rather than configuring a shared test platform. Docker is great for local testing, but there are other benefits for developers, including faster developer on-boarding, leveraging the immutable server pattern (eliminating the *"works on my machine"* situation), full stack local testing, and fast/efficient cluster-based integration testing.

Using Docker for faster developer on-boarding

Docker supports faster developer on-boarding; developers only need to install Docker and everything else can run in (isolated) containers. While some developers may still install an IDE and local JDK for testing and debugging their Java code, any developer can clone a source code repository, build the application, and run it locally in minutes with only Docker installed. This is a huge improvement for defect remediation in a large team environment where a random team member may be assigned to fix a bug.

Using Docker to improve software development cycles

Imagine a scenario where a bug has been reported in a production system and is assigned to the next available developer. The developer reviews the bug report, clones the source code repository for the production version of the application, builds the application locally, and begins testing on their development workstation. Notice that they didn't have to install any special development tools locally, or adjust the version of tools already installed; they just needed Docker running on their workstation. Now, they identify the bug, modify the source code, and rebuild and retest the application locally. This remediation cycle, even for a developer who is new to the team, can take less than 10 minutes in a Dockerized development environment.

Now, the developer can confidently check in their changes and author a pull request. In contrast, if a developer needs to configure their local environment with the correct version of all the tools required for the current production version, it could take days, with no guarantee of it matching production. For most informed development teams, it becomes clear that incorporating Docker into a software development environment makes a lot of sense.

Docker Containers as a Service (CaaS)

Now, let's think for a moment about a team starting a new development project. Normally, you would do some research and begin installing different components on your development workstation. From there, you would begin to tweak those components to get them to work together. Then, once you have them working, you probably want to have some sort of architectural review done by a senior developer for approval. Once you have the green light, now you have to try to recreate the installation instructions for the rest of your team and hope they get the same version you have running on your machine. This can be sort of a hassle, especially when you consider every team doing it on their own. Now, let's think about that same development team in a Docker Enterprise environment.

In a Docker world, the team can view the **Docker Trusted Registry(DTR)** for the correct base image. Hopefully, the system administrators have created an application base container for the team to start with. If not, the team can work with system administrators to locate a candidate base image from Docker's public image repository, Docker Hub. Docker Hub literally has tens of thousands of application platforms already configured for developers to use. When a suitable candidate image is identified, the team can work with the system administrator to add the new base image to the enterprise catalog for teams to use. This approach is sometimes referred to as **Containers as a Service (CaaS)**, and it improves security, efficiency, and time to market.

Because these images are scanned by the system administrators before teams use them, critical vulnerabilities will have been addressed before most teams begin development. Once the team has a base image, they just need to focus on building and testing their components using the base image. Because these images are shared across multiple teams, you will likely have a high number of cache hits when deploying Dockerized applications onto test and production clusters. Finally, the base images have been pre-approved by the system administrative team, so there will be less resistance to putting them in production quickly. This can be a big advantage in a microservices environment where teams often introduce fresh platforms with every release.

In the following diagram, we can see a sample base image hierarchy from an article on `https://success.docker.com/article/mta-best-practices#imagehierarchy`. This example starts off with two root images, one for Linux containers and one for Windows containers. Following the example for Linux, it uses a CentOS 7.2 Linux distribution. From the CentOS root image, three different application images are derived for an Apache application, a Java application, and a PostgreSQL database server. Further more, we can see how the Java application has three different application server varieties, including one JBoss version and two Tomcat versions. On the right-hand side of the picture, the green shaded images are managed by the application teams, but based on one of the blue enterprise base images from the left as their base image.

The application teams add their code to create an application image. As a result, only the outer layers of the image will vary for each application while the rest are common for all teams using a common base image:

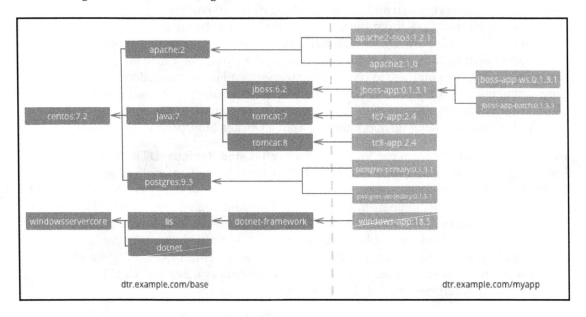

Figure 1: Sample Image Hierarchy-Copyright © 2013-2018 Docker, Inc. All rights reserved.

Again, since Docker uses a layered filesystem to run containers, it is advantageous to share base images. Essentially, the **tc7-app** and **tc8-app** application images share two common base layers: CentOS and Java, meaning that when these application images are pulled down from a central repository, those layers are likely to already be resident on the Docker node, and therefore, can skipped for efficiency.

The final point regarding the use of Docker for software development is to address the age-old, *"it works on my machine"* syndromes. The problem occurs when a developer's platform is different than a test platform because, during the process of development, the developer either upgraded one of their local components, or installed a new local component. Now, their local machine is different from the test environment. In this situation, the software developer pushes the code to the source code control system where it is then deployed to a test platform. Because of the missing or changed component, the test fails, and when the developer is asked about the failure, the developer will show the tester how the application runs correctly on their local machine. Docker's inherent ability to package the application, and all of the required component dependencies, essentially, eliminates this problem.

What you need to know about distributed applications

Traditionally, most application developers are accustomed to developing monolithic applications, or using a monolithic application deployment model, where several applications share the same platform components, such as IIS and .NET, or Java and Tomcat. Containers give developers the opportunity to break their applications into smaller, independently deployable units. For that reason, Docker has become an essential tool for microservice development teams. Breaking applications into smaller components has a lot of advantages, but at the same time, it introduces some additional complexity.

These advantages include being able to efficiently divide application development of the discrete application components across a large development team, where developers can work more independently. Also, these smaller components provide opportunities for horizontal scaling with better performance and availability in a clustered environment. Conversely, some complexities arise from wiring up all of these independent components at runtime. Therefore, we will discuss some key topics from distributed application development principles as they pertain directly to containers.

Key principles for container application design

Before we build our application, there are a few things we need to understand so that we can build an orchestrated container solution. For the sake of simplicity, we will provide details and examples using Docker in this chapter. Later in this book, in Chapter 10, *More on Kubernetes with Docker Enterprise*, we will come back and look at using Kubernetes to accomplish the same tasks with the Kubernetes constructs and APIs.

Docker Swarm services

Both Swarm and Kubernetes rely on the concept of services as a key orchestration element, and a durable endpoint for the collection of like containers. By like containers, we mean they share the exact same image for all container instances. For example, if a container running in your cluster needs to call an API running in another container, the caller can use the API container's service name, rather than using a container IP. This is really important because, in an orchestrated environment, containers can be replaced by the orchestrator at any time, and the resulting container will have a new IP. Therefore, using the service name assures the caller a connection to a running version of the container, which they need.

The following diagram demonstrates how a calling container accesses a container using a service endpoint. In this case, the caller makes a remote call using the API's service name. The service name resolves through the orchestrator's DNS service to a VIP for the API service. The call's VIP resolves through round robin load balancing to either Container 1, 2, or 3. Docker service endpoints can also be of type **DNS round robin (DNSRR)** instead of VIP:

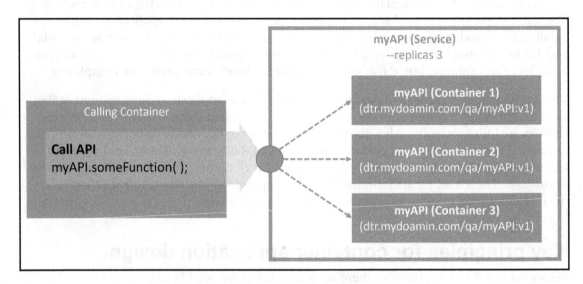

Figure 2: Service Endpoint for myAPI

The DNSRR name is a little confusing since it is really its counterpart, the **Virtual IP (VIP)** service endpoint, that automatically round robin load balances requests, whereas DNSRR leaves any load balancing up to the client. With DNSRR, the calling client receives a list of IPs for the underlying service's containers, and then may manually load balance using something like the last response time for each container to choose the fastest container's IP, or passing traffic to the IP with the least connections. Presumably, DNSRR is designed to integrate with upfront load balancers that expect multiple IPs from their DNS lookup. While there are certainly cases for DNSRR, it is considered a better practice to, instead, design your containers to be as stateless as possible and to use VIP.

There are some significant benefits when using VIP for stateless services with multiple replicas. First of all, the replicas can be scaled up or down (horizontal scaling) to meet load demands. Also, if a container fails, the orchestrator can remove the bad container and replace it with a new one. In either case, using the service name instead of a container IP protects you from referencing dead containers. It should be noted that, when the orchestrator detects a failed container, it removes it from the load balancer's backend pool. Also, when a new container starts, it is added to the load balancer's backend pool, only after it is determined to be running and healthy. We will talk about health checks a little later.

With Docker Swarm, the service is a first class citizen in the Docker API. Therefore, you may easily create a service using a command, as shown in the following diagram. Please note that the following command needs to be run from a Docker manager node, or using a Docker Enterprise command like bundle corresponding to a user with the correct privilege:

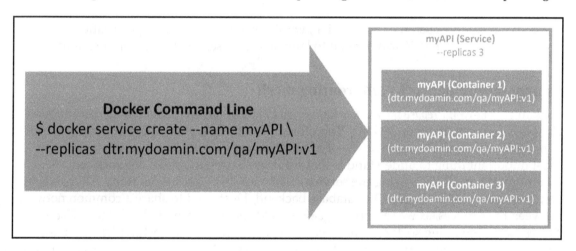

Figure 3: Create Docker Service from Command Line

Also, as a first step, we will list services by using `docker service ls`, as shown in the following code snippet:

```
admin@docker-CLI$ docker service ls
ID              NAME    MODE        REPLICAS     IMAGE
m10ynu62iv02    myAPI   replicated  3/3
dtr.mydoamin.com/qa/myAPI:v1
```

Here, we can see the unique ID of the service, the name of the service, and the three replicas running, as well as the image the service is running for each container.

If we want additional information from the Swarm orchestrator regarding the placement of our containers and their current state, we can use the `docker service ps` command, as shown in the following code snippet. Since my tests are from a single node Swarm cluster (my development laptop), all of the node names are the same—`linuxkit-00155d16dc03`:

```
admin@docker-CLI$ docker service ps myAPI

ID              NAME            IMAGE                           NODE
DESIRED         CURRENT
STATE           STATE
5qs15ifju352    myStack_myAPI.1 dtr.mydoamin.com/qa/myAPI:v1
linuxkit-00155d16dc03 Running       Running
p64jp0asuzes    myStack_myAPI.2 dtr.mydoamin.com/qa/myAPI:v1
linuxkit-00155d16dc03 Running       Running
xuber5oqgtkq    myStack_myAPI.3 dtr.mydoamin.com/qa/myAPI:v1
linuxkit-00155d16dc03 Running       Running
```

Later, in our sample customer application, we show the services API specification via a `docker-compose` file in YAML format to launch, compose, and Swarm applications.

Swarm service networks and routing mesh

Back in `Chapter 4`, *Prepare the Docker Enterprise Pilot Cluster*, we provided an introduction to cluster-based container networking. Therefore, we will not repeat it here and we will briefly summarize the most important areas of application networking in a Swarm cluster. The most important thing to understand is that services sharing the same network can communicate on all ports using the service's name for DNS resolution. If my API needs to communicate with a PostgreSQL database backend, I just need to share a common network between the services, as we saw in `Chapter 8`, *First Application in Production with Docker Enterprise*. When doing so, there's no need to expose ports for the PostgreSQL database since the common network will give the caller access to all ports. Please note, unless ports are explicitly exposed with some form of -P/-p, the service will only be available to other services via a shared network, and will not be not exposed externally.

When we are dealing with Docker Swarm and we publish a port for external access, we end up with IPVS mapping a port on the Swarm ingress network (the ingress network is set up by Docker when the cluster is initialized, then connected to cluster nodes as they join the cluster) that spans all nodes in the cluster. This means that, if I expose port 8000 of a service running in a Swarm cluster using -p 8000:80, a request to any node in the cluster on port 8000 will be forwarded to port 80 inside one of the running containers behind this Swarm service. If the service has multiple replicas, by default, the request will be load balanced between each of the backing container replicas:

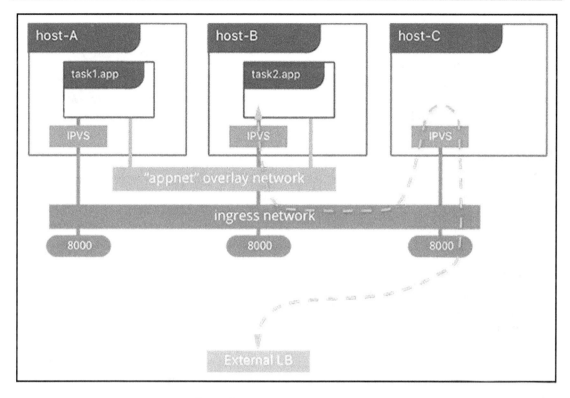

Figure 4: Copyright © 2013-2018 Docker, Inc. All rights - Ingress Networking

 It's important to note that Docker service networking (by default, Docker Overlay networks are backed by VXLAN) and Docker routing mesh are available as a part of the Community Edition Swarm implementation. These features do not require Docker Enterprise, but they're commonly used in both CE and EE settings.

So, for internal networking between components of your application, add them to a common network. For external access to services, you must publish a port (-p) for the service and it will be added to the ingress network—referred to as the Swarm routing mesh, where a cluster-unique port number is routed to service VIP for load balancing.

When using Docker Swarm routing mesh, keep the service's published ports unique across all services in the cluster. This can be a little confusing to developers who are moving from containers to services because we can reuse the same port number across as many containers as we want, since each container has a unique IP address. However, for the service mesh, the port number is registered with every node's adapter in the cluster, and therefore, non-unique port numbers will cause a port conflict on the nodes adapter.

Docker Enterprise layer 7 routing

Imagine that a developer is attending their morning stand-up meeting, and the product owner asks for a new feature. Developer goes back to their desk and implements the feature as they understand it. They can then use Docker Enterprise layer 7 routing, deploy their feature branch to the cluster, and send a URL to the product owner to review. This feature branch is completely isolated from all other stacks running in the cluster, and it's immediately available with either a unique host name in the request header for the future branch, or a special path for the feature branch.

Docker Enterprise provides a layer 7 routing infrastructure using a reverse proxy configuration (backed by either HAProxy or NGINX) with Interlock 2, or simply layer 7 routing. This technology is really efficient for managing cluster base deployments, particularly in non-production clusters, because a new application stack can be deployed and made accessible to users without any upstream DNS or load balance reconfiguration.

When enabled, Docker Enterprise's **Universal Control Plane (UCP)** will create a `ucp-interlock` overlay network, and attach the `ucp-interlock` and `ucp-intelock-extension` services to the network. The `ucp-interlock` service monitors Docker system events and looks for services with deployment labels using the prefix of `com.docker.lb`. When an event is published with a matching label, `ucp-interlock` calls `ucp-interlock-extension` to configure the `ucp-interlock-proxy` as a reverse proxy to route traffic based in the inbound user's request header and/or path to corresponding Swarm service's VIP.

Later on in this chapter, you will see a working example where our AtSea application uses Docker Enterprise layer 7 routing. Later we will demonstrate the use of service labels to figure a layer 7 reverse proxy using the NGINX extension. There are simple and production configuration for the Interlock 2 deployment. In this chapter, for the pilot, you will use simple implementation. Later in our getting ready for production chapter, we will reconfigure Interlock 2 for high availability production mode.

 For more information on the configuration of Interlock, see `https://docs.docker.com/ee/ucp/interlock/architecture/`.

There is a great reference architecture article by Anoop Kumar on this topic: `https://success.docker.com/article/ucp-service-discovery`. In the article, Anoop describes how a Docker Enterprise layer 7 routing is enabled and configured by an administrator.

We will revisit this topic and further discuss the highly available proxy configuration later in this book when we get our application ready for production.

Defensive coding

Services are great for providing a durable and reliable employee. However, when an application is deployed by an orchestrator, services will come online quickly, but not simultaneously. Therefore, we can run into some timing issues when a caller is online before its dependent services.

We saw an example of this situation in the last chapter when our wiki application started before the Postgres database was ready. As a result, we created an entry point script to start the wiki application. The entry point script polls the Postgres database port until it was ready. When the database is ready, the entrypoint script starts the wiki's Tomcat server in the foreground using the `catalina.sh run` command.

Here is the `entrypoint.sh` we used to wait for the Postgres DB to start:

```
#!/bin/bash
while :
do
    echo "Probing postgres:5432 ..."
    nc -z -w 1 postgres 5432 </dev/null
    result=$?
    if [[ $result -eq 0 ]]; then
        echo "postgres is reachable!"
        break
    fi
    sleep 5
done

echo "starting tomcat catalina in 10 seconds..."
sleep 10
catalina.sh run
```

Subsequently, we had to update the wiki's Dockerfile to launch the `entrypoint.sh` script instead of the Java command directly. We did so by adding the following commands at the end of the Dockerfile:

```
COPY entrypoint.sh /usr/local/tomcat/
CMD ./usr/local/tomcat/entrypoint.sh
```

Beyond start off, there's another important aspect of defensive coding, and that is making sure that your application calls are resilient to failure.

In a monolithic application, if a method call fails, that usually means something is seriously wrong with the application since the caller and the method being called are running in the same process space. When this sort of failure occurs, it would be typical to throw an exception, dump a stack trace, and exit the application. In a distributed application environment, these failures are pretty common and are often related to transient timing issues where downstream containers are starting up or being replaced by the orchestrator. So, for robust, distributed applications, we don't want the calling application to crash. Instead, we want the caller to back off and retry again, where we increase the back off time between attempts as the number of failed attempts increases in an effort not to overwhelm the failed service. Doing so can lead to your own, albeit unintentional, denial of service attack.

Since this is not a programming book per se, we will not go into great detail with these examples, but adopters of Docker Enterprise who are building distributed applications need to know about these concepts, and research their implementation options. Most programming environments have some built-in features or extensions to assist developers with retry logic in a clean way. If you are using JavaScript, you might want to look at promise exceptions, and if you are using Java, you might want to look at Spring Retry. Links for these are included in the *Further reading* section at the end of this chapter.

It is important to know that there are comprehensive frameworks and evolving technology devoted to managing remote system calls in very sophisticated ways, and usually, doing so by implementing a circuit breaker pattern. One popular framework for this is Netflix's Hystrix. Hystrix provides a proxy to wrap your remote call. The proxy is instrumented with response time data associated with the target remote API. If the remote API response times are exceeding preset parameters, the proxy will trap the call and return a failure immediately. This is called an open circuit and may close of the API recovers.

Finally, the most sophisticated and comprehensive approach built to support large scale microservices running in Kubernetes clusters is Istio from Google. Istio runs as a service in a Kube cluster, enabled with sidecar containers adjacent to your application service pods, to create a highly engineered service mesh. Istio is still in the early stages and is overkill for most container adopters, but is likely to influence how future Google-scale applications are designed and deployed with Kubernetes.

Centralized logging

In `Chapter 10`, *More on Kubernetes with Docker Enterprise*, we will talk more about monitoring, logging, and alerting in a Docker Enterprise environment. However, in this chapter, we do need to discuss the application side of logging in a Docker environment. Traditionally, most applications use some sort of framework to log to a local filesystem. This is great when you know exactly where your application is running and when its dependent components are co-located on the same server. If there is a problem, you just need to review the logs on the host server to figure out what happened. Distributed, cluster-based applications are different.

In a distributed environment, particularly when an orchestrator is distributing workloads across the cluster, we look toward a centralized logging design. This means that applications no longer log to a local file. Rather, these containerized applications should write their logging information to standard error and standard output, and allow the Docker Engine to capture the logged messages. That said, as you might imagine, a consistent logging message structure across applications makes it much easier to filter logs and construct reasonable log queries without a PhD in regular expressions.

Secrets

The final concept for cluster base application development and deployment is secrets. Secrets provide a means of storing special private data elements in a cluster. They are created by a secret holder and stored in a encrypted format within the cluster. Later, the secret can be delivered to a target container (encrypted in transit) at a specified location (by default, `/run/secrets`) where it can be accessed in an unencrypted format inside the container. This is very useful for storing passwords, authorization tokens, private keys, and certificates.

Here is a simple example where, from a Swarm manager node, we create a secret called `my_secret_data`:

```
$ echo "secret-secret" | docker secret create my_secret_data -
```

Then, we create a service that uses `my_secret_data` in the default target location `/run/secrets/my_secret_data`:

```
docker service create --name redis --secret my_secret_data redis:alpine
```

To verify that the secret was delivered to the Redis container, we want to list the contents of `/run/secrets/my_secret_data`, but we need the ID of the container running behind the service. We can accomplish this by using `docker container ls` with a `--filter` flag to list our Redis container's info and the `-q` parameter to only return the container's ID. Finally, we nest the container ID filter expression inside of the `docker container exec` command:

```
$ docker container exec $(docker container ls --filter name=redis -q) cat
/run/secrets/my_secret_data

secret-secret
```

We can see the result of our `cat` command, showing the contents of `my_secret_data` that matches our secret.

Secretes are available to use in Docker Engine-Community Swarm and Kubernetes.

For more information on using Docker secrets, see the Docker documentation at `https://docs.docker.com/engine/swarm/secrets/`.

Later in this chapter, we will use certificates to store our SSL certificate and private key for the AtSea website when we deploy to our cluster.

Docker tools for the local development and testing of the AtSea application

For our example application, we are going to adapt AtSea, a well-known sample application from the `dockersamples` public GitHub repository at `https://github.com/dockersamples/atsea-sample-shop-app`. AtSea is a really interesting application because it demonstrates many popular and interesting features, as follows:

- Reactapplication frontend
- A RESTful API written with Java Spring Boot
- PostgreSQL backend Database
- A payment gateway support service
- A reverse-proxy service for TLS termination

AtSea application structure

As a first step, we clone `atsea-sample-shop-app` to our development workstation. With the source code on our local development machine, we will be able to build the application images locally. Please note the application structure in the following abbreviated file tree. Notice how each main folder has its own `Dockerfile` to build a separate Docker image for each component.

The main application components are in the `app` directory, and they include the `react-app` folder for the JS frontend and the `src` folder for the Java Spring Boot API. Please note the collocation of the JavaScript and Java applications in the same folder, reflecting a design decision to run them both in a single Tomcat web/app server instance, rather than separating them. You will see this more clearly when we look at the `app/Dockerfile`. The `app` folder has the Maven `pom.xml` file for the application as well a `Dockerfile` and `Dockerfile-dev`. The `Dockerfile-dev` is used to build a special version of the image, where the application is driven from a remote debugging session to test the API from an IDE like IntelliJ or Eclipse. The folder and file structure will be similar to the following structure:

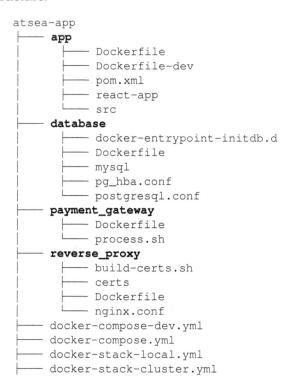

```
atsea-app
├── app
│       ├── Dockerfile
│       ├── Dockerfile-dev
│       ├── pom.xml
│       ├── react-app
│       └── src
├── database
│       ├── docker-entrypoint-initdb.d
│       ├── Dockerfile
│       ├── mysql
│       ├── pg_hba.conf
│       └── postgresql.conf
├── payment_gateway
│       ├── Dockerfile
│       └── process.sh
├── reverse_proxy
│       ├── build-certs.sh
│       ├── certs
│       ├── Dockerfile
│       └── nginx.conf
├── docker-compose-dev.yml
├── docker-compose.yml
├── docker-stack-local.yml
├── docker-stack-cluster.yml
```

The `database` folder holds the Postgres configuration and initialization files, as well as the `Dockerfile` that's used to build the Postgres database image, which we will discuss shortly. The `payment_gateway` folder holds the startup script for the payment gateway, as well as the `Dockerfile` that's used to build the `payment_gateway` image. The `reverse_proxy` folder is only used locally for testing. When we deploy the application to the Docker Enterprise cluster, we will use Docker Enterprise's Interlock 2 for layer 7 routing, as well as the proxy's SSL termination capability.

Finally, we have four different YAML files being used to build and deploy the application with the Docker API. These files are covered in the following sections.

Using docker-compose as a Makefile

We reviewed the application components, but now, we will look at how they are put together. To do this, we will look at the first of two `docker-compose` files, `docker-compose-dev.yml`, by viewing the contents of the following code block. Again, this is a special compose file that's used during the development process, hence the `-dev` filename suffix. At the highest level, the file lists the services making up the local debug version of application, that is, the `database` and `appserver` services. Notice that the `payment_gateway` and `reverse_proxy` services are missing from the file. This provides a bare minimum for local API debugging. There are two items to note about the `appserver` service definition. First, the alternate Dockerfile (`Dockerfile-dev`) is used to build the container as specified in the `build: dockerfile:` parameter. The second is exposing port `5005`, allowing the debugger to connect from host to the `appserver` container:

```
version: "3.7"

services:
  database:
    build:
        context: ./database
    image: atsea_db
    environment:
      POSTGRES_USER: gordonuser
      POSTGRES_DB: atsea
    ports:
      - "5432:5432"
    networks:
      - back-tier
    secrets:
      - postgres_password

  appserver:
```

```
build:
    context: ./app
    dockerfile: Dockerfile-dev
image: atsea_app
ports:
    - "8080:8080"
    - "5005:5005"
networks:
    - front-tier
    - back-tier
secrets:
    - postgres_password

secrets:
  postgres_password:
    file: ./devsecrets/postgres_password
networks:
  front-tier:
  back-tier:
```

In the following code block, we will take a quick look at the `docker-compose-dev.yml` files, reference, `Dockerfile-dev`, which is being used to build the debug version of the `appserver`. This file is a multi-stage build `Dockerfile` with three build stages. Remember, only the last stage remains after the build, and only a targeted subset of assets are copied from first two build stages. In this case, the contents of the `/usr/src/atsea/app/react-app/build/` directory are copied from the `jsbuild` image to the `/static` working directory of the final build stage. Also, the Java `/usr/src/atsea/target/AtSea-0.0.1-SNAPSHOT.jar` file is copied from the Maven stage to the final build stage image's `/app` directory. All of this is pretty standard issue for a React application and a Java Spring Boot application built with Maven. What is different here is the `EXPOSE` command for the debugger port `5005` and the `ENTRYPOINT` Java command for the final stage. While not required, the `EXPOSE` directive is a hint to the image user about the image expecting port `5005` to be mapped to host or cluster port. The alternate `ENTRYPOINT` command invokes remote debugging of the Java API. In this case, the `CMD` is being used as a default parameter to load the `postgres` section of the Spring profile:

```
FROM node:latest As jsbuild
WORKDIR /usr/src/atsea/app/react-app
COPY react-app .
RUN npm install
RUN npm run build

FROM maven:latest As maven
WORKDIR /usr/src/atsea
```

```
COPY pom.xml .
RUN mvn -B -f pom.xml -s /usr/share/maven/ref/settings-docker.xml
dependency:resolve
COPY . .
RUN mvn -B -s /usr/share/maven/ref/settings-docker.xml package -DskipTests

FROM java:8-jdk-alpine
WORKDIR /static
COPY --from=jsbuild /usr/src/atsea/app/react-app/build/ .
WORKDIR /app
COPY --from=maven /usr/src/atsea/target/AtSea-0.0.1-SNAPSHOT.jar .
EXPOSE 5005
ENTRYPOINT ["java", "-
agentlib:jdwp=transport=dt_socket,server=y,suspend=y,address=5005","-jar",
"/app/AtSea-0.0.1-SNAPSHOT.jar"]
CMD ["--spring.profiles.active=postgres"]
```

docker-compose-dev.yml is a file that we use with a docker-compose -f docker-compose-dev.yml   --build command to build atsea_app and atsea_db images for local testing. Then, we can use a docker-compose -f docker-compose-dev.yml up -d command to start the application for local testing with an IDE. To verify that the application started correctly, we can see that the docker-compose processes are running by using the docker-compose ps command, as shown in the following code:

```
Name                    Command                    State  Ports
-----------------------------------------------------------------------------
---------------------------------
atsea-app_appserver_1 java -agentlib:jdwp=transp ... Up
0.0.0.0:5005->5005/tcp, 0.0.0.0:8080->8080/tcp
atsea-app_database_1  docker-entrypoint.sh postgres  Up
0.0.0.0:5432->5432/tcp
```

For more information on remote debugging and the AtSea sample application, take a look at https://blog.docker.com/2017/05/spring-boot-development-docker/.

Building and running an application with Compose and Swarm

In addition to building a local dev/debug version of the application, we will now look at using the `docker-compose` YAML file to define a production image `Makefile`, primarily for local full stack testing, but perhaps for our CI scripts.

In the next section of this chapter, we will look at the CI options that usually gravitate toward one build script per repository, but might have three discrete steps for each image's build (step one to build, step two to test, and step three to push the new image). For now, we need to build a local stack that runs with the production images.

In the last section, we described the `docker-compose-dev.yml` file, where we left our the `reverse_proxy` and `payment_gateway` services. Now, we want to run all of the services locally to closely mimic production. From our local Docker desktop platform, we can run a Swarm application stack to get most of the features of our Docker Enterprise cluster. We can initialize Docker Swarm, leaving us with a single node cluster that enables overlay networks, configurations, and secretes. The only thing missing is the Docker layer 7 routing, where we are using header-based routing and TLS termination. For a reasonable local test, we can use the `reverse_proxy` service with NGINX (after all Docker Enterprise uses NGINX behind the scenes by default) to be a functional placeholder for Docker Enterprise layer 7 routing on our local host.

Mocking layer 7 routing and TSL termination for local Swarm testing

The first step in creating our mock layer 7 routing service is to generate a certificate for our test domain (for local testing, just add the `at-sea.mydomain.com` to your dev machine host file). In the following diagram, we generate the certificates with an interactive **Certificate Signing Request (CSR)** (the `openssl req` command will prompt you for the CSR parameters, and this is where you provide the common name of your domain) using the `openssl req` command to generate the certificate (`.crt`) and private key (`.key`) files that are required by NGINX for termination.

We will use Docker secrets (requires Docker Engine-Community Swarm to be initialized) to safely store the certificate and key until our `reverse_proxy` service uses them later:

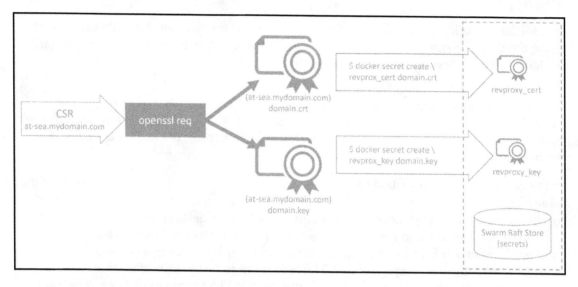

Figure 5

The following is the Bash script to generate the certificates in the `certs` directory. Then, we store the certificate and private keys as Swarm secrets, as follows:

```
#!/bin/bash
#Generate Certificates
mkdir certs
openssl req -newkey rsa:4096 -nodes -sha256 -keyout certs/domain.key -x509
-days 365 -out certs/domain.crt

#Store Certificates as Secrets in Local Swarm Cluster
docker secret create revprox_cert certs/domain.crt
docker secret create revprox_key certs/domain.key
```

After the secrets are created, you can list the secret (not the contents, of course) using the `docker secret ls` command to get the following output:

```
ID                            NAME           CREATED      UPDATED
5hhayjj711wszm9xcmym0gk6k     revprox_cert   2 days ago   2 days ago
vx5oiwizjlywuphkrz65vb7or     revprox_key    2 days ago   2 days ago
```

We will now add the `reverse_proxy` service section to our `docker-stack-local.yml` file, as shown in the following code block. Notice how the `reverse_proxy` service publishes ports `80` and `443` on the ingress network of the local tests Swarm network. We can see how the secrets we created are used by the `reverse_proxy` service. The Docker service pulls the secret name supplied as the source parameter from the cluster store and injects it into the `/run/secrets` directory, using the target parameter as the name. In a few moments, we will see where this is used when we examine the local `nginx.config` file.

Finally, we can see how the `reverse_proxy` service is connected to the front-tier network, allowing it to communicate with the `at_sea` application service (port `8080`) when it forwards requests from the `reverse_proxy` to the application's web UI:

```
services:
  reverse_proxy:
    image: reverse_proxy
    ports:
      - "80:80"
      - "443:443"
    secrets:
      - source: revprox_cert
        target: revprox_cert
      - source: revprox_key
        target: revprox_key
    networks:
      - front-tier
```

Since we don't have Docker Enterprise's Interlock 2.0 on our development workstation, we can configure a NGINX `reverse_proxy` service to handle layer 7 routing and TLS termination. We provide our own file for local testing by providing a `nxinx.conf` file when we build the image. In the following excerpt from the `nginx.conf` file, we can see the server bindings for port `80` and port `443`. Port `80` simply redirects any HTTP traffic to HTTPS on the same host with the same URI. The `443` server binding is a little more interesting.

The `443` server binding shows how the NGINX container can find the SSL certificate and key in the `/run/secrets` directory (because of these preceding secrets directives) and uses them for TLS termination. Then, the request is passed over standard HTTP protocol on the internal, isolated front-tier network to the `appserver` on port `8080`. Finally, we can see how the access and error logs are directed to the `/dev/stdout` and `/dev/stderr` where the Docker logs can pick them up:

```
server {
    listen 80;
    server_name at-sea.nvisia.io;
```

```
        return 301 https://$host$request_uri;
    }

    server {
        listen 443;
        ssl on;
        ssl_certificate /run/secrets/revprox_cert;
        ssl_certificate_key /run/secrets/revprox_key;
        server_name at-sea.mydomain.com;
        access_log /dev/stdout;
        error_log /dev/stderr;

        location / {
            proxy_pass http://appserver:8080;
        }
```

Finally, we have the Dockerfile that we will use to build a reverse proxy server. This was originally a pretty simple Dockerfile, but there were a couple of issues. First, always specify a version for a base image! Secondly, we had to add an entrypoint.sh script to eliminate a NGINX DNS resolution timing problem. Hence, we locked in on nginx:1.14-alpine as our base image, and to make that work, we just need to copy the nginx.conf file into a folder inside the container where NGINX expects to find it. Finally, instead of running the nginx binary directly from the command line, we instead run our entrypoint.sh script as the start CMD:

```
FROM nginx:1.14-alpine

COPY nginx.conf /etc/nginx/nginx.conf

# Added entrypoint.sh.
# Need to add sleep command before starting NGINX services to avoid a DNS
problem.
COPY entrypoint.sh .
CMD ./entrypoint.sh
```

The following is the tiny enterypoint.sh script for starting our reverse_proxy service. If it were more than a mock container for local testing, something more than a sleep command would seem appropriate:

```
#!/bin/sh
sleep 30
nginx -g 'daemon off;'
```

Now, our mocked layer 7 reverse_proxy service is ready for local testing, and we can put the finishing touches on the local test stack.

Final steps for local Swarm testing

To make sure that we have all the images ready for final testing, we must make sure we are using the full image name, including the private registry's FQDN/namespace, and make sure the real (not the dev) version of the Dockerfile is used for the build. To accomplish this, we create a `docker-compose-build.yml` file, as shown in the following code, with only build (no deployment) information.

We do not need a namespace, or need to push the `reverse_proxy` image, as it is only for local developer use. We add the `dtr.mydomain.com/dev` prefix to the images so that we can use the DTR's dev organization as the developer image sandbox. We add a `:local` tag to our images so that we know they are locally built and pushed. Later, automated build images will come from the CI pipeline and we will use different tags for those images.

It is fine for developers to use their private namespace, for example `dtr.mydomain.com/ssoftware`, so that they can push their own cluster-based test images as well. We used `/dev` because it can be easily shared by a group of developers who are working together on a feature branch/release:

```yaml
version: "3.7"

services:
  reverse_proxy:
    build:
      context: ./reverse_proxy
    user: nginx
    image: reverse_proxy

  database:
    build:
      context: ./database
    image: dtr.mydomain.com/dev/atsea_db:local

  appserver:
    build:
      context: app
      dockerfile: Dockerfile
    image: dtr.mydomain.com/dev/atsea_app:local

  payment_gateway:
    build:
      context: payment_gateway
    image: dtr.mydomain.com/dev/payment_gateway:local
```

Now, we can use this make-like file approach to build our images using a `docker-compose -f docker-compose-build.yml build` command and the `docker image ls` to review them.

Our final step for the local build and development machine deployment is building a `docker-stack-local.yml` file, as shown in the following code. This file is an intermediate step for a local Swarm deployment and will become the foundation for our Docker Enterprise cluster deployment stack file, which will be used by the CI system later in this chapter. Since we already discussed the `reverse_proxy` service in the previous section, we will jump right down to the database service:

```
version: "3.7"

services:
  reverse_proxy:
    image: reverse_proxy
    ports:
      - "80:80"
      - "443:443"
    secrets:
      - source: revprox_cert
        target: revprox_cert
      - source: revprox_key
        target: revprox_key
    networks:
      - front-tier

  database:
    image: dtr.nvisia.io/dev/atsea_db:local
    environment:
      POSTGRES_USER: gordonuser
      POSTGRES_DB_PASSWORD_FILE: /run/secrets/postgres_password
      POSTGRES_DB: atsea
    networks:
      - back-tier
    secrets:
      - postgres_password

  appserver:
    image: dtr.nvisia.io/dev/atsea_app:local
    networks:
      - front-tier
      - back-tier
      - payment
    deploy:
      replicas: 2
      update_config:
```

```
        parallelism: 2
        failure_action: rollback
      restart_policy:
        condition: on-failure
        delay: 5s
        max_attempts: 3
        window: 120s
    secrets:
      - postgres_password

  visualizer:
    image: dockersamples/visualizer:stable
    ports:
      - "8001:8080"
    stop_grace_period: 1m30s
    volumes:
      - "/var/run/docker.sock:/var/run/docker.sock"
    deploy:
      update_config:
        failure_action: rollback

  payment_gateway:
    image: dtr.nvisia.io/dev/payment_gateway:local
    secrets:
      - source: staging_token
        target: payment_token
    networks:
      - payment
    deploy:
      update_config:
        failure_action: rollback

networks:
  front-tier:
  back-tier:
  payment:
    driver: overlay
    driver_opts:
      encrypted: 'yes'

secrets:
  postgres_password:
    external: true
  staging_token:
    external: true
  revprox_key:
```

```
    external: true
  revprox_cert:
    external: true
```

The database service is isolated on the back-tier network, along with the `appserver`, and therefore only the `appserver` service can reach the database. The database service uses a `POSTGRES_DB_PASSWORD_FILE` environment variable to tell Postgres where to find the password file. For our sample, it is in the `/run/secrets` directory. Please note that the database secret does not specify a source and target, as specified for the `reverse_proxy` service. In this case, the secret name and the file that were created in the `/run/secrets` directory are the same and called `postgres_password`. This secret is also needed by the `appserver` service to connect to the database.

Notice that all of the services are using the full image name with the private registries FQDN, namespace (org or username), repo/image name, and tag. These, of course, match the output that is generated from using our `docker-compose-build.yml` file to build and tag our images.

The last notable feature we introduced was the deploy section of the file. This literally tells Swarm how to behave when deploying the services. Under deploy, we first set the replicas property to `'2'`, telling the orchestrator to keep two containers running the `atsea_app` image at all times.

The `deploy:>` `update config:>` parameters are related to how a service gets updated. In our case, when the service is updated (perhaps a new version of the image with some bug fixes need to be deployed), Swarm will update two containers at a time. This is a little silly for this example because we only have two replicas running, but both will be updated at the same time. `failure_action` tells the orchestrator what to do if the updated service fails. The options are `rollback` or `pause`, with `pause` being the default. The `pause` option can be helpful in debugging a `rollout` issue. The next part of the deployment specification deals with the service's `restart_policy`.

The `restart_policy` describes how, and if, the service restarts the replicas. In our example, we only restart replicas on a failure, but the options also include `none` (never restart) and `any` (to always attempt a restart, which is the default). The `delay` is how long to wait between attempts (the default is 0). The max attempts describes how many times to attempt to restart a container before giving up (the default is "never give up"). Finally, the window is the total time that's allowed for a restart to succeed.

You can find more information about Swarm deployment options here: `https://docs.docker.com/compose/compose-file/#deploy`.

Notice that I left the `visualizer` service in our stack. This is a little bit of sizzle that you might find more useful in a multi-node cluster, but essentially, this service shows the containers running in each node of your Docker cluster. The service mounts the Docker socket so that it can monitor the state of the Swarm. The visualizer needs to run on a Swarm manager node to tap into the API and get the information it needs. Since we are a cluster of one, it will be on a manager node. Otherwise, we would need to use a deployment constraint like the following:

```
deploy:
    update_config:
        failure_action: rollback
    placement:
        constraints:
            - 'node.role == manager'
```

Now, we just need to run the `docker-stack-local.yml` file on our local development machine's Swarm cluster using the `docker stack deploy -c docker-stack-local.yml at-sea-local` command to launch our new stack, called `at-sea-local`.

After launching the stack, you can run the `docker stack ps at-sea-local` command and verify the current state of the stack's process that is running. Then, you need to update your local host file too, so that the `at-sea.mydomain.com` domain name resolves to `127.0.0.1`. Then, point your browser to `https://at-sea.mydomain.com` to see the application running.

Clean up with a `docker stack rm at-sea-local` command to remove your local stack.

Deploying a custom app to the Docker Enterprise cluster

Here, we will begin to see how the development and operations roles split as we isolate a parallel set of assets for our application deployments. In doing so, we split out the deployment assets and begin to script the platform deployment in preparation for our CI pipelines in the next section. More specifically, we will now introduce scripts, along with new Docker stack files to manage the deployment of application services.

We will start by breaking out a separate deployment repository from the application deployment repository. This is the place where our deployment scripts and cluster-based test, QA, and prod stack files will live, and will be governed by the system administrators and operations team.

While the development team will help to produce these assets, all of the changes will be merged back into the `master` branch by the administrators and operators who are responsible for using them. This is where we also start to think about managing deployment resources for each environment (for example, dev, test, and prod) as well.

For this purpose, we will create an `ATSEA-DEPLOY` folder as a peer to our `ATSEA-APP`, as up here to the application assets we cloned from the `dockersamples` AtSea GitHub repository (`https://github.com/dockersamples/atsea-sample-shop-app`). The `ATSEA-DEPLOY` content structure is shown in the following tree listing. There are, of course, many ways to organize deployment assets, but this is a pretty reasonable example. In addition, you might have a `configs` folder as a peer to the `secrets` folder to swap out different config files (that is, NGINX configs and Spring properties).

Please note that the contents of the `secret` directories, perhaps with the exception of the `secrets/dev` folder, are populated after the code is pulled from source code control. These scaffolding or placeholder directories and default artifacts are not necessary, but illustrative of some of the ways to abstract environmental assets out of your deployment script file:

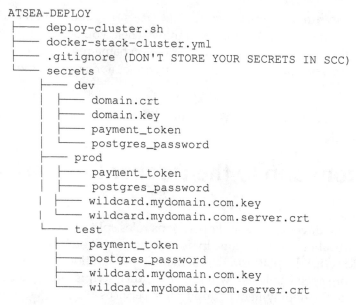

```
ATSEA-DEPLOY
├── deploy-cluster.sh
├── docker-stack-cluster.yml
├── .gitignore (DON'T STORE YOUR SECRETS IN SCC)
└── secrets
    ├── dev
    │   ├── domain.crt
    │   ├── domain.key
    │   ├── payment_token
    │   └── postgres_password
    ├── prod
    │   ├── payment_token
    │   ├── postgres_password
    │   ├── wildcard.mydomain.com.key
    │   └── wildcard.mydomain.com.server.crt
    └── test
        ├── payment_token
        ├── postgres_password
        ├── wildcard.mydomain.com.key
        └── wildcard.mydomain.com.server.crt
```

Our deployment repository will start off as a simple deployment script with a command-line parameter to deploy cluster based applications to either dev, test, or prod using Docker's stack deploy. It is here where we script the creation of all external, dependent assets as a part of the deployment. These assets typically include networks, configs, and secrets that are external to the stack. Also, I left some comments, indicating where you might pull secrets from a secure remote location into the appropriate `secrets` directory.

For instance, before we begin the process of deployment, we may want to pull some secrets from a HashiCorp vault and inject them into our Docker Swarm's TLS encrypted store. Other times, it will simply be an operator accessing secured files from the command line, and using their access rights to create Swarm secrets required by the application services. The following is a sample for the `vault` command to create a Docker Swarm secret:

```
# snippet from http://work.haufegroup.io/spring-cloud-config-and-vault/

$ vault write -f -format=json auth/approle/role/myapprole/secret-id | jq -r
'.secret_id' | \
docker secret create myapprole_secretid -
```

The following is a simple script and an updated version of our YAML stack file using the `docker-compose` file 3.x format:

```bash
#!/bin/bash
# deploy_cluster.sh

# Add your code to fetch and populate ./secrets/test ./secrets/prod using
copy or vault etc.

# Set stack name
if [[ -z "$1" ]]; then
    echo "Usage: please specify dev, test or prod";
    exit 1;
else
    export STACK_ENV=$1
    export STACK=${STACK_ENV}_at-sea
fi

# Clean up old external stuff
echo -e "Remove old stuff...\n"
echo $(docker network rm front-tier)
echo $(docker secret rm wildcard.mydomain.com.key)
echo $(docker secret rm wildcard.mydomain.com.server.crt)
echo $(docker secret rm postgres_password)
echo $(docker secret rm payment_token)

echo -e "Waiting for 5 seconds...\n" $(sleep 5) "\n\n"
echo -e "Creating new external networks and certificates...\n"
echo -e $(docker network create -d overlay front-tier) "\n"
echo -e $(docker secret create wildcard.mydoamin.com.key
./secrets/${STACK_ENV}/wildcard.mydomain.com.key) "\n"
echo -e $(docker secret create wildcard.mydomain.com.server.crt
./secrets/${STACK_ENV}/wildcard.mydomain.com.server.crt) "\n"
echo -e $(docker secret create postgres_password
secrets/${STACK_ENV}/postgres_password) "\n"
```

```
echo -e $(docker secret create payment_token
secrets/${STACK_ENV}/payment_token) "\n"

echo -e "Waiting for 5 seconds...\n" $(sleep 5) "\n"
echo -e "Launching stack..." $(docker stack deploy -c docker-stack-
cluster.yml ${STACK}) "\n"
```

We begin with the `deploy_cluster.sh` script by looking for the existence of a command-line parameter, making sure we have an environment name passed in. We are keeping the sample script brief, and just looking for the existence of a parameter, but validating that the parameter's value is actually `dev`, `test`, or `prod` would be a good addition for a real version of script. Next, we clean up the old external networks and secrets from the Swarm. From there, we create the external network, create the Swarm secrets by loading their contents from the `/secrets` files, and finally, deploy the stack.

The script sets up the dependencies and deploys the `docker-stack-cluster.yml` stack. Now, we will dive into the associated `docker-stack-cluster.yml` we are launching in the last line of `deploy_cluster.sh`.

Layer 7 routing with Docker Enterprise

Since we are moving from a local Docker Engine-Community Swarm deployment on a local developer machine to a Docker Enterprise Cluster deployment, we can take advantage of Docker Enterprise's Interlock 2 layer 7 routing feature. In addition to layer 7 routing, we can also use Interlock 2 for our TLS termination, as shown in the following diagram. Therefore, by using this feature in our application, we will replace the `reverse_proxy` service we used for our local deployment stack.

To describe how this feature works for our sample application, we can follow the inbound traffic from a remote computer, starting with the wildcard DNS entry, which resolves the `atsea.mydoamin.com` URL on port `443` on our external load balancer. The load balancer directed the inbound request to any one of the cluster nodes on port `8443`. Earlier, we used the Docker Enterprise admin settings to enable layer 7 routing on ingress ports `80` and `8443`. So, any inbound traffic into the cluster on ports `80` and `8443` is routed to the Interlock proxy service. Later, when we deploy our application with the `docker stack deploy` command, Interlock 2 detects that the service used Interlock 2's labels, starting with `com.docker.lb.*` and it uses the label values to configure the proxy (think of an `nginx.conf` update).

This configures the Interlock 2 proxy to inspect headers, and reverse proxy inbound traffic requests with the `atsea.mydoamin.com` host name to the `appserver` Swarm service's VIP on port `8080` over the front-tier network. Inside the `appserver` service, Spring's embedded Tomcat server is listening on port `8080` and responds to web requests. The response is routed back out through the same path it entered:

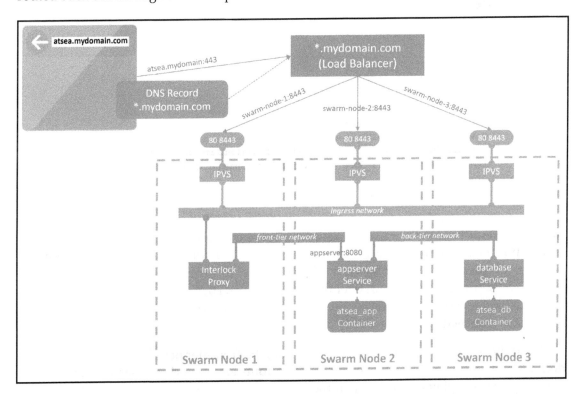

Figure 6: Layer 7 routing with AtSea

In the following code, we can see the abbreviated version of the updated stack file. Please pay attention to the `services` > `appserver` > `deploy` > `labels` section:

```
#docker-stack-cluster.yml
version: "3.7"

services:
<...>
  appserver:
    image: dtr.mydomain.com/dev/atsea_app:local
    networks:
      - front-tier
```

```
      - back-tier
      - payment
   deploy:
     replicas: 2
     update_config:
       parallelism: 2
       failure_action: rollback
     restart_policy:
       condition: on-failure
       delay: 5s
       max_attempts: 3
       window: 120s
     labels:
       com.docker.lb.hosts: at-sea.mydomain.com
       com.docker.lb.network: front-tier
       com.docker.lb.port: 8080
       com.docker.lb.ssl_cert: wildcard.mydomain.com.server.crt
       com.docker.lb.ssl_key: wildcard.mydomain.com.key
   secrets:
     - postgres_password
<...>
```

Here, we can see how Docker uses labels to configure both layer 7 routing and TLS termination. `com.docker.lb.hosts` tells Interlock to look for headers with this host name (`at-sea.mydomain.com`) and forward them to the `appserver` service on `com.docker.lb.port` (8080) over the `com.docker.lb.network` (front-tier) network. Interlock likes to have `com.docker.lb.network` as an external network, created before the stack is launched.

Notice at the end of the preceding YAML file that, the front-tier network and secrets are declared `external: true`. This means that the front-tier network and secrets must be created prior to deploying stack, and if they are not the orchestrator, will fail to deploy the services. Again, we are deploying this stack file using `docker stack deploy` from within `deploy_cluster.sh`, where we create the expected external resources.

Finally, to deploy, we use the `./deploy_cluster.sh test` command. Then, after waiting about 30 seconds for Interlock 2 to configure and update the `ucp-interlock-proxy` service, we should be able to test the site using our browser, `https://at-sea.mydomain.com`. Of course, you must make sure your DNS (either host file, internal DNS, or public DNS) record points to external load balancer. This can be a single site entry (`at-sea.mydomain.com`) or a wildcard DNS entry (`*.mydomain.com`).

Congratulations on manually deploying your custom application with layer 7 routing and DNS termination! At this point, you have deployed an application to a Docker Enterprise Docker cluster. While we are in pilot mode, our deployment targets a non-production Docker Enterprise cluster where internal users will have access to the application to evaluate its performance and function. For the most part, other than swapping out some configuration parameters, we should be very close to a production deployment. Therefore, the assets developed should be reusable across multiple deployment environments by simply changing out a script the parameter such as `test` or `prod` (for example, `./deploy_cluster.sh prod`). In our example, we use the test parameter, causing the script and compose file resources from the `secrets/test` directory. A similar pattern could be used for development and production as well.

Building and deploying the custom app with a CI pipeline

Now, our pilot-related activities are shifting into the DevOps space as we build out a continuous integration pipeline for our custom application. The goal of this section is to demonstrate how to create a Docker-based pipeline to build and deploy our application to our Docker Enterprise cluster. Armed with our new deployment repository and the application assets we have developed in the application repository, we set off on our Docker CI pipeline adventure!

Sample CI pipeline overview

Now, we are going to make our application feel more like a microservices (multi-service) application, where different people, or even teams, are working on independently deployable services. We are going to break up our custom pilot AtSea application into separate services source code repositories.

To illustrate our CI Pipeline example with a high degree of detail, we will build it out using `gitlab.com`. We are not necessarily endorsing GitLab here, but we did choose it for a couple of reasons. First, it is becoming a very popular choice in the development community. Secondly, because of its container friendliness, and finally, because it is based off of pipelines as code using a YAML definition in the root of each service repository. This philosophy keeps us out of plugin hell by using container based runners to execute our builds and deployments on our own remote servers.

We could have taken this example one step further by deploying our own GitLab CE server as a Swarm service on our Docker Enterprise cluster for the purposes of this chapter. While running a Docker Pipeline service, like Jenkins or GitLab, from inside a Docker cluster is a pretty straightforward exercise (and well documented). Doing so adds an unnecessary layer of complexity to this chapter that may be confusing, and take our focus away from important details of a CI pipeline's interactions with Docker Enterprise.

We chose to use the cloud hosted version of `gitlab.com` (formerly GitLab Cloud), but we will be deploying our own GitLab-runners to a Docker based build server that is adjacent to our EE cluster. The following diagram presents a high-level overview of our sample CI pipeline structure with GitLab:

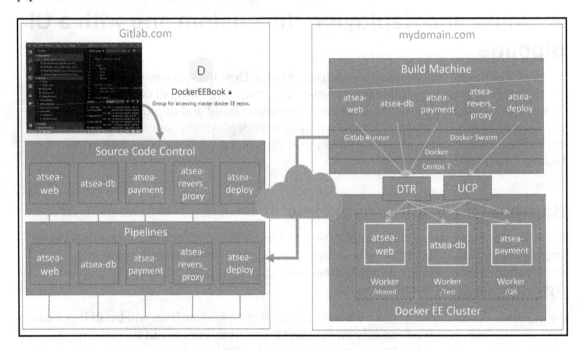

Figure 7: GitLab pipeline with Docker Enterprise

The **Build Machine** is not only running Docker, but it is also running as a single node Swam cluster, so we may test our application stack before we push any freshly built images to our Docker Trusted Registry. This build node Swarm is separate from the Swarm running in our Docker Enterprise cluster.

The preceding diagram shows the general flow of a software development life cycle through our sample CI pipeline. From a high level, the developer builds and tests their code locally, checks it in, and pushes it to the GitLab source code control system. GitLab looks for a pipeline definition file in the root of the repo (`.gitlab-ci.yml`). When found, GitLab executes the pipeline. The preceding diagram shows how we have split up the code base into separate repositories that align with each image, and each repository has a corresponding pipeline and a `.gitlab-ci.yml` pipeline definition file.

The pipeline is responsible for building and pushing the image to the Docker Trusted Registry. The pipelines themselves schedule and monitor the build activity on the remote build machine, where the GitLab Runner builds images using a local Docker Engine. Additionally, our GitLab-Runner configuration on the build machine allows our Docker containers to communicate directly with the Docker daemon of the build server host. This is a really important feature for both caching and deploying test stacks. We'll talk more about that later when we go through the details of our pipelines.

Notice the blue line going from the build machine to the pipelines, where it looks like it's going the wrong way. This represents how the runners communicate to GitLab servers, eliminating the need to proxy inbound request from the GitLab servers. Instead, the Runner checks in with GitLab every few seconds for updates—presumably checking the current state and getting any new builds. This works great because most networks allow egress from the inside out, so there's no network configuration required to support the implementation of the Runner. This is really nice!

After the image is built on the build server, it is tested, and if it passes the test, the image is pushed to the Docker Trusted Registry using the builder's credentials. Additionally, as depicted by the orange arrows at the bottom of the GitLab Pipelines, when the build successfully completes, it triggers the pipeline to deploy the test stack. In this case, the deploy pipeline uses the Universal Control Plane client bundle to deploy the stack to the test environment in the Docker Enterprise cluster using the deployer's credentials.

Connecting GitLab to Docker Enterprise

There are a variety of touch points that we need to line up for our CI pipeline to work properly with Docker Enterprise. First, the CI system has to have access through a user account to the DTR, as well as accounts with their associated client bundles, to access the universal control plane. Furthermore, we have to structure the assets in both DTR repositories, and UCP collections, to align with our CI process and access control.

This all looks easy enough, but there are a lot of moving parts that we will walk through to convey the concepts, as well as key details. Let's get started with the configuration of GitLab and the installation of the GitLab Runner.

In the following screenshot, we can see how we created a group in GitLab to house all of our related repositories (referred to as projects in GitLab) for the AtSea application. While the grouping mechanism helps to organize related repositories, it is a great place to manage shared resources and store common information for all projects in the group.

In our case, this is where we store our GitLab Runner configuration so that it can be shared across all of the repositories. This is pretty straightforward, since we are using Docker to build all of our repositories into images. Additionally, we are storing common environment variables to be used across all of the repositories. More specifically, we are sharing the builder account username and password used to access DTR by using a protected environment variable.

A GitLab protected environment variable can only be accessed from within a protected branch (for example, the `master` branch).

Therefore, it is difficult to inadvertently expose a protected variable to anyone other than a repository owner:

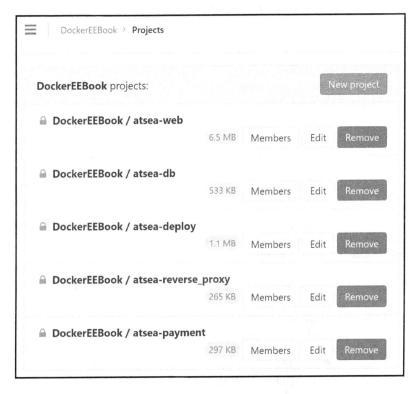

Figure 8: GitLab Projects

The preceding builder credentials are the first touchpoint to Docker Enterprise—more specifically, the DTR. We will use the builder credentials to log in to DTR, pull our base images, and push our freshly built application images. Of course, this requires a little bit of planning.

Adding a GitLab Runner to the build machine

Once we have our GitLab groups with our project structure created, our DTR builder credentials are stored at the GitLab group level (so that it can be shared across each projects pipeline) as protected environment variables. We are now ready to configure our Runner.

The Runner is a small bit of code that we will install on our build machine to bootstrap the connection between our build machine and `gitlab.com`. As we mentioned before, our building machine is a Docker host that is unaffiliated with the Docker Enterprise cluster, and runs its own standalone, single node Swarm cluster.

From the GitLab group, you can navigate to the setting for CI/CD and expand the **Runner** section. Within the **Runner** section, you will find a couple of important things. First is the link to the instructions to install a Runner on your build machine platform. Remember, in our case, we want to use the Docker service Runner: `https://docs.gitlab.com/Runner/install/docker.html`. The other important items are the link back to `https://github.com/`, and the token required to access your GitLab account from the Runner.

For our Runner, I have chosen to use just a simple Docker container that is executed with the following `docker run` command:

```
docker run -d --name gitlab-Runner --restart always \
    -v /srv/gitlab-Runner/config:/etc/gitlab-Runner \
    -v /var/run/docker.sock:/var/run/docker.sock \
    gitlab/gitlab-Runner:latest
```

This container simply starts the small application that will be using the poll `https://about.gitlab.com/` for build jobs. Thus far, we have just started the Runner's Docker container and it is waiting to do something. However, there are some points of interest regarding how the container is launched.

The first noteworthy parameter is the volume mount to the `srv/gitlab-Runner/config` local host directory. This is where the GitLab Runner stores its configuration file called `config.toml`. So, even if the container is replaced, the GitLab Runner configuration will be preserved on the host filesystem. We will talk more about the GitLab Runner configuration file soon after we get to the next Docker command for registering the Runner with our GitLab service.

The next parameter is the second volume mount of the Docker socket. Essentially, this volume mount directs any Docker command that is run inside the container to be passed through to the host's Docker Engine for execution. This allows the GitLab Runner to execute Docker commands directly against the host's engine from inside to get Runner's container while executing the pipeline. As mentioned before, this is important for two purposes on our build server:

- First, it gives all of the build jobs the ability to leverage a common cache of image layers to cut build times
- The second purpose is to allow multiple containers on the same host to communicate on the local Docker bridge network, or in our case, using the Docker Swarm overlay network to connect Swarm services

You will see how we use this during our post image build testing.

Once we have the Runner container loaded on the build server, it's time to configure it using the following Docker command:

```
docker run --rm -t -i -v /srv/gitlab-Runner/config:/etc/gitlab-Runner
gitlab/gitlab-Runner register \
  --non-interactive \
  --executor "docker" \
  --docker-image docker:stable \
  --url "https://gitlab.com/" \
  --registration-token "XXXXXXXXXXXXXXXXXX" \
  --description "docker-iscsi-Runner" \
  --tag-list "docker,ntc" \
  --run-untagged \
  --locked="false"
```

This Docker command mounts the host configuration directory so that it can update the Runner's configuration file with the parameters that are passed to the `register` command. Notice that we have the URL and the registration token from the **Runners** section of the **CI/CD** setting page. Additionally, we give the Runner a name that will come in handy to make sure that our builds are actually running on your specific Runner, instead of a shared Runner, at build time.

After registering the Runner, the Runner will show up in the GitLab UI, as shown in the following screenshot:

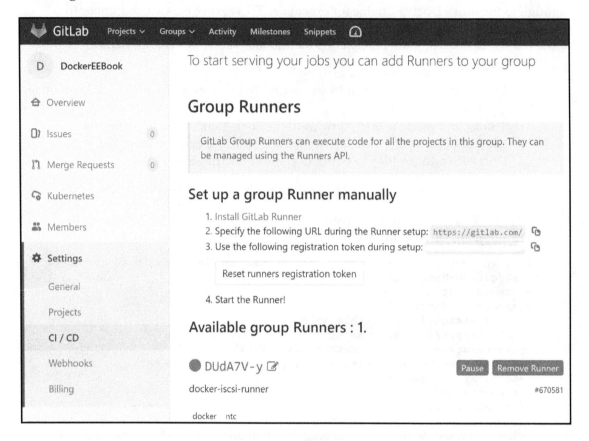

Figure 9: GitLab Runner status

Our Runner is almost there! However, we are using Docker Enterprise and we may want some sort of default access to our Docker Trusted Registry using the Runner from our build server to push our freshly built images. We can explicitly log in from our CI (we will show this in action later in this section) and/or we can add a special line into our `/srv/gitlab-Runner/config/config.toml` file to give any Runner job on the build server access to DTR as a builder. While this is convenient and may make things run a little more smoothly, you have to examine the security ramifications as well.

Normally, the build jobs will only be run from protected branches in the CI system, and the Docker commands they can issue for DTR operations are generally non-destructive, so it may not be a horrible idea, but proceed with caution.

To add the builder account as a default DTR connection, you first need to generate a DTR authentication token (this is a completely different token than we used for accessing GitLab). This token can be generated by simply logging into the DTR from your build server's command line with `docker login dtr.mydomain.com`. Then, enter your `builder` username and password so that Docker will generate an authentication token in a file called `~/.docker/config.json`. Docker then uses this authentication token to access DTR on your behalf any time you are using an asset associated with `dtr.mydomain.com`. We need to share this DTR authentication token with our Runner configuration file so it too can access the DTR on behalf of our builder user to push images.

First, we'll get the contents from our `config.json` file, as shown in the following block of code:

```
$cat .docker/config.json
{
        "auths": {
                "dtr.nvisia.io": {
                        "auth": "FDfafea434r",
                        "identitytoken": "xxxxxxxx-xxxx-xxxx-xxxx-
xxxxxxxxxxxx"
                }
        },
        "HttpHeaders": {
                "User-Agent": "Docker-Client/18.09.1 (linux)"
        }
}
```

Then, we will need to reformat the `auths` section of this file to be used in the GitLab Runner's configuration file. There are several ways to access the Runner configuration file. One way is to simply use `sudo -s` to assume root on your build server and edit the `/srv/gitlab-Runner/config/config.toml` file. An alternative way would be to start a CentOS or Ubuntu Docker container, `docker run -it -v /srv/gitlab-Runner/config:/config centos:7 bash`, and then edit the `/config/config.toml` from within that container shell. Any way you choose to do it, the objective of the exercise is to inject the following `environment = ..` line into the Runner config file so that it looks like the following code block:

```
concurrent = 1
check_interval = 0
[session_server]
  session_timeout = 1800
[[runners]]
  name = "docker-ntc-Runner"
  url = "https://gitlab.com/"
  token = "xxxxxxxxxxxxxxxxxx"
  executor = "docker"
```

```
    environment = ["DOCKER_AUTH_CONFIG={\"auths\":
{\"dtr.mydoamin.com\":{\"auth\":\"FDfafea434r\",\"identitytoken\":\"xxxxxxx
x-xxxx-xxxx-xxxx-xxxxxxxxxxxx\"}}}"]
  [runners.docker]
    tls_verify = false
    image = "docker:stable"
    privileged = false
    disable_entrypoint_overwrite = false
    oom_kill_disable = false
    disable_cache = false
    volumes = ["/var/run/docker.sock:/var/run/docker.sock", "/cache"]
    shm_size = 0
```

Please remember to substitute your individual values where we provide "xxxx" in the preceding config file.

Finally, note the tls_verify = false command parameter. This is not associated with the Runner's DTR connection. Rather, this is the Runner's TLS connection back to your GitLab server. If you are hosting your own server with self-signed certificates, make sure that you have set to false. Otherwise, the Runner may get X.509 certificate trust errors.

Now, your Runner should be good to go! Now that we have a Runner ready to execute pipelines remotely on our build server to build Docker images, we need to think about structuring our target DTR.

DTR CI integration

We will need to configure DTR's organization namespaces, users, teams, and repositories to support our pipeline process. Our image namespaces need to have logical names that flow with the pipeline stages (that is, dev, test, qa) and these repositories should only be accessible by the intended and authorized users. Remember, DTR namespaces (for example, dtr.mydomain.com/**namespace**/myrepo:tag1) use either usernames or organization names. We, of course, want to use organization names over usernames and make sure the organization names reflect the teams using them.

In our case, there are three organizations within our Docker Trusted Registry. First, we have the pilot organization we used to deploy our wiki application. Secondly, we have the dev organization where freshly built images land from our CI system, or from developers collaborating with one another. Please note that developers can always use their personal namespace for storing experimental images for testing and then deploy to the cluster within their private sandbox. However, if developers are sharing images, it is generally easier to use the dev organization's repository namespace. The one thing we want to be careful about is potentially reserving certain standards for image tags. For example, reserving any tag starting with RC- as a release candidate may be automatically promoted into the test organization's repositories. Generally, only the builder account will have access to the special dev repositories. In our case, these repositories end with _build, as follows:

- dtr.mydomain.com/dev/atsea-db_build
- dtr.mydomain.com/dev/atsea-payment_build
- dtr.mydomain.com/dev/atsea-reverse_proxy_build
- dtr.mydomain.com/dev/atsea-web_build

The final organization for this example is test. Docker Trusted Registry has the ability to promote images from one repository to another based on user-defined criteria. We want to use DTR policies to promote images from our dev repositories into our peer repositories in the test organization that mirror those in the dev organization, as follows:

- dtr.mydomain.com/test/atsea-db_build
- dtr.mydomain.com/test/atsea-payment_build
- dtr.mydomain.com/test/atsea-reverse_proxy_build
- dtr.mydomain.com/test/atsea-web_build

To promote these images from dev to test, we use a feature of the DTR called a promotion policy. The promotion policy is an event-driven task, where you determine what triggers the promotion and the criteria that need to be met. Additionally, you define the target repository, as well as any modifications to the tag, as the images are promoted from one repository to the next.

In the following screenshot, we can see the DTR web interface for configuring a repository promotion policy:

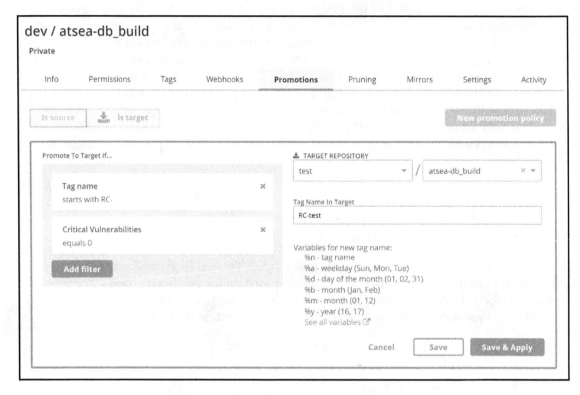

Figure 10: Docker Trusted Registry Image Promotion

Here, we are looking at an image with no critical vulnerabilities (this policy will not fire until the image scan is complete) and a tag starting with RC-. If an image matches the two criteria, it will then be promoted to the test/atsea-db_build repository with a tag name of RC-test. Please note the other options for using variables in tag names that include the original tag name, as well as other related variables.

With our repositories in place, we need to be sure that our builder account has the appropriate access rights to push images to the target repositories within the dev organization. One really simple way to do this is to give the builder organization owner privileges within the dev organization as, shown in the following screenshot:

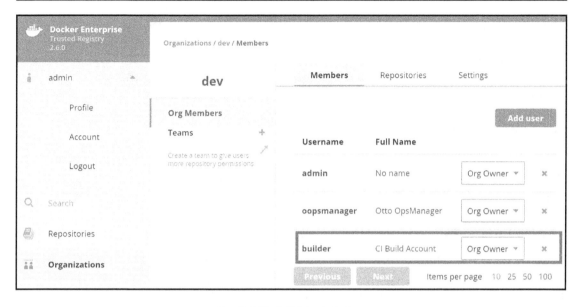

Figure 11: Builder As DTR Organization Owner

With this configuration work out of the way, we can now move on to see how our application was split into multiple service repositories, and how these repositories are turned into build pipelines.

Building our services

When we left off from our cluster deployment section earlier in this chapter, we used a simple script to create our external resources and deploy the AtSea stack to our Docker Enterprise cluster. We accomplished this with two repositories—one repository for the application artifacts and another for our initial deployment artifacts.

In this section, we will break up the application artifacts into separate repositories for each deployable service so that we can build them independently in our CI pipeline. This structure is generally a requirement for larger development teams where multiple work streams need to be supported with minimal interference between team members.

As a result, we have decomposed the application into the following repositories:

```
├── atsea-db
├── atsea-deploy
├── atsea-payment
├── atsea-reverse_proxy
└── atsea-web
```

The AtSea application stack will be made up of three primary services: the web service, the payment service, and the db service. Remember, we do not need the reverse_proxy server in our final deployment because we are using Docker Enterprise for layer 7 reverse proxy routing and TLS certificate termination. Therefore, we will focus this section on building the db, payments, and web services. Then, we will return to the atsea-deploy repository, where we will reconfigure our scripts to run from a triggered job, and deploy our stack onto the Docker Enterprise test cluster.

We are going to start off with two simpler build jobs (atsea-db and atsea-payment) and then ramp up to a more complex example of multi-stage build for the atsea-web application.

Simple build and push pipeline for atsea-db image

First, we will look at the contents of our atsea-db service repository. For the most part, the repository contains the contents from the database sub directory of the old atsea-app repository. There is, of course, one critical new addition—the .gitlab-ci.yml file:

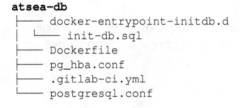

```
atsea-db
├──── docker-entrypoint-initdb.d
│   └──── init-db.sql
├──── Dockerfile
├──── pg_hba.conf
├──── .gitlab-ci.yml
└──── postgresql.conf
```

There is a special convention within the GitLab source code control system related to CI pipeline file. When code is checked into the repository with a .gitlab-ci.yml file in the root of the repository, a pipeline is created based on the contents of this file.

Of course, there is much to say about CI pipeline systems and GitLab, but that is a topic for another book. Our goal for this section is to help you understand the interaction between a CI pipeline system and Docker Enterprise in the context of a software development cycle. We believe an example is usually the best way to convey concepts with sufficient detail.

Let's get started by looking at the following simple CI pipeline definition file with a brief explanation of what is going on with our db pipeline.

The first line of the file is simply a comment for readers to associate the file content that was shown with the repository structure discussion previously. The variables section is where you define environment variables within the scope of your pipeline. For testing purposes, these pipeline variables may be overridden when the pipeline is manually run. In our case, we are using a variable to store the FQDN of our DTR server. This variable is used later in the file when we log in to DTR, and when we tag and push our images during the push process. You can see how the `DTR_SERVER` is substituted into the pipeline's `before_script` section as a parameter to the Docker login command and the `$DTR_SERVER` is referenced.

`image: docker:stable` specifies what image the Runner will use to run the following script commands. The `docker:stable` image is an official Docker image (pulled from `hub.docker.com/_/docker`) that was created for the purpose of running Docker commands from within a container. Remember, since our Runner mounts the host Docker socket (Docker-on-Docker approach), your Docker commands are actually passed to the host's Docker Engine for safe execution.

Note that this is different from the Docker-in-Docker (Docker-in-Docker—DinD) approach, where you run your container in privileged mode to fully access all host resources. This sounds great, but there are many issues, including and most commonly, data/filesystem corruption. We strongly recommend you stick with Docker-on-Docker:

```
# atsea-db .gitlab-ci.yml
variables:
 DTR_SERVER: dtr.mydomain.com

image: docker:stable

before_script:
 - docker login -u builder -p $BUILDER_PW $DTR_SERVER

stages:
 - build
 - push
 - deploy

build-image:
 stage: build
 script:
 - docker image build -t
$DTR_SERVER/dev/"$CI_PROJECT_NAME"_build:$CI_COMMIT_REF_NAME .

push-branch:
 stage: push
 script:
```

```
    - docker push $DTR_SERVER/dev/"$CI_PROJECT_NAME"_build:$CI_COMMIT_REF_NAME

push-master:
 stage: push
 script:
 - docker image tag
$DTR_SERVER/dev/"$CI_PROJECT_NAME"_build:$CI_COMMIT_REF_NAME
$DTR_SERVER/dev/"$CI_PROJECT_NAME"_build:RC-DEV
  - docker image push $DTR_SERVER/dev/"$CI_PROJECT_NAME"_build:RC-DEV
  - docker image rm $DTR_SERVER/dev/"$CI_PROJECT_NAME"_build:RC-DEV
 only:
 - master

deploy-to-test:
 stage: deploy
 before_script:
 - apk add curl
 script:
 - echo "wait for image promotion..."
 - sleep 10
 - curl -X POST -F token=xxxxxxxxxxxxxxxxxxxxx-F "ref=master" -F
"variables[DEPLOY_TARGET]=test"
https://gitlab.com/api/v4/projects/xxxxxxxxxxxx/trigger/pipeline
```

Next, we have the pipeline's `before_script` section. Here, we supply a default set of commands that will be run before each of the pipeline stages begin. Do note, however, that if there is a `before_script` defined for any specific stage, it will override the global `before_script` (the script at the top of the file). In our case, that works out great, because in our final deploy stage, we do not need to log in to DTR, but we need a `curl` command installed to fire the deployment trigger. We will come back to the deploy stage in a minute.

Pipelines are called pipelines for a good reason. They define a sequence of pipeline stages wherein each of these stages may have multiple jobs running in parallel for improved cycle times. In our case, as shown in the following screenshot, you can see our pipeline flow with the **Build**, **Push**, and **Deploy** stages that are designated in the preceding `stages:`. Inside each stage, you have our pipeline file's four jobs: **build-image**, **push-branch**, **push-master**, and **deploy-to-test**. Please notice the parallel flow during the **Push** stage of the build, where we have the **push-master** and **push-branch** job's pushed images to the DTR:

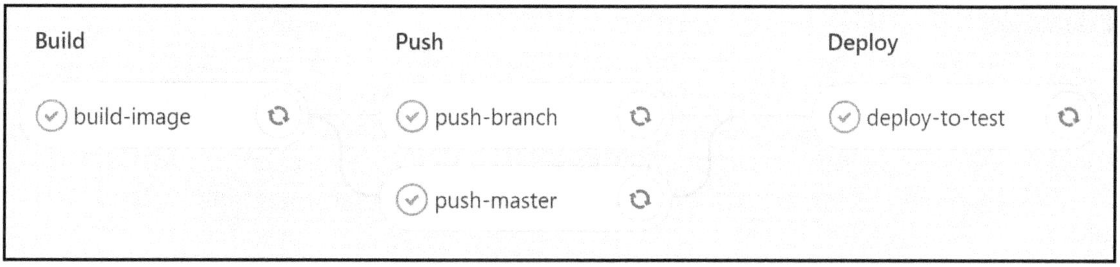

Build	Push	Deploy
✓ build-image ↻	✓ push-branch ↻	✓ deploy-to-test ↻
	✓ push-master ↻	

Figure 12: GitLab Pipeline Flow

After the stages section of the `gitlab-ci.yml` file, we have our jobs defined. Each of these jobs have stage tags to associate the job with a pipeline stage, and a script section where we list the commands that are to be executed within the job. Also, notice that we are using some built-in `CI_*` environment variables where the CI system provides a `CI_PROJECT_NAME` for the project name and `CI_COMMIT_REF_NAME` for the branch name. Since we are creating a distinct pipeline file for each repository, the project name variable is not completely necessary. However, we include it to demonstrate the variable usage, and as a step toward creating group-wide build templates.

The only project assets that are consumed directly by this build script is the Dockerfile that's used to build the `atsea-db_build` image. In our build-image job, you can see how we are running a `docker image build` to generate a DTR ready tag name, and using the local context in the `atsea-db` folder to build the image. In the local context, we find the `atsea-db/Dockerfile`, where the image is built as it was before.

After the `atsea-db_build` image is built, the push-branch pushes a copy of the image to DTR's /dev organization. The push-master job only runs if the branch being built is the master branch—designated by the `only:` tag at the end of the push-master job definition.

The master push retags the branch image with an `:RC-DEV` tag, and pushes the image to the Trusted Registry and cleans up the master image before it completes. Finally, the deploy-to-test job installs the `curl` package in the Docker container, and then it waits for some period of time for the dev image to be promoted to the test organization's repository for deployment. Rather than waiting for a specified period of time (`sleep 10`) for the promotion policy to fire in DTR, you could also use an event-driven web hook from the DTR to a GitLab trigger endpoint, but it requires a little bit of extra work.

Connecting a web hook from the DTR's `test/atsea-db_build` repository to kick off the deployment job after the image is promoted to the test repository is possible, but unfortunately, you cannot tie DTR directly to the GitLab at this time. This integration requires an intermediate web hook forwarder/filter between the DTR web hook and GitLab trigger endpoint. The forwarder/filter must remove the JSON payload from the DTR before posting to GitLab's trigger endpoint to eliminate the JSON parsing error that will otherwise occur.

For our pipeline trigger example, we are therefore driving the build and deploy from within each of the service's build pipeline files, as shown on the preceding deploy stage. When you are done, you should see fresh images in the DTR. Since we were building on the `master` branch, we have two image repositories—one for the `master` branch, and then the other for the release candidate with the `RC_DEV` tag. Remember the release candidate image will be promoted to the `test/atsea-db_build` organization's repository, and then deployed to the Docker Enterprise clusters /test collection from there:

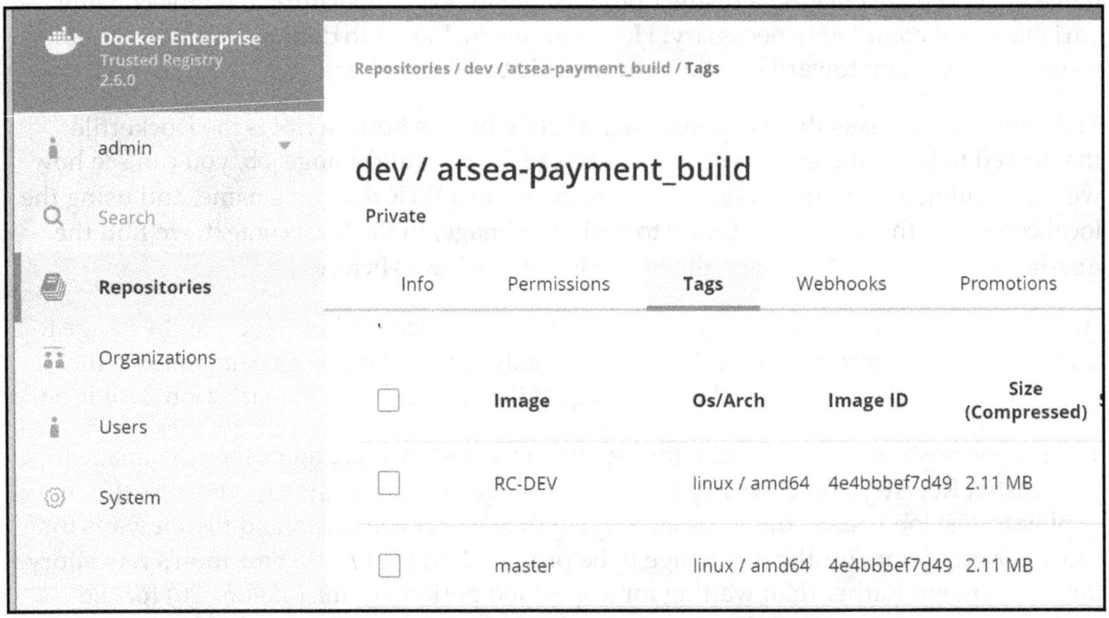

Figure 13

Now that we have a basic build and push pattern set up, let's see if we can take our pipeline file and reuse it for the payment service.

Simple build and push pipeline for the atsea-payment image

The `payment` image's pipeline file looks identical to the pipeline file for the `db` image. However, the pipeline's `docker build` command picks up the `atsea-payment/Dockerfile` from its context to build the payment image:

```
atsea-payment
├── Dockerfile
├── .gitlab-ci.yml
└── process.sh
```

Therefore, using a Dockerfile in the repositorie's root and the `$CI_` variables for the project and branch names yields the results that are shown in the following screenshot. It just works, and you can see how this simple build and push style pipeline can be reused:

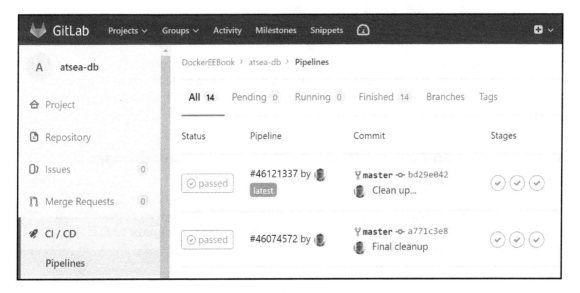

When the pipeline completes and the image below show the image was pushed to the target repository in the DTR:

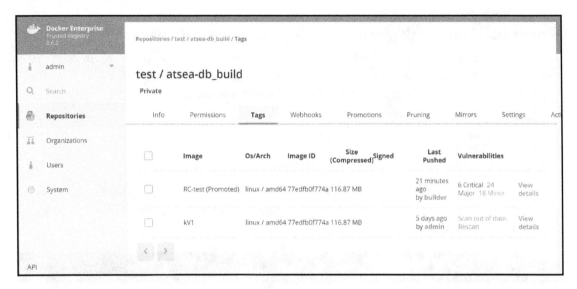

Okay, those are simple samples where the CI pipeline grabs the latest code, runs a docker build, and pushes the resulting image to your DTR. Now, it is time for us to move into a more complex pipeline, which we will demonstrate with the web application service repository.

Build, End to End Test, and Push pipeline for the atsea-web image

Now, it is time to build off of the last CI pipeline and take it to the next level. For our web application, we are raising the bar. We want to: 1) build the image, 2) run a test application stack using the new image, and 3) connect an e2e test driver to the web app stack and validate the application. If the test succeeds, then we will push the image to DTR. Otherwise, we will fail the build. Now that is cool!

Let's start by looking at the following pipeline file, where everything looks the same as before, until we get to the `deploy-test-on-swarm` job. The first line of the `deploy-test-on-swarm` script has the `docker stack deploy` command we used for our manual deploy earlier in this chapter, but there are some important additions in the abbreviated file:

```
# atsea-web .gitlab-ci.yml
<...>

deploy-test-on-swarm:
  stage: test
  script:
    - docker stack deploy --with-registry-auth -c docker-compose-e2e.yml
atsea-web-${CI_PIPELINE_ID}
    - sleep 30
    - docker container run --network atsea-web-${CI_PIPELINE_ID}_front-tier
--name local-test-driver-container-${CI_PIPELINE_ID} local-test-
driver:${CI_PIPELINE_ID}
  after_script:
    - docker stack rm atsea-web-${CI_PIPELINE_ID}
    - docker container rm -f local-test-driver-container-${CI_PIPELINE_ID}
    - docker image rm local-test-driver:${CI_PIPELINE_ID}

<...>
```

After sleeping for 30 seconds for the stack deploys on the build server, we run a testing container using the `test-driver` image we created in the build stage. When we run the test container, we connect it to our application's front-tier network. The test driver running in our test container is really simple. We will look at the code in a moment, but it simply uses `curl` to connect to the `appservice` over port `8080`, and looks for a specific string in the results. Again, we could spend a chapter or two on e2e testing, but at least here we provide the plumbing for implementing something more sophisticated like a Selenium Chrome test application.

After the test is done, we clean up the test container and remove the test application stack from the build server's local Swarm cluster.

For our Docker stack deploy to use the correct image for our app server under test, we created a special version of our `docker-compose` YAML file for the test stack. The following test stack YAML file uses the `$CI_COMMIT_REF_NAME` variable to reference the current test image for deployment based on branch. For the test stack and test-driver container, we used the `CI_PIPELINE_ID` to avoid any possible conflicts on the build server.

For all of the other images, we use the development organization's latest released candidate (RC-DEV), tagged images, for example, `dtr.mydomain.com/dev/atsea-db_build:RC-DEV`. Looking further down the file, we notice something special about the frontier network. We have included the attachable equals true parameter to the front-tier network. This allows our test-driver container to attach to the stack's internal front-tier network. Otherwise, only other services in this stack would be allowed to attach to the network.

Finally, at the end of the file, notice that we have our stack's secrets being injected into our stack's internally scoped secrets (no `external: true`) from files in our source code control system. We will talk about more options regarding stack internally scoped resources and initializing passwords when we get to discussing the `atsea-deploy` repository:

```
#docker-compose-e2e.yml

version: "3.7"

services:
  database:
    image: $DTR_SERVER/dev/atsea-db_build:RC-DEV
    user: postgres
    environment:
      POSTGRES_USER: gordonuser
      POSTGRES_PASSWORD_FILE: /run/secrets/postgres_password
      POSTGRES_DB: atsea
    ports:
      - "5432:5432"
    networks:
      - back-tier
    secrets:
      - postgres_password

  appserver:
    image: $DTR_SERVER/dev/atsea-web_build:$CI_COMMIT_REF_NAME
    user: gordon
    ports:
      - "8080:8080"
    networks:
      - front-tier
      - back-tier
    secrets:
      - postgres_password

  payment_gateway:
    image: $DTR_SERVER/dev/atsea-payment_build:RC-DEV
    networks:
      - payment
```

```
    secrets:
      - payment_token

  networks:
    front-tier:
      driver: overlay
      attachable: true
    back-tier:
    payment:

  secrets:
    postgres_password:
      file: ./devsecrets/postgres_password
    payment_token:
      file: ./devsecrets/payment_token
```

Finally, let's take a look at how we put together our end-to-end test driver container. First, we created a really simple container that is capable of running a `curl` command. Here is the Dockerfile that used to build the test-driver. We start with an Alpine (very small image), install the `curl` utility, and copy the `local-test-driver.sh` file to the image, make it executable, and set the `local-test-driver.sh` to start as PID 1:

```
#atsea-web/local-test-driver/Dockerfile
FROM alpine:3.7

RUN apk add curl
COPY ./local-test-driver.sh .
RUN chmod +x local-test-driver.sh
CMD ./local-test-driver.sh
```

Now, we will look at the script file that was executed by the Dockerfile `CMD`. Following that, we `curl` port 8080 of the `appserver` service. The service's name, `appserver`, resolves because the `test-driver` container is attached to a common front-tier with the `appserver` service. The response from `appserver` is parsed for the `Atsea Shop` string. If the string is found, the container exits successfully with a `0` error code, and the build proceeds. If the string is not found, then the container exits with a `1` (non-zero error code) and fails the build:

```
#!/bin/sh
[ $(curl --silent http://appserver:8080/index.html | grep -c "Atsea Shop")
== "1" ] || exit 1
```

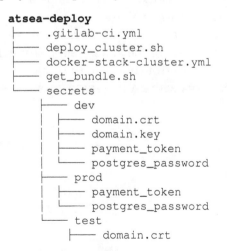

Figure 15: Left - Test fails, Right - Test succeeds

In the preceding screenshot on the left, we can see where the container test fails, and subsequently, the job and pipeline fail as expected. Because the test stage failed, the push never happens, and the defective image is never pushed to the DTR.

Pipeline deployment to Docker Enterprise

Finally, we get to the CI deployment and the final task in building our pipeline for our custom pilot application. For this, we visit the `atsea-deploy` repository. We start by building off of the scripts that we use for the manual deployment and adding a pipeline configuration file, just like the service pipelines. The following are the key artifacts in our deployment repository:

```
atsea-deploy
├── .gitlab-ci.yml
├── deploy_cluster.sh
├── docker-stack-cluster.yml
├── get_bundle.sh
└── secrets
    ├── dev
    │   ├── domain.crt
    │   ├── domain.key
    │   ├── payment_token
    │   └── postgres_password
    ├── prod
    │   ├── payment_token
    │   └── postgres_password
    └── test
        ├── domain.crt
```

```
├──── domain.key
├──── payment_token
├──── postgres_password
├──── wildcard.nvisia.io.key
└──── wildcard.nvisia.io.server.crt
```

In the beginning of the pipeline chapter in *Figure 7*, we used arrows to show that when source code is pushed, it triggers a pipeline build for each service repository. The service repository build created new images from the updated source code, pushed them to the DTR, and then triggered the application's deploy job using a deploy job from the `atsea-deploy` repository.

We are using the deploy repository as a central place for deploying our application whether it's to dev, test, prod. We could have duplicated this deployment logic at the end of each of the builds, but that would have gotten pretty messy and difficult to manage. Also, as discussed in the last section, we need the ability to trigger a deployment from a variety of events, including events outside of our CI system. So far, the only event we have seen is the deployment trigger that's fired upon the completion of a build from each of the service repositories. However, we want to position ourselves so that the deployment can be triggered from a remote script, or from the DTR as an image is promoted, or successfully scanned.

With a top-down approach, we describe our automated application deployment example, starting with how the external trigger enters the deployment pipeline, and we end up with an application stack running in a Docker Enterprise /test collection. We begin our deployment journey with the `atsea-deploy` repositories `.gitlab-ci.yml` file that's shown in the following sections.

Deployment pipeline file

We are using our Docker Runner with the `docker:stable` image. This image is based off of an Alpine 3.8 base image, and generally, works great. You may notice that we install several additional packages for the pipeline's Alpine container during the `before_script`. These are required to support the commands in our stack-deploy job's script. Let's take a detailed walk through the file:

```
# atsea-deploy .gitlab-ci.yml

image: docker:stable

stages:
  - deploy

before_script:
```

```
      - apk add unzip
      - apk add curl
      - apk add jq
      - apk add bash

  deploy-stack:
    stage: deploy
    script:
      - bash
      - chmod +x ./get_bundle.sh
      - chmod +x ./deploy_cluster.sh
      - ./get_bundle.sh
      - chmod +x ./env.sh
      - echo $DEPLOY_TARGET
      - ./deploy_cluster.sh $DEPLOY_TARGET
    only:
      - trigger
```

Again, `image: doctor:stable` tells the Runner to execute the script commands inside of Docker's official Alpine 3.8-based image with the Docker binaries installed. Remember when we registered the Docker Runner, we specified a volume (`-v /var/run/docker.sock:/var/run/docker.sock`) to mount the build server's host Docker socket. Initially, this means Docker commands executed from our pipeline container will be passed along to the build server's Docker daemon for execution. Please note that later, inside the `deploy_cluster.sh` script, we are going to override socket connection by sourcing our Bash shell to use the remote Docker daemon on one of the UCP hosts in our Docker Enterprise cluster. After the remote daemon connection is established, all of our Docker commands execute against the cluster! We will talk more about this when we get to the discussion about the `deploy_cluster.sh` script.

This deployment pipeline has one job (`deploy-stack`) and one stage (`deploy`). Therefore, the stage section, which could have been omitted since there's only one stage, simply lists the deploy stage.

In the `deploy-stack:` job, we jump right into the script section. First, we execute a Bash shell so that the rest of our commands have access to Bash's capabilities, allowing us to access the source command with our client bundle. Keep in mind that we installed the Bash Alpine package using the preceding `before_script`. Next, we want to make sure that these two scripts are executable from within our pipeline container. Use the `chmod +x` command to accomplish this. Then, we run the `get_bundle.sh` script file. This is an important feature of Docker Enterprise, where UCP provides a client bundle for remote RBAC enforced cluster access.

The following `get_bundle.sh` script creates an authorization token to connect to the remote Docker Enterprise UCP managers. `AUTH_TOKEN` is generated by hitting our Docker Enterprise's UCP API with UCP account's username and password parameters (we are passing our deployer account from a GitLab protected environment variable) in the header. This, of course, requires a pre-existing user account for our deployer to be created in the UCP authorization system. Additionally, the deployer's credentials need to have been safely stored inside of a GitLab protected environment variable. In our case, we stored the deployer username and password credentials inside an `atsea-deploy` project level protected variable, rather than at the group level like we did with the builder account credentials. We did this because the deployer credentials are only required from within the `atsea-deploy` project's pipeline. Finally, the results of the `curl`, where we pass the `AUTH_TOKEN` in data section of the client bundle post, is a `bundle.zip` file:

```bash
#!/bin/bash
export AUTH_TOKEN=$(curl -sk -d
'{"username":"'${DEPLOYER_USER}'","password":"'${DEPLOYER_PW}'"}'
https://ucp.nvisia.io/auth/login | jq -r .auth_token 2>/dev/null)
echo "Authtoken: ${AUTH_TOKEN}"

curl -sk -H "Authorization: Bearer ${AUTH_TOKEN}"
https://ucp.nvisia.io/api/clientbundle -o bundle.zip
ls -la
unzip bundle.zip
```

The `bundle.zip` file contains two types of assets—user certificates and scripts. The user certificates are used to create a secure remote connection and authenticate a specific user with UCP's **Role-Based Access Control (RBAC)**. The bundle also provides Linux and Windows scripts to connect a local shell to the remote cluster. Later, in our `deploy_cluster.sh` script, we will use the `env.sh` script to set up a secure remote shell from our pipeline shell (on the build server) to the remote Docker Enterprise cluster.

Finally, we list the contents of a directory to verify the `bundle.zip` file's size and contents, and then we unzip `bundle.zip`. Later, we will use the contents of the bundle to connect in the `deploy_cluster` script.

When we return from the `get_bundle.sh` script, we want to make sure that the `env.sh` script file is available for execution by using the `chmod +x` command, as we are going to use the `deploy-cluster` script. Now, we are ready to deploy.

As a debugging feature, and a point of discussion, we will now look at the `echo $DEPLOY_TARGET` script command. This variable is set by the caller of the remote trigger.

Our pipeline trigger was set up at the `atsea-deploy` project level in the CI/CD Setting > Pipeline triggers. When looking at the preceding `.gitlab-ci.yml` listing, notice at the bottom of the stack-deploy job specification that there is an `only:` constraint. We specified that this job is only run when initiated by a trigger. That means that to test this job, we have to use a `curl` command to trigger the pipeline and run the job.

If you recall, at the end of our service's build pipelines, we used a `curl` command to trigger our builds. One of the parameters to the trigger was the `DEPLOY_TARGET` variable `-F "variables[DEPLOY_TARGET]=test"` and, in our case, we set the parameter to `test` because we wanted to trigger a test deployment job. The test deployment takes the current release candidate images (`RC-`**test**) from our DTR test organization repositories and deploys them in a stack to the Docker Enterprise test cluster. To understand more about how this works, we can take a look at the following `deploy_cluster.sh` script file that's listed.

Inside of our `deploy_cluster.sh` file is an important comment about secrets. Here, you could use a variety of mechanisms to retrieve secrets from a remote, secure store to populate a temporary file, or inject them directly into the cluster as external secrets. In the next section, we will take a look at the `docker-stack-cluster.yml` file to see exactly how the secrets get populated at deploy time.

Next, we check to see if a parameter was passed in. Again, you could/should be more thorough with actual parameter validation. Next, we source the UCP client bundle to connect our local shell to the Docker Enterprise cluster. If the parameters are found, we create the `STACK` and `STACK_ENV` environment variables. These variables are referenced inside of the `docker-stack-cluster.yml` stack deploy file.

`IFS=` sets the internal field specifier for the shell to the default of `<space><tab><newline>`. If it is not set this way, the output of `env.sh` will not be processed properly as a `$()` sub command because the output from the `env.sh` command has no line breaks and fails. `eval $(<env.sh` runs the `env.sh` script from the UCP client `bundle.zip` file and points the shell client at the UCP remote cluster. Therefore, all subsequent Docker commands are run against the remote UCP cluster as the UCP user associated with the bundles, in our case, the deployer user.

Finally, we run the `docker stack deploy-c docker-stack-cluster.yml ${STACK}`
command to launch our stack, and use the `STACK` variable to name it:

```bash
#!/bin/bash

# Add your code to fetch and populate ./secrets/test ./secrets/prod using
copy or vault etc.

# Set stack name
if [[ -z "$1" ]]; then
    echo "Usage: please specify dev, test or prod";
    exit 1;
else
    export STACK_ENV=$1
    export STACK=atsea-deployer-${STACK_ENV}
fi

# Should fail and continue locally, but actually load the builder bundle in
CI build
IFS=
eval $(<env.sh)

echo -e "Launching stack... docker stack deploy -c docker-stack-cluster.yml
${STACK} \n"
docker stack deploy -c docker-stack-cluster.yml ${STACK}
```

We are almost there! Now, we need to take a closer look at our stack deployment YAML
file used in the following `deploy_cluster.sh`, to cover some subtle, but important, points
of interest.

First of all, we are referencing environment variables that we set in the
`deployed_cluster.sh` script. Again, that is the script that actually called `docker stack
deploy` and runs this file. Using environment variables is a convenient way to use stack
files as parameterized templates. However, there is one key restriction you should be aware
of—you cannot substitute environment variables into Swarm top level resource's names,
such as the names of services, networks, volumes, and secrets. In other words, we cannot
define `services: ${DB_NAME}-database:` or `networks: ${NET_NAME}-front-end:`
in our stack files. There are some pretty good reasons to do this, primarily to avoid
collisions on common Swarm-wide resource names, but Swarm's stack internal resource
isolation can help here. We will talk about this in the *Docker Swarm resource* section.

At the bottom of the file, we notice that our secrets are set up a little differently than before.
This time, the secrets are being read from a file directly into the secrets for the stack. Again,
these secrets could have been directly injected from Hashicorp vault or a temporary file
location.

Otherwise, this stack file looks deceptively similar to the version we used for our manual stack deployment earlier in this chapter. However, there are actually some substantial differences in this file related to internal verses external resources!

```
# atsea-deploy .gitlab-ci.yml
version: "3.7"

services:
  database:
    image: ${DTR_SERVER}/${STACK_ENV}/atsea-db_build:RC-${STACK_ENV}
    environment:
      POSTGRES_USER: gordonuser
      POSTGRES_DB_PASSWORD_FILE: /run/secrets/postgres_password
      POSTGRES_DB: atsea
    networks:
      - back-tier
    secrets:
      - postgres_password

  appserver:
    image: ${DTR_SERVER}/${STACK_ENV}/atsea-web_build:RC-${STACK_ENV}
    networks:
      - front-tier
      - back-tier
      - payment
    deploy:
      replicas: 2
      update_config:
        parallelism: 2
        failure_action: rollback
      restart_policy:
        condition: on-failure
        delay: 5s
        max_attempts: 3
        window: 120s
      labels:
        com.docker.lb.hosts: at-sea-${STACK_ENV}.mydomain.com
        com.docker.lb.network: ${STACK}_front-tier
        com.docker.lb.port: 8080
        com.docker.lb.ssl_cert: wildcard.mydomain.com.server.crt
        com.docker.lb.ssl_key: wildcard.mydomain.com.key
    secrets:
      - postgres_password

  payment_gateway:
    image: ${DTR_SERVER}/${STACK_ENV}/atsea-payment_build:RC-${STACK_ENV}
    secrets:
      - source: staging_token
```

```
        target: payment_token
      networks:
        - payment
      deploy:
        update_config:
          failure_action: rollback

networks:
  front-tier:
  back-tier:
  payment:
    driver: overlay

secrets:
  postgres_password:
    file: ./secrets/${STACK_ENV}/postgres_password
    labels:
        com.docker.ucp.access.label: /${STACK_ENV}
  staging_token:
    file: ./secrets/${STACK_ENV}/payment_token
    labels:
        com.docker.ucp.access.label: /${STACK_ENV}
  wildcard.mydomain.com.key:
    file: ./secrets/${STACK_ENV}/wildcard.mydomain.com.key
    labels:
        com.docker.ucp.access.label: /${STACK_ENV}
  wildcard.mydomain.com.server.crt:
    file: ./secrets/${STACK_ENV}/wildcard.mydomain.com.server.crt
```

Injecting secrets from a file is very convenient, but prepending labels values like the
com.docker.lb.network can be challenging.

Understanding Docker Swarm resource scoping

In the previous manual deployment example, our stack's YAML file made use of external
Swarm resources. In other words, we created the front-tier network and all of our secrets
before we launched the stack. Then, in the stack file, we marked the resources as external,
indicating to Swarm those resources are to be created outside, and prior to the scope of this
stack. This works great when you deliberately intend to share resources across multiple
stacks in a Docker Swarm. However, it's not so great if you or your build system
accidentally shares resources because they coincidentally have the same names! Luckily,
the Docker community has put some thought into this.

When deploying a stack using Docker Swarm, it achieves stack resource scoping by adding the stack's name as a prefix to all of the stack's top-level, internal resources (services, networks, and secrets not declared as `external: true`) at deploy time. Therefore, if we deploy the stack file shown previously with a stack name of `atsea-deployer-test`, the back-tier network will be created as `atsea-deployer-test_back-tier`. This is a convention Swarm uses to achieve stack resource isolation. External stack resource names do not change at deployment, and are expected to be present at stack deploy time—Swarm does not prefix them.

That is all great, but this can get a little tricky for us when setting label values that contain internally scoped resources. For instance, we use `com.docker.lb.network: front-tier` to tell Interlock which network to use. However, as we just learned, the name of the front-tier network will be changed to `atsea-deployer-test_front-tier` when the stack is deployed. The Interlock service will try to find the front-tier network and fail. In our case, we set the label to `com.docker.lb.network: ${STACK}_front-tier` to make it work.

It is worth mentioning that there are some Docker template variables you can use in stack files where you can ask Swarm for runtime values of services's attributes like hostname, mount, and env properties.

> More information can be found at `https://docs.docker.com/engine/reference/commandline/service_create/#create-services-using-templates`.

Unfortunately, the Stack properties are a level above the service, and are not available at this time. Finally, as we mentioned previously, you may not use environment variable substitution within the `compose-file` with Swarm when referring to a top-level resource names (for example, `${STACK_NAME}front-tier`) in the secrets or network sections of our file.

So, there are some trade-offs to be considered when building your Swarm stack files. You can use external resources and always be sure of the name, but you must avoid name collisions across the entire Swarm, perhaps using some sort of name spacing scheme. Or you can use Swarm's internally scoped resource names, and compensate externally, adding the stack name as a prefix.

Triggering the pipeline manually

Now, it's time to give it a try. To start a process, we must trigger a pipeline with the following `curl` command. Therefore, I will run it from a Bash shell on my local development machine and we get a long JSON response container with a link to the resulting pipeline:

```
$curl -X POST -F token=xxxxxxxxxxxxxxxxx-F "ref=master" -F
"variables[DEPLOY_TARGET]=test"
https://gitlab.com/api/v4/projects/xxxxxxxxxxxx/trigger/pipeline

{... https://gitlab.com/dockereebook/atsea-deploy/-/jobs/156752572...}
```

If we follow the line, we can see the output from the pipeline, as follows. The source code is checked out, the packages are installed, the UCP client bundle is downloaded, the files are unzipped, the shell is connected, and the stack is launched:

```
Checking out f0d8a037 as master...
Skipping Git submodules setup
$ apk add unzip
fetch http://dl-cdn.alpinelinux.org/alpine/v3.8/main/x86_64/APKINDEX.tar.gz
fetch
http://dl-cdn.alpinelinux.org/alpine/v3.8/community/x86_64/APKINDEX.tar.gz
(1/1) Installing unzip (6.0-r4)
Executing busybox-1.28.4-r3.trigger
OK: 5 MiB in 15 packages
$ apk add curl
(1/4) Installing nghttp2-libs (1.32.0-r0)
(2/4) Installing libssh2 (1.8.0-r3)
(3/4) Installing libcurl (7.61.1-r1)
(4/4) Installing curl (7.61.1-r1)
Executing busybox-1.28.4-r3.trigger
OK: 6 MiB in 19 packages
$ apk add jq
(1/2) Installing oniguruma (6.8.2-r0)
(2/2) Installing jq (1.6_rc1-r1)
Executing busybox-1.28.4-r3.trigger
OK: 7 MiB in 21 packages
$ apk add bash
(1/5) Installing ncurses-terminfo-base (6.1_p20180818-r1)
(2/5) Installing ncurses-terminfo (6.1_p20180818-r1)
(3/5) Installing ncurses-libs (6.1_p20180818-r1)
(4/5) Installing readline (7.0.003-r0)
(5/5) Installing bash (4.4.19-r1)
Executing bash-4.4.19-r1.post-install
Executing busybox-1.28.4-r3.trigger
OK: 16 MiB in 26 packages
$ bash
```

```
$ chmod +x ./get_bundle.sh
$ chmod +x ./deploy_cluster.sh
$ ./get_bundle.sh
Authtoken: xxxxxxxxx-xxxx-xxxx-xxxx-xxxxxxxxxxxxxx
total 64
drwxrwxrwx    4 root      root          4096 Feb  5 18:22 .
drwxrwxrwx    4 root      root          4096 Jan 28 14:36 ..
drwxrwxrwx    5 root      root          4096 Feb  5 18:22 .git
...
-rw-r--r--    1 root      root         11879 Feb  5 18:22 bundle.zip

Archive: bundle.zip
  extracting: ca.pem
  extracting: cert.pem
  extracting: key.pem
  extracting: cert.pub
  extracting: env.ps1
  extracting: env.cmd
  extracting: kube.yml
  extracting: env.sh
$ chmod +x ./env.sh
$ echo $DEPLOY_TARGET
test
$ ./deploy_cluster.sh $DEPLOY_TARGET
Launching stack... docker stack deploy -c docker-stack-cluster.yml atsea-
deployer-test

Creating network atsea-deployer-test_payment
Creating network atsea-deployer-test_back-tier
Creating network atsea-deployer-test_front-tier
Creating secret atsea-deployer-test_staging_token
Creating secret atsea-deployer-test_wildcard.mydomain.com.key
Creating secret atsea-deployer-test_wildcard.mydomain.com.server.crt
Creating secret atsea-deployer-test_postgres_password
Creating service atsea-deployer-test_payment_gateway
Creating service atsea-deployer-test_database
Creating service atsea-deployer-test_appserver
Job succeeded
```

Finally, here's a UCP screenshot of our service being deployed to the Docker Enterprise cluster—the services are deployed and replicated:

Figure 16: UCP shows the pipeline deployed stack

Summary

In this chapter, we covered important concepts related to developing and deploying applications with Docker Enterprise. We backed the concepts up with samples, including an end-to-end CI pipeline to build and deploy the Docker AtSea sample application onto a Docker Enterprise cluster. We covered services, networking, routing mesh, layer 7 ingress control, UCP client bundles, and integration with CI Pipelines.

As we continue on our journey, we will take a look at logging and monitoring of your new pilot application, followed by a variety topics about getting your cluster and application production ready. In this chapter, we focused on using Swarm as our orchestrator, because it is a really good starting point for most Enterprises. Later in this book, we are going to come back and redeploy our application using Kubernetes in our Docker Enterprise cluster.

Questions

1. How does Docker speed up software development cycles?
2. What are the multiple docker-compose files for?
3. How does Docker Enterprise integrate with a CI system?
4. What is the life cycle for secrets in our Build Pipeline?

Further reading

- **Article on how long to wait between failed calls**:
    - https://aws.amazon.com/blogs/architecture/exponential-backoff-and-jitter/
- **Retrying Java API calls with Spring retry**:
    - https://docs.spring.io/spring-batch/trunk/reference/html/retry.html
- **Circuit breaker patter with Netflix Hystrix**:
    - https://github.com/Netflix/Hystrix
- **This is a great reference architecture article by Anoop Kumar on Ingress Networking and Load Balancing**:
    - https://success.docker.com/article/ucp-service-discovery
- **Using Docker Swarm secrets**:
    - https://docs.docker.com/engine/swarm/secrets/
- **Using Kubernetes secrets**:
    - https://kubernetes.io/docs/concepts/configuration/secret/#creating-a-secret-using-kubectl-create-secret
- **Dockerfile best practices**:
    - https://docs.docker.com/develop/develop-images/dockerfile_best-practices/
- **Remote debugging with Java**:
    - https://blog.docker.com/2017/05/spring-boot-development-docker/
- **Docker Enterprise 2 Ingress with Interlock 2**:
    - https://docs.docker.com/ee/ucp/interlock/architecture/

- **Storing configs in Swarm**:
  - https://docs.docker.com/engine/swarm/configs/
- **Service template variables and variable substitution**:
  - https://docs.docker.com/engine/reference/commandline/
    service_create/#create-services-using-templates
  - https://docs.docker.com/compose/compose-file/#variable-
    substitution.
- **Using variable substitution in compose (docker-compose and docker stack deploy)**:
  - https://docs.docker.com/compose/compose-file/#variable-
    substitution
- **Gitlab Runner introduction**:
  - https://docs.gitlab.com/Runner/
- **Post on injecting external Spring configs**:
  - https://stackoverflow.com/questions/46057625/
    externalising-spring-boot-properties-when-deploying-to-
    docker
- **Docker In Docker verses Docker On Docker**:
  - https://jpetazzo.github.io/2015/09/03/do-not-use-docker-
    in-docker-for-ci/

7
Pilot Docker Enterprise Platform Monitoring and Logging

As we wind down our pilot phase, we need to think about how we are going to support our pilot application during the internal pilot. Beyond the external access metrics like `https://www.site24x7.com/` and others do so well, we need to get start getting real experience in container logging and monitoring.

Logging and monitoring is a transformational area where we have to be careful **not** to pave the cowpath. In other words, it would be easy to carry some old habits into the new world of containers, but it could be problematic. Traditionally, we set up our application servers to handle logging. We usually did this in one of two ways. We either used logging frameworks to write logs to the application server's filesystem, or we installed agents on each of these servers to monitor the logging activity. Because we had a relatively small number of application servers set up to host monolithic, multi-application deployments, it made sense and worked pretty well.

While the logging and agent approaches will still technically work in a container world, they are not necessarily a good fit for the ephemeral nature of containers where each application has one or more containers. Let's say you had an old application server running five applications (each with a web app and restful API) that turns into 10 containers (5 x 2). Now, imagine that those 10 containers are spread across a five node cluster. Just imagine trying to figure out where the container ran last and where it wrote the logs. Or, think about having to instrument every container in your cluster with a log agent and figure out the licensing for 10 running and perhaps 30 stopped containers!

Don't panic! Along with this great container technology stack came a lot of innovative and cost-effective solutions.

In this chapter, we will cover the following topics:

- Docker Engine-Community logging
- Logging and monitoring distributed container applications with ELK
- Logging and monitoring with Docker Enterprise
- Open source logging and monitoring with Prometheus/Grafana
- Commercial logging example with Sysdig

Logging and monitoring distributed, containerized applications

First, we will start with the basics of Docker logging by looking at logging on a single host Docker node, as shown in the diagram that follows. As you may recall, Docker automatically captures the standard error and standard output streams from running containers and directs them to the Docker log files. In this section, we will explore what that really means in terms of where the logs go, and how to get to them.

This diagram represents the default log configuration settings for a Docker Linux daemon. On the left-hand side of the diagram, you can see a Docker Engine represented with a box. Underneath the Docker Engine box, we can see how the Docker Engine uses `systemd` to write to the system logs on the host's `systemd-journald` log. The system captures the output from the Docker daemon to this log, where it can be accessed with the `journalctl` command, as shown in the Terminal window.

Default Docker Engine logs

Inside of the Docker Engine box, we can see two containers running and how their logs are being written to the host filesystem in JSON format. These logs can be accessed from the Docker container logs command, as shown in the Terminal window:

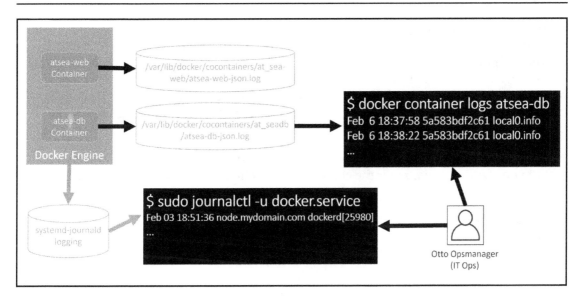

Figure 1: The settings for Docker contain

The settings for Docker container logging can be adjusted by modifying a file located in the /etc/docker directory called daemon.json. Looking at the following listing, you can see the listing from a sample daemon.json file that I would strongly recommend as a default configuration. In the following file, you can see that the log-driver is set to json-file. That is the default when Docker is installed on a Linux-based system. The log-opts vary for each driver. In our case, we are using the max-size option to set the maximum size of a log file to 10 MB and the max-file option to specify how many log files to keep. This means Docker will rotate the log files so that when a file reaches 10 MB, it starts a new file and it keeps only the latest three logs files in storage.

This is really important as one serious issue we see at customer sites is when log files are not rolled. They can then grow out of control and consume all of the disk space on a Docker node. The node can become none-responsive, but this can easily be avoided by using these options. Never set an engine's logging level to debug without verifying you have some sort of log truncation or rolling scheme in place. At a debug level of logging, you can collect gigabytes of logs in just hours.

Also, notice the live restore option that's set to true on this node. This configuration file is taken from my standalone (non-swarm) Docker load balancer node, where HAProxy is handling all inbound traffic to the cluster, and I, therefore, do not want this container going down, even if the Docker Daemon stops. Please note there are some side effects that can affect things like upgrades, where you will want to take your container down manually to perform the upgrade so that we're sure that no resources are locked during the upgrade process.

Please know that if you make any changes to your daemon JSON file, you will have to restart your Docker daemon for the changes to take effect. Generally speaking, a `sudo service docker restart` should do the trick, as follows:

```
$ sudo cat /etc/docker/daemon.json
{
"log-driver": "json-file",
"log-opts": {
    "max-size": "10m",
    "max-file": "3"
    },
"live-restore": true
}

# Get the current logging driver
$ docker info --format '{{.LoggingDriver}}'
json-file

# Get a list of available logging plugins
$ docker info --format '{{.Plugins.Log}}'
[awslogs fluentd gcplogs gelf journald json-file local logentries splunk
syslog]
```

The following is a list of the standard logging drivers included with an out-of-the-box install of the Docker Engine-Community Linux Daemon. Remember, if there is no `/etc/docker/daemon.json` file, or it is empty, the default driver is `.json` file. You can check your logging file, as shown in the preceding code block, with the `docker info --format '{{.LoggingDriver}}'` command.

Finally, you can see all of the available logging drivers, including any drivers installed by third-party logging plugins, by using the `docker info --format '{{.Plugins.Log}}'` command.

You can get more information on the log options for each standard driver by visiting the Docker documents page found here: `https://docs.docker.com/config/containers/logging/configure/`:

Log driver	Description
None	No logs are available for the container and Docker logs do not return any output.
json (https://docs.docker.com/config/containers/logging/json-file/)	The logs are formatted as JSON. The default logging driver for Docker.
syslog (https://docs.docker.com/config/containers/logging/syslog/)	Writes logging messages to the syslog facility. The syslog daemon must be running on the host machine.
journald (https://docs.docker.com/config/containers/logging/journald/)	Writes log messages to journald. The journald daemon must be running on the host machine.
gelf (https://docs.docker.com/config/containers/logging/gelf/)	Writes log messages to a **Graylog Extended Log Format** (**GELF**) endpoint such as Graylog or Logstash.
fluentd (https://docs.docker.com/config/containers/logging/fluentd/)	Writes log messages to fluentd (forward input). The fluentd daemon must be running on the host machine.
awslogs (https://docs.docker.com/config/containers/logging/awslogs/)	Writes log messages to Amazon CloudWatch logs.
splunk (https://docs.docker.com/config/containers/logging/splunk/)	Writes log messages to splunk using the HTTP Event Collector.
etwlogs (https://docs.docker.com/config/containers/logging/etwlogs/)	Writes log messages as **Event Tracing for Windows** (**ETW**) events. Only available on Windows platforms.
gcplogs (https://docs.docker.com/config/containers/logging/gcplogs/)	Writes log messages to **Google Cloud Platform** (**GCP**) logging.
logentries (https://docs.docker.com/config/containers/logging/logentries/)	Writes Log messages to Rapid7 Log entries.

Centralized logging

Docker logging works great for a single node, but what if I have a cluster of 10, 20, or even 100 nodes? How are we supposed to manage all of those logs across all of those nodes? The answer is centralized logging!

There are a couple of different approaches to implementing centralized logging. One method is a **publish model**, where all of the metric endpoints publish their logs to a central server. An ELK Stack is a good example of an open source solution using the publish model. A second method for centralized logging is a **polling model**, where the central logging server polls all the targeted metric endpoints. Prometheus is a popular example of an open source solution using a polling model.

Publish approach with an ELK Stack

The ELK in ELK Stack is an acronym representing the components in the logging stack. E is for Elasticsearch, L is for Logstash, and K is for Kibana. It turns out that these three open source technologies make an outstanding centralized logging stack. Logstash can take a massive pipeline of data, normalize it, and deliver it to Elasticsearch at scale. Logstash is sometimes referred to as a powerful ingestion tool for Elasticsearch. Elasticsearch indexes huge amounts of log data and makes them searchable in real time, while Kibana provides very cool infographic style visualisations and graphs from your log data.

The publish model relies on log structure to not only understand the metrics, but equally as important is what the metric's source was. Because the logs are pushed to the central server, there is no easy and reliable way to determine the source. The server knows nothing about the metric sources as a matter of configuration, so only through convention of the log tags/structure can the source information be determined. This is why we emphasize the importance of a good logging structure for application development teams. While architects may no longer dictate which logging framework to use when building distributed systems (or even microservices), they should insist on the following:

- Conventions in the logging format
- Logs are always written to standard out and standard error

So let's take a look at how an ELK Stack works in a Docker cluster. We need to start each node's configuration for the local Docker Engine logging driver. In our following example, in the following diagram, we are no longer using the default `json`-file driver. Instead, we have switched over to the `journald` log driver. This means all container logs are saved in the local host's `systemd-journald` logs. So now, all container logs and Docker daemon services are captured in the same local log file.

Now, we need to get the logs from our local log file to the log stash service running on the ELK server. In our diagram, this flow is represented by the red arrows, and is facilitated by something called Journalbeat (`https://github.com/mheese/journalbeat`). Journalbeat runs in a container, mounts the local system logs, and pushes the new entries to the Logstash service on the remote ELK server host. Then, all of the new logs from each of the nodes are quickly indexed and stored. Finally, Otto, our operations manager, can use the Kibana UI to look for any problems or anomalies in log data from any container on any node:

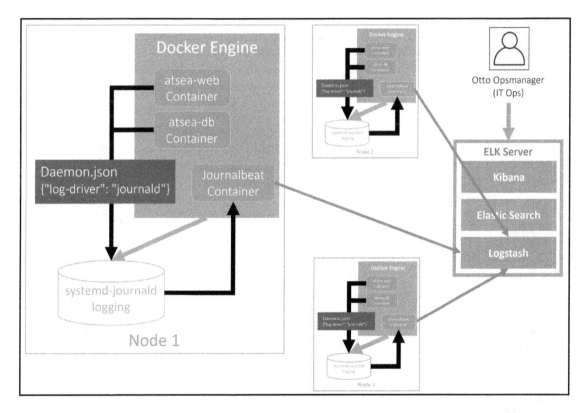

Figure 2: ELK Stack Central Logging

That is pretty cool, but it is just the beginning of the central logging journey. In fact, the plumbing is the easy part of this platform setup. The difficult part is structuring the queries to discover problems and anomalies, and making sure that the application teams are logging the appropriate information at the right time.

Polling approach with Prometheus

The second common centralized logging approach is a **polling** model, where the central logging server polls all of the targeted metric endpoints. In this scenario, the central server is aware of its metric endpoints as a matter of configuration and polls them, storing the results in a central database. One popular example of the polling model is Prometheus, a very popular, open source monitoring platform.

Prometheus is an open source monitoring platform that is simple to configure and use. In the following diagram, we are showing a very basic setup, with a Prometheus server being configured through a YAML configuration file, and polling an application container on a test server. The YAML file describes the server's behavior, such as how often the server scrapes/polls the endpoints. Most importantly, it describes the target endpoints as jobs and the server uses the HTTP path, IP address, and port number to collect metrics. On the test server side, we have something called an exporter.

There are a number of exporters that you can plug into your application's deployment platform, where you deploy the export alongside your application to get access runtime metrics without changing your application code. For instance, the Prometheus JMX exporter's (`https://github.com/prometheus/jmx_exporter`). `jar` file can be downloaded into your Tomcat deployment as a separate application, and expose key JVM metrics to the Prometheus server. This works great for lift and shift applications, but there is way more you can do if you wish to build your own metrics endpoint.

Prometheus has official and unofficial client libraries for a wide variety of programming languages: `https://prometheus.io/docs/instrumenting/clientlibs/`. You can use these client libraries to create your own metrics, such as the number of widgets shipped, or burgers ordered. This opens the door to using a whole new collection of business metrics where you can create a dashboard for your business users. A word of caution, though; the maintainers of Prometheus do not guarantee the type of metric traceability you would need for something like a billing system. So, while you can use it for internal metrics of all kinds, be careful if lawyers are involved! We recommend Elton Stoneman's Pluralsight class (`https://www.pluralsight.com/courses/monitoring-containerized-app-health-docker`) as a great place to get started with the Prometheus client libraries.

Simple Prometheus setup

Once you have this simple setup in place, Otto can use Prometheus's Web UI to configure graphs and alerts based on the metrics provided by the Prometheus export app on port 9323:

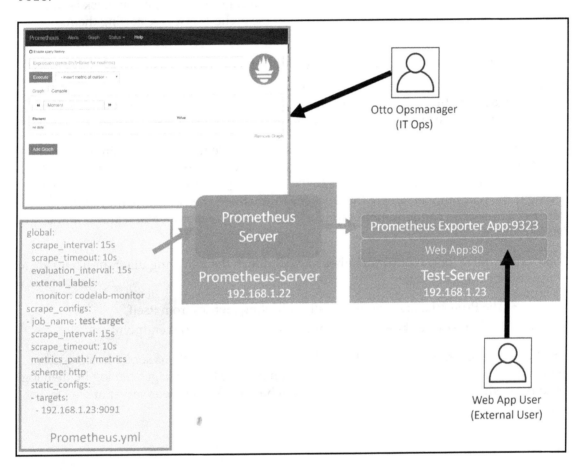

Figure 3: Simple Prometheus Web Application Monitor

Okay, but what does that have to do with Docker? It turns out that Docker has exposed a Prometheus metrics endpoint within the Docker Engine. So, you can collect a wealth of information, like the number of containers in various states (paused, running, stopped), or number of failed health checks—do not overlook the value of the failed health checks. Remember that Swarm will restart containers that fail, and therefore, it can mask issues where containers crash after a period of time and the orchestrator is restarting them.

Prometheus on Docker and checking Docker

Now that we know Docker has a Prometheus metrics endpoint, we will set up a quick demo from a Prometheus server running as a Docker container, on the same node where we are monitoring the Docker metrics! This is well-documented here.

In the following diagram, we take a look at a few critical items that are required to make this setup work. First, we have to get the Docker Engine to expose the Prometheus endpoint on a specific port. This requires changes to the `daemon.json` file. The first configuration setting is the port number, where the Docker's Prometheus metrics endpoint can be reached. The second configuration setting allows access to experimental features in the Docker Engine.

Next, take a quick look at our Prometheus YAML file in the following diagram. There are a couple of key things to note:

- The Prometheus server is actually collecting metrics from itself
- We can also see how it is monitoring the Docker metrics endpoint

The following diagram illustrates the deployment of the Prometheus server in a container with a `docker container run` command and how Otto Opsmanager can log in, then log in to Prometheus's Web UI and see metrics from both the Prometheus server and a Docker endpoint:

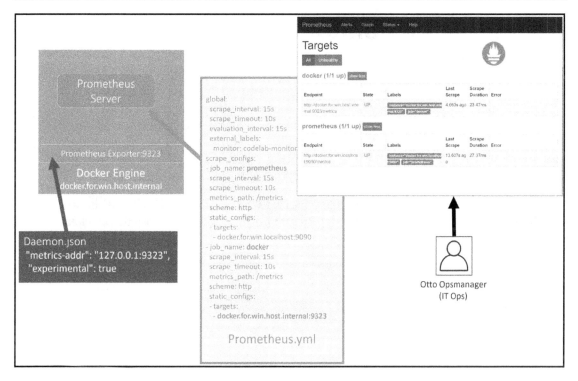

Figure 4: Prometheus Pulling Metrics From Docker Engine Endpoint (Experimental)

That is cool enough, but I'm sure I lost most of you at **experimental** mode! Experimental mode implies experimental features in the Docker Engine that are not production-ready. Therefore, using this sort of direct monitoring of the Docker Engine endpoint might work fine for local development, but it is not so acceptable an approach for production environments.

Next, we will look at monitoring a Docker Enterprise cluster with more production grade solutions. We will build off of the Prometheus concepts we discussed in this section, as well as look at a sample commercial solution.

Logging and monitoring in Docker Enterprise

Docker Enterprise does a great job of walking a tightrope between providing enough essential, out-of-the-box, enterprise features, and flexibility through integration and extensibility. Monitoring is a really good example of this balancing act. You get the basic information you need for operating your Docker Enterprise cluster, but the flexibility to bring your own tools to the game. For monitoring, Docker uses an internal packing of Prometheus to provide some essential metrics through the UCP dashboard.

The following screenshot shows a metrics overview from UCP's Web UI Dashboard, where the data all comes from a Kubernetes deployment of Prometheus across the Docker Enterprise Manager Nodes:

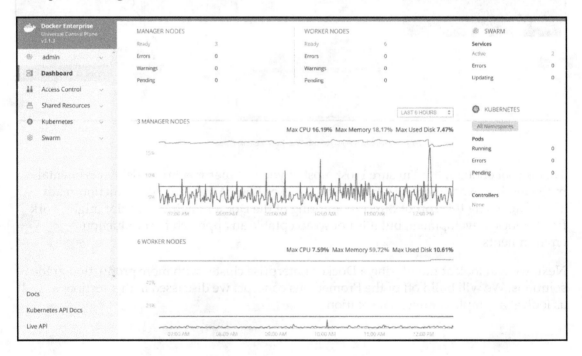

Figure 5: UCP Dashboard Using Prometheus

The UCP metrics give cluster operators the ability to quickly see if there are issues with their cluster. While this is perhaps not a great long-term solution, it really helps during the pilot phase as the operations team figures out what sort of metrics will be important in the container world. Then, Docker gets out of the way and encourages you to implement pretty much any solution you would like, including Prometheus and Grafana running in your cluster, alongside their internal Prometheus implementation.

We intentionally say that Docker encourages extension and integration, because they provide solution briefs in conjunction with certified partner solutions. Docker certified solution briefs are step-by-step guides to help you extend and integrate Docker with third-party, Docker certified technology providers you already use.

Docker Enterprise UCP and Prometheus

Looking at Docker's implementation of Prometheus for UCP's metrics provides some pretty interesting insights into how Prometheus can be used in a production setting. Interestingly enough, in Docker UCP version 3.1, UCP metrics are collected through a Kubernetes deployment of Prometheus to each UCP Manager node. The goal of their implementation is to collect up to 24 hours worth of running metrics from UCP events and resources to assist operators to triage problems. In other words, if there's a problem, you can pop into the UCP's UI to look at the metrics and this can lead you toward problem diagnostic and resolution. However, it is not designed to displace your primary toolset for logging, monitoring, and alerting the system.

In addition to Docker's use of Kubernetes to deploy UCP's Prometheus metrics, they also added a UCP API endpoint (`metricsdiscovery`) to support their implementation. This endpoint reveals all of the metric endpoints Prometheus needs. If you are interested in seeing this in action, log in to the UCP Web UI, click on the live API link, navigate to `metricsdiscovery`, try it, then execute. You will see a response body that looks like the following:

```
[
  {
    "targets": [
      "10.10.1.38:12376",
      "10.10.1.39:12376",
      "10.10.1.40:12376",
      "10.10.1.40:443",
      "10.10.1.43:12376",
      "10.10.1.43:443",
      "10.10.1.37:12376",
      "10.10.1.37:443",
      "10.10.1.44:12376",
```

```
        "10.10.1.45:12376",
        "10.10.1.41:12376",
        "10.10.1.42:12376"
      ]
    }
  ]
```

Notice how the IP address is different for the manager's nodes (port `443`—UCP's API) and workers (port `12376`— `ucp_proxy`). Docker then uses an inventory container (inside the metrics pod), uses the UCP API's `metricsdiscovery` service to pull the exporter endpoints, and saves them to a share volume, where the Prometheus server configuration can pick them up.

Now that we've seen how Docker does it, let's figure out the best approach for a pilot setup.

Docker Enterprise with Prometheus and Grafana

When it comes to using Prometheus and Grafana with Docker Enterprise, there are a couple of options since Docker Enterprise's UCP is already using Prometheus. One approach is where we piggyback on Docker Prometheus's exporters/endpoint and just add our own Prometheus server to poll them. That will work, of course, and it is well-documented (`https://docs.docker.com/ee/ucp/admin/configure/collect-cluster-metrics/`), but then we rely on the underlying endpoint structure to remain the same as Docker upgrades their UCP metrics implementation over time. A safer way would be to deploy our own Prometheus server and exporters so that we can deploy independently of the Docker's Prometheus implementation.

 Neither of these approaches use the Docker Engines experimental endpoint. They both use discrete exporters, separate from the Docker Engine, to probe the system for metrics, and therefore avoid the use of any experimental features.

This approach to implementing Prometheus and Grafana is documented in a Docker solution brief. I will walk you through a quick streamlined version using Docker Swarm to deploy our Prometheus exporters, as well as the server. The full article is available here: `https://success.docker.com/article/grafana-prometheus-monitoring`.

The article starts off by talking about the major components required for the solution. Fundamentally, we will deploy one server stack (Prometheus/Grafana/NGINX) and a set of two exporters to each node in the cluster.

This topology is easy to achieve with both generic Swarm or Kubernetes. In Swarm, you can use **global** replication, while in Kubernetes, you can use a daemon set for the exporters. However, UCP restricts the types of workload that run on a certain node. For instance, worker nodes are marked as Swarm, Kubernetes, or Mixed. Furthermore, UCP can be set to disallow user workloads on DTR workers and UCP manager nodes. Fortunately, there are some clever workarounds. Luckily, there's a little hack to work around this problem with Swarm, as long as you have SSH access to one of the UCP manager nodes in your cluster. This hack bypasses UCP and uses Swarm CE by going directly to the UCP manager's Docker socket—disabling environmental variables during the stack deploy with `env -i` does the trick. Unfortunately, if you just have a UCP client bundle and no manager node SSH, you will have to go with the Kubernetes daemon set approach for the exporters as pods.

With respect to the two types of exporters, the first is called cAdvisor and is used to collect container related statistics. The second type is called Node Exporter, and it collects system metrics from each host. Swarm global replication will make sure that each of these containers is running on all nodes at all times—even if new workers are added to the cluster after deployment.

The server stack (Prometheus/Grafana/NGINX) is comprised of three components. The first component is an NGINX server to provide basic auth access to the Prometheus Web UI server. The second component is the Prometheus server itself, which we've seen before. Finally, we have Grafana to display our dashboard. We will only expose two ports outside of our stack. Port `33090` is used to access the Prometheus Web UI via the NGINX basic auth from end, and port `33000` is used to access Grafana's Web UI.

Setting this up with swarm is actually pretty simple. We need to complete the following steps:

1. SSH into a UCP Manager.
2. Create a `prometheus` subdirectory, `cd` into it, and copy these files:
    - `nginx.conf` (`https://success.docker.com/api/asset/.%2Fpublish%2Fgrafana-prometheus-monitoring%2F.%2Fsamples%2Fnginx.conf`)
    - `docker-entrypoint.sh` (`https://success.docker.com/api/asset/.%2Fpublish%2Fgrafana-prometheus-monitoring%2F.%2Fsamples%2Fdocker-entrypoint.sh`)
    - Dockerfile (`https://success.docker.com/api/asset/.%2Fpublish%2Fgrafana-prometheus-monitoring%2F.%2Fsamples%2FDockerfile`)

3. Build and push an NGINX basic auth proxy image to your DTR repo:
    1. `docker image build --rm --no-cache --tag dtr.mydomain.com/admin/monitoring-nginx:v1 .`
    2. `docker image push dtr.mydomain.com/admin/monitoring-nginx:v1`
    3. You may have to `docker login dtr.mydomain.com` before you push

4. Create a swarm secret, as follows:

```
echo 'YourPasswordHere'| docker secret create prometheus-password -
```

5. Update the `docker-compose` file, as follows:
    1. Update the image name of the NGINX image to `dtr.mydomain.com/admin/monitoring-nginx:v1`
    2. Remove the ports specification from the `monitoring-cadvisor` and `monitoring-node-exporter` services as they are not needed, and may cause port conflicts

6. Deploy the stack. Here's the hack:

```
env -i docker stack deploy -c docker-compose.yml grafana-prometheus
```

7. Log into Prometheus by using any cluster node's IP and port `33090`:
    1. Use the the password you saved in the secret back in step 4.1
    2. Check **Status** | **Targets** to see if your nodes are up

8. Log into Grafana using any cluster node's IP and port `33000`:
    1. The `admin/admin`
    2. Reset password

9. Set up a Prometheus data source using your basic auth Prometheus credentials

10. Import a sample dashboard using the following URL: `https://grafana.com/dashboards/893`

11. Enjoy the magic!

Here is my cleaned up version of the `docker-compose` file, broke into a few pieces:

```
version: '3.4'

services:
  monitoring-nginx:
```

```
image: dtr.mydomain.com/admin/monitoring-nginx:v1
hostname: monitoring-nginx
environment:
  PROMETHEUS_PASSWORD_FILE: '/run/secrets/prometheus-password'
secrets:
  - prometheus-password
deploy:
  restart_policy:
    condition: any
    delay: 5s
    max_attempts: 5
networks:
  - monitoring-frontend
  - monitoring-backend
ports:
  - "33090:19090"
```

The preceding `monitoring-nginx` service is used as a load balancer frontend, and provides a basic auth wrapper in front of the Prometheus Web UI.

The following code block shows the setup for Grafana and Prometheus:

```
monitoring-grafana:
  image: grafana/grafana:latest
  hostname: monitoring-grafana
  networks:
    - monitoring-frontend
    - monitoring-backend
  ports:
    - "33000:3000"
  volumes:
    - grafana-data:/var/lib/grafana

monitoring-prometheus:
  image: prom/prometheus:latest
  hostname: monitoring-prometheus
  networks:
    - monitoring-backend
  command:
    - '--config.file=/etc/prometheus/prometheus.yml'
    - '--storage.tsdb.path=/prometheus'
  volumes:
    - prometheus-metrics-data:/prometheus
  configs:
    - source: prometheus.yml
      target: /etc/prometheus/prometheus.yml
```

The following code block shows the configuration for our two types of monitoring probes that are deployed on every node:

```
monitoring-cadvisor:
  image: google/cadvisor:latest
  hostname: monitoring-cadvisor
  networks:
    - monitoring-backend
  deploy:
    mode: global
  volumes:
    - /:/rootfs:ro
    - /var/run:/var/run:rw
    - /sys:/sys:ro
    - /var/lib/docker/:/var/lib/docker:ro

monitoring-node-exporter:
  image: prom/node-exporter:v0.15.0
  hostname: monitoring-node-exporter
  networks:
    - monitoring-backend
  deploy:
    mode: global
```

In the following code, we have the local volumes, networks, config, and secret that are used by Prometheus and Grafana:

```
volumes:
  prometheus-metrics-data:
  grafana-data:

networks:
  monitoring-frontend:
    driver: overlay
    attachable: true
  monitoring-backend:
    driver: overlay
    attachable: true

configs:
  prometheus.yml:
    file: ./prometheus.yml

secrets:
  prometheus-password:
    external: true
```

As you can see, there are endless options for creating Prometheus graphs and Grafana dashboards, but you still have some work to do to get it where you need to go. Also, from Grafana, check out the alert setting as well. It's very cool and useful! Here is my dashboard:

Figure 6: Grafana Dashboard

Again, this is really cool, but do pay attention to the numbers. Remember to compare Prometheus/Grafana numbers with the UCP metrics and queries from your UCP client bundle with a UCP admin user role (that is, `docker container ls -aq | grep -c --regex "^[0-9,a-f]"`). The default, albeit a sample, shows a 1006 container, but the UCP Web UI and the client bundle queries show `281`. Also, the nodes being listed are the Swarm networks IPs of the Exporters. So, make sure you know what you are looking at and how to navigate from a dashboard problem discovery to troubleshooting a node or container.

We just covered a popular open source option, so now let's look at a commercial option.

Commercial example – Sysdig

The traditional monitoring tools market is abundant and mature. Chances are, you probably already have one or more existing tools in place. You already bought them, you know how to use them, and for the most part, they might work just fine for some of your container-based monitoring needs. However, there are some fundamental differences between traditional infrastructure/application monitoring and container platform monitoring.

The first difference between traditional and container monitoring is that containers are ephemeral and can be short-lived. Once the container is gone, it is difficult to understand what might have happened. You need to make sure that your monitoring platform takes into account the ephemeral nature of containers, and the difficulties in using agent-based solutions, where agents are not only constantly starting and stopping, but also understanding how to monitor the related container platform components.

The second difference between traditional and container monitoring is the move from monolithic applications to microservices. In this twelve factor application age, where service components are dynamically bound together at runtime, it is very helpful if your monitoring solution can navigate this dynamic typology.

In this section, we wanted to use an example of a commercial solution, and the one I'm most familiar with is Sysdig Monitor and Sysdig Secure. This is not an official endorsement of Sysdig, nor am I saying they are the only ones to provide such features, however it has become my tool of choice because of their container first approach and their open source community roots. Sysdig comes from the creators of Wireshark and its roots are in the Falco open source community.

First, any monitoring tool is of limited value if it can't help us to determine the root cause of an event. So, we are looking for something to go deep when there is a problem. To this end, Sysdig has a feature called capture that lets you go back in time prior to a critical event and review everything that was going on in the environment. You can correlate events across multiple channels on a common timeline to track down what was happening (host, network, file, and container related events) prior to a particular event. We have included the following screenshot to help you view this, and there's a great demonstration video to check out here: `https://sysdig.com/blog/sysdig-inspect/`:

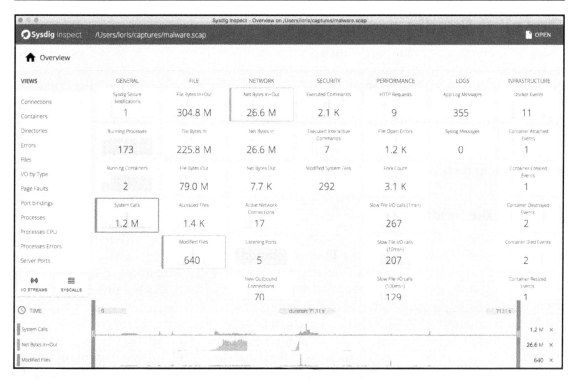

Figure 7: Sysdig Inspect of Event Capture

Our intent here is not to hijack this section and turn it into a big sales brochure; rather, it is to help raise the awareness of all types of tooling that are very useful in an ephemeral container environment. In a nutshell, the Sysdig platform provides the ability to monitor or inspect a variety of host, network, filesystem, and container metrics. Then, based on rules, the system generates alerts and captures detailed metrics leading up to an event.

Now, back to our pilot! At this point, we have rolled out a couple of applications:

- Our confluence Wiki
- Our custom Java application that we developed in the last chapter

As a practical matter, and because we have opened our containerized wiki application up to internal users, we would like to make sure things are working properly. Therefore, we need a better view of what's happening with our new wiki application. So, we will walk through the process of using a free trial of Sysdig to monitor the wiki as it runs on our Docker Enterprise platform.

Our pilot Sysdig architecture

The Sysdig monitoring solution we are using for our pilot is the cloud-based version of their monitoring platform, and there is a free trial available. This is convenient for a pilot because you don't need to buy anything (yet) and you will only need to install the probe agents onto your Docker host and you will be ready to go. Please note that, for higher traffic, or more highly secure environments, Sysdig offers a variety of configurations for their cloud-based solution, as well as an on-prem version. During your pilot, we would recommend the cloud version, leaving the server hosting to Sysdig—you can always move to the on-prem version later after you have kicked the tires.

Installing the Sysdig agents

When installing Sysdig on Docker Enterprise 2.1, there are a couple of different approaches. One of the approaches is covered in a Docker solution brief (`https://success.docker.com/article/sysdig-monitoring`). The Docker solution brief uses a Kubernetes daemon set to install the agents in the Docker Enterprise cluster. On the surface, this is a pretty straightforward implementation where you can simply create a Kubernetes secret and then apply a Kubernetes YAML file from a UCP client bundle to perform the magic. However, like many things Kubernetes, there can be some complications. In our case, these complications are related to the required kernel module and our bare metal on-prem Docker Enterprise hosting. So, **if you are just using Swarm at this point in your pilot and running on-prem**, I would strongly recommend using the simple container-based install as a more straightforward and bulletproof approach to installing the agents in your cluster. As long as you have SSH access to your Docker cluster hosts using a user in the Docker group (you need to run a Docker command), this will take about one minute per host node.

 Hey Kubernetes fans, do not fret! We will come back to the Kubernetes deployment with Kube-State monitoring later in this book.

Before you can install anything, please visit `https://sysdig.com/` and click on the **get started** button. From there, you can start your free trial of monitor. Just sign up, and then follow the instructions up to the agent install. You will need to copy your access key as it is a parameter for our Docker container-based installation.

After acquiring your access key, you simply need to log in to each of your Docker host nodes in the cluster and use the following Docker run command with your access key (replace the following xxxxxxxxxxxxxxx with your access key):

```
docker run -d --name sysdig-agent \
--restart always \
--privileged \
--net host \
--pid host \
-e ACCESS_KEY=xxxxxxxxxxxxxxxxxxxxxxx \
-e SECURE=true \
-e TAGS=example_tag:example_value \
-v /var/run/docker.sock:/host/var/run/docker.sock \
-v /dev:/host/dev \
-v /proc:/host/proc:ro \
-v /boot:/host/boot:ro \
-v /lib/modules:/host/lib/modules:ro \
-v /usr:/host/usr:ro \
--shm-size=512m \
sysdig/agent
```

There are some important points to highlight in the preceding Docker command. Again, make sure you use your own free trial access key from the https://sysdig.com/ website. Secondly, you may have noticed that we are running the agent as a privileged container. This is not a trivial matter and is not something you should normally consider. This allows anything running in that container to have complete access to your host! Also, take a look at the volume mounts that include read-only access to process any kernel module directories. This is required because Sysdig uses a kernel module to capture event data using syscalls. This allows for deep host integration, but is certainly a security consideration you should **absolutely discuss with your SecOps team prior to installing**.

The Wiki pilot dashboard

Within a few minutes, after installing the agents, you will be able to see your cluster's data appearing on your Sysdig monitor dashboard. There are a variety of resources to get you up to speed: https://sysdig.com/resources/. If you wait about 15 minutes after the data starts to flow into the Sysdig monitor site, you can look at the bottom left of your web interface for a little red button called the spotlight. Sysdig looks at the type of metrics being collected and makes recommendations for pre-built dashboards. More times than not, after logging into the monitoring dashboard of a fresh Docker Enterprise cluster that appears to be running just fine, we quickly discover some issues. This is really helpful!

Now, let's take a look at the pilot dashboard I put together for the wiki application that I wanted to monitor. The reason we say pilot is because, when we work with the application, we will definitely make changes to both the dashboard and the alerts as a part of the learning process:

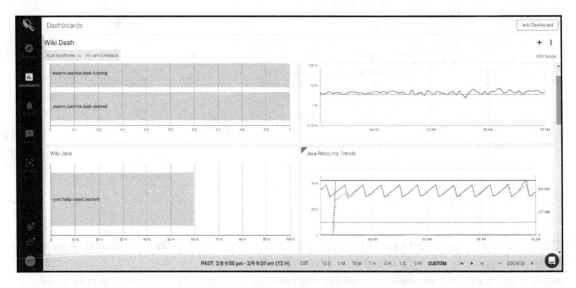

Figure 8: Monitoring for Pilot Wiki Application

On the top part of my dashboard is the tracking information related to Swarm services and the wiki app's JVM usage. The actual numbers in the graphs on the right-hand side of the dashboard are far less important than trends. We can use these trends to correlate metrics to performance problems or crashes. Please note there are custom dashboard JVM metrics, which gives you a bird's-eye view of all Java apps in your cluster.

The next part of my dashboard, as shown in the following screenshot, relates to the postgres backend database for the wiki. I was able to grab most of these metrics from a standard Postgres database dashboard. I just had to restrict the scope to the wiki application:

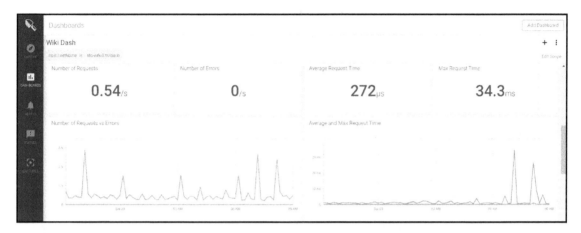

Figure 9: Monitor Request Tends for the Wiki

So, now we have something to look at if there is a problem, but how do we know there is a problem? We could wait for the users to complain, but we want to be more proactive than that.

Setting up alarms

For our pilot, there is one more thing we need to accomplish with Sysdig monitor—we need some alerts. To get started with our pilot alerting, we need to set up three different alarms. One alarm is specific to the wiki service and the other two are generally a good idea in a cluster, as you will see.

The first alarm looks to see if a Swarm service is down within the scope of our wiki stack. If you remember, we launched our wiki application from a Docker stack deploy for two services: a web app and a database app. If either of these services go down for more than one minute, an alarm will be triggered:

Figure 10: Wiki Service Down Alert

As shown the preceding screenshot, we can see the next alarm. This alarm triggers if any nodes in our cluster with a prod node label is down for more than two minutes. This is where you have to consider the idea of maintenance windows. You can set up site maintenance windows for server reboots so that alarms are ignored during that window. If you do that, you can use much tighter windows for failure than the two minutes I have here. Also, for this alarm, I set up a capture event, as shown in the following screenshot:

Figure 11: Production Docker Node is Down Alert

If the prod worker goes down, we will capture all the events for the 15 second period prior to the outage. Again, this can be very useful when trying to figure out why the servers went away:

Figure 12: Capture All Events Around Node Down Event

Our final alarm is a general Swarm alarm. This one looks a little odd, but essentially, if there is a service with no task (a thin wrapper and Swarm's atomic deployable unit) running for 3 minutes, this alarm will trigger. The reason for the 3 minutes is in case a large image needs to be pulled from the registry. While pulling the image, the task will be in the preparing state:

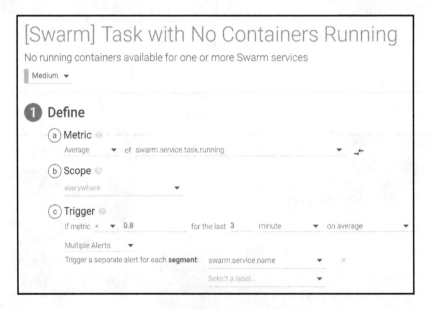

Figure 13: Task is Schedule No Container Running Alert

Summary

We started out with basic Docker Engine logs where we provided a recommended default configuration for your Docker Engine's `etc/docker/daemon.json` file. Otherwise, you would need to roll/truncate the log files on your own. If you fail to do so, the logs can consume the entire host filesystem and cause the system to lock up. We talked about centralized logging and how important it is in the cluster-based environment, and especially with distributed systems.

We covered two open source approaches to central logging and monitoring, as well as sharing the UCP's role in monitoring and logs. We discussed the ELK Stack as a powerful central logging solution. Then, we spent some time covering monitoring with Prometheus. Finally, we talked about a commercial solution as a means to monitor our wiki pilot application.

One thing that is sort of interesting here is that if your monitoring tool gives enough information to narrow your problem focus, you may not need centralized logging. As an example, if a service crashes and you're alerted, you can log in to your monitoring tool, figure out the circumstances around a specific container's demise, and check the logs from your UCP bundle. Yes, you can use a `docker container logs` command without logging in to a specific node where the container was running, because the UCP bundle allows you to review logs or exec into any container in the cluster from your local shell that's connected with the UCP bundle. Alternatively, you can always fall back to the UCP Web UI once you have the diagnostic clues from your premier monitoring tool.

At this point in our journey, you have your pilot applications running and a platform for monitoring them as your internal pilot users begin testing your new Docker Enterprise platform, as well as your newly found logging, monitoring, and troubleshooting skills.

Next, we will start talking about preparing for production.

Questions

1. In what file is the Docker daemon logs configuration kept?
2. Should you use a Prometheus endpoint that is built into the Docker Engine?
3. What monitoring tools are used by Docker Enterprise UCP?

Further reading

- **Configuring Docker log drivers**: https://docs.docker.com/config/containers/logging/configure/

- **Article from success website on logging best practices**: https://success.docker.com/article/logging-best-practices

- **Journalbeat**: https://github.com/mheese/journalbeat

- **ELK Stack freemium information**:
  - **Kibana**: https://www.elastic.co/products/kibana
  - **Elasticsearch**: https://www.elastic.co/products/elasticsearch
  - **Logstash**: https://www.elastic.co/products/logstash
  - **Support info**: https://www.elastic.co/subscriptions

- **Prometheus**:
  - **Overview**: https://prometheus.io/docs/introduction/overview/
  - **Exporters**: https://prometheus.io/docs/instrumenting/exporters/
  - **JMX exporter**: https://github.com/prometheus/jmx_exporter

- **Elton Stoneman's Pluralsight course**:
  - https://app.pluralsight.com/library/courses/monitoring-containerized-app-health-docker/table-of-contents

- **Sysdig**:
  - **Docker solution brief**: https://success.docker.com/article/sysdig-monitoring
  - **Sysdig resources**: https://sysdig.com/resources/

Section 3: In Production with Docker Enterprise

This section covers how organizations approach Docker adoption at the enterprise level.

The following chapters are included in this section:

- Chapter 8, *First Application in Production with Docker Enterprise*
- Chapter 9, *Important Docker Enterprise Production Topics*
- Chapter 10, *More on Kubernetes with Docker Enterprise*
- Chapter 11, *Taking the Docker Enterprise Platform into the Future*

8
First Application in Production with Docker Enterprise

Getting your first application ready for production and preparing a production cluster for its live debut is an important step in the container-adoption process. This is where we see rookie mistakes damage the reputation of very smart technologists. In one case, without running **High Availability (HA)** for non-production, the customer built their first HA cluster for production, not practicing with the non-production cluster first and did it with just two managers nodes. Had they started in non-production the failure would have been much less visible (remember, an even numbers of managers means trouble)! Some key lessons learned here were to keep your non-production and production cluster architectures very similar and always try new things in the non-production cluster first.

In this chapter, we will look at important topics related to the security and reliability of the Docker Enterprise production cluster, but the material in this chapter is only intended to supplement your current security practices and not to replace them. Please allocate adequate time for pre-launch security reviews, scans, pen-tests, and audits. In the end, most organizations find their container platforms not only surpass their current security standards, but they are also easier to keep secure.

In this chapter, we will cover the following topics:

- Design considerations for a production Docker Enterprise platform
- Strategies for managing production data
- Getting the pilot application production ready
- Maintaining and updating your production cluster

Docker Enterprise production cluster

So far in our Docker Enterprise adoption journey, we have been working with our non-production Docker Enterprise cluster. Now it's time to build out a Docker Enterprise production cluster, factoring in everything we have learned from our pilot experience along with current corporate security standards/polices and the topics covered in this chapter.

Having internally released our pilot application, we have gotten familiar with the many capabilities and challenges of container-based application deployment and operations. Our thoughts tend to shift toward topics such as container-based application data management (backing up or migrating the app data), application updates, Docker software updates, and host-node OS updates. Now we are going to add a production cluster into this mix. How will this all work?

High-level cluster flow and concepts

In this section, we want establish an understanding of our software supply chain by looking at the end-to-end life cycle of an application as it moves into production. This should help us to visualize the relationship between our non-production and production clusters. We will start with a sample non-production-to-production cluster flow diagram:

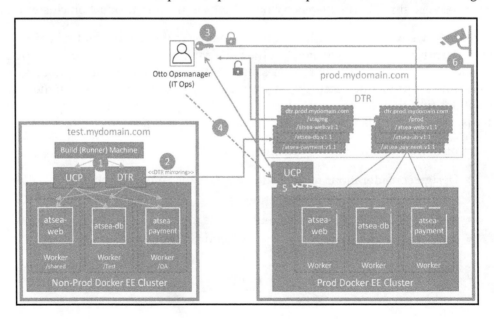

Software Supply Chain Non-Production to Production

On the left side, we see our familiar non-production cluster with our build machine, where we host a GitLab runner. The process begins when developers push their changes into source code control; the GitLab runner builds and deploys images into the non-production cluster with the non-production **Docker Trusted Registry (DTR)** and **Universal Control Plane (UCP)** (shown as *step 1* in *Figure—Software Supply Chain Non-Production to Production*). Eventually, the images are tested and make their way through the repository promotion process to end up in the final non-production **DTR** organization, called **QA**.

In *Figure—Software Supply Chain Non-Production to Production*, *step 2* depicts how the **QA** organization's repository (that is, `dtr.test.mydoamin.com/qa/atsea-web:v1.1`) mirrors images to the production **DTR**.

Image mirroring

In *step 2* of *Figure—Software Supply Chain Non-Production to Production*, please notice the line connecting non-production **DTR** to the production **DTR**. This is a DTR mirror link, a DTR feature used to push (or pull) images between multiple DTRs.

In our case, we move our **atsea-web** image from the non-production DTR to the staging repository in the production cluster DTR—`dtr.prod.mydomain.com/staging/atsea-web:v1.1`. When using DTR mirrors, we designate a target and trigger, much like a promotion policy, but instead of just adding the image to another local repository, the image is pushed to a different (in our case, the production) DTR registry.

In *Figure—Docker Trusted Registry Mirroring,* we see how the mirror is configured:

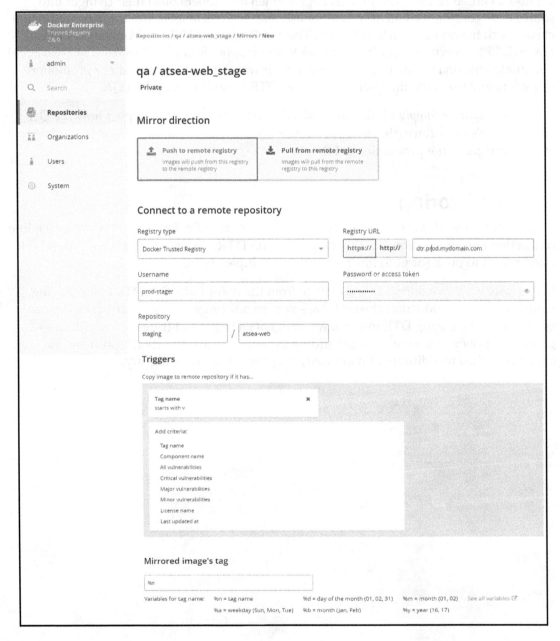

Docker Trusted Registry Mirroring

Mirroring can be accomplished by either pushing images from the source registry or pulling images from the target registry. In our example, we are pushing from the non-production DTR, but it requires storing DTR production credentials in our non-production DTR's mirroring information. Alternatively, we could have logged in to our production DTR and mirrored a pull from the non-production DTR QA repo. This might be preferred by some, because you are then storing non-production DTR credentials in the production DTR, which is more locked down.

One last note on mirroring. The metadata attached to the image, such as the signing information, is not passed along to the target registry (at this time—that may change). Therefore, in our preceding example flow, we sign the image with Otto's valid UCP production key after pushing it to the production DTR.

Image signing

Now back to *Figure—Software Supply Chain Non-Production to Production*. We look at *step 3*, where Otto (the operations manager) pulls the unsigned **atsea-web** image from the production DTR's staging organization repo, and retags the image for production using `docker image tag dtr.prod.mydomain.com/`**staging**`/atsea-web:v1.1 dtr.prod.mydomain.com/`**prod**`/atsea-web:v1.1`. Then, using this UCP production cluster signing key, Otto digitally signs the image and pushes the signed image to the DTR's production organization repository, `dtr.prod.mydomain.com/prod/atsea-web:v1.1`.

Configuring image signing can be a bit tedious. The signer needs to install the notary client, add the (production) UCP certificate, initialize each of the target DTR repositories, rotate their snapshot keys, and make sure the appropriate delegation keys are set up for the signer's DTR users.

 For a nice tutorial on image signing with DTR using an automated deployment GitLab pipeline, check out Andy Clemenko's article: `https:/ /success.docker.com/article/secure-supply- chain#dockertrustedregistry`.

UCP production scheduling with Docker Content Trust

Now we examine *step 4* back in *Figure—Software Supply Chain Non-Production to Production*, where Otto uses his UCP **production** client bundle to update the existing production stack's images using the `docker stack deploy -c docker-stack-prod.yml existing_stack_name` command. The latest version of the production `docker-stack-prod.yml` file will use the new, signed v1.1 image tags, usually using an environment variable and a script. At this point, our repository tag is likely to correspond to a source code system-release tag for the production release, such as v1.1. Later, when you get to a CI pipeline deployment, you can use GitLab's `${CI_COMMIT_TAG}` in the `docker-stack-prod.yml` file.

The following code is a sample of a `docker-stack-prod.yml` file where we use `${CI_COMMIT_TAG}` to set the correct image version. This assumes all of the `atsea` services images are all tagged and built with the same version tag as `atsea-deploy` repo.

In the following code block, we show how we use the `${CI_COMMIT_TAG}` variable to set the image version to be deployed:

```
# atsea-deploy docker-stack-prod.yml
version: "3.7"

services:
  database:
    image: ${DTR_SERVER}/prod/atsea-db_build:${CI_COMMIT_TAG}
    environment:
      POSTGRES_USER: gordonuser
      POSTGRES_DB_PASSWORD_FILE: /run/secrets/postgres_password
      POSTGRES_DB: atsea
    networks:
      - back-tier
    secrets:
      - postgres_password

  appserver:
    image: ${DTR_SERVER}/prod/atsea-web_build:${CI_COMMIT_TAG}
    networks:
      - front-tier
      - back-tier
      - payment
<...>
```

There are a couple of important things to note in this deployment scenario. First, the signing key Otto uses is from the production cluster. Each Docker UCP cluster has its own **certificate authority** (**CA**) and subsequently a different set of keys. Therefore, we cannot use signing keys from the non-production cluster in the production cluster or vice-versa. This is important because we are using UCP's **Docker Content Trust** feature to restrict the scheduling of workloads in the production cluster. We only allow images that were signed by a member of the production UCP's operations team to which Otto belongs. Therefore, without Otto's UCP production signature on the image, UCP would not have to deploy it to the production cluster.

In the following screenshot, we see the UCP **Admin Settings** dialog with the **Docker Content Trust** tab selected:

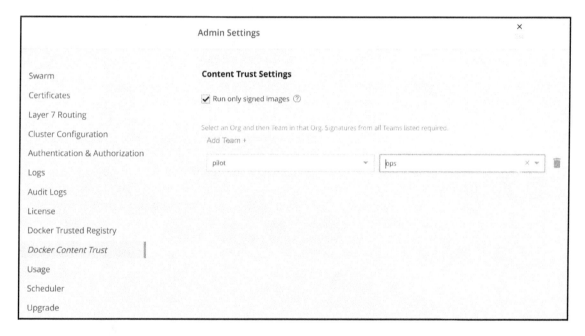

Universal Control Plane Content Trust Setting

Notice that a member of the ops team must sign the images before deployment. **Docker Content Trust** is a great security feature, but it is not always used, at least initially. Luckily, there is another pragmatic measure in Docker Enterprise to provide some basic protection against image tampering.

Immutability for DTR repos

While some organizations mature to use Content Trust, some organizations decide not to use image signing in their production clusters. In this situation, a pragmatic security feature in DTR is shown in *Figure—Docker Trusted Registry Immutability Setting*, called tag immutability, and it is highly recommended for production repositories. It means no one can push a different manifest using the same tag name as an existing image. Ultimately, this makes it more difficult for a "bad actor" to inject nefarious binaries using older trusted image tags. Do note, if image signing had been used here, it would have blocked the tampered image from being deployed to the production cluster.

The image immutability feature is really just enforcing a general best practice of not reusing tags, such as the latest tag. When you reuse tags, you might get a different version of the image with the same tag, especially in a cluster with lots of nodes and each potentially storing lots of old versions.

Docker Enterprise's swarm orchestrator avoids this ambiguity by appending the tag with the unique `sha` hash of the image. The only way it will use the cached image is if it's a hashed match. Here is a sample image name used in UCP:

`dtr.mydomain.com/test/atsea-web_build:RC-test@sha256:547e4e568593fd98b5d824f6fa76e0ee1da8b7644b953b02030505f63c1e108b.`

The following screenshot shows DTR immutability being turned **On**:

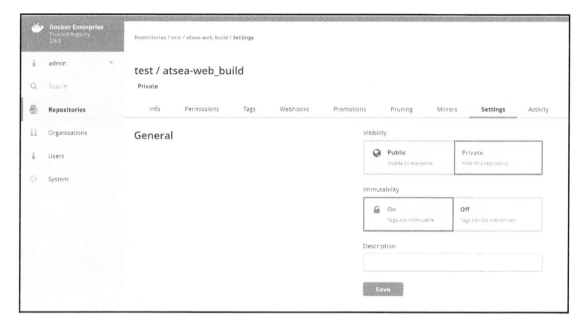

Docker Trusted Registry Immutability Setting

Finally, back in our cluster diagram we see the camera icon at the top right of *Figure—Software Supply Chain Non-Production to Production*. This represents some additional tools being used in a production environment. In our case, we'll take a quick look at how the Sysdig Secure platform helps to maintain a secure production environment. We will talk a little bit more about that later.

Image scanning in production

Image scanning in your production cluster is a very good idea. Docker Enterprise Advanced has a couple of important scanning features. It updates its vulnerability database every night and then reviews all image components in DTR for previously unknown vulnerabilities. In other words, an image can scan as clean on the first scan, but later vulnerabilities may have been discovered. Docker Enterprise's advanced version of DTR can alert you to new vulnerabilities as they are discovered in your registry as well as highlight running services/containers that are running vulnerable images in your (production) cluster.

The following screenshot shows the DTR scan results of our `atsea-payments` service. It reveals two major vulnerabilities:

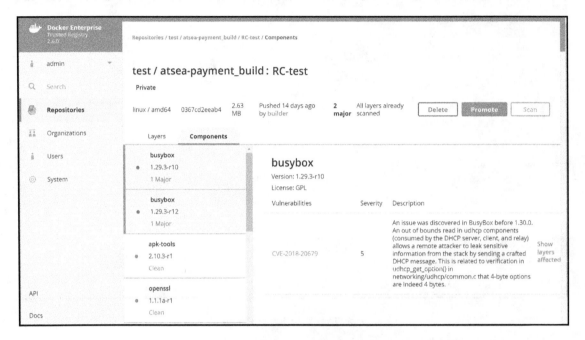

Docker Trusted Registry Image Scanning

The following screenshot shows how vulnerabilities are revealed in UCP with our atsea application stack. We see not only all of the problems, but the payment service shows the two major vulnerabilities from DTR:

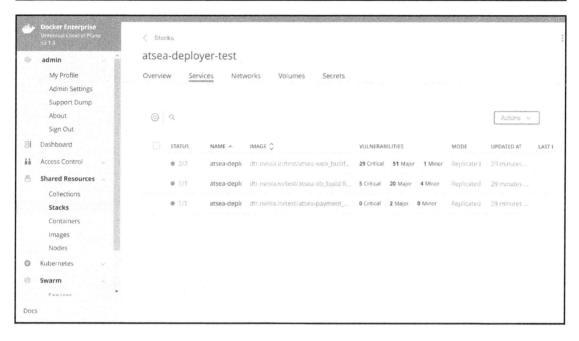

UCP Services Showing Image Vulnerabilities

In a nutshell, this illustrates a simple, but fairly typical, Docker Enterprise flow for a first production application. We securely promote images from a non-production cluster to a production cluster. We suggest a manual deployment method—in this case, Otto handles it—for the initial production application deployments. Once your team is comfortable with that approach, it is easy enough to create a production version of your deployment pipeline using the production UCP client bundle.

Now that we understand the flow, let's talk about setting up the production cluster.

Production cluster considerations

As you move to production, your level of sophistication and understanding will naturally grow. Therefore, as you discover new options and features in the production phase of your journey, you should consider first applying them in your non-production cluster. Again, we need to test as much as possible with our non-production cluster before applying it to our production environment.

As you move beyond the pilot, it may be tempting to set up several additional clusters. After all, we are used to having separate environments for dev, test, QA, staging, and production. Take the time to configure UCP RBAC with node isolation so you only need two nodes, non-production and production.

Avoiding cluster sprawl

Back in `Chapter 2`, *Docker Enterprise – an Architectural Overview*, we talked about a two-cluster design (non-production and production), as opposed to having separate dev, test, QA, staging, and production clusters. Again, this is possible because of the Docker Enterprise and Kubernetes role-based access control systems, which enforce resource isolation in Docker Enterprise clusters. Using features such as Docker Enterprise advanced cluster isolation helps to avoid cluster sprawl and vast numbers of under-utilized servers.

Early on, cloud-native development teams thought it would be easy to spin up and shut down their clusters. However, they quickly learned that clusters, at least manager and master nodes, are a lot more like pets than cattle.

The story goes that many of these clusters stuck around longer than expected. However, the biggest contributors to cluster sprawl appear to be a lack of security and our understanding of cluster security. Hence, for most organizations, cluster access is an all-or-nothing proposition. So if you have a certificate/key to access a cluster's master/manager nodes, you have unlimited privileges. This fine-grained control left teams reluctant to share their clusters with other teams and hence there were clusters everywhere.

Production-installation considerations

If we are following best practices when setting up our pilot environment, we already have experience setting up and operating at least three manager nodes for a high availability configuration. So the point of this section is to build off of our pilot knowledge and experience, fundamentally repeating what we did with the pilot cluster, but adding some additional items to our list of important considerations.

One anti-pattern in moving from the pilot to production phase is deciding not to maintain a high availability configuration for non-production. It's generally a bad idea. One reason is you need the ability to practice and/or validate your updates, backups, and recovery procedures against an identical, non-production cluster. If your clusters lack sufficient symmetry between the non-production and production clusters (that is, high availability), you will have two sets of one-off procedures. This is why we strongly recommend keeping them as similar as possible.

> One question we often hear is, Do I really need high availability for my non-production cluster? The answer is generally yes. The non-production cluster often becomes busier and larger than the production cluster. Without high availability, the cluster will have to be brought offline for any sort of maintenance, including routine updates. This is generally unacceptable, particularly when you get into continuous integration and test appointments on your non-production cluster.

Production manager nodes

The first question is: how many manager nodes do you need in production? Three is usually a good place to start, but you have to keep in mind what that means in terms of fault-tolerance. For instance, with three manager nodes, your fault-tolerance is just one manager node. This means we can take one manager out for maintenance and updates while the other two carry on. However, if something were to happen to one of the two remaining managers while the third was undergoing maintenance, the managers would lose quorum (they lack the minimum two votes necessary for a raft consensus group to make changes to the cluster) and you will be unable to make changes to the cluster. If you lose quorum, all of your services and containers will continue to run, but you would not be able to make any changes to the cluster.

The following table is a summary of a cluster's fault-tolerance based on the number of swarm managers. It is from Docker's docs swarm admin guide (`https://docs.docker.com/engine/swarm/admin_guide/`):

Number of managers	Majority	Fault-tolerance
1	1	0
3	2	1
5	3	2
7	4	3
9	5	4

For many organizations, the three-node configuration is generally acceptable. However, some enterprises need their production environment to be rock solid and/or to make frequent changes to their services. In this situation, consider moving to a five-manager configuration, which allows you to tolerate the loss of two managers. Generally, there's no need to go beyond five nodes until you're operating at a very large scale.

Node sizing

Without following the prescribed agile adoption model which includes, PoC, pilot, and production adoption approach, this step can be very intimidating. Imagine if you were starting your Docker Enterprise adoption by building out a production cluster, without having the experience of running your first internal pilot application.

We have been in this situation with customers, dealing with their angst when we cannot use our crystal ball to tell them exactly how much hardware they will need for their cluster. This is one important reason we strongly recommend monitoring as part of the pilot phase.

When we started implementing our pilot platform, we just took a guess at some middle-of-the-road hardware specs and started there. The stakes were relatively low and we allowed ourselves some room to fail as it was a pilot. As we moved to production, we saw our cluster perform in our environment while running our pilot application and we collected baseline metrics by using our monitoring platform. The agile adoption process positioned us well for our first production application deployment!

In *Figure—Sysdig Resource Trends for Pilot Application*, we have our cluster performance metrics:

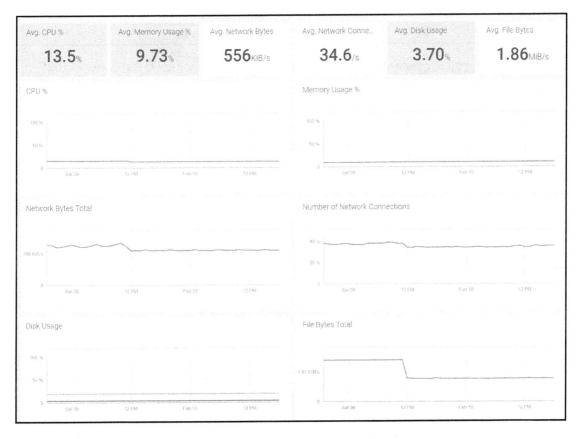

Sysdig Resource Trends for Pilot Application

Docker lists the following requirements and recommendations for the **Universal Control Plane** (**UCP**) manager nodes and DTR (worker) nodes:

UCP	DTR
Minimum UCP requirements: • 8 GB of RAM for manager nodes • 4 GB of RAM for worker nodes • 2 vCPUs for manager nodes • 4 GB of free disk space for the /var partition for manager nodes	**Minimum DTR requirements**: • 16 GB of RAM for nodes running DTR • 2 vCPUs for nodes running DTR • 10 GB of free disk space

Recommended production requirements: • 16 GB of RAM for manager nodes • 4 vCPUs for manager nodes • 25-100 GB of free disk space	Recommended production DTR requirements: • 16 GB of RAM for nodes running DTR • 4 vCPUs for nodes running DTR • 25-100 GB of free disk space

 If you are planning on scanning images, consider the DTR recommended production requirements a minimum. Specifically, to avoid problems with DTR scanning jobs failing or backing up, you will need at least 16 GB of RAM.

Armed with your pilot non-prod cluster metrics and Docker's guidelines for manager and DTR nodes, you should be able to confidently size your cluster nodes.

Finally, use SSDs if possible for production drives, especially for the /var/lib/docker/swarm mount point. This is the swarm directory and it stores the swarm state. We want updates to process with minimal latency.

Setup and installation considerations

Rather than starting from scratch, we can build off of the process we used to create the non-production cluster. We are not going to repeat that here. However, we are going to talk about some additional considerations for your production cluster.

Center for Internet Security (CIS) docker benchmarks

After you prepare your nodes and install the Docker Enterprise engine on your cluster nodes, it would be a good idea to run a CIS benchmark on each of the nodes and review the results with your security team. CIS is a not-for-profit organization dedicated to the promotion of cyber-defence best practices. They provide the framework for developing tests for specific platforms, such as Docker. In our case, the benchmark was produced by the Docker community.

The following code is a sample CIS Docker Benchmark report. Start with the following Docker command to run the report:

```
# https://github.com/docker/docker-bench-security
$ docker run -it --net host --pid host --userns host --cap-add
audit_control \
    -e DOCKER_CONTENT_TRUST=$DOCKER_CONTENT_TRUST \
    -v /var/lib:/var/lib \
    -v /var/run/docker.sock:/var/run/docker.sock \
    -v /usr/lib/systemd:/usr/lib/systemd \
    -v /etc:/etc --label docker_bench_security \
    docker/docker-bench-security
```

The first part of the output displays version information and the host configuration report section:

```
# --- Summarized for Docker Enterprise Book Listing! ---

# ----------------------------------------------------------------------
----- # Docker Bench for Security v1.3.4 /etc:/etc --label
docker_bench_security d #
# Docker, Inc. (c) 2015-
#
# Checks for dozens of common best-practices around deploying Docker
containers in production.
# Inspired by the CIS Docker Community Edition Benchmark v1.1.0.
# ----------------------------------------------------------------------
-----

Initializing Wed Feb 13 14:16:31 UTC 2019

[INFO] 1 - Host Configuration
...
[WARN] 1.6 - Ensure auditing is configured for Docker files and directories
- /var/lib/docker
[WARN] 1.7 - Ensure auditing is configured for Docker files and directories
- /etc/docker
[WARN] 1.8 - Ensure auditing is configured for Docker files and directories
- docker.service
[WARN] 1.9 - Ensure auditing is configured for Docker files and directories
- docker.socket
...
```

Let's take a quick look at a couple of highlights from our CIS benchmark output, starting with `1 - Host Configuration`. There are a variety of informational messages omitted, but we wanted to point out the 1.6 to 1.9 warnings, related to auditing or specific directories. We want to make sure that no containers mount these directories and tamper with their contents. This is something we can easily monitor with tools such as Sysdig Secure, Aqua Security, or Twistlock. Later in `Chapter 9`, *Important Docker Enterprise Production Topics*, in *Production monitoring* section, we will take a look at how Sysdig Secure monitors any write activity to these special directories with a `sensitive_mount` policy:

```
[INFO] 2 - Docker daemon configuration
...


[INFO] 3 - Docker daemon configuration files
...


[INFO] 4 - Container Images and Build File
[WARN] 4.1 - Ensure a user for the container has been created
[WARN] * Running as root: sysdig-agent
[WARN] * Running as root: gitlab-runner
...


[INFO] 5 - Container Runtime
[WARN] 5.1 - Ensure AppArmor Profile is Enabled
[WARN] * No AppArmorProfile Found: sysdig-agent
[WARN] * No AppArmorProfile Found: gitlab-runner
[WARN] 5.2 - Ensure SELinux security options are set, if applicable
[WARN] * No SecurityOptions Found: gitlab-runner
[PASS] 5.3 - Ensure Linux Kernel Capabilities are restricted within
containers
[WARN] 5.4 - Ensure privileged containers are not used
[WARN] * Container running in Privileged mode: sysdig-agent
...
```

Section 4, `Container Images and Build File`, refers to the best practice of using non-root users to run inside of containers. Many official images create non-root users (you can see this in their Docker file) for binary execution within their container, such as the Postgres official image Dockerfile:

```
[INFO] 6 - Docker Security Operations
[INFO] 6.1 - Avoid image sprawl
[INFO] * There are currently: 48 images
[INFO] 6.2 - Avoid container sprawl
[INFO] * There are currently a total of 62 containers, with only 3 of them
currently running
...
```

```
[INFO] 7 - Docker Swarm Configuration
[WARN] 7.1 - Ensure swarm mode is not Enabled, if not needed
[PASS] 7.2 - Ensure the minimum number of manager nodes have been created
in a swarm
[WARN] 7.3 - Ensure swarm services are binded to a specific host interface
[WARN] 7.4 - Ensure data exchanged between containers are encrypted on
different nodes on the overlay network
[WARN] * Unencrypted overlay network: atsea-web-46141311_front-tier (swarm)
[WARN] * Unencrypted overlay network: ingress (swarm)
```

The following is an example of how the user is set up for the `postgres` official base image:

```
# https://github.com/docker-library/postgres/11/Dockerfile
# explicitly set user/group IDs
RUN set -eux; \
  groupadd -r postgres --gid=999; \
#
https://salsa.debian.org/postgresql/postgresql-common/blob/997d842ee744687d
99a2b2d95c1083a2615c79e8/debian/postgresql-common.postinst#L32-35
  useradd -r -g postgres --uid=999 --home-dir=/var/lib/postgresql --
shell=/bin/bash postgres; \
```

In the `postgres` startup script (`docker-entrypoint.sh`), the `gosu` command is used to run as the `postgres` user (same UID) as configured inside of the container.

> By setting up and running a non-root user inside of a container, you mitigate the damage from a breakout attack. A breakout attack is very rare, but a recent flaw in runc (`https://nvd.nist.gov/vuln/detail/CVE-2019-5736`) reminds us they are real. When a process is able to break out of the container's isolation it may gain access to the host. This is clearly a bad situation, but it very bad if the container process was running as root. If a container process running as root breaks out of isolation, they will become root on the host and your security will be compromised. On the other hand, if the breakout process is running as a non-root user and the non-root user is not set up on the host, the breakout process will have no privileges. That is the motivation for running as a non-root user inside of a container.

There are some topics you're going to want to get your security operations team up to speed on as soon as possible. Additionally, in the spirit of becoming an informed user, I would look at evaluating one of the industry-leading container security platforms, including but not limited to Sysdig Secure, Twistlock, and Aqua Security. Just playing around with these tools in your non-production cluster will be very enlightening!

Locking down SSH access

One bad habit of early Docker users was freely giving SSH access to Docker nodes. This was understandable as a lot of early Docker deployments were developer-led initiatives and subsequently, developers needed remote access to the Docker nodes all the way through production. However, now you are adopting Docker Enterprise to operationalize your Docker environments. Therefore, the only folks that should have access through SSH to the production systems are operators who are responsible for performing maintenance, such as OS patches and Docker Engine updates. Other than these operators, all other access should be managed through Docker UCP client bundles to leverage Docker Enterprise's role-based access control and auditing.

No public access to Docker nodes

During the PoC, we set up our host with a public IP address (if you recall, it was a cloud setup). This was a practical matter, so we could easily SSH in each node to install and configure Docker. In our pilot configuration, all external access to the cluster was routed through a firewall and then an internal load balancer. This included the remote UCP, DTR, Kubernetes API access, as well as access to any application running in the cluster. Our sample Docker cluster is also running on its own subnet and controls all access through the subnet's interface with firewall rules.

Figure—Pilot Platform Infrastructure, provides a review of our pilot platform infrastructure:

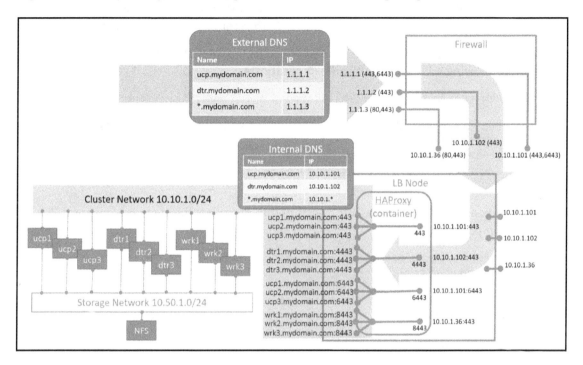

Pilot Platform Infrastructure

Notice how all traffic enters the cluster through the **LB Node**. All external network traffic resolves to firewall public IPs and is NAT-ed to the LB Nodes' internal IP addresses. Internal access is handled with split DNS and resolved directly to the LB Nodes' internal IP addresses.

Production UCP configuration

As you get started with your production UCP, you can start with a snapshot of your non-production cluster by leveraging UCP's configuration file feature. You can modify the file and use it to install UCP in the production cluster.

This saves you the frustration of clicking through the UCP Web UI. An explanation for all of the following UCP configuration options can be found here: https://docs.docker.com/ee/ucp/admin/configure/ucp-configuration-file/#configuration-options.

The following code block shows the process for cURLing a UCP configuration file from a manager node using a UCP client bundle of certificates:

```
# cd into the folder where you unzipped a UCP Admin's client bundle

# get the test configuration file from the test UCP using an UCP Admin's
certs and private key files
$ curl --cacert ca.pem --cert cert.pem --key key.pem
https://ucp.test.mydomain.com/api/ucp/config-
toml > ucp-config.toml
```

Now let's look at the output of the auth section that describes the system access and authorization parameters:

```
# List the contents of the ucp-config.toml file
$ cat ucp-config.toml
[auth]
  default_new_user_role = "restrictedcontrol"
  backend = "managed"
  samlEnabled = false
  samlLoginText = ""
  [auth.sessions]
    lifetime_minutes = 60
    renewal_threshold_minutes = 20
    per_user_limit = 10
  [auth.saml]
    idpMetadataURL = ""
    spHost = ""
    rootCerts = ""
    tlsSkipVerify = false
```

Here, we see how UCP is integrated with DTR:

```
[[registries]]
  host_address = "dtr.test.mydomain.com"
  service_id = "8c599992-8996-43b5-b511-f26c94631fea"
  ca_bundle = "-----BEGIN CERTIFICATE-----\n ...<<SNIP-REMOVED>>... o=\n---
--END CERTIFICATE-----\n"
  batch_scanning_data_enabled = true

[scheduling_configuration]
  enable_admin_ucp_scheduling = false
  default_node_orchestrator = "swarm"
```

```
[tracking_configuration]
  disable_usageinfo = true
  disable_tracking = true
  anonymize_tracking = false
  cluster_label = ""
```

Here is the section with the content trust settings:

```
[trust_configuration]
  require_content_trust = false

[log_configuration]
  level = "INFO"

[audit_log_configuration]
 level = ""
 support_dump_include_audit_logs = false

[license_configuration]
  auto_refresh = false

[cluster_config]
  controller_port = 443
  kube_apiserver_port = 6443
  swarm_port = 2376
  swarm_strategy = "spread"
  kv_timeout = 5000
  kv_snapshot_count = 20000
  profiling_enabled = false
  external_service_lb = "ucp.test.mydomain"
  metrics_retention_time = "24h"
  metrics_scrape_interval = "1m"
  rethinkdb_cache_size = "1GB"
  cloud_provider = ""
  cni_installer_url = ""
  pod_cidr = "192.168.0.0/16"
  calico_mtu = "1480"
  ipip_mtu = "1480"
  unmanaged_cni = false
  nodeport_range = "32768-35535"
  azure_ip_count = ""
  local_volume_collection_mapping = false
  manager_kube_reserved_resources = "cpu=250m,memory=2Gi,ephemeral-
storage=4Gi"
  worker_kube_reserved_resources = "cpu=50m,memory=300Mi,ephemeral-
storage=500Mi"
```

While any of these values could be tweaked, remember we want our clusters to be as similar as possible. With that in mind, we will walk you through the file and highlight the items of particular interest as you move to production:

Config Item	Description	Comments
default_new_user_role = "restrictedcontrol"	The role that new users get for their private resource sets. Values are admin, viewonly, scheduler, restrictedcontrol, or fullcontrol. The default is restrictedcontrol.	For your production cluster, you may want to default to viewonly. We should not have users running workloads in their private collection (sandbox) on the production cluster.
backend = "managed"	The name of the authorization backend to use is either managed or ldap. The default is managed.	You want a small number of users with access to the production cluster. Consider managed, using a UCP built-in user DB. This may help avoid LDAP mistakes and the Just-In-Time User-Provisioning issue where revoked LDAP users can still access the cluster using their UCP Client bundle.
[[registries]] array	An array of tables that specifies the DTR instances that the current UCP instance manages.	Skip this at because DTR is not yet installed.
require_content_trust = false	Set to true to require images be signed by content trust. The default is false.	As discussed in the image signing section of this chapter, setting this to true will only allow signed images to run in your cluster. You will define the require_signature_from option to designate who has to sign the images.
[audit_log_configuration] section	Configures audit-logging options for UCP components.	This is often a request to production when compliance is involved. If used, consider sending a custom driver for the UCP controller logs to sent to the remote, secure server. If you don't ship them, make sure the standard logs are rotated and truncated as they will get large. Every HTTP action gets audit logged!
log_configuration table	Configures the logging options for UCP components.	If you are not using a central log scheme for your Docker Engine, you may want to send logs for the UCP component to a remote location by configuring this section.
enable_admin_ucp_scheduling = false	Set to true to allow admins to schedule on containers on manager nodes. The default is false.	We do not want workloads on the production manager or masters.
[tracking_configuration]	Specifies the analytics data that UCP collects.	We typically disable these for production clusters.

It is a really good idea to use third-party client certificates from a trusted authority for UCP and DTR. This will get us away from using no TLS or untrusted settings. After you install your Doctor Trusted Registry in the production cluster make sure that you go to the UCP scheduling settings and disallow workloads on the DTR servers to avoid resource contention. This is especially important if you're running DTR image scanning.

Production DTR configuration

We've discussed a number of points related to the DTR's production configuration. A typical production deployment would include three DTR replicas for high availability, the use of a third-party certificate from a trusted certificate authority, and the repositories would have tag immutability enabled. Finally, the three DTR replicas would be tied to the production cluster and running within the production cluster. I bring this up because we often are asked about sharing one DTR across both clusters.

You could attempt to share your non-production DTR between the non-production and production clusters (or vice versa), but we strongly suggest you do not share even an HA DTR between clusters. While it looks possible in theory, there is a fair amount of cohesion when it comes to the UCP orchestrator pulling images to cluster nodes. You don't want to log in to DTR from every cluster node as admin to pull images. It is therefore both ill-advised and **unsupported**. Not to mention you want to be able to test updates on your non-production cluster before moving to production.

Data management

One of the most challenging topics related to deploying containerized applications is data management. There are various approaches to managing container volumes in a clustered environment. Some designs are simple and straightforward, but lack flexibility. Other designs are highly sophisticated, but have lots of moving parts to align. Most of the time the answer is somewhere in the middle.

Host volume mounts

One simple and straightforward approach to handling container data persistence in a cluster is with a host-mounted volume. In a nutshell, the orchestrator randomly schedules the container to run on node A in your cluster. When a container runs, it mounts a specified directory on node A's filesystem and writes its data. Very simple, but what if the orchestrator redeploys the container to a different node next time it runs? When the new container starts on node B, it will find an empty volume because its data is still back on node A, where it ran last time. Luckily, there is a way to make this work.

Both Swarm and Kubernetes have mechanisms that constrain or persuade the orchestrator's placement of containers on cluster nodes. They label nodes in the cluster and then instruct the orchestrator to match those labels when scheduling the containers in the cluster.

In the following code block, we add a `com.mydomain.wiki.stage=prod3` label to worker #3 in our production cluster:

```
$ docker node update --label-add com.mydomain.wiki.stage=prod3 prod-
wrk-3.mydomain.com
```

We show the stack file for deploying our application to worker #3 using the `com.mydomain.wiki.stage=prod3` label as a deployment constraint. Notice the `deploy: placement: constraints:` section and how we added it to both our `wiki` service and the `postgres` database. This ensures the database is always running on the same node and can find its data. We placed the `wiki` on the same node for a couple of reasons. The first reason is low network latency, because they're on the same node and the traffic never leaves the host interface. The second reason is the Wiki application also needs to mount the host filesystem to save documents stores for users.

The following code block shows the Docker stack YAML file for deploying `wiki` and the `postgres` stack to production node#3:

```
version: '3.5'

services:
  wiki:
    image: dtr.prod.mydomain.com/pilot/wiki:v1.1.2
    volumes:
      - /var/local/atlassian-
data:/opt/j2ee/domains/mydomain.com/wiki/webapps/atlassian-confluence/data/
    ports:
      - 8080:8080
    networks:
      - wiki_net
    deploy:
      placement:
        constraints:
          - node.labels.com.mydomain.wiki.stage==prod3

  postgres:
    image: dtr.nvisia.io/pilot/postgress:v1.0.1
    environment:
      - POSTGRES_PASSWORD=JnB8nUuT
    volumes:
      - /var/local/wiki-db-data:/var/lib/postgresql/data
      - /var/local/wiki-init-data:/docker-entrypoint-initdb.d
    networks:
      - wiki_net
    deploy:
      placement:
```

```
        constraints:
          - node.labels.com.mydomain.wiki.stage==prod3
networks:
  wiki_net:
```

Keep in mind that the host mount point can be either a folder in the host filesystem or it can be a mounted device on the host. This means we could have our container data stored in a mounted (possibly portable) block storage device or any sort of network storage that uses a host mount point as its interface. Yes, this means you can host mount an NFS, NAS, SAN, or iSCSI file/block device.

Please note, if you host mount NFS the standard way, where you map your local mount point into a specific folder on the NFS host at mount time, you will need separate mounts for each isolated NFS folder and that's a bit clunky. So, in the next section, we will talk about a more flexible approach to leveraging NFS using a Docker volume plugin.

Docker NFS volume plugin

The next approach is taking advantage of a cluster-based filesystem, in this case NFS. This is a very popular option for on-premises implementations where you have full control over the network. For cloud implementations where your noisy neighbors may cause network latency, you should consider an alternative solution designed for a cloud platform. We'll talk about some options in the next section, *Other volume storage solutions*.

In order to use the NFS volume plug-in from Docker, you will have to have the NFS client software set up on each Docker node.

The following code block shows an example of installing the NFS client software using the `nfs-utils` package on Centos:7.5:

```
## FOR EACH CLUSTER NODE ##
#*********************************************
#* NFS client Setup - just add nfs-utils *
#*********************************************
sudo yum install -y nfs-utils
```

After the client is installed on each node, you can test it. It's a pretty simple process where you create a Docker volume, mount the volume with a test container, and create a `test-file.txt`.

Please notice the `--opt` parameters we use when we create the volume with the local driver. We set the driver type to `nfs`, provide the address of the remote NFS server, and map the volume into a spot on the NFS filesystem. With this approach, we do not need anyone to configure the NFS host mount point ahead of time. Instead, we use the Docker API to create the volume, use the volume, mount the volume, and remove the volume.

In the following code block, we use the Docker NFS volume driver to write a file to NFS from inside of a container on node A:

```
###########################
## SSH to worker node A ##
#*******************************************
#* Test NFS client with Docker Volume access*
#*******************************************
$ docker volume create --driver local \
--opt type=nfs \
--opt o=addr=test-iscsi-1.mydomain.com,rw \
--opt device=:/var/nfsshare/apps \
apps

# Create test-file.txt on NFS drive
docker run -it --rm -v apps:/apps centos:7 touch /apps/test-file.txt

# List file on apps volume from inside a cento:7 container
docker run -it --rm -v apps:/apps centos:7 ls /apps

# Clean up your volume
$ docker volume rm apps
```

In this code block, we use the Docker NFS volume driver to read a file to NFS from inside of a container on node B:

```
###########################
## SSH to worker node B ##
## Remember to install nfs-utils on this node
$ sudo yum install -y nfs-utils

$ docker volume create --driver local \
--opt type=nfs \
--opt o=addr=test-iscsi-1.mydomain.com,rw \
--opt device=:/var/nfsshare/apps \
apps

# List file on apps volume from inside a cento:7 container
$ docker run -it --rm -v apps:/apps centos:7 ls /apps
$ docker volume rm apps
```

Once you have NFS working and verified on all of your cluster nodes, it is time to move on to the next step of getting your deployment ready to take advantage of the Docker NFS plugin.

The key to making the volume plug-in work in your YAML stack file is in the volumes section at the bottom. Here is an excerpt from a file using NFS volume mounts with Docker Enterprise.

In the following code block, you can see how the AR test parameters translate into an actual volume driver configuration:

```
volumes:
  wiki-init-data:
    driver: local
    driver_opts:
      type: nfs
      o: addr=ntc-iscsi-1.mydomain.com,rw,hard
      device: ":/var/nfsshare/apps/wiki/db-init"
  wiki-db-data:
    driver: local
    driver_opts:
      type: nfs
      o: addr=ntc-iscsi-1.mydomain.com,rw,hard
      device: ":/var/nfsshare/apps/wiki/db-data"
```

Be sure to test all the applications that are using the NFS connection. Not so much for Docker-related issues, but to discover any NFS related. For instance, in the preceding code block, I had two NFS volumes defined: one for the Wiki service file storage and another for the postgres data files. The postgres database worked just fine, but the Confluence Wiki application encountered a file-sharing issue due to NFS file-locking incompatibility. I tracked it down to "Cannot resolve reference to bean 'luceneConnection'".

If you recall, this Wiki application was my lift and shift application from the beginning of the Chapter 5, *Prepare and Deploy a Docker Enterprise Pilot Application, The sample pilot Wiki application* section. As such, the point was to *not* change any code, just containerize it and deploy it. Therefore, we can go back to putting a label on a node and using the deployment constraint on the Wiki service, but perhaps allow the database to use NFS if that seems helpful. However, since losing the node means the Wiki container will completely fail anyway, you might as well just pin both the database and the Wiki to the same node as we did earlier in Chapter 5, *Prepare and Deploy a Docker Enterprise Pilot Application*. Then of course you enjoy lower latency for being on the same node.

Going back to an earlier point about making sure that the non-production and production clusters are as similar as possible, NFS is a good example of something you want in both clusters so you may test applications thoroughly before moving them into production.

Other volume storage solutions

If you are hosting a Docker Enterprise cluster in the cloud, you may have already discovered other volume storage plugins. These plugins are part of the docker4x (as in, Docker Engine-Community for Azure and Docker for AWS) ecosystem and can be installed in your cloud environment by following Docker Certified Infrastructure. In Chapter 9, *Important Docker Enterprise Production Topics*, we will explore AWS and Azure installs with Docker Enterprise.

Cloudstore is a powerful plugin that allows you to access cloud-native resources for the Docker API. For instance, on AWS, you can specify an **elastic block store** (**EBS**) backed volume for the container to mount. If the workload migrates to a different node, AWS will move this volume and attach it to the new instance. If you're crossing availability zones, AWS will copy the contents you have in your EBS volume into a new volume in the new AZ and mount it into the instance where your container is running. While this approach may seem a little clumsy, it does have its advantages as you can specify very high performance EBS IOPS volumes to meet the needs of some demanding applications.

Another way to implement cloud storage on AWS is in a shared mode where the volume is backed by **elastic file storage** (**EFS**). In this case you can have multiple containers sharing the same back end file system. Certainly very flexible and convenient, but it may not have the performance your application requires.

In addition to the cloud provider storage plugins, there are about 20 Docker-certified plugins from various storage vendors. Some of these have free back end implementations, but many of them are designed to integrate with the storage solutions the vendors provide. This includes a lot of on-premises vendors such as VMware, NetApp, and Nutanix.

Backing up data

Obviously, backing up data is critical for any production environment. In our Docker Enterprise discussion, we will talk about three areas for backup—UCP, DTR, and application data.

Consult the most recent documentation from Docker regarding backups, but if you are running UCP 3.1.0 - 3.1.2 you must run the following script prior to running the UCF you back up! There is a clean-up job you should have as a part of a cron tab to regularly clean up `ucp-kubelet` mounts.

The following code block show Docker's pre-backup clean-up script:

```
SHM_MOUNT=$(grep -m1 '^tmpfs./dev/shm' /proc/mounts)
while [ $(grep -cm2 '^tmpfs./dev/shm' /proc/mounts) -gt 1 ]; do
 sudo umount /dev/shm
done
grep -q '^tmpfs./dev/shm' /proc/mounts || sudo mount "${SHM_MOUNT}"
```

UCP backup needs to be run from the manager nodes. An operator or an operator using a script needs to log in to the UCP nodes and perform the following:

1. Stop the Docker service using the following command:

   ```
   $ sudo service docker stop
   ```

2. Back up the `/var/lib/docker/swarm` to a safe location
3. Restart the Daemon (`$ sudo service docker start`) and wait for the node to stabilize
4. Back up UCP (described in the following section)

Backing up UCP

After the Docker service restarts and the UCP node returns to health, the backup is started by running the following command, noting the TAR file that is created. Do not leave it on `/tmp`. Specify an alternate safe directory or immediately `scp` the file to a remote backup location.

The UCP backup command is shown in the following code block:

```
## SSH Into each manager node.
UCPID=$(docker run --rm -i --name ucp -v
/var/run/docker.sock:/var/run/docker.sock docker/ucp id)

# Create a backup, encrypt it, and temporarily store it on /tmp/backup.tar
docker container run \
  --security-opt label=disable \
  --log-driver none --rm \
  --interactive \
  --name ucp \
  -v /var/run/docker.sock:/var/run/docker.sock \
```

```
        docker/ucp:3.1.2 backup \
        --id $UCPID \
        --passphrase "secret" > /tmp/backup.tar

    # Decrypt the backup and list its contents
    $ gpg --decrypt /tmp/backup.tar | tar --list
```

Please note the `--security-opt label=disable` parameter is for `SELinux`. To verify run the `cat /etc/docker/daemon.json` and look for `"selinux-enabled":"true"` in the output. Also, the `passphrase` is set to `"secret"`. You probably want to adjust that as well.

When running a UCP backup, please note that all of the UCP containers are stopped in order to capture a reliable backup snapshot. This means the UCP being backed up will stop running temporarily. If you are in a high-availability configuration, the cluster should continue running normally. For this reason, it is generally a good idea to back up during periods of low activity and, of course, only back up one node at a time. Also, because the UCP containers need to start running again after the backup is complete, always give the manager nodes a few minutes to recover. Verify the node is healthy (the UCP dashboard is a good place to verify this) before proceeding to back up the next node.

Backing up DTR

Unlike the UCP backup, DTR backups can be done remotely using the UCP admin's client bundle. This method is very simple and causes minimal disruption. Please note this backup includes your DTR's metadata about the organization, teams and repos, but it does not include the actual binary image layers. Those are stored by the backup filesystem that you set up when you installed DTR. For on-premises implementations, the DTR backup is probably NFS and that is where the blobs are stored for the images.

Here is Docker's office list of what is backed up during a DTR backup:

Data	Backed up	Description
Configurations	Yes	DTR settings
Repository metadata	Yes	Metadata such as image architecture and size
Access control to repos and images	Yes	Data about who has access to which images
Notary data	Yes	Signatures and digests for images that are signed
Scan results	Yes	Information about vulnerabilities in your images
Certificates and keys	Yes	TLS certificates and keys used by DTR
Image content	No	Needs to be backed up separately; depends on DTR configuration

Data	Backed up	Description
Users, orgs, teams	No	Creates a UCP backup to back up this data
Vulnerability database	No	Can be re-downloaded after a restore

The following code block is a script to run the Docker DTR backup from a UCP admin client bundle and store them in the `dtr-backup-files` subdirectory. Start with this simple sample to get running, but do be careful as this script has an admin password embedded within the parameters:

```bash
#!/bin/bash

#get current ucp certificate
curl -4k https://ucp.nvisia.io/ca > ucp.ca

# list docker replicas
dtr_replicas=($(docker container ls --format "{{.Names}}" | grep dtr-
registry | awk -F- '{print $NF}'))

for i in "${dtr_replicas[@]}"
do :
   echo "backing up:$i"
   docker run --log-driver none -i --rm \
     docker/dtr:2.6.0 backup \
     --ucp-url https://ucp.mydomain.com \
     --ucp-ca "$(cat ucp.ca)" \
     --ucp-username admin \
     --ucp-password XXXXX \
     --existing-replica-id $i > ./dtr-backup-files/backup-$i-metadata.tar
   echo -e "backup complete\n\n"
done
```

These scripts take a few minutes to run.

Backing up application data

This section is basically a placeholder to remind you to back up your application data. Containers do not automatically back themselves up, and hopefully you have learned to not store data that you care about inside of your containers. Therefore, you should be using Docker volumes to store your data on the host filesystem or with NFS. So if you are doing a simple host mount, you are going to have to copy the data from the worker node to a central, safe, and secure place. When live backups are an option, consider using `rsync` to synchronize the files to a remote location.

Updates can be found at `https://docs.docker.com/ee/ucp/admin/install/upgrade/`.

Applying OS and Docker updates

Here are some general procedures for updating your cluster. The example are geared toward centOS, but ideas can easily be applied to most cluster configurations and minor updates. If you are working through a larger upgrade process, you obviously want to set aside a maintenance window and start with your non-production cluster. After you upgrade your non-production cluster, please perform thorough testing before proceeding to do any upgrades on the production cluster.

OS and Docker Enterprise Engine updates

First, make sure that your cluster is in a steady and healthy state. This means no major changes to the cluster nodes or configuration just prior to your update. Do not add, remove, promote, or demote nodes. Also, do not adjust UCP or DTR settings just before updates as any of these changes can take several minutes to complete and we do not want to start an update before it is completely propagated and the cluster is stabilized.

The strategy here is to make sure that all of the Docker Engines are the latest version prior to making updates to the UCP and DTR software, as they are expecting the latest version of the Docker Engine.

UCP manager nodes

Perform these steps on each UCP manager node:

1. Stop Docker Engine using $ `sudo service docker stop`.
2. Upgrade the OS and Engine with $ `sudo yum update -y`.
3. Reboot if required using $ `sudu reboot`, or start Docker Engine using $ `sudo service docker start`.

4. From a UCP manager node, use $ `sudo docker node ls` to verify the node is ready and healthy.

After the node is back and healthy, move on to the next manager. Once all the managers have been upgraded, proceed to the DTR servers.

Worker nodes

Perform these steps on each of the cluster's worker nodes:

1. From a UCP manager node, use `$ sudo docker node update --availability drain {name of node to update}`.
2. On the node to be updated, stop the Docker Engine using `$ sudo service docker stop`.
3. Upgrade the OS and Engine with `$ sudo yum update -y`.
4. Reboot if required using `$ sudu reboot`, or start Docker Engine using `$ sudo service docker start`.
5. From a manager node, use `$ sudo docker node update --availability active {name of node just updated}`.
6. From a UCP manager node, use `$ sudo docker node ls`, then wait for the node to be ready and healthy.

Upgrading the UCP software

After the OS and Engine updates are completed on all nodes, log in to UCP **Admin Settings** | **Upgrade** and look for available upgrades. If the upgrade is available, proceed.

Here, the UCP setting | Update screen shows that the UCP is the latest version:

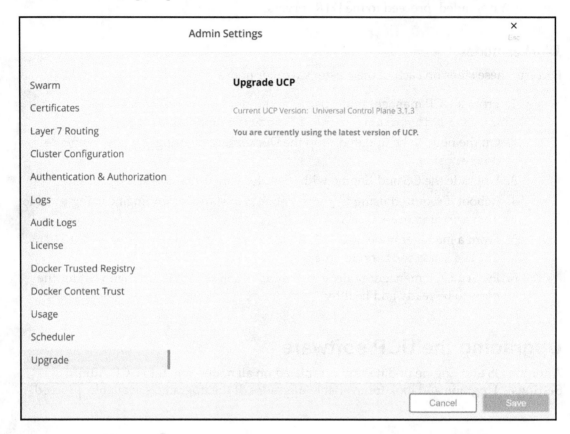

UCP Upgrade Screen

Upgrading the DTR software

With UCP updated, log in to DTR and see whether there are any updates pending. The following screenshot shows we need to update our DTR software:

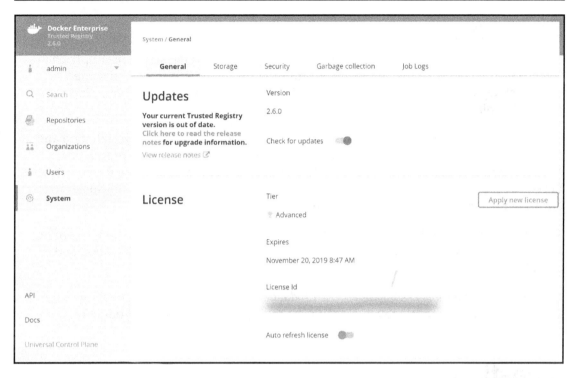

Docker Trusted Registry System General Settings

Navigate to `https://docs.docker.com/ee/dtr/admin/upgrade/`. This process allows us to pull the latest DTR container and run the upgrade command. The upgrade command will update all of the replicas in the cluster. Please be aware that this process takes about 10-20 minutes.

Summary

In this chapter, we walked you through the high-level flow on the software supply chain, from CI's initial build all way to the image-running production. We covered some important key topics as we walked through the pipeline. Then we started building the production platform.

Building upon what we learned in the pilot about the Docker Enterprise installation and configuration, we discussed some additional factors to consider for your production environment. Finally, we talked about data management and maintenance for your Docker Enterprise clusters. Remember, you want to start with your non-production cluster to test out all of the new changes prior to updating your production systems.

This should be enough to get started with your first application in production. However, we still have a few important topics to cover related to deploying the application and operating the Docker Enterprise platform.

In Chapter 9, *Important Docker Enterprise Production Topics*, we will dive deeper into the Docker Enterprise concepts related to running multiple applications in production.

Questions

1. What are the main differences between your non-production and production DTRs?
2. Why should you not run as root inside of a container?
3. How can you get to your cluster if it is behind a firewall?

Further reading

Check out the following resources for more information on the topics covered in this chapter:

- **Docker Enterprise Reference Architectures**:
    - https://success.docker.com/architectures
- **Running Docker Enterprise at Scale**:
    - https://success.docker.com/article/running-docker-ee-at-scale

- **Swarm Cluster Admin**:
  - https://docs.docker.com/engine/swarm/admin_guide/
- **Docker UCP Backup, Restore, and Recovery**:
  - https://docs.docker.com/ee/ucp/admin/backups-and-disaster-recovery/
- **Fixing an Unhealthy DTR Replica**:
  - https://docs.docker.com/ee/dtr/admin/disaster-recovery/
- **Using Cloudstor on AWS**:
  - https://docs.docker.com/docker-for-aws/persistent-data-volumes/
- **Using Cloudstore in Azure**:
  - https://docs.docker.com/docker-for-azure/persistent-data-volumes/
- **Docker Enterprise Backup and Restore Best Practices Article**:
  - https://success.docker.com/article/docker-ee-best-practices#backupandrestore

Important Docker Enterprise Production Topics

9

While we covered some of the bare essentials for getting our first application into production with Docker Enterprise
in Chapter 8, *First Application in Production with Docker Enterprise*, there are still many important concepts related to running multiple production applications on a shared, stable Docker Enterprise platform. It is not possible to cover every production deployment scenario, but this chapter's topics will be important when deploying multiple production applications to your production cluster.

In Chapter 8, *First Application in Production with Docker Enterprise*, we talked about getting the first application into production, but as you deploy subsequent applications, how can you make sure the applications have sufficient resources? How do you know that dead containers won't be used to serve incoming ones? What if there is a problem when we update an application service? In this chapter, we will answer these questions and many more.

In this chapter, the following topics will be covered:

- Exploring some important features of orchestrators used in production
- Understanding simple blue/green application deployments
- Production monitoring
- Getting help from the experts at Docker

Working with orchestrators in production

Over the last several years, both the Swarm and Kubernetes communities have continued to add important features to improve application performance, scalability, and reliability. Orchestrators play a key role in maintaining application health, managing resources, and ensuring that applications are in their desired state.

As we start deploying to production, we need to cover several important topics related to how container orchestrators interact with running applications. In this section, we will explore how to configure our Docker Enterprise orchestrators to support application health and cluster efficiency.

Health checks

One key feature of a container orchestrator is making sure our applications are in their desired state, as specified when the workload is scheduled. For example, if my application deployment file or API call specifies that five instances of an NGINX web server are to be running at all times, it is up to the orchestrator to make sure that happens.

Both Swarm and Kubernetes monitor the status of their scheduled containers or pods to make sure they are up and running by constantly comparing the current state with the desired state within the cluster. If there is a discrepancy, the orchestrator schedules a compensating action to achieve the desired state. However, in order for this to happen, the container's health needs to be observed by the orchestrator. Therefore, we need to instrument our container with health checks for the orchestrator to call.

Health checks are a special bit of code provided by the container creator. The health check code is periodically run by the Docker Engine inside the container and it reports the health status to the orchestrator. If the health check fails, the orchestrator subsequently removes the unhealthy container and creates a new one in its place.

Often, these checks are based on a cURL command, which is OK in some circumstances, but has some drawbacks (see Elton Stoneman's post in this topic: `https://blog.sixeyed.com/docker-healthchecks-why-not-to-use-curl-or-iwr/`). It is usually a better idea to build a custom health check endpoint or leverage something such as Spring Boot's Actuator sub-project.

Adding Spring Boot's Actuator to your Java applications gives you out-of-the-box API endpoint implementations for probing and managing your application over HTTP. The built-in endpoints allow a query for a wide variety of information about the status of your application, but most important for our conversation is the /health endpoint. The /health endpoint returns the HTTP 200 status code when the application is healthy. Additionally, /health can be customized, allowing developers to define their own specific criteria for the /health response.

In some cases, we have seen this used in creative ways. In one scenario, to compensate for a memory leak in a third-party code library, the health check was configured to respond with an unhealthy response when the memory usage reached a predefined threshold. In this situation, when memory hit the predefined limit, the endpoint returned a failed health check, causing the orchestrator to kill the old, bloated container and start a new, clean container.

Ephemeral containers and orchestration

Because orchestrators start and stop containers on a regular basis, the concept of an ephemeral container becomes important. There are two key aspects with ephemeral containers:

- They are stateless
- They have relatively fast startup and shutdown times

By stateless, we mean all requests are only dependent on information that is included in the request (parameters or fields) and not on any previous interactions with a service. Therefore, a request with the same parameters or fields will always yield the same final state of the service. This is sometimes called being idempotent. Statelessness makes horizontal scaling possible and for orchestrators it means multiple containers can safely run behind a single service with requests load-balanced across the group of backing containers. If one of these containers stops working, the orchestrator removes it from the load balancer, kills it, and starts another. During this process, service requests are directed to alternate containers by the service's load balancer.

The other aspect of ephemeral containers is fast startup and shutdown times to avoid long gaps between the container's PID 1 starting and the container passing its health check and being ready to serve traffic. During this time period, the container is not available to callers, but occupies a task slot, meaning one of your service container instances is out of service during startup.

Application startup and health checks

By default, both Swarm and Kubernetes provide very simple health check mechanisms when a custom health check is not defined. In this default case, both orchestrators simply use PID 1's status as an indicator of container health. Subsequently, the orchestrators assume if PID 1 is running, the container is ready for traffic. However, there are many situations where this behavior is unacceptable. In other words, we need the orchestrator to withhold traffic from our new container until it is completely started and ready to process requests. To accomplish this, both orchestrators leverage custom health checks.

The custom health check principle is pretty straightforward. The orchestrator starts a new container and waits for it to pass the health check before adding it into the service's load balancer to serve requests. In *Figure 1*, you can see a Swarm service is started with three replicas:

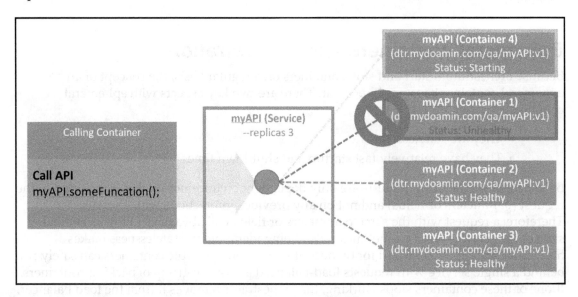

Figure 1: Docker Swarm in the process of replacing an unhealthy container

As you can see, one of the replicas, container 1, fails its health check. Then, the orchestrator retries the prescribed amount of times and eventually kills container 1. Please note, during this failure time window (the container is not responding, but orchestrator is waiting for health check to time out—maybe 3 tries that are 10 seconds apart), the caller may get a connection to the dead container. This is why we stressed defensive programming principles for distributed services in Chapter 6, *Design and Pilot a Docker Enterprise CI Pipeline*, in *Defensive coding* section.

While the new container is starting up, Swarm will wait for the duration specified in the `--start-period` parameter (the default is `0`) before it starts running health checks. So, for a longer startup application, you would want to override the default to something appropriate, perhaps 60 or 90 seconds. Imagine, however, that a new release of your service has a longer startup time. It is very possible that the `--start-period` will elapse and the health checks will fail before the application starts. In fact, the orchestrator will kill it before it ever becomes healthy, and it will try to start another one. This leaves you in a continuous restart loop and no container running for your service. While this is easy to fix by extending the `--start-period` parameter, Kubernetes provides a more elegant solution for the problem.

Kubernetes provides two types of health checks: a liveliness probe and a readiness probe. The liveliness probe is used to determine whether the application is running, while the readiness probe determines whether the service is ready to serve traffic. As you can see, this can be very useful during a long-running startup process where we have some middle ground between healthy and unhealthy. Not until the pods liveliness probe fails, will the orchestrator replace the pod. Additionally, you get the benefit where the service's load balancer can quickly remove a container from its backend pool as soon as the readiness profiles. There are two interesting failure conditions in Kubernetes: when a readiness probe has failed, stop traffic flow from the service, and if Nto the liveliness probe has failed, the pod is unhealthy and needs to be replaced.

Kubernetes allows us to define health checks in a few different ways. A command-style probe, such as we saw with Docker's health checks, where the command is executed inside of the container and an exit code of `0` indicates a healthy container. The second type is an HTTP probe, where Kubernetes pings you applications on the unspecified port/path and looks for a 2xx or 3xx response code to indicate a healthy container. The third type of probe is a TCP probe that attempts to make a TCP connection on a specified port and if the connection is made, Kubernetes assumes a healthy container.

In `Chapter 10`, *More on Kubernetes with Docker Enterprise*, we will work through a Kubernetes example application that includes a health check, but now let's look at a Swarm health check example.

Swarm service health check for AtSea-web

Docker allows a health check to be defined in the Dockerfile or the Swarm stack YAML file. When we add HEALTHCHECK to a Dockerfile, the check adds a simple health indicator to standalone containers (the $ docker run command) or as a Swarm service (the $ docker service create command). While running a heath check on a standalone container does not take any corrective action automatically, it does reports the status of the health check when you list your containers using the $ docker container ls command.

The following code block shows how a standalone container run from an image with a healthcheck directive showing a health status:

```
$ docker container ls
CONTAINER ID IMAGE          COMMAND                     CREATED         STATUS
f90e97819351 hc-db:test "docker-entrypoint.s..." 30 seconds ago Up 29 seconds
(healthy)
```

You could go to the trouble of writing a script that monitors Docker Engine events to restart unhealthy standalone containers, but that is what Swarm already does for us! Therefore, we will focus our attention on a Swarm example using the AtSea-web application we built in Chapter 6, *Design and Pilot a Docker Enterprise CI Pipeline*.

For our example, we could put the healthcheck command inside either the Dockerfile or our docker-stack-cluster.yml file. Since we are likely to specify custom health check parameters in the docker-stack-cluster.yml file anyway, we will just put it there. Otherwise, we end up having health check-specific information spread across both the Docker file and the docker-stack-cluster.yml file, which seems both unnecessary and messy.

So, while we are not adding the health check directive, healthcheck, to our Dockerfile, we do need to update the Dockerfile with the appropriate dependencies to support a cURL healthcheck command. In our case, this requires installing the apk curl package on our Alpine JDK base image. Remember, this is a multistage build file and we only need to install our curl package in the final stage as it will be the base for our service container.

The following Dockerfile code block shows how we are using the apk package manager to install the curl package to support our cURL-based health check:

```
FROM node:latest AS jsbuild
WORKDIR /usr/src/atsea/app/react-app
COPY react-app .
RUN npm install
RUN npm run build
```

```
FROM maven:latest AS mavenbuild
WORKDIR /usr/src/atsea
COPY pom.xml .
RUN mvn -B -f pom.xml -s /usr/share/maven/ref/settings-docker.xml
dependency:resolve
COPY . .
RUN mvn -B -s /usr/share/maven/ref/settings-docker.xml package -DskipTests

FROM java:8-jdk-alpine
RUN apk --update add curl
RUN adduser -Dh /home/gordon gordon
WORKDIR /static
COPY --from=jsbuild /usr/src/atsea/app/react-app/build/ .
WORKDIR /app
COPY --from=mavenbuild /usr/src/atsea/target/AtSea-0.0.1-SNAPSHOT.jar .
ENTRYPOINT ["java", "-jar", "/app/AtSea-0.0.1-SNAPSHOT.jar"]
CMD ["--spring.profiles.active=postgres"]
```

Now, we have to add the `healthcheck` section to our `appserver` service in our stack file, as shown in the following code block:

```
appserver:
  image: ${DTR_SERVER}/${STACK_ENV}/atsea-web_build:RC-${STACK_ENV}
  networks:
    - front-tier
    - back-tier
    - payment
  healthcheck:
    test: ["CMD", "curl", "-f", "http://localhost:8080/index.html"]
    interval: 30s
    timeout: 5s
    retries: 3
    start_period: 40s
  deploy:
    replicas: 2
    update_config:
      parallelism: 2
      failure_action: rollback
    restart_policy:
      condition: on-failure
      delay: 5s
      max_attempts: 3
      window: 120s
    labels:
      com.docker.lb.hosts: at-sea-${STACK_ENV}.nvisia.io
      com.docker.lb.network: ${STACK}_front-tier
      com.docker.lb.port: 8080
      com.docker.lb.ssl_cert: wildcard.mydomain.com.server.crt
```

```
        com.docker.lb.ssl_key: wildcard.mydomain.com.key
    secrets:
      - postgres_password
```

Not only did we provide the `test: ["CMD"...` using the `curl` we specified, we also included some additional parameters to define how the checks are run and to determine what constitutes a failure. The first parameter is the interval, which specifies the time between checks. The second is the timeout parameter, which indicates how long the test should wait for a response. The **retries** parameter specifies how many times to retry the test before failing. The `start_period` parameter, as we discussed in the Application startup and heath checks section of this chapter, is how long the orchestrator will wait before running the first health check at startup.

Passing signals into containers

There are some important semantics related to the CMD when building your images with a Dockerfile and running them with an orchestrator. When people get started with Docker, they generally gloss over the concept of the shell versus exec forms of CMD. Often, they just think of it a JSON versus command-line style of formatting. In fact, there are several other differences that are important, but for our conversation with orchestration, we need to talk about signal forwarding.

The Docker docs talk about the main CMD forms, as follows:

- `CMD ["executable","param1","param2"]` (the `exec` form; this is the preferred form)
- The `param1 param2 CMD` command (shell form)

The first and preferred form is the `exec` form; as the commands process is not wrapped inside a shell process and subsequently all signals are forwarded to any child processes. This is important because if an orchestrator issues a `SIGTERM` signal to a container, you will want your processes to receive the signal and have the opportunity to respond with an orderly shutdown. If, however, you are using the shell form, the signal will not be forwarded past the shell to the child processes. This can be problematic if you are running an `entrypoint.sh` style script that needs a shell, such as bash, to run and you want the commands, such as Java, to get signals from the host. Fortunately, there's a well-know workaround for this, using something called `tini`. In fact, Docker uses `tini`.

If you run into any issues related to signals not getting past the shell or zombie processes in the shell, look at using tini. I would suggest starting with this article: `https://github.com/krallin/tini`.

Managed and unmanaged cluster resources

Most examples of running applications in a cluster do not include any information about resource needs or limits for the application's workload. Without information about resource needs and limits for the workload, the orchestrator is unable to effectively manage cluster resources. This **unmanaged** approach leaves cluster operators to rely heavily on their monitoring infrastructure to avoid resource starvation by dynamically scaling their cluster up and down as required.

In a cloud-native environment of boundless elastic resources, an unmanaged approach may be workable, but it is both expensive and wrought with potential application performance inconsistencies. So, we recommend limiting the use of unmanaged clusters to non-production environments—even for cloud platforms. Furthermore, with unmanaged non-production clusters, seriously consider using Docker Enterprise Advanced Edition's **collections** to manage node-level isolation to reduce resource starvation situations for performance testing and user acceptance environments in the non-production cluster.

We strongly recommended that you take a managed approach to resource management in your production clusters, as discussed in the next section.

Orchestrators and resource management

In `Chapter 8`, *First Application in Production with Docker Enterprise*, we discussed the concept of scheduling preferences and constraints for Swarm scheduling. When we need our data-related services to consistently run on the same nodes where their data volumes resided, we used node labels in conjunction with deployment constraints to tell Swarm where to place the data-related services. Now, we're going to talk about another orchestrator scheduling topic and learn more about how Swarm and Kubernetes manage available resources.

Both Swarm and Kubernetes keep track of the resources reserved (requested in Kubernetes) by containers as they are scheduled on each node (additionally, Kubernetes keeps track of the entire namespaces/cluster to manage quotas). Essentially, when a container is scheduled on a node, the orchestrator reduces its record for that node's available capacity by the amount reserved/requested for the deployed containers.

Let's talk through a simple example. In our example, we have three worker nodes: node A, node B, and node C. Each node has 16 GB of memory and four CPU cores. Now, the orchestrator has placed three containers on node A and each container reserved/requested 3 GB of memory and 0.5 CPU cores. Through simple math, the orchestrator knows that *7 GB (16 GB - 3 GB x 3)* of memory and *2.5 CPU cores (4 cores - 0.5 x 3)* remain available on node A. If the next scheduling requests exceeds 7 GB or 2.5 CPUs, the orchestrator will have to find a different node. If no other nodes have the capacity, the scheduler will log an error indicating there are no suitable nodes to satisfy the scheduling request.

Container reservations, requests, and limits

To accomplish resource management, orchestrators rely on two concepts: **reservations** (called requests in Kubernetes) and **limits**. Essentially, the orchestrator uses the resource reservations (called requests) for its internal accounting system to keep track of available node resources. Limits are used to enforce the amount of resources a container is allowed to consume when running. The best practice is to set your reservations equal to your limits to avoid potentially over-scheduling a cluster node.

How can a node be over-scheduled in a managed resource model? Here is an example. Our nodes each have 16 GB of memory. The orchestrator schedules four containers where each container requires 2 GB of memory and sets a limit at 3 GB of memory. This makes sense to us because we require a 2 GB minimum to run our container properly, but it could go up to 3 GB of memory at peak times. However, keep in mind the orchestrator is planning on 2 GB of consumption for each. Therefore, the orchestrator schedules all four containers on the same node. As soon as the container averages more than 2 GB of memory usage, you get an over-scheduled, resource-starved cluster node. However, if we had set our limit and a reservation to be equal, we would have avoided over-scheduling, but then we may get an error of under-utilization. However, in a production environment, it is much better to have resources under-utilized than to have applications deprived of resources!

 There's a significant difference between how the limits on CPU and memory are handled. CPU limits throttle a container's CPU utilization, allowing it to continue running at the CPU limit specified. Memory limits, on the other hand, will trigger an **Out-of-memory Exception** (**OOME**) in the container and shut the container down. This is important to understand. To avoid unexpected container restarts, pick your memory limits carefully, especially in a production environment!

Now that we've described the concepts of the managed and unmanaged cluster approaches, let's look at how to use the managed approach.

Setting CPU and memory reservations

For a Swarm example, we will go back to our AtSea custom web application deployment and add a reservation and limit to the `appserver` service. The `appserver` service is running a spring boot application in a Java 8 environment. So, we have a couple of things to contend with in this situation. The first is related to a version of Java prior to Java 10, where the JVM disregarded the container's `cgroup` memory restrictions. As a result, the JVM behaved as though all of the host's memory was available to the JVM, instead of what was allocated to the container through `cgroup`. This would usually cause the JVM to allocate memory beyond the container limit and to cause the container to fail with an OOME. So to work around this, we added the `JAVA_OPTS` environment variable to the following code block to set the maximum memory for the JVM to 1 GB with the `-Xmx1G` flag.

Now, let's take a look at deploying our `appserver` service with some sensible limit reservations:

```
# atsea-deploy docker-stack-cluster.yml
version: "3.7"

services:
  appserver:
    image: ${DTR_SERVER}/${STACK_ENV}/atsea-web_build:RC-${STACK_ENV}
    environment:
      JAVA_OPTS: -Xms512M -Xmx1G
    networks:
      - front-tier
      - back-tier
      - payment
    healthcheck:
      test: ["CMD", "curl", "-f", "http://localhost:8080/index.html"]
      interval: 30s
      timeout: 5s
      retries: 3
      start_period: 40s
    deploy:
      resources:
        limits:
          cpus: '1'
          memory: 1.5G
        reservations:
          cpus: '1'
```

```
      memory: 1.5G
  replicas: 2
  update_config:
    parallelism: 1
    failure_action: rollback
  restart_policy:
    condition: on-failure
    delay: 5s
    max_attempts: 3
    window: 120s
  labels:
    com.docker.lb.hosts: at-sea-${STACK_ENV}.nvisia.io
    com.docker.lb.network: ${STACK}_front-tier
    com.docker.lb.port: 8080
    com.docker.lb.ssl_cert: wildcard.nvisia.io.server.crt
    com.docker.lb.ssl_key: wildcard.nvisia.io.key
secrets:
  - postgres_password
...
```

In the previous code block, notice the resources section under deployment. Here, we can find where the resource limits and reservations are set. We set the reservations and limits the same as in our previous strategy. The CPUs are set to one core and the memory is set to 1.5 GB.

Because we created a CI pipeline to deploy this application, all we need to do is change the `docker-stack-cluster.yml` file, commit it, and push it to GitLab. Finally, we trigger the build with our `curl` GitLab command:

```
curl -X POST -F token=xxxxxxxxxxxxxxxx-F "ref=master" -F
"variables[DEPLOY_TARGET]=test"
https://gitlab.com/api/v4/projects/10552558/trigger/pipeline
```

Now we can head over to the, under **Swarm** | **Services**, and click on `atsea-deployer-test_appserver` to watch the status of our deployment. In *Figure 2*, you can see the service information in the **Universal Control Plane(UCP)** web UI:

Figure 2: Service information in the UCP web UI

When we look at the service status previously in the UCP, we see the green button indicating the service is healthy for two out of two replicas. Then, if we scroll down, we will see the limits and reservations exactly how they were specified in the stack deployment file.

Another way to look at the service to verify the reservations would be to use the UCP client bundle, as shown in the following code block in the abbreviated output from the `service inspect` command:

```
$ docker service inspect atsea-deployer-test_appserver
[
    {
        "ID": "vqqoaglk897x0pewagj11rwyz",
        "Version": {
            "Index": 640839
        },
...
            "Resources": {
```

```
                    "Limits": {
                        "NanoCPUs": 1000000000,
                        "MemoryBytes": 1610612736
                    },
                    "Reservations": {
                        "NanoCPUs": 1000000000,
                        "MemoryBytes": 1610612736
                    }
                },
        ...
```

Now, let's take a look at applying the same principles to a Kubernetes pod. In this case, we are just using a trivial `nginx` example, and we limit the memory to 128 MB and the CPU to 250 millicores (1/4 of a core).

The following code block shows the sample `kube-limits.yaml` file used to launch our test pods with requests and limits:

```
# kube-limits.yaml
apiVersion: v1
kind: Pod
metadata:
  name: frontend
spec:
  containers:
  - name: proxy
    image: nginx:1.14-alpine
    resources:
      requests:
        memory: "128Mi"
        cpu: "250m"
      limits:
        memory: "128Mi"
        cpu: "250m"
```

In the following code block, we use `kubectl` from our UCP client bundle to deploy the frontend pods with limits and requests. After the pods deploy, we again use `kubectl` to look at our new pod deployment. We have highlighted the limits and requests section in the following output:

```
$ kubectl apply -f kube-limits.yaml
pod/frontend created

$ kubectl describe pod frontend
Name: frontend
Namespace: default
Priority: 0
```

```
PriorityClassName: <none>
Node: ntc-wrk-3.mydomain.com/10.10.1.45
Start Time: Tue, 19 Feb 2019 00:12:43 -0600
...
    Limits:
      cpu: 250m
      memory: 128Mi
    Requests:
      cpu: 250m
      memory: 128Mi
...
```

As you can see, the mechanism for deploying reservations, requests, and limits is very simple. The challenging part is figuring out what numbers to provide as parameters for the limits/reservations. Again, this is where your monitoring tools will come in handy, especially with Java applications.

Figure 3 shows a metrics screen from the Sysdig monitor for the newly deployed `appserver`:

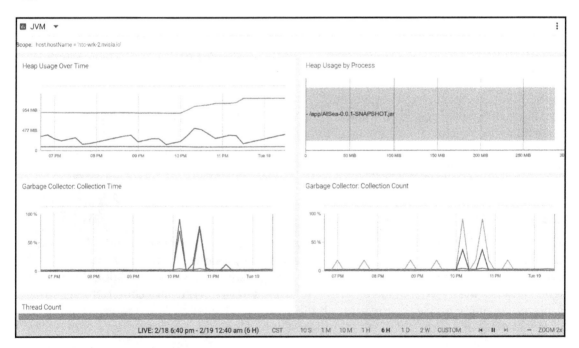

Figure 3: Metrics screen

At the end of the day, many cloud-native DevOps teams are comfortable with the **dynamic** nature and technical complexity of scaling unmanaged resources in their cluster. More traditional IT operations teams find the **deterministic** nature of using reservations, requests, and limits to manage resources essential in their production environments.

Production ingress

When it comes to production ingress, we find ourselves facing the same **dynamic** versus **deterministic** decisions. On the one hand, we enjoy the dynamic nature of various tools for layer 7 routing, as we have shown previously in `Chapter 6`, *Design and Pilot a Docker Enterprise CI Pipeline,* when we used labels with UCP's Interlock 2 and configuration of our reverse proxy server (usually NGINX these days) is automatically configured by simply deploying your service to the cluster. Unfortunately, this approach requires a lot of moving parts, which is not a good thing in a production environment where simplicity and securities reign supreme. Both Swarm and Kubernetes give you a few models for deploying applications, including dynamic routing (layer 7), simple port-based routing (layer 4 IPVS), and static host deployments.

Ingress model overview

In these three sections, we will give a brief overview of each of the ingress models. Then, we will go into some specific implementation details of the most common approaches. At one end of the spectrum, we have very dynamic models with lots of moving parts, and at the other end, we have deterministic models that require more manual configuration and are potentially more brittle.

Layer 7 dynamic routing

For layer 7, we have UCP's Interlock 2, the Kubernetes ingress controller and other great similar layer 7 services such as Traefik. These technologies monitor the orchestrator's events, keying off of labels, and adjust the reverse proxy servers' configuration dynamically when services are deployed. Layer 7 reverse proxy wrappers are very cool in the sense that can send all of my ingress traffic through the layer 7 controller and the requests end up in the right place. It's very cool when it works reliably. However, we have seen a variety of issues related to networking (phantom networks) and security (port blocking) where these controllers may not be 100% reliable, or convergence times (the time it takes for the changes to propagate) are too long.

To illustrate this feature, we've used Interlock 2 in our Swarm AtSea application's appserver service configuration throughout this book. However, while Interlock 2 might be an option for our single production application in `Chapter 8`, *First Application in Production with Docker Enterprise*, we are still not sold on its stability for higher scaling implementations.

With both Swarm and Kubernetes, you can also deploy your own reverse proxy servers using NGINX and implement your own ingress scheme. The trick with the custom approach is to update the configurations dynamically and deal with possible service disruptions during controller updates. The Kubernetes community is pushing the technology envelope with some advanced, mergeable ingress models (`https://github.com/nginxinc/kubernetes-ingress/tree/master/examples/mergeable-ingress-types`), but unfortunately these more complex ingress schemes are out of the scope of this book.

Layer 4 simple port-based routing

Both Swarm and Kubernetes provide a simple, port-based, cluster-wide routing mechanism that is both efficient and reliable. With this model, you essentially point your external load balancers into the cluster using a specific port number (a unique port for each exposed service) with an IP or DNS name belonging to any node in the cluster. The layer 4 routing captures the request from any node's network adapter on the specific port number and forwards it to the correct cluster service with load balancing using IPVS. This is a good balance between managed ingress and dynamic workload placement, because the orchestrator transparently handles the specific details of the container and pod placement.

We will see some examples of these later in section Key concepts of blue/green deployments when we look at blue/green deployments section.

Static host deployments

The static host deployment model is the old-school approach to deployments. This is generally how we deployed our first production websites. This model is highly deterministic and subsequently takes very little advantage of our container platform features. For many organizations that are just getting started with production containers at scale, they will often start here. While that is completely understandable, be careful about applying old models to new container technology platforms. You could end up with much of the risk and none of the benefits of containers if you're not careful.

In a static host model, your services are deployed to a specific host using a label (as we did for our Wiki PoCP application), and the service's ingress port is mapped directly from the host's adapter (usually on an ephemeral port to avoid port conflicts) to the service.

Once the service is deployed to the server and the port is mapped, you configure the application load balancer with that host node's IP address or DNS name + ephemeral port number. In this configuration, you update your load balancer with information for each node hosting the service. Again, this is very deterministic and the network path is very efficient (no IPVS hops on the way in and out), but certainly more cumbersome and brittle.

Key concepts of blue/green deployments

If you are concerned about downtime while making updates to your running production applications, you are not alone. That is why the blue/green deployment model has become popular. With a blue/green deployment, you are able to stand up the new version of the application, and verify it is ready and working before directing external traffic to the application.

Earlier in Chapter 3, *Getting Started – Docker Enterprise Proof of Concept*, we talked about concept of rolling out a stack of new services into production with Swarm, but we did not discuss the options for migrating application updates. In this section, I want to explore a very simple model that will work for your early production applications. We will illustrate it with both Swarm and Kubernetes.

Blue/green deployments with Swarm

First, we will talk about the Swarm blue/green deployment, where we will use a load balancer in conjunction with two versions of a Docker service. The load balancers could be external to our cluster or actually running in a container within our cluster. For the sake of our discussion, let's say it's an external application load balancer that's sitting in front of our cluster.

Figure 4 shows how the process works for Swarm:

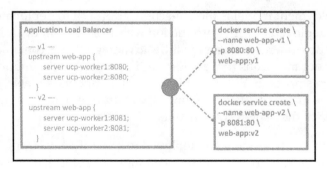

Figure 4: The Swarm blue/green migration process

Prior to the update, only items in green are present. Traffic is coming to the load balancer and being forwarded over port `8080` to the `web-app-v1` service. When it's time to release a new version of our web app, we deploy the `web-app-v2` service to the cluster. When the new service is up and ready for traffic, we reconfigure the load balancer to direct traffic on `8081`. This effectively cuts off traffic to the old version and redirects it to the new version.

If there's a problem with the new version of our application, we can reverse the process and send traffic back to the old version. However, once we are convinced the new version is working properly, we can spin down version 1 and remove it from the cluster.

Kubernetes blue/green deployment

Now, we can take a look at the Kubernetes blue/green deployment process. Notice for the Kubernetes process that we do not use an external load balancer; it is all handled with Kubernetes resources within the cluster:

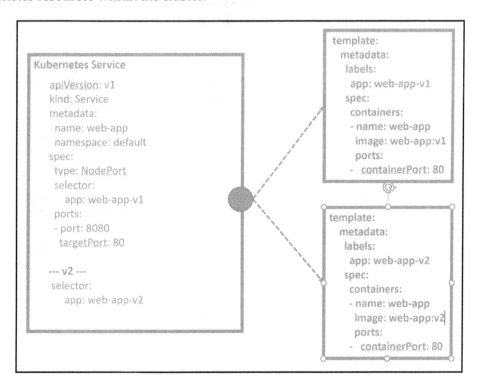

Figure 5: Kubernetes blue/green deployment process

On the left, we see a Kubernetes `NodePort` service, again showing the green configuration for version 1. Version 1 of the service is bound to the green pod on the right using selector matching pods with the `web-app-v1` app. When it's time for the upgrade, we deploy `web-app-v2` the pod(s). Then, we update the selector in the Kubernetes `web-app` service to match version 2 of the web app: `web-app-v2`. We apply the change to the `web-app` service and traffic now flows to web app V2.

We will talk about how this could be accomplished in the *Layer 4 routing in production* section.

Layer 7 routing in production

As mentioned in our Ingress model overview section, the use of layer 7 routing in production, at least right now, feels risky. If you are exploring the use of layer 7 routing in your production environment, we strongly recommend thorough testing through many application deployments, updates, and rollbacks. When using Interlock 2, make sure that you follow the instructions for Interlock 2's production deployment (`https://docs.docker.com/ee/ucp/interlock/deploy/production/`) and verify that all networks are being cleaned up properly after un-deploying unused application stacks from the cluster.

Another appealing feature with layer 7 routing is the ability to terminate SSL certificates using the layer 7 reverse proxy server. This is really cool and could make life really easy. Because of the additional complexity this adds to the automatic reverse-proxy reconfiguration process, make sure you thoroughly test this in your production environment.

Also, if you're interested in layer 7 routing without some of the overlay networking requirements, you can use a host mode deployment of Interlock 2. Keep in mind that when you shift to host mode, you are directly accessing host ports where the Interlock components are deployed. Therefore, if you have firewalling enabled on your cluster nodes (we recommend that you do), you will have to open up a port range for the ephemeral ports used for proper operation. The need to open firewall ports for a range of ephemeral host ports within the cluster may be a showstopper for many security professionals.

I created some step-by-step instructions to update the `ucp-interlock` service to use host mode. Please note you will need the following:

1. Ephemeral ports opened
2. A UCP Admin Settings | Scheduler check in the box to Allow administrators to deploy containers on UCP managers or nodes running Docker Trusted Registry(DTR)

Here are my instructions: `https://github.com/PacktPublishing/Mastering-Docker-Enterprise/tree/master/Production/Ingress/Interlock2-Swarm`.

Layer 4 routing in production

Layer 4 routing is a very common model that is used across production and non-production environments. It provides an excellent balance between control and flexibility. You can control the flow of your traffic into the cluster, while having the flexibility to change the service implementations details, such as where containers are running and how they're connected.

The final implementation of our AtSea application for production has been updated to use a layer 4 model. In *Figure 6*, we see a high-level diagram of the AtSea application's configuration:

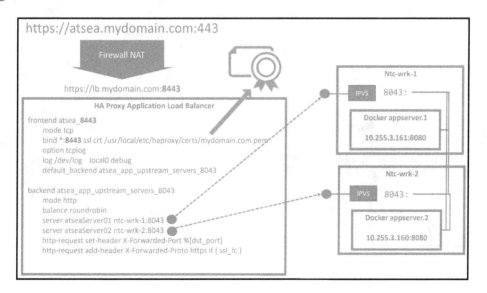

Figure 6: AtSea application configuration

Requests enter the site with the application's public URL, `https://atsea.mydomain.com`, where our wildcard (`*.mydomain.com` DNS a record) brings them to the firewall. The request passes through the firewall using Network Address Translation NAT (`atsea.mydomain.com:443 >> lb.mydomain.com:8443`), where it is picked up by the load balancer. The load balancer's frontend terminates the TLS connection, using the `*.mydomain.com` wildcard certificate.

The `.pem` file used to secure the site is located in `/usr/local/etc/haproxy/certs/nvisia.io.pem` and is composed of the following three sections:

- Server certificate
- Intermediate CA certificate
- Private key

When you access the site, you should see the secure site indicator in your browser, as shown in *Figure 7*:

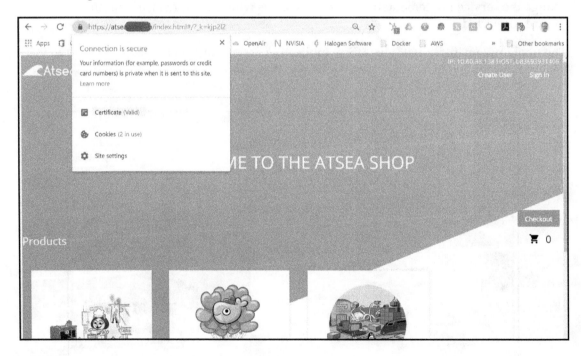

Figure 7: Secure site indicator

This looks good so far, but I have been fooled by this before, where the browser shows a secure icon, but I still get x.509 certificate errors. To be sure, use an SSL checker such as `https://ssltools.digicert.com/checker/views/checkInstallation.jsp` or `https://www.sslshopper.com/` (the output is in *Figure 8*) to verify the certificate is completely correct.

> Validate your third-party certificates, even if the browser lock looks good. Certificate validation is especially important when you install third-party client certificates for DTR and UCP as well, because the Docker CLI is very fussy about how the certificate chains.

When you check your certificate, it should look same as *Figure 8*:

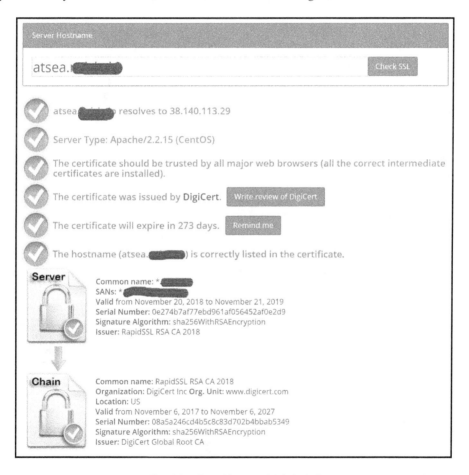

Figure 8: https://www.sslshopper.com/ssl-checker.html

Now, we can direct our attention to the backend of our pool. Since our TLS connection was terminated in the frontend, the rest of our path is unencrypted within our network. This will not be acceptable for many organizations. In cases where it is not, consider terminating TLS inside your containers. Alternatively, you can terminate in the frontend with an external certificate, and re-encrypt it with an internal certificate from the load balancer to the container to find the service. With this sort of scheme, the key for the internal certificate can be used to monitor traffic inside the network, but the internal certificate is of no use outside of the data center.

From the backend, the traffic flows to the appserver service on port 8043. IPVS is listening on port 8043 and load balances the request to 10.255.3.160:8080 and 10.255.3.161:8080 on the ingress network. Let's look at how we configure this with Swarm.

In the following code block, you can see a partial stack file (only the appserver service is shown) to demonstrate how simple this is with Swarm:

```
# atsea-deploy docker-stack-cluster.yml
version: "3.7"

services:
  appserver:
    image: dtr.nvisia.io/prod/atsea-web_build:v1
    environment:
      JAVA_OPTS: -Xms512M -Xmx1G
    ports:
      - 8043:8080
    networks:
      - back-tier-app
    healthcheck:
      test: ["CMD", "curl", "-f", "http://localhost:8080/index.html"]
      interval: 30s
      timeout: 5s
      retries: 3
      start_period: 40s
    deploy:
      resources:
        limits:
          cpus: '1'
          memory: 1.5G
        reservations:
          cpus: '1'
          memory: 1.5G
      replicas: 2
      update_config:
        parallelism: 1
```

```
        failure_action: rollback
      restart_policy:
        condition: on-failure
        delay: 5s
        max_attempts: 3
        window: 120s
    secrets:
      - postgres_password
...

networks:
  back-tier-app:

secrets:
  postgres_password:
    file: ./secrets/test/postgres_password
  staging_token:
    file: ./secrets/test/payment_token
```

All we have to do is specify the port mapping of 8043 as the external port and 8080 as the internal container port. By default, Docker uses this VIP to load balance between instance replicas and publishes port 8034 on the ingress network. These ports can be TCP or UDP, but TCP is the default. As a side note, Docker's default overlay network driver does not support multi-cast, but the Weave Net V2 plugin (https://www.weave.works/docs/net/latest/install/plugin/plugin-v2/) does and it supports Swarm. Also, notice we removed the labels required to engage the Interlock 2 ingress controller.

For our Atsea pilot application in Chapter 6, *Design and Pilot a Docker Enterprise CI Pipeline*, we used labels to indicate our Interlock 2 ingress network name, the internal container port and SSL certificate information for termination at the Interlock 2 reverse proxy server. This was an interesting idea, but we were not comfortable with it for our solution implementation. Now, since we terminated upstream at our application load balancer, we no longer need the certificate information with the appserver service.

Docker service updates

When the time comes to update your application, there are a few common approaches. The first is a simple Docker service update, the second is a blue/green deployment, and the third is a canary deployment.

The simple Docker service update is a relatively straightforward approach to updating your service with the Docker API's service update command. You can do this on a service-by-service basis from the command line or a script, but the best way is to use the Docker stack file to apply the updates.

The updated Docker stack file may include changes to Docker image versions or service deployment parameters. You simply update the stack file and apply them with the `docker stack deploy` command using the current service name, just like when you started the application. When you run the `deploy` command the second time, it compares the desired state in the new stack file with the state of the running stack. From there, it applies updates, based on the updated configuration for each service.

In the previous stack file, look at how the `appserver` service specifies an `update_config` section with two parameters to override the defaults. The first one is parallelism and it defines how many containers will be updated at a time; in our case we want to update one at a time. The default is to update all containers at once which can be disruptive and the reason most people want rolling updates. The next parameter is the failure action, it describes what the orchestrator should do if a service fails during the update. In our case, we set it to roll back to the previous version.

Layer 4 blue/green deployment

When we are ready to deploy a new version of our application to the cluster, we can use layer 4 routing with your load balancer to perform a blue/green deployment. First, stand up your new service on a new port number and then move the load balance to point to the new port. For further clarity, let's walk through an example.

Earlier in section Layer 4 routing in production, we rolled out the first version of our `appserver` on port `8043` using `docker stack deploy -c docker-stack-cluster.yml atseaV1`. Then, we configured our load balancer's backend servers to point to our Swarm nodes using the `appserver 8043` port and the application was running fine, but a bug was discovered. The development team fixed the bug and ran the changes through the pipeline to create a new version of the image in the prod DTR, `dtr.nvisia.io/prod/atsea-web_build:v2`.

The following code block shows how we updated our `docker-stack-cluster.yml` file to reflect the new image name and new port number:

```
# atsea-deploy docker-stack-cluster.yml
version: "3.7"

services:
  appserver:
    image: dtr.nvisia.io/prod/atsea-web_build:v2
    environment:
      JAVA_OPTS: -Xms512M -Xmx1G
    ports:
      - 8044:8080
```

Now, it is time to stand up the new `atseaV2` stack next to the old `atseaV1` stack. We use `$ docker stack deploy -c docker-stack-cluster.yml` **atseaV2** and wait for the service to converge.

Then, to smoke test the new stack, we run `$ curl -v http://cluster-node:8044/index.html` to see the unformatted stream of HTML, as shown in the following code block:

```
<!doctype html><html lang="en"><head><meta charset="utf-8"><meta
name="viewport" content="width=device-width,initial-scale=1"><title>Atsea
Shop</title><link href="/static/css/main.d25422c6.css"
rel="stylesheet"></head><body><style>body{max-width:100vw;overflow-
x:hidden}</style><div id="root"></div><link rel="stylesheet"
href="//fonts.googleapis.com/css?family=Open+Sans"/><script
type="text/javascript"
src="/static/js/main.7dc2a38c.js"></script></body></html>
```

It responded as expected! Now, let's migrate the rest of the traffic to the new version of the service. We head to our load balancer's backend server pool, replace the existing `8043` port entries with the new service port number, `8044`, and reload the load balancer to cut over the new service.

The following code block shows the changes required to redirect traffic to a new application stack on port `8044`:

```
backend atsea_app_upstream_servers
        mode http
        balance roundrobin
        server atseaServer01 ntc-wrk-1:8044
        server atseaServer02 ntc-wrk-2:8044
        server atseaServer03 ntc-wrk-3:8044
        http-request set-header X-Forwarded-Port %[dst_port]
        http-request add-header X-Forwarded-Proto https if { ssl_fc }
```

Check the logs and check your monitoring console to make sure everything looks good. Remember, the old stack is still there if you want to roll back.

Finally, do not forget to clean up the old stack! When you feel good about the new stack and you are sure you will not need to roll back, remove the old stack with `$ docker stack rm atseaV1`.

Layer 4 canary deployment

Okay, perhaps you are a little concerned about a full cut-over from blue to green. Instead, you would like to send just a little traffic to the new application stack to see how it goes. This is called a canary deployment and it's a great way to see how the new stack will respond to traffic. With most load balancers, this is pretty easy to accomplish.

We reconfigure our load balancer to do the following:

- Add the new server, `atseaCanaryServer01`
- Add weighting to the backend pool servers to effectively create a canary deployment

The following code block shows a canary deployment with 10% of the traffic going to the new application stack on port `8044`:

```
backend atsea_app_upstream_servers
        mode http
        balance roundrobin
        server atseaServer01 ntc-wrk-1:8043 weight 15
        server atseaServer02 ntc-wrk-2:8043 weight 15
        server atseaServer03 ntc-wrk-3:8043 weight 15
        server atseaCanaryServer01 ntc-wrk-3:8044 weight 5
        http-request set-header X-Forwarded-Port %[dst_port]
        http-request add-header X-Forwarded-Proto https if { ssl_fc }
```

Production monitoring

In Chapter 7, *Pilot Docker Enterprise Platform Monitoring and Logging*, we introduced logging and monitoring tools to serve several key purposes. First of all, this was to help us better understand what was happening in the cluster with respect to resources such as processor, disk, and networking across the cluster. We wanted to quickly identify and diagnose otherwise difficult-to-find problems. We also wanted to keep a close eye on the health of our pilot application. Finally, understanding resource consumption across our non-production cluster over a reasonable amount of time gives us some confidence in sizing nodes when building out our production cluster.

Now, as we move into production, we need to keep a keen eye on the health of our applications and the cluster, but we also need to pay close attention to security and compliance. To this end, I want to take a quick look at some of the things you should expect in production-level monitoring with policy management. Again, I'll be leaning on the tools from Sysdig, this time their secure product.

I do not want to turn this into a Sysdig tool brochure or infomercial. Rather, we would just like to show a couple of examples regarding container-based policies and compliance.

In the following example, I have enabled one of Sysdig's built-in policies, which detects when someone has executed a Terminal shell process inside of a container. This is often regarded as a serious threat. With this policy in place, we can be alerted whatever anyone executes a Terminal shell in a container and furthermore, we can stop or pause the container where the intrusion is taking place. Even if we allow the container to continue running, we can capture everything that's happening on that node and in that container when the event occurs:

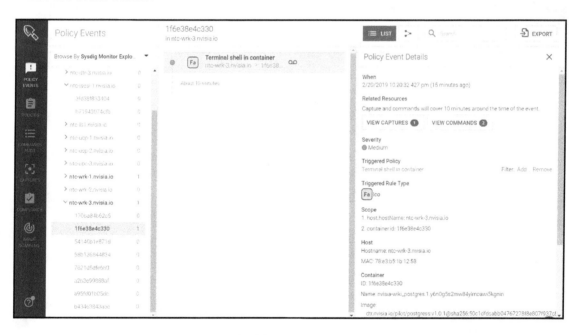

Figure 9: Terminal shell in container

Then, we can take a look at the commands they ran inside of the container. In *Figure 10*, you can see they executed the shell and an `LS` command inside the shell:

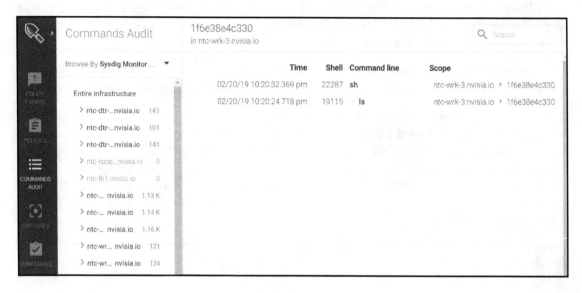

Figure 10: Execution of ls command

We can also show a timeline from the capture that occurred when the event was triggered. We can see a wide variety of activities before and after the event, down measure in milliseconds, as shown in *Figure 11*:

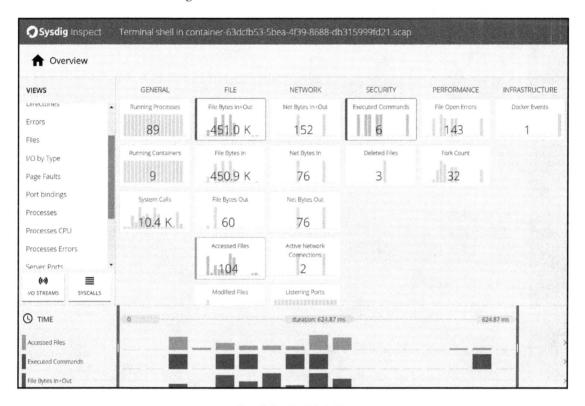

Figure 11: Overview of the timeline

You can adjust the timeline at the bottom of the screen to narrow down the events that occurred within that window. All of the boxes on the screen allow you to drill into the details behind them.

In addition to event tracking and policies, I added a CIS Docker benchmark test as a compliance tool. Not only does it show you whether you passed or failed a test, it shows trends over time. Since you'll never have a perfect score, it is helpful to know how you are trending against your baseline in terms of tests that have been passed or failed:

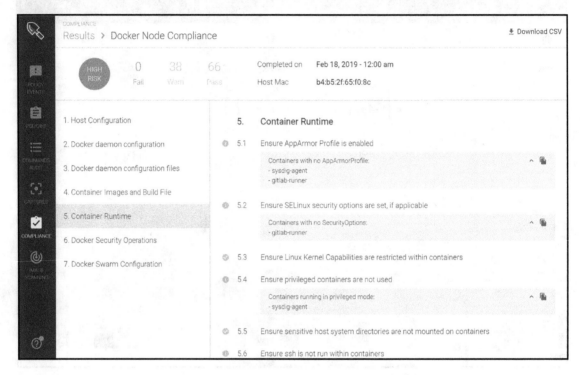

Figure 12: Docker node compliance

Again, this is not to show off or endorse any particular tool. We present this only to raise awareness regarding the capabilities of container-based production monitoring tools.

Summary

In this chapter, we introduced another round of concepts, techniques, and tools for moving you closer to your production Docker Enterprise environment. We attempted to give some practical advice regarding production architecture and deployment models. Again, this is not a comprehensive or complete list by any means, as there are so many variables within each industry, business, and regulatory realm. However, it should be helpful in moving you toward a successful production environment.

In `Chapter 10`, *More on Kubernetes with Docker Enterprise*, we are going to take a closer look at running Kubernetes applications under a Docker Enterprise cluster.

Questions

1. What do you mean by health checks in Docker EE ?
2. Which are the three production ingress models ?
3. How does the blue / green deployment help ?

Further reading

Check out the following resources for more information on the topics covered in this chapter:

- **Health check in Dockerfile**:
  - https://docs.docker.com/engine/reference/builder/#healthcheck
- **Health check in the compose file**:
  - https://docs.docker.com/compose/compose-file/#healthcheck
- **Tini discussion—signals and zombies in Docker containers**:
  - https://github.com/krallin/tini
  - https://github.com/krallin/tini/issues/8
- **Limiting container resources**:
  - https://docs.docker.com/config/containers/resource_constraints/
- **Docker Enterprise at scale article**:
  - https://success.docker.com/article/running-docker-ee-at-scale
- **Kubernetes best practice videos**:
  - https://www.youtube.com/playlist?list=PLIivdWyY5sqL3xfXz5xJvwzFW_tlQB_GB
- **Docker Enterprise ingress article**:
  - https://success.docker.com/article/ucp-service-discovery#theswarmlayer7routing(interlockproxy)

10
More on Kubernetes with Docker Enterprise

So far in this book, we have focused on Swarm for our orchestration. That was intentional, because it is generally much easier to get started with Swarm, and since Docker Enterprise supports both orchestrators, you can use either or both. In this chapter, we turn our attention to using Kubernetes on the Docker Enterprise platform. With its popularity and rich ecosystem, Kubernetes deployments will likely grow and represent a significant portion of your applications. After getting our first application into production with Swarm, it's time to circle back and take a look at running Kubernetes applications on your Docker infrastructure. In this chapter, we will introduce Kubernetes and walk through examples of deploying applications with it.

The following topics will be covered in this chapter:

- Docker Enterprise with Kubernetes features and integrations
- Understanding how to leverage Docker Desktop with Docker Enterprise for an end-to-end Kubernetes experience
- Core third-party Kubernetes tools with Docker Enterprise
- Using Kubernetes persistent volumes and the layer-7 ingress controller

Overview of Docker Enterprise with Kubernetes

Kubernetes is integrated into the Docker Enterprise platform. It is installed by default and is becoming an increasingly important part of Docker Enterprise's own tooling. For instance, Docker Enterprise 2.1 relies on Kubernetes to deploy Prometheus metrics. I strongly suspect Docker's dependence on Kubernetes will continue to increase with their Enterprise platform.

From a strategic point of view, this is very important, especially if you are considering Docker Enterprise, but wondering about Docker's long-term commitment to Kubernetes. The answer is pretty clear: Docker does not just support Kubernetes; it relies on it as a part of its Enterprise solution—that is commitment!

Since we talked about the Docker Enterprise architecture in Chapter 2, *Docker Enterprise – an Architectural Overview*, we will jump right into the Kubernetes highlights. *Figure 1* shows Docker Enterprise's architecture, with the Kubernetes components in green:

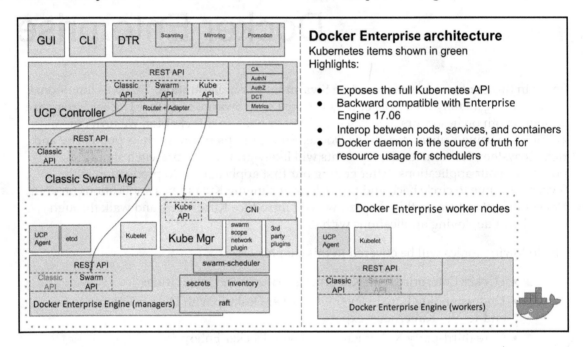

Figure 1: Docker Enterprise 2 Architecture-Copyright © 2019 Docker, Inc. All rights reserved.
https://docs.docker.com/ee/images/docker-ee-architecture.svg

In *Figure 1*, we can see how Kubernetes is actually integrated directly into the orchestration fabric of Docker Enterprise. It is not a bolt-on module. Looking at the items in green, we have the Kubernetes API deployed on the master node that piggybacks its UCP/Swarm managers. So, if we have three UCP managers, we will have three Kubernetes masters. The Kubernetes API is accessed with the same UCP client bundle as the Docker/UCP API. It is seamless. When using a remote client bundle, you can use the `docker` and `kubectl` commands to manage the remote EE cluster's Swarm or Kubernetes resources. However, you do need to have port 6443 rerouted to your manager nodes to make this work.

Next, we will look at the green CNI box.

CNI networking

By default, Docker ships with Kubernetes v1.11.5 and installs Calico v3.5. Furthermore, Docker has chosen to implement Calico's BGP/IP-in-IP networking implementation in an effort to insulate the platform from the underlying network details. In most cases where you have control of the network, this is really helpful. However, when you are at the mercy of a cloud provider's policy (cloud providers make these policies for good reasons, of course), the default CNI plugin configuration might not work at all. For example: Azure does not allow IP-in-IP traffic on their network, and therefore the Docker Enterprise default CNI plugin is not an option. For this reason, Docker gives you a choice of CNI plugins with managed/unmanaged networks. In fact, Docker makes it very easy to swap out CNI plugins.

All CNI plugins must adhere to the following:

- All containers can communicate with all other containers without NAT.
- All nodes can communicate with all containers (and vice-versa) without NAT.
- The IP that a container sees itself as is the same IP that others see it as.

Let's see how we can configure Docker Enterprise's CNI plugins.

Docker Enterprise install – Kubernetes

Docker provides several options related to Kubernetes networking, including which CNI provider to use. In fact, there are several important options to consider when using Kubernetes at scale. The following table contains a list of Kubernetes-related install options:

Option	Description
`--kube-apiserver-port`	Port for the Kubernetes API server (default: `6443`).
`--cni-installer-url`	A URL pointing to a Kubernetes YAML file to be used as an installer for the CNI plugin of the cluster. If specified, the default CNI plugin is not installed. If the URL uses the HTTPS scheme, no certificate verification is performed.
`--pod-cidr`	The Kubernetes cluster IP pool for the pods to allocate IPs from (default: `192.168.0.0/16`).
`--unmanaged-cni`	The default value of `false` indicates that Kubernetes networking is managed by UCP with its default managed CNI plugin, Calico. When set to `true`, UCP does not deploy or manage the life cycle of the default CNI plugin—the CNI plugin is deployed and managed independently of UCP. Note that when `unmanaged-cni=true`, networking in the cluster will not function for Kubernetes, until a CNI plugin is deployed.

The `kube-apiserver-port` and `pod-cidr` must be considered when designing the initial network implementation for your Docker Enterprise install. The CNI-related parameters are more advanced decisions related to your platform (that is, Cloud or on-premises) and you will need to gain experience with your applications at higher scale before making CNI decisions for high-scale production environments. So, for a pilot or early production cluster under lighter workloads, most of these options should work well.

CNI providers offer a Kubernetes YAML file for setup, and the following code block shows a truncated file provided by Weaveworks:

```
apiVersion: v1
kind: List
items:
  - apiVersion: v1
    kind: ServiceAccount
    metadata:
      name: weave-net
      annotations:
        cloud.weave.works/launcher-info: |-
          {
            "original-request": {
              "url": "/k8s/net?k8s-<...>",
              "date": "Sat Feb 23 2019 17:51:08 GMT+0000 (UTC)"
            },
            "email-address": "support@weave.works"
          }
      labels:
        name: weave-net
      namespace: kube-system
<...>
```

This format should look very familiar to Kubernetes users. A link (saved as `CNI_URL`) to this file is actually included in the following UCP install commands.

Now, to actually apply this file to a UCP install, you can use these commands:

```
#Set CNI_URL to Weave's Kubernetes YAML file.
$
CNI_URL="https://cloud.weave.works/k8s/net?k8s-version=Q2xpZW50IFZlcnNpb246
IHZlcnNpb24uSW5mb3tNYWpvcjoiMSIsIE1pbm9yOiI5IiwgR2l0VmVyc2lvbjoidjEuOS4zIiw
gR2l0Q29tbWl0OiJkMjgzNTQxNjU0NGYyOThjOTE5ZTllYWQzYmUzZDA4NjRiNTIzMjNiIiwgR2
l0VHJlZVN0YXRlOiJjbGVhbiIsIEJ1aWxkRGF0ZToiMjAxOC0wMi0wN1QxMjoyMjoyMVoiLCBHb
1ZlcnNpb246ImdvMS45LjIiLCBDb21waWxlcjoiZ2MiLCBQbGF0Zm9ybToibGludXgvYW1kNjQi
fQpTZXJ2ZXIgVmVyc2lvbjogdmVyc2lvbi5JbmZve01ham9yOiIxIiwgTWlub3I6IjgrIiwgR2l
0VmVyc2lvbjoidjEuOC4yLWRvY2tlci4xNDMrYWYwODAwNzk1OWUyY2UiLCBHaXRDb21taXQ6Im
FmMDgwMDc5NTllMmNlYWUxMTZiMDk4ZWNhYTYyYNGI0YjI0MjBkODgiLCBHaXRUcmVlU3RhdGU6I
mNsZWFuIiwgQnVpbGREYXRlOiIyMDE4LTAyLTAxVDIzOjI2OjE3WiIsIEdvVmVyc2lvbjoiZ28x
```

```
LjguMyIsIENvbXBpbGVyOiJnYyIsIFBsYXRmb3JtOiJsaW51eC9hbWQ2NCJ9Cg=="

$ docker container run --rm -it --name ucp \
  -v /var/run/docker.sock:/var/run/docker.sock \
  docker/ucp:3.1.2 install \
  --host-address <node-ip-address> \
  --cni-installer-url ${CNI_URL} \
  --unmanaged-cni <true|false> \
  --interactive
```

It is worth noting that you can reconfigure Calico to not use IP-in-IP and instead only use Calico's policies and rely on the underlying network. Make sure that Kubernetes will function properly without it. For example: make sure you can get routable IP addresses for pods. Just be aware of the underlying network's possible limitations, such as the number of pods per node.

Advanced Kubernetes networking philosophy

When it comes to container-based networking, there are two competing and primary concerns. The first is reachability, where pods/containers can communicate freely across the cluster and things just work! The second, and opposing, concern is policy enforcement, where we need to manage and control the traffic between pods/containers.

Not too long ago, this was not very difficult, because we relied purely on perimeter security. We would lock down the perimeter of our network and let everything flow freely inside. However, in today's world, we have to be just as vigilant about attacks from within our own network. Therefore, both encryption and policy management become very important, especially in the Kubernetes world, where, by design, everything is running in a flat-network space.

 For key insights in this section, I want to thank Christopher Liljenstolpe, evangelist for the Calico project and founder and CTO of Calico's premium product company, Tigera.

There is a lot going on in this space, especially since Kubernetes entered the Enterprise space.

Coexistence – Swarm and Kube

Another interesting observation when looking at the architecture of Docker Enterprise is the coexistence. Both Swarm and Kubernetes are in the same cluster. Many people think of this as an either/or situation, when in reality you can leverage them running side by side in the same cluster.

Swarm and Kubernetes will run quite happily on the same node; however, their respective schedule's resource management has no awareness of the other scheduler's resource commitments. Therefore, you could easily end up with an over-scheduled situation, even if you were using Swarm reservations at Kubernetes' request. Therefore, do not use mixed node, Swarm and Kubernetes for worker nodes in a production environment.

One of the most difficult things is dealing with very different networking philosophies, as Swarm and Kubernetes are so different in this respect. Essentially, every Swarm stack has its own isolated network, and potentially additional networks for additional isolation. From a shift-left perspective, where developers can use software-defined networks to architect their multi-service application's interactions, this is a great thing. However, this requires extremely ephemeral networking, where an IP address's life cycle may be measured in minutes instead of years and may be recycled often on a given day.

In Kubernetes, all resource run on the same network. This is one of the key features of CNI plugins, especially the premium ones, such as Tigera, with a sophisticated multi-layer policy management. This kind of policy as code technology is becoming a standard for modern infrastructure and must be considered when designing a Docker Enterprise Kubernetes network.

Docker Enterprise Kubernetes role-based access control

Back in Chapter 5, *Prepare and Deploy a Docker Enterprise Pilot Application*, we introduced the concept of **Role-Based Access Control (RBAC)** in Docker Enterprise. Our earlier discussion was limited to locking down Swarm-related resources using a construct called **collections**. Let's revisit a similar scenario in *Figure 2*, where we have added a test namespace. *Figure 2* represents how we can apply the exact same subject, role, and resource RBAC model to Kubernetes assets, using namespace instead of collections as the target resource groupings:

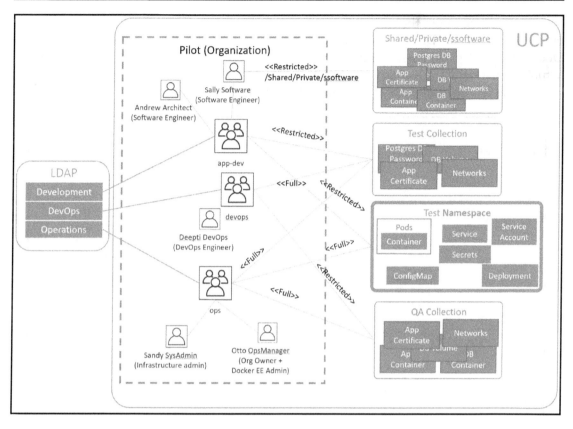

Figure 2: Docker Enterprise RBAC with Kubernetes

As we look at the diagram, on the left, we have an LDAP server integrated with our teams and users. We went into some detail regarding the configuration of UCP with LDAP integration in Chapter 5, *Prepare and Deploy a Docker Enterprise Pilot Application*. I only revisit it here to reinforce the fact that Docker Enterprise ties a centralized security system into Kubernetes RBAC.

To support Kubernetes, the role attributes need to reflect the structure of the Kubernetes environment. In fact, Docker uses native Kubernetes RBAC (`Roles` and `ClusterRoles`) in Docker Enterprise. So, when defining the Kubernetes role for Docker Enterprise, you can actually use a standard Kubernetes YAML format. Once applied to the Docker Enterprise Kubernetes cluster, they appear as shown in *Figure 3*:

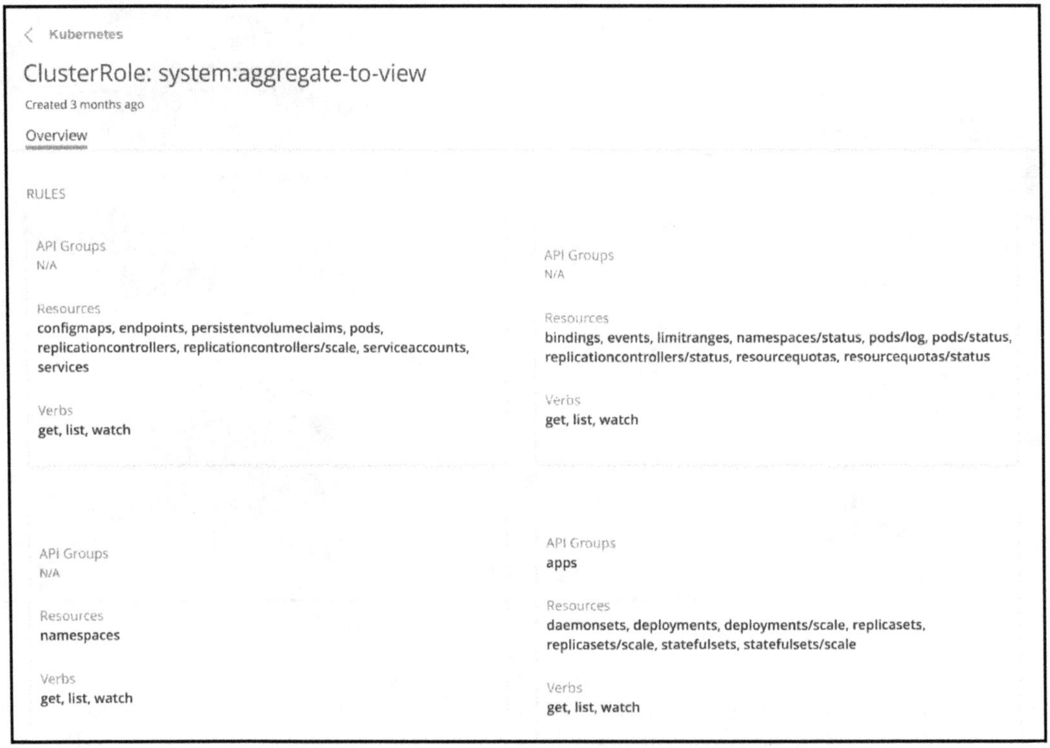

Figure 3: Universal Control Plane ClusterRole

In addition to user access to collection or namespace resources, we can also tie a namespace to a node restriction (through a collection). This means, you can restrict a Kubernetes namespace to only run on specified nodes. This can be useful for staging namespaces where unredacted data might be used for final testing. Node isolation is part of the Docker Enterprise Advanced feature set.

Alternatively, we could introduce additional clusters for isolation, but that takes us back to underutilized resources and a phenomenon we call cluster sprawl. Generally, you are better served by thinking through your security model and using it to manage a smaller number of large clusters.

Kubernetes persistent volume management

In our experience, persistent volume management in the Docker Enterprise world is pretty much native Kubernetes. Generally, you would like to have some sort of persistent volume auto-provisioning service to handle the management of common storage resources across the cluster, such as NFS.

 Plese read the Kubernetes docs for a better understanding of the Kubernetes persistent volume life cycle: `https://kubernetes.io/docs/concepts/storage/persistent-volumes/`.

There are of course some very simple methods, such as using an NFS type volume directly from a pod/container, where, when a pod is deployed, the pod's container essentially performs a Docker host volume mount with a local, node-based NFS driver. While the end result is the same (multiple pods sharing the same filesystem mount point regardless of where they're deployed), it can be difficult to control (bypassing RBAC-controlled resources, for example) and centrally manage usage. Later in section *Kubernetes persistent volumes with an existing NFS server* we will walk through an example of an existing NFS server to auto-provision Kubernetes persistent volumes based on persistent volume claims.

Docker Desktop to Docker Enterprise Kubernetes

In `Chapter 6`, *Design and Pilot a Docker Enterprise CI Pipeline*, we spent time building our AtSea custom Java application. It only seems appropriate now to use the same images and redeploy them as a Kubernetes application. Additionally, we will demonstrate how to build and test a Kubernetes application on a developer desktop (without Minikube!), and apply it to our Kubernetes cluster running on Docker Enterprise.

In this section, we are going to convert our AtSea Swarm application into a Kubernetes application and deploy it to our pilot cluster, alongside the Swarm version of the application that is still running. Furthermore, we will actually perform a blue/green deployment, where we perform a live migration from the Swarm application to the Kubernetes application.

Docker Desktop – Converting AtSea to Kubernetes

Earlier in the book, we used Docker Desktop to build and test images on the local development machine using Swarm to simulate the stack running the same way it would be in production. So, we are going to do the exact same thing, but this time with Kubernetes. Also, there's no need to rebuild our images, as we already have those.

Our approach here, much like the first time when we built the application, is from the bottom to the top. *Figure 4* shows how we set up our local development:

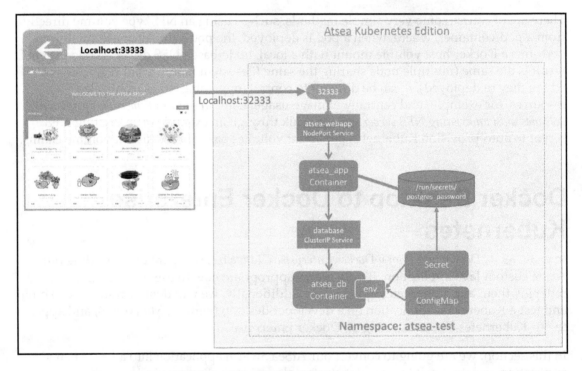

Figure 4: Atsea application in Kubernetes

We will start with the database container, create a pod deployment, and inject both `ConfigMap` and `Secret` properties into the database container's environment variables. This is exactly where the database container expects to find them, as it is identical to the Swarm application's use of environment variables. Then, we will create a database `ClusterIP` service (only visible within the cluster) as a durable endpoint to connect to the database.

Please note that the `ClusterIP` service has the same database as the Swarm application's database service. This allows the web app to reference the same DNS name for the database. Hence, we will make no code changes to any of our images.

Next, we create a deployment for the `atsea_app` container and inject the `postgres-password` from our Kubernetes secret into a local volume mount, where again the application is expecting to find the secret—in the same location where the Swarm application injected the secret. Then, we add the `NodePort` service to the front of our AtSea `web_app` pods. The `NodePort` service use IPVS to publish a port on all non-master nodes in the cluster. This way, the AtSea application load balancer can direct traffic to any non-manager node in the cluster on port `3233`, and the AtSea web app `NodePort` service will forward the request to the web app pod(s).

You can find the code examples for the section in the GitHub repository: `https://github.com/PacktPublishing/Mastering-Docker-Enterprise/tree/master/chapter10/atsea-kube`.

Setting up Docker Desktop with Kubernetes

Let's start by making sure that your Docker Desktop environment is correctly configured to run Kubernetes on your workstation or laptop. If you have Docker Desktop installed, there is no longer any need (that I know of) to use Minikube. To do that, right-click on the well in your system tray and select **Settings**, as shown in *Figure 5*:

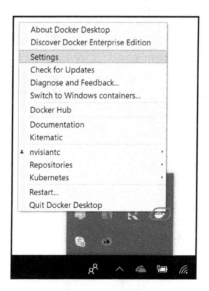

Figure 5: Docker Desktop Context menu

Then click on the **Kubernetes** tab on the left side of the dialogue, as shown in *Figure 6*. Make sure the **Enable Kubernetes** box is checked; after checking it, wait for Kubernetes to start and the dot at the bottom left of the dialogue to turn green:

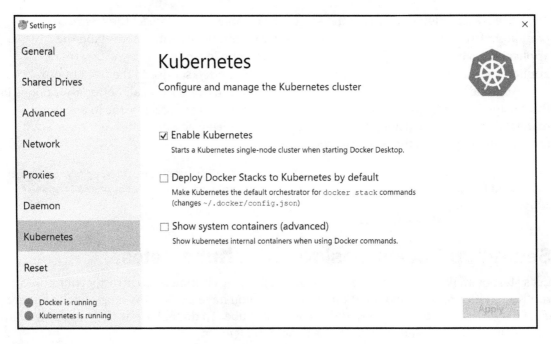

Figure 6: Enable Kubernetes

Once Kubernetes is running, close the dialog, open a PowerShell or Bash shell, and run the following $ kubectl get nodes command. It looks pretty much the same for either Bash or PowerShell, as you can see, but, in either case, you should see docker-for-desktop Ready master 40d v1.10.11:

```
# Windows Powershell
PS > kubectl get nodes
NAME STATUS ROLES AGE VERSION
docker-for-desktop Ready master 40d v1.10.11

# Bash Shell
@xps-bash$ kubectl get nodes
NAME STATUS ROLES AGE VERSION
docker-for-desktop Ready master 40d v1.10.11
```

As a side note, Kubernetes in the Desktop version is a little bit old. Surprisingly, it's older than the EE Kubernetes version of 1.11.5. I point this out because you could run into a situation where things behave differently on your Desktop than they do on the cluster. This is also true for versions of Docker.

You are all set!

Configuring an application with Kubernetes (Namespace/Secrets/ConfigMaps)

Let's get started by creating a namespace for our application. We are going to put all of our Kubernetes resources into the atsea-test namespace. This makes it very easy to isolate and clean up our local machine when we have finished. We can see the YAML file we will use to create the namespace:

```
apiVersion: v1
kind: Namespace
metadata:
  name: atsea-test
```

Then we use the Kubernetes command-line tool, $ kubectl, to declaratively apply resources in our create-app-namespace.yaml file to the cluster. The result is a new namespace on our local Kubernetes desktop cluster:

```
$ kubectl apply -f create-app-namespace.yaml
namespace/atsea-test created
```

Now we can walk through the ConfigMap file. ConfigMaps are used to store configuration information separately from other deployment artifacts. This allows you to swap out files based on your target—different configs between the dev, test, and qa environments. In the following data section, we store the data key-value pairs we are going to use when deploying our application. The metadata section stores the config's name and also the namespace where ConfigMap will be stored. In the Swarm version of our application, we stored these literal values in our stack file:

```
apiVersion: v1
kind: ConfigMap
data:
  db: atsea
  user: gordonuser
metadata:
  name: dbconfig
  namespace: atsea-test
```

Now we need to apply our `configmap` to the cluster and we can use $ `kubectl get configmap` to verify the cluster state:

```
$ kubectl apply -f configmap.yaml
configmap/dbconfig created

# Verify the configmap..
$ kubectl get configmap dbconfig -o yaml
apiVersion: v1
data:
  db: atsea
  user: gordonuser
kind: ConfigMap
metadata:
  creationTimestamp: "2019-02-22T17:32:14Z"
  name: dbconfig
  namespace: default
```

`ConfigMap` provides a very nice separation of the deployment values from the configuration. For the record, Swarm also has configs that could be used in a similar, but less sophisticated, way. Therefore, this is not a feature difference, but instead a small design upgrade made during the conversion to Kubernetes. The same is true for the following `Secret` YAML:

```
apiVersion: v1
kind: Secret
metadata:
  name: atsea-postgres-password
  namespace: atsea-test
type: Opaque
stringData:
  postgres_password: "gordonpass"
```

Here, we can see where `postgres_password` is saved as a `Secret`.

> Be very careful when using Kubernetes' secrets, as they are not encrypted, and only `base64` encoded! Consider using a third-party product, such as **hashicorp vault**, to secure your passwords, certificates, and other secrets. From the following code block, you can see how easily it can be retrieved and then decoded.

Finally, we apply our secret to the cluster and then review it. By default, Kubernetes' secrets are not encrypted, just `base64` encoded. This is why many Kubernetes users use a vault of some sort in place of, or in conjunction with, Kubernetes' secrets:

```
$ kubectl apply -f secret.yaml
secret/atsea-postgres-password created

# Verify password
$ kubectl get secret atsea-postgres-password -o yaml
apiVersion: v1
data:
  password: Z29yZG9ucGFzcw==
kind: Secret
metadata:
  name: atsea-postgres-password
  namespace: default

# Look at password - scary! It is just base64 encoded!
$ echo 'Z29yZG9ucGFzcw==' | base64 --decode
gordonpass
```

Now let's move to database deployment to see how we use the `ConfigMap` and `secret`.

Converting and testing the DB

Let's start by looking at the first section of our database pod deployment file:

```
apiVersion: apps/v1
kind: Deployment
metadata:
  name: atsea-database
  namespace: atsea-test
spec:
  selector:
    matchLabels:
      run: atsea-database
  replicas: 1
  template:
    metadata:
      labels:
        run: atsea-database
```

The first section of the file is the deployment section. It lets us describe how we want our pod set rolled out and how many we want to stay running (replica set). In our case, we have replicas set to `1`, because this a database and it is stateful.

In the following code block, we will take a look at the container specification to see how the `ConfigMap` and `secret` are used:

```
spec:
  containers:
  - name: database
    image: dtr.mydomain.com/test/atsea-db_build:kV1
    ports:
      - containerPort: 5432
    env:
      - name: POSTGRES_USER
        valueFrom:
          configMapKeyRef:
            name: dbconfig
            key: user
      - name: POSTGRES_DB
        valueFrom:
          configMapKeyRef:
            name: dbconfig
            key: db
      - name: POSTGRES_PASSWORD
        valueFrom:
          secretKeyRef:
            name: atsea-postgres-password
            key: postgres_password
```

Finally, in the last section of the database pod deployment file, we added resource management to our database server container:

```
resources:
  limits:
    cpu: "1"
    memory: 1Gi
  requests:
    cpu: "1"
    memory: 1Gi
imagePullSecrets:
- name: regcred
```

We have limited the database to one CPU and 1 gig of RAM. Notice that we set the request to the same level. As discussed in `Chapter 9`, *Important Docker Enterprise Production Topics*, this is definitely a best practice for both Swarm and Kubernetes scheduling.

Finally, at the bottom of the file, notice the `imagePullSecrets` section; there's one item called `regcred`. You may need to use this if you have an `imagepullbackoff` error while deploying your pods. All the great examples you are pulling public images that require no Authentication. However, our Kubernetes cluster and our local desktop Kubernetes need to pull private images from our private DTR.

So, to make this work, we need to create a `secret` called `regcred`:

```
$ kubectl create secret -n atsea-test docker-registry regcred --docker-server=dtr.mydomain.com --docker-username=admin --docker-password=xxxxxxxxx --docker-email=sysadmin@mydomain.com
```

Now we can deploy our database `pod`:

```
$ kubectl apply -f db-pod.yaml
deployment.apps/atsea-database created

# Check Pod
$ kubectl get pods
NAME                              READY  STATUS  RESTARTS  AGE
atsea-database-6bf74cbc4b-7n5d7  1/1    Running  0        25s
```

We can see that the database pod is running.

Creating the DB ClusterIP

Now we will put the `ClusterIP` service in front of our database. While we could have the application connect directly to the pod, that does not protect us from the pods being replaced by the orchestrator. Instead, we use a `ClusterIP` service in a durable endpoint for our application to make database requests. This way, if the pod goes away and is replaced, the web apps, endpoint remains the same.

Also note the `ClusterIP` service is only reachable from within the cluster. Since we are not exposing the database outside of the cluster, this is a good choice for security reasons.

The following code block shows the deployment file for the database cluster IP service:

```
apiVersion: v1
kind: Service
metadata:
  name: database
  namespace: atsea-test
  labels:
    run: atsea-database
spec:
```

```
    type: ClusterIP
    ports:
    - port: 5432
      targetPort: 5432
      protocol: TCP
      name: http
    selector:
      run: atsea-database
```

First, we see the name of the service, which is important for DNS purposes. This is the DNS name the web application will use to access the database. The ports section shows what port the service is accessed on and what port maps to the inside of the database container. Finally, the selector is what is used to bind this service to the database pod. If you look back `metadata: > labels:` section of the database pod deployment file, you will see a label run: `atsea-database`.

Now we have to apply our database service to the cluster:

```
$ kubectl apply -f db-service.yaml
service/database created

$ kubectl describe svc/database
Name: database
Namespace: default
Labels: run=atsea-database
<...>
Type: ClusterIP
IP: 10.109.222.29
Port: http 5432/TCP
TargetPort: 5432/TCP
Endpoints: 10.1.0.28:5432
<...>
```

First, we apply the changes our changes made to the cluster, adding the database service. After the deployment of the database service, it is a good idea to make sure the service is bound to our database pod. Seeing the endpoints with an IP address and port number is a really good sign. Otherwise, the `Endpoints` would empty, indicating it was unable to use a selector to bind to the pod(s).

Converting the web app

Next, we will get started on converting the web application. In the following code block, we have the first section of the web application deployment file:

```yaml
apiVersion: apps/v1
kind: Deployment
metadata:
  name: atsea-web
  namespace: atsea-test
spec:
  selector:
    matchLabels:
      run: atsea-web
  replicas: 1
  template:
    metadata:
      labels:
        run: atsea-web
```

The previous snippet describes the deployment and replica set specifications. Other than some name changes, it's very similar to *Converting and testing the DB* section. In the following code block, we see the container specification for the AtSea web application:

```yaml
spec:
  containers:
  - name: atsea-web
    image: dtr.mydomain.com/test/atsea-web_build:kV1
    ports:
      - containerPort: 8080
    volumeMounts:
      - name: secret
        mountPath: "/run/secrets"
        subPath: postgres_password
        readOnly: true
    resources:
      limits:
        cpu: "1"
        memory: 1.5Gi
      requests:
        cpu: "1"
        memory: 1.5Gi
    env:
      name: JAVA_OPTS
      value: -Xms512M -Xmx1G
  volumes:
  - name: secret
    secret:
```

```
            defaultMode: 0666
            secretName: atsea-postgres-password
      imagePullSecrets:
        - name: regcred
```

The web application handles `secret` a little differently. You might recognize the `/run/secrets` directory from our Swarm implementation. That is the default directory where Docker Swarm places secrets. To emulate that behavior with Kubernetes, we mounted the path into the container at the same location. Then, in the last section, we create the volume and inject the `secret` into the volume.

Again, we created a resources section to specify limits and requests. In this case, we are throttling the container at one CPU and putting a limit of 1.5 gigs of memory. Remember, if the container attempts to surpass the memory limit, the Docker Engine will be able to kill the container with an out-of-memory exception. The request is telling Kubernetes the amount of resources the container will consume on the node where the container is deployed, helping the Kubernetes orchestrator keep track of the available remaining resources on each node.

One last reminder about Java applications running in containers: Before version 10 of Java, you need to define the maximum amount of memory (Xmx) as a parameter or environment variable to the JVM. Without this, the Java container will attempt to take the majority of available resources on the entire node, not respecting any limits set for the container. In this situation, you are likely to encounter an out-of-memory exception if a limit is used without the JVM parameter. In our example, we use both the limit and the JVM Xmx parameter.

Creating the webapp NodePort

Now we need to expose the web application with a service outside the cluster, allowing our application load balancer to reach the web application. To accomplish this, we use a different kind of service, a `NodePort` service. The following code block shows the specs for our web application's `NodePort` service:

```
apiVersion: v1
kind: Service
metadata:
  name: atsea-webapp
  namespace: atsea-test
  labels:
    run: atsea-web
spec:
  type: NodePort
  ports:
    - port: 8080
```

```
        nodePort: 32666
  selector:
    run: atsea-web
```

Again, we see a set of ports specified. Port 8080 inside the cluster, and port 32666 is the access port from outside the cluster. As a result, we can send a request from our desktop browser to port 32666, using the localhost and a web application when we receive the request.

Later, when we deploy to the Kubernetes cluster running on Docker Enterprise, there will be two differences. The first difference is the port number for nodePort, as the default ephemeral port range for Kubernetes on Docker Enterprise is 32768 to 35535. We will use port 33333 when deploying to the cluster. The second difference is rather than pointing a browser at the NodePort service, we will instead send traffic our application load balancer.

Finally, we need to start a webapp pod and the NodePort service, using the commands in the following code block. Again, we want to make sure that the services are started properly. We see both services and their port address:

```
$ kubectl apply -f webapp-pod.yaml
deployment.apps/atsea-web created

$ kubectl apply -f webapp-service.yaml
service/atsea-webapp created

$ kubectl get svc
NAME           TYPE       CLUSTER-IP      EXTERNAL-IP   PORT(S) AGE
atsea-webapp NodePort   10.104.35.106 <none>        8080:32666/TCP 29s
database       ClusterIP 10.109.43.119 <none>        5432/TCP 1m
```

Our application is now running on Kubernetes!

Testing locally

To verify that the application is working, we are now ready the use our browser to connect to `http://localhost:32666`, add items to the register, and check out:

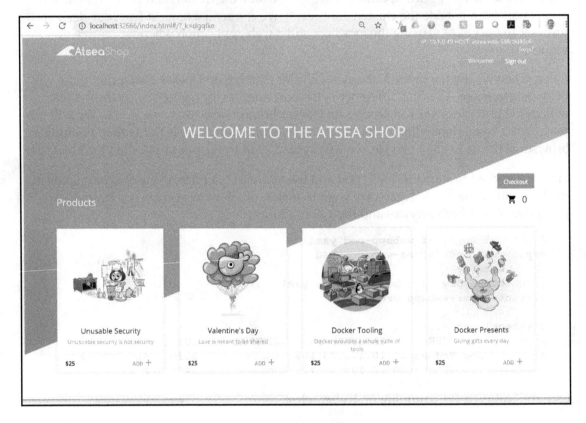

Figure 7: Atsea Kubernetes local test success

Docker Enterprise for a pilot release of AtSea Kubernetes

Now that we have prepared the Kubernetes version of our AtSea application, we can prepare to deploy it to our Docker Enterprise Kubernetes cluster. Additionally, we want to demonstrate the ability to isolate our `atsea-test` namespace with Docker RBAC and Kubernetes.

First, we will create our `atsea-test` namespace. Then, we will create a non-administrative user, `mpanthofer`, and using a Docker RBAC grant, we will allow `mpanthofer` to have administrative rights only within the `atsea-test` namespace. Now we are all set to deploy our application using the `mpanthofer` user account and client bundle.

Setting up Docker RBAC for the atsea-test namespace

After logging into the universal control plane as the administrator, navigate to the namespaces menu. From there, click on the **Create** button in the upper-right corner, as shown in *Figure 8*:

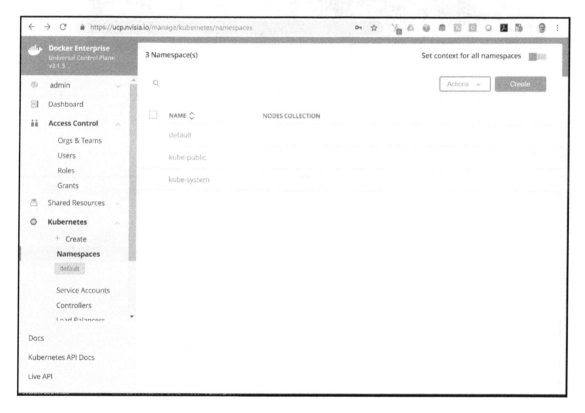

Figure 8: UCP Kubernetes namespaces

In *Figure 9*, we see the Kubernetes object-creation dialogue in the UCP web interface. Here, we can paste the code we used to create the `atsea-test` namespace on our desktop. Then we click on **Create**:

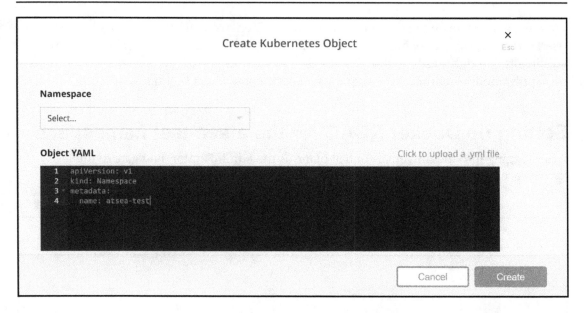

Figure 9: UCP Add Kubernetes namespace

We can see the `atsea-test` namespace has been created in *Figure 10:*

Figure 10: New atsea-test Kubernetes namespace

Figure 11 shows how we create the non-admin user account for `mpanthofer` from the **Access Control** ǀ **Users** ǀ **Create dialog**:

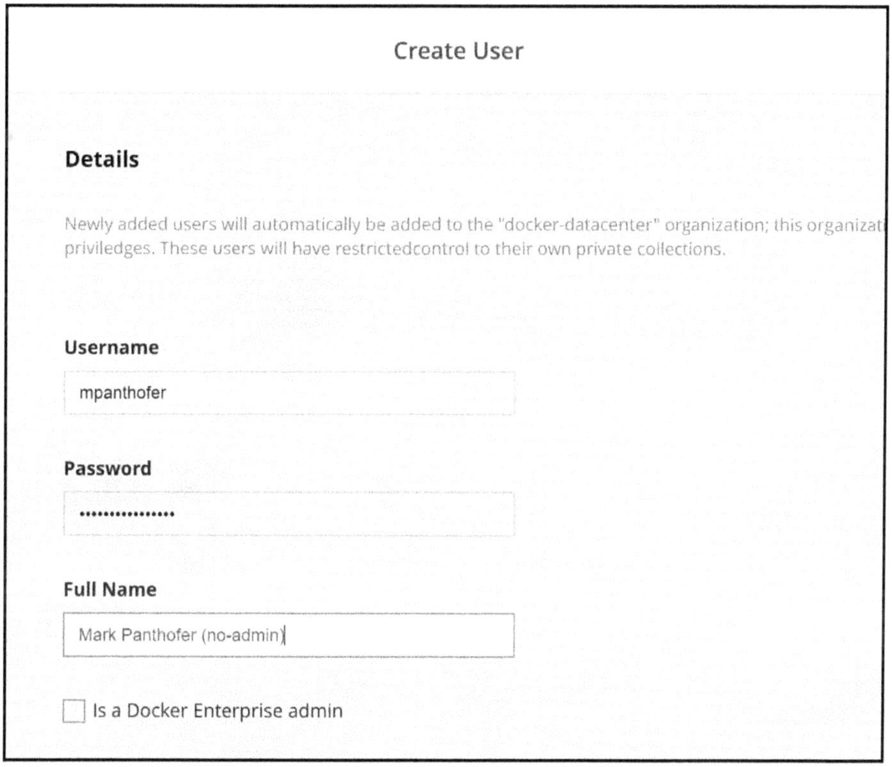

Figure 11: Create non-admin UCP user

Finally, we add assign this user admin access to just the `atsea-test` namespace, as shown in *Figure 12*:

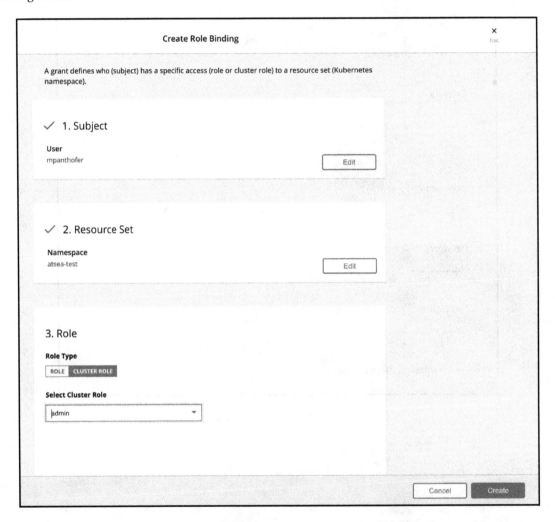

Figure 12: Bind mpanthofer as admin to atsea-test

We now create a client bundle for the `mpanthofer` (no-admin) account from UCP, and download it to a local machine. We unzip the files and `$ source env.sh` to connect to the cluster. Then, we run a quick test. First, we try to list the resources from the default namespace, where we did not grant any access rights. We are denied with a long list of forbidden warnings. Now let's try the same thing against our empty at sea namespace. As you can see in *Figure 13*, it behaves as expected:

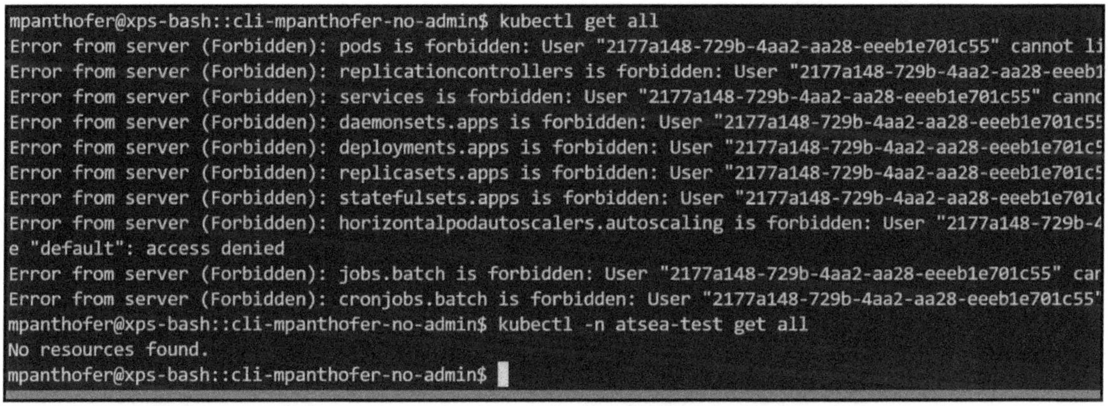

```
mpanthofer@xps-bash::cli-mpanthofer-no-admin$ kubectl get all
Error from server (Forbidden): pods is forbidden: User "2177a148-729b-4aa2-aa28-eeeb1e701c55" cannot li
Error from server (Forbidden): replicationcontrollers is forbidden: User "2177a148-729b-4aa2-aa28-eeeb1
Error from server (Forbidden): services is forbidden: User "2177a148-729b-4aa2-aa28-eeeb1e701c55" canno
Error from server (Forbidden): daemonsets.apps is forbidden: User "2177a148-729b-4aa2-aa28-eeeb1e701c55
Error from server (Forbidden): deployments.apps is forbidden: User "2177a148-729b-4aa2-aa28-eeeb1e701c5
Error from server (Forbidden): replicasets.apps is forbidden: User "2177a148-729b-4aa2-aa28-eeeb1e701c5
Error from server (Forbidden): statefulsets.apps is forbidden: User "2177a148-729b-4aa2-aa28-eeeb1e701c
Error from server (Forbidden): horizontalpodautoscalers.autoscaling is forbidden: User "2177a148-729b-4
e "default": access denied
Error from server (Forbidden): jobs.batch is forbidden: User "2177a148-729b-4aa2-aa28-eeeb1e701c55" car
Error from server (Forbidden): cronjobs.batch is forbidden: User "2177a148-729b-4aa2-aa28-eeeb1e701c55"
mpanthofer@xps-bash::cli-mpanthofer-no-admin$ kubectl -n atsea-test get all
No resources found.
mpanthofer@xps-bash::cli-mpanthofer-no-admin$
```

Figure 13: Test permissions of mpanthofer

Now let's deploy our application with the `mpanthofer no-admin` account.

Blue/green deployment of AtSea to the Docker Enterprise Kubernetes cluster

First, we are going to have to add a `regcred` secret to our new namespace so the Kubernetes orchestrator can access our private registry:

```
$ kubectl create secret -n atsea-test docker-registry regcred --docker-
server=dtr.mydomain.com --docker-username=admin --docker-password=xxxxxxxxx
--docker-email=someuser@mydomain.com
secret/regcred created
```

Now we will run through the rest of our deployment commands, using the command-line bundle to target our Docker Enterprise cluster, using our `mpanthofer` account:

```
$ kubectl apply -f configmap.yaml
configmap/dbconfig created

$ kubectl apply -f secret.yaml
secret/atsea-postgres-password created

$ kubectl apply -f db-pod.yaml
deployment.apps/atsea-database created

$ kubectl apply -f db-service.yaml
service/database created

$ kubectl apply -f webapp-pod.yaml
```

```
deployment.apps/atsea-web created

$ kubectl apply -f webapp-service.yaml
service/atsea-webapp created
```

Now we need to check our deployment:

```
$ kubectl -n atsea-test get all
NAME READY STATUS RESTARTS AGE
pod/atsea-database-66848b4897-2jn5s 1/1 Running 0 3m
pod/atsea-web-59774bc8c9-6trcl 1/1 Running 0 3m

NAME TYPE CLUSTER-IP EXTERNAL-IP PORT(S) AGE
service/atsea-webapp NodePort 10.96.203.92 <none> 8080:33333/TCP 2m
service/database ClusterIP 10.96.71.70 <none> 5432/TCP 3m

NAME DESIRED                          CURRENT UP-TO-DATE AVAILABLE AGE
deployment.apps/atsea-database        1 1 1 1 3m
deployment.apps/atsea-web             1 1 1 1 3m

NAME                                         DESIRED CURRENT READY AGE
replicaset.apps/atsea-database-66848b4897 1 1 1 3m
replicaset.apps/atsea-web-59774bc8c9         1 1 1 3m
```

It appears that everything is up and running correctly.

Smoke-testing the AtSea Kubernetes application

I will log into the load-balancer node and run a quick cURL test against one of the worker nodes using port 33333. If it checks out, I'll head over to the load balancer and start directing traffic to the new implementation:

```
$ curl -v http://10.10.1.39:33333/index.html
* About to connect() to 10.10.1.39 port 33333 (#0)
* Trying 10.10.1.39...
* Connected to 10.10.1.39 (10.10.1.39) port 33333 (#0)
> GET /index.html HTTP/1.1
> User-Agent: curl/7.29.0
> Host: 10.10.1.39:33333
> Accept: */*
>
< HTTP/1.1 200
< X-Content-Type-Options: nosniff
< X-XSS-Protection: 1; mode=block
< Cache-Control: no-cache, no-store, max-age=0, must-revalidate
< Pragma: no-cache
< Expires: 0
```

```
< X-Frame-Options: DENY
< Last-Modified: Tue, 05 Feb 2019 00:07:40 GMT
< Accept-Ranges: bytes
< Content-Type: text/html
< Content-Length: 462
< Date: Sun, 24 Feb 2019 07:16:45 GMT
<
* Connection #0 to host 10.10.1.39 left intact
<!doctype html><html lang="en"><head><meta charset="utf-8"><meta
name="viewport" content="width=device-width,initial-scale=1"><title>Atsea
Shop</title><link href="/static/css/main.d25422c6.css"
rel="stylesheet"></head><body><style>body{max-width:100vw;overflow-
x:hidden}</style><div id="root"></div><link rel="stylesheet"
href="//fonts.googleapis.com/css?family=Open+Sans"/><script
type="text/javascript"
src="/static/js/main.04755338.js"></script></body></html>
```

The `curl` command succeeded as we hoped. You can tell by the HTML at the bottom of the code block.

Configuring the load balancer for blue/green deployment

Let's reconfigure the backend of our load balancer to start sharing the load between the new implementation and our old Swarm implementation, which is still running in our cluster.

Here's what the load balancer's backend profile looks like now:

```
backend atsea_app_upstream_servers_8043
        mode http
        balance roundrobin
        server atseaServer01 ntc-wrk-1:33333
        server atseaServer02 ntc-wrk-2:8043
        server atseaServer03 ntc-wrk-3:8043
        http-request set-header X-Forwarded-Port %[dst_port]
        http-request add-header X-Forwarded-Proto https if { ssl_fc }
```

Before we restart the load balancer, we take a screenshot of our AtSea Swarm application's page, zooming in on the upper-right corner to show where it lists the IP address, from Swarm's address pool:

Figure 14: Zoomed view of Atsea on Swarm

Now we restart the load balancer, refresh the page a couple of times, and get the AtSea Kubernetes application's page:

Figure 15: Zoomed view of AtSea on Kubernetes

Both applications are running, and the new application appears to be running well. Now we will direct all traffic to the Atsea Kubernetes application and remove Atsea Swarm. Our Kubernetes conversion project is complete and deployed!

Third-party Docker Enterprise Kubernetes integrations

The Kubernetes ecosystem has exploded with all kinds of extensions and integrations, and it seems as if we are just getting started. However, one thing you might run into are some slight issues with the installation process of third-party Kubernetes-based tools that run on Docker Enterprise. These issues are usually minor and have to do with how Docker decided to install and configure its version of Kubernetes.

Helm charts on Docker Enterprise Kubernetes

One really popular tool in the Kubernetes community for softer distribution is **Helm charts**. Often called the **Kubernetes package manager**, Helm makes application installation and maintenance with a Kubernetes cluster pretty simple. There are Helm charts for just about every popular software package. You can find more here: https://hub.helm.sh/. While I am fairly new to Helm charts, I wanted to share some tweaks to get you started, using Help with Docker Enterprise.

Let's walk through setting up Helm with Docker Enterprise. It turns out there are just a couple of pieces missing from the Docker deployment of Kubernetes that are normally part of the Kubernetes standard distribution. First, we are missing a `rolebinding` and `clusterrolebonding` which need to be added before installing Helm:

```
$ kubectl create rolebinding default-view --clusterrole=view --
serviceaccount=kube-system:default --namespace=kube-system

$ kubectl create clusterrolebinding add-on-cluster-admin --
clusterrole=cluster-admin --serviceaccount=kube-system:default
```

Then, we need to create a `ServiceAccount` for `tiller` (Helm's remote agent that lives inside your cluster). Finally, we need to bind the `tiller` service account to the `cluster-admin` role, as shown in the following code block (you can find the code at https://github.com/PacktPublishing/Mastering-Docker-Enterprise/tree/master/chapter10/Helm-DockerEE):

```
apiVersion: v1
kind: ServiceAccount
metadata:
  name: tiller
  namespace: kube-system
---
apiVersion: rbac.authorization.k8s.io/v1
kind: ClusterRoleBinding
metadata:
  name: tiller
roleRef:
  apiGroup: rbac.authorization.k8s.io
  kind: ClusterRole
  name: cluster-admin
subjects:
  - kind: ServiceAccount
    name: tiller
    namespace: kube-system
```

Apply the `tiller` service account and `clusterrolebinding` with the `$ kubectl create -f rbac-config.yaml` command.

Now we need to grab the install script, set the permission on the script, and run it. When you have finished, initialize Helm and do not forget the service account option:

```
$ curl https://raw.githubusercontent.com/helm/helm/master/scripts/get > get_helm.sh

$ chmod 700 get_helm.sh

$ ./get_helm.sh

$ helm init --service-account tiller
```

Helm should be ready to go! If you're following along, make sure you leave Helm running, as we will use it to install our NFS Client persistent volume provisioner and our NGINX ingress controller.

GitLab and Docker Enterprise Kubernetes

We love GitLab! However, there are a couple of issues that led me away from using its Kubernetes integration to our Kubernetes cluster. The GitLab integration appears to be set up primarily to work with GCP out of the box, but we were able to integrate using our UCP Client bundle certificate access to our on-premises Docker Enterprise Kubernetes cluster.

I could not get the GitLabs Kubernetes application integration to install on our cluster (not that I would want to use that, since we already installed helm/tiller in *Helm charts on Docker Enterprise Kubernetes* section). When I looked at installing the Kubernetes version of the `gitlab-runner`, using Helm, out of security and stability concerns, I aborted the plan. From what I read in the GitLab docs, the current implementation requires privileged mode for running Docker in Docker. We are not comfortable running Docker in Docker using privileged mode because of security issues and potential filesystem corruption.

Currently, we are very happy with our stand-alone GitLab-runner box, using Docker on Docker to mount the Docker socket and avoiding privileged mode issues.

Kubernetes persistent volumes with an existing NFS server

Earlier in the chapter, we discussed persistent volumes with Kubernetes. We presented a simple, alternative approach of using an NFS volume mount within each pod. Therefore, the solution presented in this section uses a more sophisticated volume auto-provisioner for a centralized, managed approach.

The first challenge here was trying to find something that was built to work with an existing NFS server. Many of the solutions out there, particularly the cloud-based ones, are designed to integrate with Cloud filesystems and present Kubernetes persistent volume as requested. That's cool, but we wanted a solution to work with an existing NFS server. It turns out this is called an NFS client.

 You can find the files I used for my setup here: `https://github.com/ PacktPublishing/Mastering-Docker-Enterprise/tree/master/ chapter10/NFS`.

Attaching your UCP Kube cluster to an existing on-premises NFS server

We use use our new installation of Helm to help us install our NFS provisioner for Kubernetes. The provisioner dynamically creates persistent volumes when a persistent volume claim is made.

Our setup is based on the following and requires an existing NFS server to work: `https:// github.com/helm/charts/tree/master/stable/nfs-client-provisioner`.

If you do not have an NFS server and want to auto-provision cloud resources from your Kubernetes cluster, there is another chart for that. We do not cover it in the book, but you might want to check it out: `https://github.com/helm/charts/tree/master/stable/nfs-server-provisioner`.

The setup

Be sure to use your own `nfs.server` and set `nfs.path` by replacing the `{sample values}` in the `helm install` command:

```
$ helm install --name my-release --set nfs.server={10.50.1.46} --set
nfs.path={/var/nfsshare/apps} stable/nfs-client-provisioner

$ kubectl apply -f nfs-pvc.yaml

$ kubectl get pvc
NAME STATUS VOLUME CAPACITY ACCESS MODES STORAGECLASS AGE
nfs-claim Bound pvc-eb937812-3767-11e9-88f4-0242ac110007 1Mi RWX nfs-client
20h
```

Let's take a look at UCP's Kubernetes storage list:

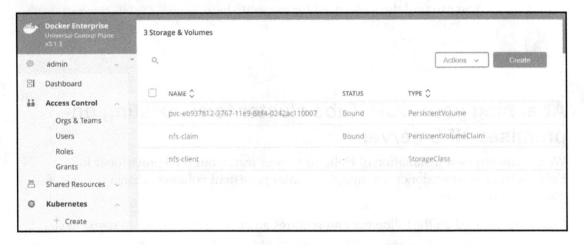

Figure 16: UCP Kubernetes storage and volumes

Here, we see the three items that were created. `nfs-client` was created by the Helm chart. Then, we made an NFS persistent volume claim, which generated the actual persistent volume, where our data resides and is backed by the NFS filesystem.

Let's take a look at the PVC in the following code block:

```
kind: PersistentVolumeClaim
apiVersion: v1
metadata:
  name: nfs-claim
  annotations:
    volume.beta.kubernetes.io/storage-class: "nfs-client"
spec:
  accessModes:
    - ReadWriteMany
  resources:
    requests:
      storage: 1Mi
```

Let's look at a few items inside our persistent volume claim class. The first one is of course the name—you'll see why that's important in a minute. II is the storage class. This needs to point to the storage class that we installed, `nfs-client`. In the last item is the request, which of course reduces the amount of available resources by this amount.

Now we can take a look at actually using our freshly-minted persistent volume. Here's the test we are going to use verify that are NFS is functioning properly:

```
kind: Pod
apiVersion: v1
metadata:
  name: test-pod
spec:
  containers:
  - name: test-pod
    image: gcr.io/google_containers/busybox:1.24
    command:
      - "/bin/sh"
    args:
      - "-c"
      - "touch /mnt/SUCCESS && exit 0 || exit 1"
    volumeMounts:
      - name: nfs-pvc
        mountPath: "/mnt"
  restartPolicy: "Never"
  volumes:
    - name: nfs-pvc
      persistentVolumeClaim:
        claimName: nfs-claim
```

The first thing to note is the actual command that runs inside the pod. If this actually works, I would expect to see a file called SUCCESS on the NFS server's export. The important part related to the persistent volume is at the bottom of the test file in the previous code block. Here, we see how it uses the persistent volume claim's name. So, nowhere do we actually use the auto-generated persistent volume's name. Rather, we just refer to it by the claimName.

Now we will run our test pod and see what happens:

```
$ kubectl apply -f test-nfs.yaml

$ kubectl get pods
NAME                                                   READY STATUS RESTARTS
AGE
my-release-nfs-client-provisioner-bb77bb766-rhz6x      1/1 Running 0 21h
test-pod                                               0/1 Completed 0 20h
```

Here, we can see that the test pod ran and completed. So all that's left is to go over to our NFS server and see whether our SUCCESS directory appeared:

```
[/var/nfsshare/apps]# tree -L 2
.
├── default-nfs-claim-pvc-eb937812-3767-11e9-88f4-0242ac110007
│   └── SUCCESS
```

It's interesting to see what happened here. Under our export directory, a new directory was created with the name for the persistent volume claim and ID. Beneath that is the SUCCESS file. We can see how it works by injecting an intermediate directory with the PVC's name.

Ingress controller

In this section, we will talk about using the NGINX ingress controller with Docker Enterprise Kubernetes. For this section, I have set up the following environment:

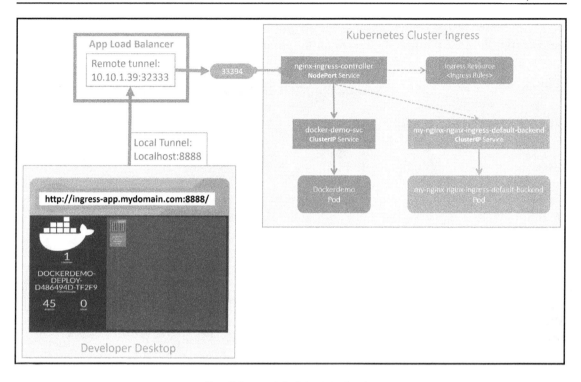

Figure 17: Ingress controller desktop test configuration

Since our cluster is behind a firewall, we will use an SSH tunnel to pass through our app load balancer to access cluster nodes. From there, our request passes to the `nginx-ingress-controller` where it uses ingress rules to determine the routing for the request based on the host name in the header. In our case, we have created a rule to pass requests with a host name header of `ingress-app.https://www.mydomain.com/` to the `docker-demo-service`, which are then passed on to the `docker-demo` pod—very cool!

Installing the NGINX ingress controller

For the implementation of our Kubernetes ingress controller, we will again rely on Helm. We start by installing the NGINX ingress controller chart (`stable/nginx-ingress`), as shown in the following code block:

```
$ helm install stable/nginx-ingress --name my-nginx --set rbac.create=true
<... You will see the initial status after the install here ...>
```

You will see the initial status after the install, but you need to wait about five minutes for help to complete the deployment. You can use the UCP web UI to validate that the pod is running:

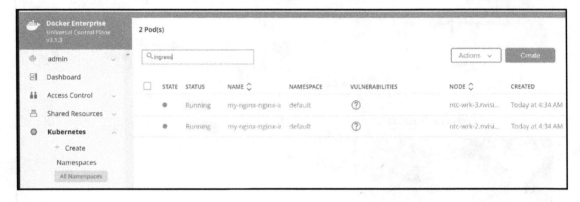

Figure 18

We can also use Helm to check the status after waiting five minutes, as shown in the following code block:

```
$ helm status my-nginx
LAST DEPLOYED: Sun Feb 24 04:34:34 2019
NAMESPACE: default
STATUS: DEPLOYED

RESOURCES:
==> v1beta1/ClusterRole
NAME AGE
my-nginx-nginx-ingress 6h28m

==> v1beta1/ClusterRoleBinding
NAME AGE
my-nginx-nginx-ingress 6h28m

==> v1beta1/Role
NAME AGE
my-nginx-nginx-ingress 6h28m

==> v1beta1/RoleBinding
NAME AGE
my-nginx-nginx-ingress 6h28m

==> v1/ConfigMap
NAME DATA AGE
my-nginx-nginx-ingress-controller 1 6h28m
```

In the previous block, we see how the Helm installed the Kubernetes RBAC properties as well as the `ConfigMap`. Next, we can see how the deployment and service relates resources in the following block:

```
==> v1/Service
NAME TYPE CLUSTER-IP EXTERNAL-IP PORT(S) AGE
my-nginx-nginx-ingress-controller LoadBalancer 10.96.154.150 <pending>
80:33394/TCP,443:34275/TCP 6h28m
my-nginx-nginx-ingress-default-backend ClusterIP 10.96.18.88 <none> 80/TCP
6h28m

==> v1beta1/Deployment
NAME DESIRED CURRENT UP-TO-DATE AVAILABLE AGE
my-nginx-nginx-ingress-controller 1 1 1 1 6h28m
my-nginx-nginx-ingress-default-backend 1 1 1 1 6h28m

==> v1/Pod(related)
NAME READY STATUS RESTARTS AGE
my-nginx-nginx-ingress-controller-5655d75c9c-9r5h5 1/1 Running 0 6h28m
my-nginx-nginx-ingress-default-backend-898d5489b-t5m7x 1/1 Running 0 6h28m

==> v1/ServiceAccount
NAME SECRETS AGE
my-nginx-nginx-ingress 1 6h28m
```

We can see how Helm deployed the `my-nginx-nginx-ingress-controller` service as the `LoadBalancer` type (that is what it is doing, after all), and `my-nginx-nginx-ingress-default-backend` of the `ClusterIP` type. We use bolding to indicate the abbreviated names used in *Figure 17*. This will make it easier to match up this previous output with *Figure 17*.

Please notice the following pending state:

```
my-nginx-nginx-ingress-controller LoadBalancer 10.96.154.150 <pending>
80:33394/TCP,443:34275/TCP 6h28m
```

For our setup, this is perfectly fine, because we are not expecting our load balancer to automatically wire itself up with this endpoint. Instead, it will do that manually. Since we use a wildcard DNS scheme, we just need to do this once. The automatic `LoadBalancer` wiring is generally implemented by cloud providers as part of their Kubernetes integration.

Now we can test the set up.

Using the Docker demo application to test our ingress setup

As shown in *Figure 17*, we are going to use a special application to test our ingress setup. We found the application on Docker's website in an article about configuring layer-7 routing with Docker Enterprise Kubernetes. While there are some issues with the setup files in this article, we really liked the test application. So, in the end, we opted to use the Helm Chart installation for our NGINX ingress controller and use the Dockers cool sample application to test it.

Here is a link to the Docker documentation page: `https://docs.docker.com/ee/ucp/kubernetes/layer-7-routing/`. Use the test application, but be careful with the installation, as it may not work properly (port conflict in the configuration file).

To get our test ready, we start by deploying the `dockerdemo` pods a `ClusterIP` service as its frontend.

Installing the dockerdemo application and docker-demo-svc

In the following code block, we show the deployment file for the `dockerdemo` application:

```
kind: Service
apiVersion: v1
metadata:
  namespace: default
  name: docker-demo-svc
spec:
  selector:
    app: dockerdemo
  ports:
  - protocol: TCP
    port: 8080
    targetPort: 8080
---
apiVersion: apps/v1beta2
kind: Deployment
```

```
metadata:
  namespace: default
  name: dockerdemo-deploy
  labels:
    app: dockerdemo
spec:
  selector:
    matchLabels:
      app: dockerdemo
  strategy:
    type: Recreate
  template:
    metadata:
      labels:
        app: dockerdemo
    spec:
      containers:
      - image: ehazlett/docker-demo
        name: docker-demo-container
        env:
        - name: app
          value: dockerdemo
        ports:
        - containerPort: 8080
```

In the `Service` definition at the top of the file, there is no type declared for the service. By default, Kubernetes will create a `ClusterIP` type of service. Everything else in the file appears to be very straightforward—some pod(s) bound to a cluster IP service for deployment.

Now we need you to deploy the pods and the service defined in the file by using the following command:

```
$ kubectl apply -f ingress-test-app.yaml
service/docker-demo-svc created
```

We see our `dockerdemo` application is created. You can use `$ kubectl get all` to verify the status.

Configuring ingress rules to dockerdemo

Now we will take a look at the configuration file used to set the ingress rules, as shown in *Figure 17*:

```
apiVersion: extensions/v1beta1
kind: Ingress
```

```
metadata:
  name: dockerdemo-ingress
  namespace: default
  annotations:
    kubernetes.io/ingress.class: "nginx"
spec:
  rules:
  - host: ingress-app.mydomain.com
    http:
      paths:
      - path: /
        backend:
          serviceName: docker-demo-svc
          servicePort: 8080
```

The most important setting for us is under the `rules: -host:` property, where we set the hostname for this rule. When the rule is applied, the ingress controller will look at the incoming request header's hostnames to see whether they match any of the rules. If they do, the controller passes it through to the backend, using `serviceName` and `servicePort`. In our case, `serviceName` will resolve to the `ClusterIP` service we deployed with our `dockerdemo` application.

Now we can apply the rule to the cluster and verify it:

```
$ kubectl apply -f ingress-test-conf.yaml
ingress.extensions/dockerdemo-ingress created

$ kubectl get ingress
NAME                HOSTS                     ADDRESS PORTS AGE
dockerdemo-ingress ingress-app.mydomain.com          80    3h
```

Great! Now we have our ingress controller configured to route traffic to our `dockerdemo` application. Now we need to see whether it works.

Testing the ingress controller flow

From a node in our infrastructure, I used the app load-balancer node—where we can access our cluster node adapters—so we can run a special `curl` command to see whether our ingress is working properly and our request will make into the `dockerdemo` pod:

```
$ curl -H "Host: ingress-app.mydomain.com" http://10.10.1.39:33394
<!DOCTYPE html>
<html lang="en">
    <head>
        <meta charset="utf-8">
        <title></title>
```

```
        <meta http-equiv="X-UA-Compatible" content="IE=edge,chrome=1" />
        <meta name="viewport" content="width=device-width, initial-
scale=1.0, maximum-scale=1.0">
        <meta name="author" content="Evan Hazlett">
        <meta name="description" content="Docker Demo">
        <script
src="https://ajax.googleapis.com/ajax/libs/jquery/2.2.4/jquery.min.js"></sc
ript>
        <link rel="stylesheet" type="text/css"
href="static/dist/semantic.min.css">
        <link rel="stylesheet" type="text/css"
href="static/css/default.css">
        <script src="static/dist/semantic.min.js"></script>
        ...
```

Notice the `http://10.10.1.39:33394` used in the `curl` command. The IP can be any non-master node in the cluster because the `ingress-controller` is a `NodePort` service. I chose the IP address of my first worker nodes in the cluster. Secondly, notice the port address that corresponds to our ingress controller. Finally, we have the `-H "Host: ingress-app.mydomain.com"` parameter, which is used to add the host to the request header, allowing the ingress controller to match the host header and fire a `docker-demo-svc` backend rule.

As you can see from the cURL response, it worked perfectly!

I also took this a step further. On my developer laptop, I created a record in my `Hosts` file for our test domain, as follows:

```
# localhost name resolution is handled within DNS itself.
# 127.0.0.1 localhost
# ::1 localhost
127.0.0.1 ingress-app.mydomain.com
```

Then, I used putty to create an SSH tunnel through my load-balancer node. This is what the putty setup looks like:

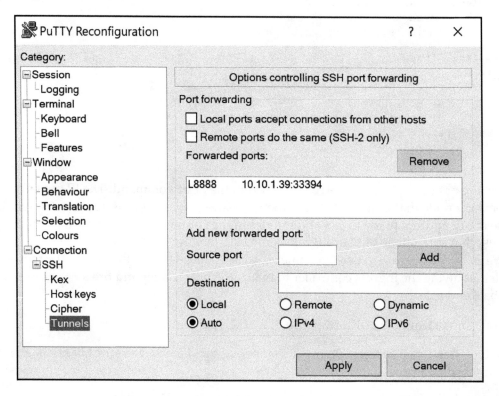

Figure 19: Set up putty tunnel to load balancer

Then, for my developer workstation, I opened my browser using `ingress-app.mydomain.com:8888` to see the following screen:

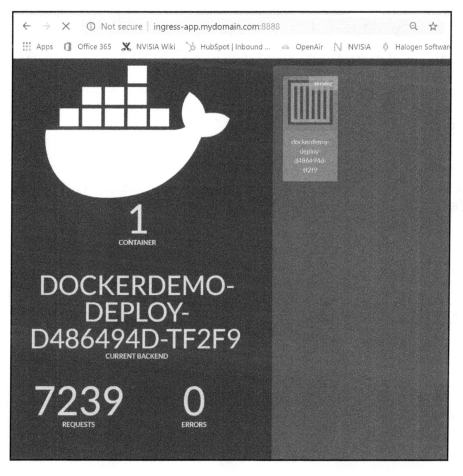

Figure 20: Ingress controller test

That's it! Our ingress controller is up and running.

Summary

In this chapter, we saw our Docker Enterprise's Kubernetes features in action. We witnessed the coexistence of Swarm and Kubernetes, as we performed a canary + blue/green deployment from our AtSea Swarm application stack to our AtSea Kubernetes application. We integrated Docker Enterprise RBAC into our AtSea Kubernetes deployment.

Finally, we saw how off-the-shelf Kubernetes extensions perform with our Docker Enterprise cluster. We were able to demonstrate the use of Helm Charts with `tiller` in our Kubernetes cluster by installing an NFS volume provisioner and an NGINX ingress controller.

Questions

1. Can I run Swarm and Kubernetes together in the same cluster?
2. What does Kubernetes provide for default networking?
3. How can I run Kubernetes locally on my desktop?
4. What is the difference between a `ClusterIP` and `NodePort` service in Kubernetes? Which one is the default?
5. Can you run Helm/Tiller on Docker Enterprise additions Kubernetes?
6. What is the best way to implement access to an external NFS server in a Kubernetes cluster?
7. What is a handy way to implement your own Kubernetes load balancer?

Further reading

Check out the following resources for more information on the topics covered in this chapter:

- **Information on the Docker CNI plugin installation and configuration**:
    - https://docs.docker.com/ee/ucp/kubernetes/install-cni-plugin/
- **Project Calico**:
    - https://docs.projectcalico.org/v3.5/reference/cni-plugin/configuration#ipam

- **Docker Enterprise RBAC tutorial**:
  - `https://docs.docker.com/ee/ucp/authorization/ee-advanced/`
- **Helm chart for installing the NGINX ingress controller**:
  - `https://hub.helm.sh/charts/stable/nginx-ingress`
- **Docs for Kubernetes ingress**:
  - `https://kubernetes.github.io/ingress-nginx/examples/tls-termination/`
- **Docker Enterprise layer-7 routing for Kubernetes (the Docker demo is cool, but the install scripts might need some tweaking)**:
  - `https://docs.docker.com/ee/ucp/kubernetes/layer-7-routing/`
- **Docker article on Kubernetes network encryption**:
  - `https://docs.docker.com/ee/ucp/kubernetes/kubernetes-network-encryption/`

11
Taking the Docker Enterprise Platform into the Future

Containers are a core-enabling technology for microservices, serverless, ML/AI, streaming, blockchain, and IoT, but they are also playing a key role in reducing the operational and support costs of traditional applications on Windows and Linux platforms. That said, it appears that containers will impact any organization that hosts web-based APIs, and service/headless applications. So, whether you are an old line business reinventing yourself or a cutting edge technology company, containers are most likely in your future. So, what's your container strategy?

I used to talk about container-first strategies, but I am reminded of Peter Drucker's famous quote:

> *"Culture eats strategy for breakfast."*

In my experience, there is a lot of truth in these words. So, maybe you should consider adding a container-first culture to your company's lunch menu, because container adoption is likely to be more of a culture thing than a strategy thing. So, in this closing chapter, we will share some final thoughts on container-first cultures and where they can take you your company with Docker Enterprise.

The following topics will be covered in this closing chapter:

- Understanding and supporting a container culture
- How the Docker Enterprise PoC, pilot, and production adoption support a container-first culture
- A glimpse into the future of a container-first enterprise

Container-first culture

First, let's define what we mean by a container-first culture. In a container-first culture, containers are the default platform for any, and all, software implementations. Whether the software comes from a vendor or is developed by an in-house team, the default delivery channel is containers. So. unless there's a really good reason to do so, containers are always used. Furthermore, when container-first is done right, you should not care where your containers are deployed, be it in the cloud or on-premises.

Life before a container-first culture

Before the container-first culture, it would take several days to provision a new test server. Our infrastructure team would need to understand exactly what SQL Server versions of each piece of software were and how to install them. For example, a typical .NET application deployment would first require the installation of SQL Server, being very careful to choose the correct version. Then, we have to make sure that the correct version of the .NET framework is installed. Finally, we would need to install the appropriate version of IIS. After this was all complete, we could install our application and hope that all of the versions match up and there are no missing pieces. Unfortunately, a lot of things to go wrong, as they often do.

When infrastructure teams ran into deployment problems, they would go back to the developer with the problem, and the developer would show them how it runs perfectly on their machine. This situation is sometimes referred to as the it works on my machine syndrome.

Because of the complex application deployment cycle, we were only able to release software on a quarterly release cycle, and the releases very rarely rolled out smoothly.

Life after a container-first culture

After adopting a container-first culture, the picture changes considerably. Applications are packaged into container images and pushed to a central image registry called the **Docker Trusted Registry (DTR)**. Rather than having the infrastructure team create an entirely new test server, the DevOps team can simply pull the latest application images down from a centralized DTR and deploy them to any server where Docker is installed. If an additional server is required, the infrastructure team only needs to install Docker. Subsequently, a new software released can be deployed to any test box in a matter of minutes and in most cases the continuous integration system actually deploys the test application as a byproduct of its standard pipeline process.

Subsequently, because the software is decoupled and isolated from the server using containers, applications can run on the same server alongside older versions of the same application; there are no more monolithic deployments. This flexibility means application teams are able to deploy their containers on their own schedule, which in some cases is a daily release cycle.

Container-first culture for developers

Developers love containers. It gives them the ability to run anything they want on other development workstations without installing anything. Containers give us the ability to experiment with cutting-edge technology, such as machine learning, serverless computing, NoSQL databases, and a variety of different no Node.js applications running on different versions without interfering with our development environment.

In addition to experimenting, we can try out the latest technology on our development workstations, and perform integration testing on our local desktops. This used to be confined to two specially provisioned test machines. Finally, container technology allows developers to make a shift to the left. Not only can developers use containers for a variety of new testing scenarios, including integration testing, but they can also implement policy insecurities as code to test other local development machines.

Container-first for DevOps

In a container-first world, DevOps is a different game. Since containers wrap up the application code and all of its dependencies in one bundle, you are working with complete deployable units and no longer dealing with a bunch of small moving parts. This reduces complexity and increases reliability.

Also, in the world in DevOps, container-first will also benefit from the just Docker principle, as you now use Docker to handle your builds, your test deploys, and binary code management. Since you're building in a Docker environment, you can stand up the entire multi-service application as a part of your build pipeline for end-to-end testing prior to pushing your image to the central image repository. Finally, to make sure the entire software supply chain is secure, you can sign images as a part of your build and approval process.

Container first for operations

In a container first-world, operations teams also benefit from just Docker; well, to be completely accurate, just Docker for Windows and just Docker for Linux. In other words, we can take all of our Windows workloads, regardless of framework versions and IIS versions, and run them side-by-side on the same machines. The same goes for Linux, where we can have Ubuntu, Alpine, and CentOS instances running on the same Docker Linux node.

So, there are a lot of benefits, but what are some of the things that get in the way overachieving a productive container-first culture?

Container-first adoption challenges

Because containers improve software development, DevOps, operations, and security, the impact of container adoption is significant and potentially daunting. However, because containers come from the open source software community, the barrier to trying container technology is very low. Subsequently, container experimentation will occur organically in pockets throughout the entire organization, whether you want it to or not. Additionally, the information from this organic adoption will come from different sources, where some will be more reliable and current than others.

The cloudy path to organic adoption

Chances are you've heard much more about cloud first than you have about container-first. That leads us to the next challenge with container adoption. Organic adoption through an enterprise's cloud partner appears to make container adoption as easy as dropping an item from your cloud service catalog into your shopping cart. While there's nothing inherently wrong with the cloud providers' implementation of containers (there is usually Docker in there somewhere), it's sort of like buying all of your bottled water from the Domino's delivery guy. It doesn't take long for people to think you have to order a pizza to get a bottle of water. Have heard teams say, *my application isn't running in the cloud, so I can't use containers*? I wonder if they like pizza?

Sadly, many organizations believe the only reasonable way to adopt container technology is in the cloud and to let your cloud provider handle the details. However, like any enterprise technology platform, the details are important! Once you get past the hello world application, you discover the container-related services are not what you thought they would be. For example, you can expect to encounter older versions of both Docker and Kubernetes, do-it-yourself raw networks, limitations on how many container or pods you can run per node, and the inability to extend the Kubernetes platform to meet your needs. However, it is easy to get started and easy to integrate the cloud provider's services with your container platform. This is all great, unless you have to move your workload from that provider.

Finally, moving to the cloud first requires that all of your teams invest in learning the specifics of the cloud provider's platform in order to build solutions for it. These skills are becoming increasingly hard to find, and there is a substantial learning curve. On the other hand, if you start with container-first, the prevalent skillset will be the Docker and Kubernetes APIs that you can deploy on any cloud platform or in your own data center. You only need hardcore cloud infrastructure skills to deploy your container platform (also known as just Docker). And if you decide to move your workload somewhere else, only this small platform team is impacted in the rest of your development and the DevOps team continues to interact with the Docker and Kubernetes APIs.

Please don't get me wrong here; the cloud is awesome and I continue to be impressed by the technology the cloud providers are delivering at scale. They have a business to run by providing value-added services and many of the popular services these days are related to containers. Just understand that there's more to containers than just the cloud, and the benefits of containers begin at the developer's desktop.

Trying to move everyone in the same direction

These days, anyone who reads an internet article or works through some demo code in a blog post feels like an expert. In a way, that's good. It's a great way to learn and gain confidence as a individual, but as an organization, you need to develop a container culture through your own experiences and informed decisions. That requires a collaborative learning environment supported by a common set of tools.

Container-first target application areas

What are the key areas to invest in when adopting a container-first culture, and what are the typical objectives?

The first area is new application development and is likely the most challenging area because of the potential skills gap between your current staff and what is required to design and build distributed container-based applications. Quite often, this is where you bring in some fresh talent as either full-time employees, which is often preferable, or experienced consultants. The objective for the new applications development area is to forge and validate future application patterns, such as microservices, and streaming technologies, such as Kafka.

The next area is legacy applications that are no longer being actively developed. The strategy here is to containerize the applications without changing code if possible. Once containerized, these applications are easily maintained and migrated because all of their fussy dependencies have been rolled up inside of the container with the application itself. This is how many organizations are dealing with Windows 2003 and 2008 applications as the vendor support closes.

The last application area is modernizing traditional web applications and APIs. These are applications that run on older .NET and Java platforms but are still actively modified and maintained. The goal here is to start off much like the legacy applications by containerizing them. From there, you take a look at which code is frequently modified and isolated from the rest of the code and factor out some of the components into separate containers. This reduces the amount of testing required when making those typical modifications.

Considerations for building a container culture

First of all, keep in mind the scope of the transition to state-of-the art containers. For many organizations, there is a lot to learn about this new world and, as we already mentioned, skill gaps can be wide, including modern, Git-based source code control; pipeline as code; distributed application design; and of course, Docker, overlay networking, cluster storage, and container orchestration, such as Swarm and Kubernetes.

Keeping it simple in the beginning

Keep in mind that not everybody is Google or Netflix, nor do you need to be. Especially when you are starting down the container path, keep it as simple as possible. For instance, consider starting with Docker's Swarm orchestrator and then move to Kubernetes when you need it. All the cool kids will tell you that Kubernetes is the only way to go and that Swarm is dead, but I assure you Swarm is alive and well and it is baked right into the Docker engine. Remember, these orchestrators are not mutually exclusive, and in fact, most people run Kubernetes on top of Docker engines where Swarm is already included. Giving your team a choice in choosing the right tool along their learning path will become important, and this is a key feature of the Docker Enterprise, as it supports both Swarm and Kubernetes out of the box.

Recognizing enthusiastic learners and committed adopters

Any cultural transformation requires leadership to emerge from the rank-and-file developers, DevOps, and operations teams. Leading this transformation is not a 9-to-5 job and requires both commitment and dedication to improving your organization's software platform. These are the people who stay late at night and work on problems over the weekend in an effort to make your container-based platform succeed. These leaders are always trying to find a way to say yes and they are backing it up with heroic attempts to solve the problem in the best possible way. Given the right climate, these players will emerge and need to be recognized if you are going to succeed.

Establishing a learning culture

Learning new technologies is a lot of fun, but putting them to work in a real situation will involve some mistakes. Are you going to punish people for these mistakes? Are you going to reward them for making mistakes? Or are you going to reward them for learning quickly by embracing a fail-fast mindset within your organization? This is an environment where you are honest and transparent about the success and failures within each sprint or development cycle.

In addition to the usual code reviews and possibly even pair programming, as team members get started, is formalized collaboration and sharing. Looking at ways to promote internal and external presentations or lightning talks on very specific technology topics related to your team development efforts can be a great growth opportunity. This naturally helps developers, DevOps, and operations team members to gain recognition, while forcing them to think through problems with a high level of detail. It's one thing to give someone a fancy demo, but it is entirely another thing to show them your code and talk them through the process of how you made it work.

The last areas I will cover as a part of the learning culture are tools and training. Make sure the teams have the tools they need to be successful, starting with Docker Desktop for Mac and Windows. Docker recently announced Docker Desktop Enterprise, which will follow more traditional enterprise software distribution models, also allowing administrators to lockdown the networking and proxy settings. Docker Desktop is really all you need for local container-base development, as it includes the latest Community Edition Docker Engine with both Swarm and Kubernetes support built in. All you need to do is check the **Enable Kubernetes** box to install and start a local single-node Kubernetes cluster on your your development machine for testing. This is much easier than the traditional Minikube setup (and maintenance).

Another great learning tool is the hackathons in science projects with a sandbox of some sort. This is another great feature of the Docker Enterprise, where you can provide the development team with UCP client bundles to access an isolated sandbox on the Enterprise non-production cluster. This is usually accomplished using a combination of collections and namespaces for Kubernetes resources. Again, the nice part is that there's really nothing to install; it's just a matter of allocating space on a shared, managed cluster.

On the training front, I strongly recommend that everyone involved with the container initiatives attends the authentic Docker, Inc. Fundamentals class. This class covers an amazing amount of ground in 2 days, including both Swarm and Kubernetes. It is a lot to absorb, but even developers with Docker experience get a lot out of the class. Furthermore, I suggest looking into an on-site version of the class so the instructor can tailor the discussions toward your specific challenges. Additionally, Docker offers advanced classes for developers, operations, and security, but they all have the prerequisite of the Docker Fundamentals class.

Docker Enterprise managed clusters

We have spent most of this book talking about the Docker Enterprise's various features, with a lot of detail and examples, but where does Docker Enterprise fit in to support a container-first culture? We can describe Docker Enterprise's contribution to a container-first culture along three lines:

- Consistent access
- Security
- Efficiency

Consistent access means you can get to the container cluster resources for integration testing or support purposes using the same mechanism, whether your cluster is running on-premises or on the cloud. Docker gives you two means of accessing the cluster. The first way is to access the cluster using the Universal Control Plane's web UI and logging in with your role-based access control credentials. The second way is to use the **Universal Control Plane(UCP)** client bundle, as we've discussed in the book. So, if a developer launches a container in the dev collection of the cluster, they can use either the web UI or their local terminal to show to access the container in the cluster.

Secure access means seamless RBAC for Docker Enterprise and Kubernetes resources, and, additionally, the BRAC system integrated into an Enterprise security system, such as Active Directory, LDAP, or SAML 2.0 single sign-on solution. Therefore, centralized control over Enterprise resource access systems is maintained and synchronized with your Docker. Additionally, all of your Enterprise images are stored in a private secure registry using DTR.

Efficiency refers to the Docker Enterprise's ability to isolate resources within a cluster. This allows you to essentially have two clusters, as described earlier in the book. One is your non-production cluster that may contain isolated dev, test, QA, training and sandbox environments, and the production cluster we're staging and final production. Docker Enterprise's RBAC and isolation for both Swarm and Kubernetes is a great defense against cluster sprawl we see so often in cloud environments, which can lead to significant deficiencies and massive monthly bills.

Agile adoption for containers and beyond

Throughout this book, we have talked about the agile approach to adopting the Docker Enterprise. The approach starts with a **proof-of-concept** (**PoC**) as a means of learning what we don't know, before attempting to make decisions we aren't prepared to make. We limit these PoC efforts to short 2-or-3 week efforts with stated objectives and measurable key results. Next, we use Docker Enterprise to deliver an internal release. Then, we move the internal release to production on a Docker Enterprise platform.

Agile Docker Enterprise adoption and container-first

The agile Docker Enterprise adoption approach discussed throughout this book intentionally supports the development of a container-first culture in the following ways. First, we structure learning through the process of doing, particularly in the early stages. Starting with the proof of concept, we focus on learning and gaining real experience with Docker Enterprise. Then we encourage honest feedback and factor it into the planning for the pilot phase of the project. In the short PoC window, we allow ourselves to try things and fail in an effort to figure out the very best way to implement the platform.

Building your future on the platform

Once you have established the container-first culture with the Docker Enterprise, you are in a great position to tackle almost all of the emerging technologies, as most of them thrive in a container environment. Machine learning, blockchain, serverless, and IoT all work better in containers.

The following diagram illustrates how Docker Enterprise's managed clusters provide a great foundation for emerging technology adoption:

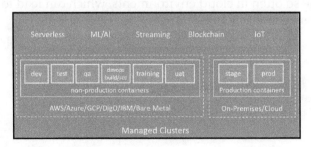

Figure 1: Managed clusters supporting emerging technology

Finally, the very same approach we used for adopting the Docker Enterprise and supporting our container-first culture can also be applied to emerging technologies, starting with PoC, then pilot, then production. Furthermore, they can all be run on your Docker Enterprise cluster.

Serverless and containers

Serverless computing is getting a lot attention these days. The concept of saying here's my function, deploy it somewhere and give me an endpoint is very appealing. Furthermore, you will hear two kinds of debate, should I be all in with containers, or all in with serverless? Hopefully by now we have learned enough to know we probably need both. If you have adopted a container first culture with Docker Enterprise, you are in good shape because serverless is generally implemented using containers. Therefore, there are lots of container based serverless frameworks you can deploy to your Docker Enterprise cluster.

One of the more popular frameworks we hear about is OpenFaaS® (Functions as a Service). This framework builds serverless functions using Docker and Kubernetes. They have packaged both Swarm stack and Kubernetes deployments.

You can find them here:

- `http://docs.openfaas.com/deployment/kubernetes/`
- `http://docs.openfaas.com/deployment/docker-swarm/`

I found a great overview of serverless and containers which was from Winder Research and Development Ltd and you can read it here: `https://winderresearch.com/a-comparison-of-serverless-frameworks-for-kubernetes-openfaas-openwhisk-fission-kubeless-and-more/`.

So, before you get yourself locked into a particular vendors serverless infrastructure, you might want to check out what you can do with your own Doctor Enterprise cluster first.

Summary

Containers are literally changing the world of software development and deployment. Building an effective container-first culture will play a key role in the success of your software organization in the future. While a cloud-first approach is the popular norm for most IT organizations, the container-first approach is picking up steam because of the cloud's portable nature and concerns over cloud vendor lock-in.

We believe the Docker Enterprise will become the platform of choice for informed enterprise buyers in the years to come. With its ability to support both Swarm and Kubernetes, it gives organizations a lot of options for starting and growing their container expertise and scale. Furthermore, container platforms are becoming foundational to most emerging technologies, including serverless, machine learning, blockchain, streaming, and IoT.

Further reading

- **Article**: Where containers, cloud, blockchain, and AI are headed in 2019:
    - https://enterprisersproject.com/article/2019/1/where-cont ainers-cloud-blockchain-and-ai-are-headed-2019
- **Article**: Serverless frameworks on Kubernetes:
    - https://winderresearch.com/a-comparison-of-serverless- frameworks-for-kubernetes-openfaas-openwhisk-fission- kubeless-and-more/

Assessments

Chapter 1: Making the Case for Docker Enterprise

1. Container foundations reach back to 2000, but **Linux containers (lxc)** were released in 2008 and Docker, Inc. packaged up the container ecosystem, making them user-friendly in 2013.

2. In 2013, they started to create tools of mass innovation. They are behind Docker Engine-Community, which is free, and Docker Enterprise, and commercially-support Docker with enterprise tooling.

3. **Docker Engine-Community** is community-based and has a community support model. It's used for non-production development and by small, highly technical teams. **Docker Enterprise** is a commercially-supported, subscription-based product with enterprise-class support and SLAs, as well as **Universal Control Plane (UCP)** and **Docker Trusted Registry (DTR)**.

4. Docker provides the engine that runs most containers, including must Kubernetes applications. Kubernetes in an orchestrator used to manage collections of containers across multiple container hosts. Docker has its own orchestrator, Docker Swarm, that is built into the Docker Engine.

5. Generally, Docker's Swarm.

6. Docker is the engine for most Kubernetes deployments, but Docker Enterprise 2 Standard and Advanced tiers come with Kubernetes installed.

7. It forces a shift left, where it is accountable for wiring up applications and scripting the deployment configuration (as a `.yaml` file in the source code control).

8. Cloud administration is focused at the container's platform level and not the application level.

Chapter 2: Docker Enterprise – an Architectural Overview

1. Enterprise container platforms.
2. Gives developers the ability to build, test (locally on development workstations, as well as on a remote development cluster), and deploy secure multi-container applications at will:

    - Provides an efficient, secure, developer-managed CI pipeline
    - Allows the operators (DevOps, TechOps, and SecOps) the ability to efficiently secure, manage, monitor, and scale multiple environments for development, test, QA, and production applications
    - Supports compliance requirements at the platform level – not just at the application level

3. The risks of going all-in with a cloud provider's container platform are as follows:

    - Being held back by older versions of Docker and Kubernetes
    - Expensive, complex cluster sprawl
    - Lock-in making it difficult to migrate to another cloud provider or on-premises

4. Docker Engine-Community is free. Docker Enterprise is sold as a subscription service.
5. 10 nodes for a basic Docker Enterprise HA-Cluster.
6. Shifting left generally means empowering developers to engage in more downstream activities, such as testing and integration.

Chapter 3: Getting Started – Docker Enterprise Proof of Concept

1. A four-node setup is highly recommended for PoCs to demonstrate UCP, DTR, and multiple worker nodes.

2. The PoC application shortlist defines a backlog of possible applications to containerize during your PoC. It is generally a good idea to have at least three or four applications identified. That way, if you run into an obstacle with one application, you can just move on to the next. The point here is to get an application into a container and deploy it to the PoC cluster. As a rule of thumb, if it is taking longer than two days to containerize the PoC application, it is time to move on to the next application on your shortlist.

3. Here are the four parts of a fully-qualified Docker image name:
   - A the registry URL (that is, **dtr.mydomain.com**/dev/web-app_build:v1.2)
   - Username or organization namespace (that is, dtr.mydomain.com/**dev**/web-app_build:v1.2)
   - The repository name (that is, dtr.mydomain.com/dev/**web-app_build**:v1.2)
   - A tag (that is, dtr.mydomain.com/dev/web-app_build:**v1.2**)

4. Follow these two steps:
   1. Retag the image as `docker image tag my-db-image:latest dtr.mydomain/dev/db-image:v1`
   2. Push the image as `docker image push dtr.mydomain/dev/db-image:v1`

Chapter 4: Prepare the Docker Enterprise Pilot Cluster

1. Here are the differences between the Docker0 default network and the custom bridge network:
   - The default network does not provide DNS
   - Customer networks provide DNS using the container's explicit name (using the `--name` parameter)

2. Yes, if you are running in Swarm mode. Create two Swarm services and connect them to the same overlay network.

3. Here are two recommended ways for a cluster user (such as a developer, DevOps, or system administrator) to access the cluster:

    - UCP web UI
    - UCL client bundle

4. The UCP Controller runs on the (Swarm) manager nodes.

5. Clock skew causes problems when validating a certificate-based connection. UCP uses certificates to secure the cluster communications and it does not take too much for the difference in clocks to drift outside of a certificate's validity window.

Chapter 5: Prepare and Deploy a Docker Enterprise Pilot Application

1. Here are the responsibilities of the pilot coordinator:

    - Schedule training for the pilot team
    - Document pilot project objectives and measurable key results
    - Establish a schedule and timeline for pilot project
    - Lead the pilot kickoff meeting

2. No. You can use the UCP's configuration file, `ucp-config.toml`.

3. Some basic refactoring during a pilot is expected. However, begin with a containerized version of the current system, and then start your refactoring so you have a fallback. Also, it is usually easier to refactor and test containerized applications.

4. Yes, during our PoC, it was OK to use self-signed certificates generated by the Universal Control Plane. However, as we move into the pilot phase, it's a good time to introduce third-party certificates issued from a trusted source.

5. Usually on a host or NFS volume. If you do use NFS, be sure to thoroughly test your application's compatibility with NFS.

Chapter 6: Design and Pilot a Docker Enterprise CI Pipeline

1. You don't have to install any special development tools locally or adjust the version of tools already installed. You only need Docker running on their workstation. Also, full stack testing on the developer's workstation requires fewer resource, is easier to set up, and catches bugs earlier.

2. We have multiple `docker-compose` files for the following uses:

   - A makefile for building all of the image with one command
   - Launching a local development and debugging stack
   - Launching a local test stack
   - Deploying our stack to the cluster

3. The Docker Enterprise integrates with a CI system:

   - The build pipeline pushes images to the Docker Trusted Registry
   - When running end-to-end tests, images are pulled from the Docker Trusted Registry
   - During deployment, the build pipeline deploys to UCP using a client bundle

4. The life cycle for secrets in our build pipeline:
   1. The secrets are pulled from a secure location
   2. The secrets are injected into the cluster at deploy-time
   3. The services read the unencrypted secrets from inside their container

Chapter 7: Pilot Docker Enterprise Platform Monitoring and Logging

1. `/etc/docker/daemon.json`
2. Not for production, as it an experimental feature
3. Prometheus

Chapter 8: First Application in Production with Docker Enterprise

1. Here are the differences between your non-production and production DTRs:
   - Repository immutability
   - Image signing

2. If there's a breakout attack, the container user will map to the host user. If that user is root, they have full access and control of the host.

3. Get to your cluster if it is behind a firewall:
   - The UCP Client bundle for Swarm access
   - UCP and DTR Web UIs
   - A Jump or Bastion host

Chapter 9: Important Docker Enterprise Production Topics

1. Health checks are a special bit of code provided by the container's creator. The health check code is periodically run by the Docker Engine inside the container and it reports the health status to the orchestrator. If the health check fails, the orchestrator removes the unhealthy container and creates a new one in its place.

2. Layer 7 dynamic routing, layer 4 simple port-based routing, and static host deployments. Layer 4 port-based routing and static host deployments are the most reliable and deterministic, making them the best choice for production implementations at this time. Layer 7 is very powerful, but has lots of moving parts and should be used with caution in production environments until you're very comfortable with its operation at scale.

3. With a blue/green deployment, you are able to stand up the new version of the application and verify it is ready and working, before directing external traffic to the application.

Chapter 10: More on Kubernetes with Docker Enterprise

1. Yes. However, in a production environment, you should designate the worker nodes as either Swarm or Kubernetes and not as mixed mode.

2. Kubernetes itself does not have a network. You need to use a **Container Networking Interface** (**CNI**) from a provider and install it yourself. The Docker Enterprise Kubernetes platform automatically installs Calico as its default CNI provider. There is an installation parameter with Packer Enterprise Edition if you'd like to install a different CNI network plugin.

3. Simply install Docker Desktop and enable Kubernetes. There is no need to install any other software to run the Kubernetes applications locally.

4. A cluster IP service is only reachable from inside the cluster, whereas a `NodePort` service, such as a Swarm service with VIP layer 4 routing, can be reached from outside the cluster through the published port number on any (worker) node's interface. `ClusterIP` is the default.

5. Yes, it works great, but there are a couple of minor RBAC configuration settings they will need to apply before installing Helm.

6. The best way is to integrate with Kubernetes' persistent volume-management system; all storage requests are handled the same way and using the same storage constructs. This requires a `nfs-client` storage provisioner.

7. Use the Kuberntes NGINX Ingress controller with wildcard DNS.

Other Books You May Enjoy

If you enjoyed this book, you may be interested in these other books by Packt:

Docker Cookbook - Second Edition
Ken Cochrane, Jeeva S. Chelladhurai, Neependra K Khare

ISBN: 978-1-78862-686-6

- Install Docker on various platforms
- Work with Docker images and containers
- Container networking and data sharing
- Docker APIs and language bindings
- Various PaaS solutions for Docker
- Implement container orchestration using Docker Swarm and Kubernetes
- Container security
- Docker on various clouds

Deployment with Docker
Srdjan Grubor

ISBN: 978-1-78646-900-7

- Set up a working development environment and create a simple web service to demonstrate the basics
- Learn how to make your service more usable by adding a database and an app server to process logic
- Add resilience to your services by learning how to horizontally scale with a few containers on a single node
- Master layering isolation and messaging to simplify and harden the connectivity between containers
- Learn about numerous issues encountered at scale and their workarounds, from the kernel up to code versioning
- Automate the most important parts of your infrastructure with continuous integration

Leave a review - let other readers know what you think

Please share your thoughts on this book with others by leaving a review on the site that you bought it from. If you purchased the book from Amazon, please leave us an honest review on this book's Amazon page. This is vital so that other potential readers can see and use your unbiased opinion to make purchasing decisions, we can understand what our customers think about our products, and our authors can see your feedback on the title that they have worked with Packt to create. It will only take a few minutes of your time, but is valuable to other potential customers, our authors, and Packt. Thank you!

Index

A

Agile adoption
for containers and beyond 450
Agile Docker Enterprise adoption
and container first 450
future, building 450
Amazon Elastic Container Service for Kubernetes
(Amazon EKS) 20
application layer, Docker Enterprise operation
architecture
cluster, interacting 46
architecture-related benefits, Docker Enterprise
choice, benefits 36, 37
computational efficiency benefits 36
container-first benefits 38
Docker support benefits 36
Docker Trusted Registry (DTR) benefits 37
rapid innovation 37
Universal Control Plane (UCP) benefits 37
architecture
cluster, interacting 48
AtSea application
services, building 261
structure 231, 232
testing 230

B

bare metal cluster network setup example
about 134
certificate structure and termination plan,
defining 135
domain name, defining 135
hostname structure, defining 135
load balancer configuration design 139, 141
load balancer setup 138
network infrastructure, designing 136
network infrastructure, implementing 137
blue/green deployment 384
Build Machine 251

C

Certificate Signing Request (CSR) 235
certificates, Docker Enterprise
external client certificates 131
internal cluster certificates 131
CI pipeline deployment, to Docker Enterprise
about 272
deployment pipeline file 273, 275, 277
Docker Swarm resource scoping 279
pipeline, triggering manually 281, 283
Cloud Native Computing Foundation (CNCF) 11,
18
cloud vendor-based container platforms
about 31
cons 31
pros 31
Cloudstor
reference 15
cluster nodes, Docker Enterprise pilot platform
additional DTR replicas, adding 158, 159
cluster-based storage considerations 143
Docker Enterprise engine, installing on each
cluster node 147, 148, 150
Docker Enterprise engine, installing on nodes
146
Docker Enterprise pilot bare metal 144
DTR, installing 156, 158
final configuration, of load balancers 159
first manager node, installing 151, 153
initial DTR 1 and worker 1 nodes, joining 154,
155
network adapters considerations 142
network timing and node synchronization 144

NFS server node, setting up 150
node sizing consideration 142
preparing 142
cluster-based container networking
  about 121, 122, 123
  Kubernetes DNS 123
  management and control planes 125, 126
  service discovery 124
  Swarm 123
components, Docker Enterprise 2
  exploring 53, 54
components, Docker Enterprise operation
  architecture
  Docker Enterprise Engine 40
  Docker Trusted Registry (DTR) 40
  Swarm mode 38, 39
  Universal Control Plane (UCP) 40
components, PoC application
  containerizing 88
  database, containerizing 88, 89, 90, 91, 93
  testing 88
  Webforms application, containerizing 93, 96, 97, 98
considerations, storage 44
Container Network Model (CNM) 116
Container Networking Interface (CNI) plugin 122
container platform categories
  cloud vendor-based container platforms 31
  extensible technologies 32
  OS platform vendor stacks 30
  virtualization vendor container platforms 29
container-culture, building
  committed adopters 447
  considerations 446
  enthusiastic learners, recognizing 447
  keeping it simple 447
  learning culture, establishing 447
container-first culture
  about 442
  cloudy path, to organic adoption 444
  container-first adoption challenges 444
  for developers 443
  for DevOps 443
  for operations 444
  life after 442

life before 442
same direction, moving in 445
container-first target application areas 446
container-first
  about 22
  using, as cloud adoption strategy 23
containerization process, sample pilot wiki
  application
  about 189
  collect and document application assets 189, 190
  images, pushing 205
  postgres DB, containerizing 191, 192
  postgres DB, testing 194, 195
Containers as a Service (CaaS) 219
containers
  about 10
  application deployment 11, 13
  application development 11, 13
  application modernization 24
  compliance 24
  DevOps support 24
  microservices support 24
  popularity 13
  strategic impact 22
  workloads, migrating back from public cloud 23
continuous integration (CI) pipeline 217
custom app
  building, with CI pipeline 249
  deploying with CI pipeline 249
  deploying, to Docker Enterprise cluster 243, 244, 245

D

data management
  about 343
  application data, backing up 351
  data, backing up 348, 349
  Docker NFS volume plugin 345, 347, 348
  DTR software, upgrading 354, 355
  DTR, backing up 350
  host volume mounts 343, 344
  OS and Docker Enterprise Engine Updates 352
  OS and Docker updates, applying 352
  UCP manager nodes 352, 353

UCP software, upgrading 353, 354
UCP, backing up 349
volume storage solutions 348
worker nodes 353
DB ClusterIP
  creating 409
defensive programming 202
deployment process, sample pilot wiki application
  about 205
  application flow 206
  deployment architecture 207, 208
  pilot application strategy 206
Dev 21
Dev workstation
  PoC application, containerizing 85, 86
  PoC application, testing 85, 86
DevOps 21, 22
distributed applications
  about 221
  key principles, for container application design
  221
DNS Round Robin (DNSRR) 107
Docker Application Converter (DAC) 86
Docker Community Edition (Docker CE)
  about 11, 14, 15
  edge channel 14
  features 16
  key capabilities 15
  nightly channel 14
  running, on AWS 15
  running, on Azure 15
  stable channel 14
Docker Content Trust 324
Docker Desktop, to Docker EE Kubernetes
  about 401
  application, configuring 405, 407
  AtSea, converting to Kubernetes 402, 403
  DB ClusterIP, creating 409
  DB, converting 407, 408
  DB, testing 407, 408, 409
  setting up 403, 405
  testing locally 414
  web app, converting 411
  webapp NodePort, creating 412
Docker EE 2.0 25

Docker EE Kubernetes integrations
  Gitlab and Docker EE Kubernetes 424
  Helm charts 423, 424
  Ingress controller 428
  persistent volumes, with existing NFS server 425
  setting up 426, 427, 428
  third-party 422
  UCP Kube cluster, attaching to existing on-
    premises NFS server 425
Docker EE, for pilot release of AtSea Kubernetes
  about 414
  blue/green deployment of AtSea to Docker EE
    Kubernetes cluster 419
  load balancer, for blue/green deployment 421,
    422
  setting up 415, 416, 418, 419
  smoke-testing 420
Docker EE, with Kubernetes
  about 393, 394
  advanced Kubernetes networking philosophy
    397
  CNI networking 395
  Docker EE install 395
  Kubernetes persistent volume management 401
  role-based access control 398, 400
  Swarm and Kube, coexistence 398
Docker Enterprise CLI bundle
  about 104, 105
  Bash, using with Docker API 105
  PowerShell, using with Docker APIo get CLI
    bundle 106
Docker Enterprise cluster architecture
  simple view 50, 51, 52, 53
Docker Enterprise cluster plumbing
  about 116
  cluster-based container networking 121
  Docker Enterprise pilot network implementation
    127
  Docker single-node networking 116
  No Domain Name System (DNS), for Docker0
    default network 119, 120
Docker Enterprise cluster
  PoC application, deploying to 103, 106, 109
Docker Enterprise Edition
  features 16
  support 16

Docker Enterprise Engine
  about 40
  installing, on nodes 63, 65, 66
Docker Enterprise managed clusters 449
Docker Enterprise operation architecture
  application layer 46
  infrastructure 40, 41, 42
  infrastructure layer 43
  layers 40, 42
  platform 40, 42
  platform layer 45
Docker Enterprise pilot bare metal
  overview 144
Docker Enterprise pilot network implementation
  about 127
  bare metal cluster network setup example 134
  certificate termination 133
  certificates 131
  DNS 131
  end users, of Docker Enterprise-hosted
    applications 129, 130
  highly available cluster 130
  hostnames, for Docker cluster nodes 134
  internal cluster users 127
Docker Enterprise pilot platform
  about 141
  cluster nodes, preparing 142
Docker Enterprise platform, for PoC step
  Docker Enterprise Engine, installing on nodes 63
  Docker Trusted Registry (DTR), installing 79, 80
  Docker's Universal Control Plane, installing 72, 73
  four-node cluster, preparing 60
  PoC, configuring 81
  RBAC, configuring 81
  trial license, uploading 74
  UCP web interface, logging to 74
  Windows 2016 Docker engine, installing 70, 71
  work nodes, adding to UCP cluster 74
Docker Enterprise platform
  preparing, for PoC step 60
Docker Enterprise PoC cross-functional team
  assembling 58, 59, 60
Docker Enterprise production cluster,
  considerations

about 329, 330
  cluster sprawl, avoiding 330
  node, sizing 332
  production cluster, considerations 331
  production manager nodes 331
  production-installation, considerations 330
Docker Enterprise production cluster, setup and
  install considerations
  about 334
  Center for Internet Security (CIS) docker
    benchmarks 334, 335, 337
  Docker nodes, no public access 338, 339
  Production DTR configuration 343
  Production UCP configuration 339, 340, 342
  SSH access, locking down 338
Docker Enterprise production cluster
  about 320
  high-level cluster flow and concepts 320
Docker Enterprise RBAC system
  collection, for pilot team 182
  organizations, setting up 179
  team member sync, LDAP used 180, 182
  teams, setting up 179
  working with 175, 177
Docker Enterprise reference architecture 48, 49
Docker Enterprise
  30-day trial license, obtaining 63, 64
  alarm, setting up 311, 312, 313, 314
  architectural overview 27
  architecture-related benefits 35
  economics 34
  features 34
  key components 34
  monitoring 298
  operational architecture 38
  pilot application development, with 218
  pilot Sysdig architecture 308
  storebit URL, obtaining 63, 64
  Sysdig agents, installing 308, 309
  Sysdig, commercial example 306, 307
  UCP and Prometheus 299
  Wiki pilot dashboard 309, 310, 311
  with Prometheus + Grafana 300, 301, 302, 304, 305
Docker in Docker (DinD) 72

Docker single-node networking
  about 116, 118
  container network troubleshooting 116
Docker tools, for local development 230
Docker Trusted Registry (DTR)
  abolut 17
  about 34, 37, 40, 219
  installing 79
Docker-based applications
  production platforms 28
docker-compose
  using, as Makefile 232, 234
Docker
  history 10, 11
DTR pilot settings
  accessing 184, 185, 187
DTR repos 326
DTR software
  upgrading 354
DTR System's Garbage Collection UI tab 188

E

economics, Docker Enterprise Edition
  direct cost 34, 35
  pricing illustration 35
End User Licensing Agreement (EULA) 90
enterprise container adoption
  sample principles and practices 9
extensible technologies
  about 32
  cons 33
  pros 32

F

Federal Information Processing Standard (FIPS) 24
four-node cluster
  preparing 60
  setting 61
Fully Qualified Domain Name (FQDN) 129

G

GitLab connection, with Docker Enterprise
  developing 252
  DTR CI integration 258, 260, 261

GitLab connection, with Docker Enterprise 258
GitLab Runner, adding to build machine 253, 255, 257

H

HAProxy start script 138
Helm charts 423
high availability (HA) 35
high-level cluster flow, Docker Enterprise
  production cluster
  DTR repos, immutability 326, 327
  image mirroring 321, 323
  image scanning, in production 327, 328
  image signing 323
  UCP production scheduling, with Docker Content Trust 324, 325, 326

I

Image2Docker 86
infrastructure layer, Docker Enterprise operation
  architecture
  computational nodes 43, 44
  network 43, 45
  nodes 43, 45
  operational network 43
  storage 43, 44, 45
Ingress controller, Docker EE Kubernetes
  integrations
  Docker demo application, using to test 432
  dockerdemo application, installing 432
  flow, testing 434, 436
  ingress rules, configuring to dockerdemo 433
  NGINX ingress controller, installing 429, 430, 432
ingress model
  about 374
  blue/green deployments with Swarm 376, 377
  blue/green deployments, key concepts 376
  Docker service updates 383
  Kubernetes blue/green deployment 377
  Layer 4 blue/green deployment 384
  Layer 4 Canary deployment 386
  Layer 4 routing, in production 379, 383
  Layer 4 simple port-based routing 375
  Layer 7 dynamic routing 374

Layer 7 routing, in production 378
overview 374
static host deployments 375

K

key principles, container application design
  about 221
  centralized logging 229
  defensive coding 227, 228
  Docker Enterprise layer 7 routing 226
  Docker Swarm services 221, 222, 223, 224
  secrets 229, 230
  Swarm service networks and routing mesh 224,
    225
Kubernetes
  about 17
  IaaS provider 20
  moving, to mainstream 20
  PaaS provider 20
  Swarm 19, 20
  Swarm orchestration 18

L

Layer 4 routing 379
layer 7 routing
  about 378
  with Docker Enterprise 246, 248
Linux Containers (LXC) 11
Linux worker nodes
  joining, to UCP cluster 75, 76
local Swarm testing
  final steps 239, 240, 242, 243
  mock layer 7 routing service, creating for 235

M

manager nodes 45
mock layer 7 routing service
  creating, for local Swarm testing 236, 237, 238
My-2-tier network 42

O

Open Container Initiative (OCI) 11
operations 22
orchestrators 17

orchestrators, Docker Enterprise Production
  about 360
  and resource management 367
  application startups and health checks 362
  cluster resources, managed 367
  cluster resources, unmanaged 367
  container reservations 368
  CPU, setting 369, 374
  Ephemeral containers and orchestration 361
  Health checks 360
  limits 368
  memory reservations 369, 374
  requests 368
  signals, passing into containers 366
  Swarm service health check, for AtSea-web 364,
    366
OS platform vendor stacks
  about 30
  cons 30
  pros 30

P

PaaS provider 21
pilot application development, with Docker
    Enterprise
  Docker Containers as a Service (CaaS) 219,
    220
  Docker, used for developer on-boarding 218
  Docker, used for improving software development
    cycles 218
pilot application
  planning for 164, 165
Pilot Docker Enterprise Platform
  about 288
  centralized logging 291, 292
  Default Docker Engine logs 288, 289, 290
  Docker, checking 296
  ELK Stack, publish approach 292, 293
  Prometheus setup 295, 296
  Prometheus, on Docker 296
  Prometheus, polling approach 294
platform layer, Docker Enterprise operation
    architecture
  about 45, 46
  DTR 45

Universal Control Plane (UCP) 45, 46
PoC application deployment, to Docker Enterprise
    cluster
    Docker Enterprise CLI bundle 104, 105
PoC application
    about 82
    containerizing, on Dev workstation 85, 86
    deploying, to Docker Enterprise cluster 103,
        106, 109
    deployment files, creating 99, 100
    deployment files, testing 99, 100
    Docker, installing on local workstation 84
    documentation, reviewing 87, 88
    images, pushing 100, 101, 102, 103
    selecting 82, 83
    testing, on Dev workstation 85, 86
    updating 110, 111
PoC DTR
    connecting to 101
PoC environment
    overview 61, 62, 63
PoC step
    Docker Enterprise platform, preparing for 60
production platforms, Docker Enterprise
    landscape of emerging container platforms 29
production
    monitoring 386, 390
Professional Services (PS) team 58
Proof of Concept (PoC) project 57

R

Responsible, Accountable, Consulted, and
    Informed (RACI) 164
Role-Based Access Control (RBAC) 53, 168

S

sample application
    building, with Compose and Swarm 235
    running, with Compose and Swarm 235
sample CI pipeline overview 249
    about 251
sample pilot planning
    core team 166
    DTR pilot settings 184
    execution 166

objectives 166
overlapping key activities 167
RBAC, in Docker Enterprise 175, 177
UCP pilot settings, configuring 168, 169, 171,
    173, 175
sample pilot wiki application
    about 188
    containerizing 189, 196, 198
    deploying 209, 211, 212, 213
    deploying, to pilot cluster 205
    testing 198, 200, 202, 204
Service Level Agreements (SLAs) 16
services, AtSea application
    build, for atsea-web image 268, 269
    building 262
    End to End test, for atsea-web image 269
    push pipeline, for atsea-web image 271
    simple build and push pipeline, for atsea-db
        image 262, 264, 266
    simple build and push pipeline, for atsea-payment
        image 267
Setup and installation considerations
    node, sizing 334
Subject Alternative Names (SANs) 132
Swarm orchestration 18
Swarm service health chec 364

T

tc7-app 220
tc8-app 220
tiers, Docker EE
    advanced tier 17
    basic tier 17
    standard tier 17
Transport Layer Security (TLS) 131

U

Ubuntu Docker engine
    installing 67, 68, 69
UCP Client bundle 74
UCP cluster
    Linux worker nodes, joining to 75, 76
    Windows server 2016 worker node, joining to 77,
        78
    worker nodes, joining to 76

UCP layer 7 routing settings 170
UCP manager node 156
UCP Prometheus metrics 299
Universal Control Plane (UCP)
  about 17, 37, 40, 50, 226
  backing up 349
  software, upgrading 353

V

virtual IP (VIP) service endpoint 222
Virtual Machines (VMs) 115
virtualization vendor container platforms

about 29
cons 29
pros 29

W

webapp NodePort
  creating 412
wildcard certificates 132
Windows server 2016 worker node
  joining, to UCP cluster 77, 78
worker nodes
  joining, UCP cluster 76

www.ingramcontent.com/pod-product-compliance
Lightning Source LLC
Chambersburg PA
CBHW060643060326
40690CB00020B/4496